THE INSURANCE AFTERSHOCK

The Christchurch Fiasco Post-Earthquake 2010-2016

2nd Edition

Sarah-Alice Miles

First Published 2012
By Dunmore Publishing Ltd

This Edition Published 2016
by Labyrinth Publishing
85 Shepherd Avenue
West Melton, Christchurch
New Zealand

National Library of New Zealand Cataloguing-in-Publication Data

Miles, Sarah-Alice.
The Insurance Aftershock: The Christchurch Fiasco 2010-2016 /
Sarah-Alice Miles.
ISBN 978-0-473-35101-9 (Soft cover);
ISBN 978-0-473-35012-3 (Kindle);
ISBN 978-0-473-35011-6 (Epub)
1. Canterbury Earthquake, N.Z., 2010-2016.
2. Insurance Aftershock, N.Z., 2010-2016.
3. Earthquake Insurance Claims—New Zealand—Canterbury.
4. Natural Disaster—New Zealand—Canterbury.
5. Earthquake insurance—New Zealand.
I. Title.

Disclaimer: This book is the result of extensive research and represents the findings and subsequent ideas and opinion of the author. The information herein is not intended to be and should not be a substitute for one's own research with regard to individual or unique policy information or legal advice. Every attempt has been made to ensure that the information in this book is as accurate as possible, up to date and accounted for. This book cannot address homeowners' policies unique to specific insurers, nor does it address how individual insurers interpret their own policies or any particular provisions within those policies. The publisher, Labyrinth Publishing, the author and any distributors of this work are not engaged in rendering professional services and hence this book cannot provide any guarantee or warranty. Neither the publisher, author nor distributor shall be liable for any loss of profit or any other commercial damages, including but not limited to special, incidental, consequential or other damages.

The Aftermath

As exhaustion takes over my body. I sit here and wonder, should we just
    leave this place?
Should we let go of this City we once loved, once thriving, now just an
    empty space.
Our land Green/Blue, an asset we would gift our children, is now just a
    damaged burden,
While Orange and White's futures still remain uncertain.

How can they just sit there and smile, as the people weep?
If earthquake wasn't enough, the wound the Government has caused is
    deep.
The east side of our City, broken, our City a barren ghost town,
Whilst they waste months taking the Grand Chancellor down.

Red zones start to say goodbye, to a place they raised their young,
Heartbroken mothers, fathers, daughters and sons.
Is there land available? The answer obviously no,
Where are these poor people expected to go?

Our home cries as it rains, and it drips from the ceiling,
While Gerry, John and Bob are wheeling and dealing.
To keep the rich happy, and keep us in line,
They ignore us, the people, when we try and speak our mind.

Earthquakes continue for decades they say,
Green/Blue, Red zoning has just been delayed.

Darla Hutt

CONTENTS

THE AUTHOR

Sarah-Alice Miles

Sarah-Alice Miles is a multidisciplinary professional with an arts degree in Modern Languages and Linguistics (Mandarin Chinese and Italian). She also holds a Law degree from Otago University, New Zealand. At Otago she was awarded a scholarship to pursue postgraduate studies in comparative private international law at the International Court of Justice in The Hague, The Netherlands. Always interested in the human condition she also holds degrees in Psychology and Psychotherapy (Gestalt) and has worked in this field for the past ten years in Christchurch. She also is qualified with a Bachelor of Commerce in Dispute Resolution (Mediation) and utilizes these skills in mediation settings within the clinical environment. She was an active participant in a specialized community 'Flying Squad' after the February 2011 earthquakes, a team of professionals specializing in psychological triage for the most seriously traumatically affected citizens.

Prior to her return from the Netherlands to New Zealand in 2004, she worked in the investment banking industry for ING Bank as a lawyer in both London (primary legal adviser in the area of e-commerce) and The Netherlands (with responsibilities for legal enforceability of financing structures, collateral structures, inter-bank loans and syndication). In 2002 she was employed as part of the Senior Management Team for the holding company, Aon B.V. Holdings in Rotterdam, The Netherlands with responsibility for matters relating to the merger and acquisition of foreign interests in Africa and Eastern Europe.

Among her interests, Sarah-Alice is a qualified viticulturist and oenologist (Post Grad) and has been involved in the development and production of special viticulture techniques for growing Pinot Noir in marginal climates. With a keen interest in art, she is also an accomplished and exhibiting artist and attended and obtained a Master of Mosaics qualification from Venice, Italy. With a good command of Dutch and Italian, Sarah-Alice has lived in Italy (5 years), Spain (4 years), The Netherlands (8 years), Ghana in West Africa (3 years) and the United Kingdom (2 years) and for the last 12 years in New Zealand.

Sarah-Alice is author of *The Insurance Aftershock*: *the Christchurch Fiasco Post-Earthquake 2010-2016* and a dedicated reporter and social commentator. Her post-earthquake Blog – *the Christchurch Fiasco* has proved popular and pivotal in the exposure of the many anomalies and idiosyncrasies of the post-earthquake recovery situation in Christchurch.

Website: www.theinsuranceanalyst.com
Gmail: theinsuranceanalyst@gmail.com
Blog: http://thechristchurchfiasco.wordpress.com/
Facebook: https://www.facebook.com/theinsuranceanalyst/
Twitter: https://twitter.com/InsurancAnalyst
LinkedIn: https://nz.linkedin.com/in/sarah-alice-miles-5a717737

ACKNOWLEDGEMENTS

Writing this book has at times felt a solitary task. I was regularly reminded of my own insurance battle and the process of immersing myself in the topic sometimes made me feel impatient and annoyed. Nevertheless, throughout the writing process I have remained focused and constantly on alert for new and interesting information.

One of my greatest challenges was to decide when to stop writing and hence my decision to continue on with a second edition. The events in Christchurch are an ongoing story; and even though this story has ended on paper, the battle for justice and a return to 'normality' for the people of Christchurch continues and will do so for the years to come.

So although I wrote alone, I wish to express my gratitude to many people, who in one way or another helped to bring this book to life.

Thank you –

To my husband, Herman van der Kloot Meijburg, who provided me with the time and space simply to do what had to be done. His gentle solid support is unconditional.

To my father, Perry Edward Miles, who for the last five years has been very generous and patient. He housed us while we tried to settle our earthquake insurance claim with State Insurance (IAG).

To Simon van der Sluis for his friendship and efforts in the design of the book cover.

To my Dutch family and friends.

To Herman Wijffel for his generosity in contributing the foreword and taking the time to share his thoughts and ideas with me.

To Barry Brailsford and Cushla Denton for their ongoing friendship and encouragement in the pursuit of my dreams and goals.

To Rebecca and Jerry Larason, our neighbours, who have offered friendship and support (and their gym equipment) while they too have struggled with their own insurance claims with State Insurance (IAG).

To the many Cantabrians who have taken the time to tell me their stories and have assisted in the process of gaining a greater comprehension of the problems we face in Canterbury, both with the insurance industry and EQC. Among these are many hundreds of people on Facebook with whom I have daily contact. Participating in the group and sharing information continues to be insightful and supportive.

To all those brave Cantabrians who have tried tirelessly to make themselves heard and who have been silenced or ignored. Your enduring courage has not gone unnoticed by those of us who understand the battle we face.

To my reviewers who were both receptive and encouraging.

Without these people and their support this book would not have been possible.

Sarah-Alice Miles
February 2016

FOREWORD

This book could have easily been written in anger. It is a credit to the author, Sarah-Alice Miles, that it was not.

In the wake of a devastating series of earthquakes and aftershocks, which destroyed much of the city of Christchurch and its surrounds, the author followed the protracted and seemingly unnecessary suffering of neighbours and the population at large. She then linked what she saw others undergo with her own personal experiences. Her motive for writing this book was driven by the question, "Why is this happening to us, living in a modern first-world democracy?" Her persistent search for answers resulted in compiling this publication, which contains, among other disclosures, an in-depth analysis of the role of the private insurance companies operating in Canterbury in the years following the initial 7.1 earthquake in September 2010. Her main focus is the Insurance industry and its handling of the resultant claims and their failure to respond in good faith and in a timely fashion. This book reviews five years of struggle by the people of Christchurch – a struggle not only with the reluctance of the insurers to deliver on their glossy promises, but also with the Government's inability/unwillingness to first of all support and meet the needs of its citizens in their hour of need. The Government response has been biased and has featured a lack of leadership, infighting, altering and stretching (building) guidelines, poor prioritising, and complicity at the expense of the urgent needs of its population and businesses. The author also presents facts which illuminate how financially precarious are both the insurance industry itself and the underwriting by the Government of the costs of this catastrophe.

Although this book finds its footing in a New Zealand case-study, it also addresses an issue of global significance and relevance. The present global constellation of corporate business is not well set up to adequately respond to natural disasters of the magnitude we have seen over recent years. It has become apparent that in the case of big natural disasters the people affected can no longer rely on the private market to come to their aid; their interests are best served through the public domain, through those public organisations which represent the people of the land and which have their interests at heart. Shareholder capitalism and profit-making imperatives make it virtually impossible for the corporate world to act in anything other than a self-serving way. The conclusion is drawn that the insurance industry does not hold policyholder protection as its top priority.

In the bigger scheme of recent, global, developments the contents of this book are pertinent as well. There is growing public disillusionment with the globally weakening corporate paradigm. The impact of the "occupy movement", although often portrayed in the media as being of minor importance, can be seen as significant in its own right as a testimony to the birth of a new consciousness. Traditional paradigms and ideologies supporting present-day corporatism are being challenged and called into question by the self-organising ability of these and similar movements. They are further enhanced by new communication technologies such as the internet, YouTube, Facebook and Twitter.

An important aspect of this book is that the author also provides proposals to mitigate the shortcomings of the present situation. She argues that the current insurance paradigm is unnecessary and should be replaced by more efficient arrangements. She advances an enlightened proposal that would ensure the meaningful guarantee of policyholder protection. She recommends a fresh look at the methodology of catastrophe management, principally in New Zealand, but also with wider global application. Such revision would offer no space for corporate manipulation and would, at the same time, involve substantial overhaul of and a changed focus for the New Zealand Earthquake Commission as the national entity responsible for catastrophe management. This would occur in combination with a radically different approach to government financial planning and fund management for natural disasters.

New Zealand is a seismic nation – this fact will not change. Future seismic events and other disasters are a certainty; only their timing and their scale are unknown. The author concludes that public confidence could be improved substantially as a result of an overhaul of the national catastrophe management system. A precursor, however, is that citizens confront their responsibility to inform themselves about the various proposals presented and trust their self-organising ability to bring about the necessary change in both society and government.

This book needed to be written; given national and global developments it has an urgent message. It is hoped that its contents will be shared and widely discussed. It will be for local authorities and national governments to act for the greater good – the honest and full protection of the nation's citizens. I commend the book to all New Zealanders and Australians.

Herman Wijffels, Professor of Sustainability and Social Change at Utrecht University, The Netherlands

H.H.F. "Herman" Wijffels is a Dutch economist and politician. From 1981 to 1991 he worked for the Rabobank, ultimately as chairman of the board of directors, and from 15 March 1999 until 1 April 2006 he was chairman of the Social Economic Council. From 2006 to 2008 he was Dutch representative at the World Bank.

WHY THIS BOOK?

At 4.35am on September 4, 2010, I was jolted out of sleep as a 7.1 magnitude earthquake struck our property; the epicentre was only seven kilometres away, the impact enormous. I found my husband lying on the floor next to a door-frame; he had been catapulted from bed and had sustained a blow to the head leaving him disoriented. As for myself, I awoke on my feet to the thundering noises and incredible lurching motion of the floor and ground beneath us. We spent the next minutes crawling out of our house through the carnage of books, water rushing from a displaced header tank, congealing food and broken glass. As one might expect with such force, our home suffered major damage. This jolt was the first of many thousands of earthquakes we were to experience over the next 2 years. This was also only the beginning of our insurance nightmare, the initial traumatic months turning to many years.

As a Christchurch resident, therapist and 'survivor' of the Canterbury earthquakes, along with my husband, I volunteered as part of the recovery response teams (in the 'Flying Squad') after the February 22, 2011 earthquake. This experience gave me insight into the extent of damage in the city and the ability of its local population to cope with their new circumstances. It was evident that Christchurch has a large vulnerable population who require a good deal of support in re-establishing themselves, working through the quagmire that is the insurance industry and ensuring that their rights are protected. Some groups within our society quickly proved ill equipped to negotiate with authorities and large corporations, either due to old age, infirmity, lack of resource or lack of tenacity and experience. And those of us who were more able, have been left deeply shocked at the treatment we have received, and the underhandedness with which we have been treated. Throughout the past five years, while I proactively waited for a decision to be made about our property, I have been truly alarmed by the way in which we and many others have been 'dealt with' by the New Zealand Government and the private insurance industry and industries affiliated to the 'Canterbury earthquake recovery'. It is on the basis of this experience that I have felt compelled to write this book.

Sixty months have now passed since the September 4, 2010 earthquakes in Canterbury and I have only recently settled my claim with my insurance company, IAG (State Insurance). It took five years for the insurer to honour its contractual obligations under a full-replacement policy. I am not alone – there are thousands of Cantabrians in the same situation. Tens of thousands of people have struggled and continue to struggle with both the Earthquake Commission and private insurers over the wording and extent of policy cover, *still* in limbo as they await the final decisions on their quake-damaged lives and homes. These are good people who in equally good faith signed insurance policies and paid their premiums to insurance companies over often many, many years.

As the years have rolled by and the stories and experiences have been shared amongst affected policyholders, what emerges is an insidious similarity in the way in which we have been treated. Affected Christchurch residents have become faceless numbers, mattering only in terms of how they might impact upon insurers' 'bottom-lines'. The quality of our lives and the possibilities for our futures appear to be of little concern. Only their profit margins matter. As I dutifully honoured my insurance premium commitments, I believed that my chosen insurance company would be there to help me in my time of greatest need. Instead, I, along with many others, have faced one 'road block' after another. A broken home is not simply about facts and figures but about the re-establishment of lives and acceptable living circumstances. Do they not understand? Do they not care?

The recent earthquake events in this region represent New Zealand's most severe property losses since the 1920–40s. The Canterbury earthquakes also form one of the biggest natural disaster insurance claims worldwide. Canterbury had a population of 390,300 prior to the earthquakes, is the largest region by area in New Zealand and was the second-largest region by population. Although this book is about the province of Canterbury, its principal city Christchurch, its citizens and the earthquakes of 2010–16, it is also the story of many other citizens in other countries around the globe who have found themselves abandoned by their insurers after natural disasters.

Earthquakes are not unheard of in Canterbury, though Christchurch City and environs had experienced only three moderate earthquakes in the past forty years. Yet major earthquakes in New Zealand are said to occur, on average, every eighty or so years. In recent times, two factors have combined to make the current upsurge in earthquakes and other severe weather events more relevant to New Zealand – these are increases in population wealth and changed population patterns. For most, these have made the need for property insurance unavoidable and in some instances mandatory.

There are as many experiences and stories of the Canterbury earthquakes and their aftermath as there are people in the wider provincial area. Several fine pictorial books have documented the devastation and immediate aftermath of the quakes and emphasised how the community pulled together in its hour of need. Accounts of these remarkable people and their deeds have been recorded for posterity; many moving stories of kindness and generosity. Yet these have proven to be only a part of a true account of the Canterbury earthquakes and their aftermath. Though much has been written about the loss, heroism and selfless efforts of Cantabrians immediately following the major disaster which struck Christchurch City, it transpires this disaster has exposed the best and the worst of human nature.

It is important for our future in this country to see the complete picture, the fact that despite the efforts of the remarkable citizens of Christchurch, many are still living in a state of limbo regarding their contractual rights. None suspected that in such circumstances they would find themselves in the battle of their lives for something they thought had been paid for in good faith in order to protect themselves. This is the story the national media is not fully investigating. This is a fiasco the Government is ignoring. We ask why.

Every day the media presents some new saga of events transpiring within the central city of Christchurch and its environs and every day more stories of insurance-industry and government ineptitude towards the affected population emerge. For many Cantabrians these events represent still greater confirmation of their own nightmarish experiences.

They are recounted here for all to see, so that debate will ensue and change occur. I believe that individual action can bring collective, often colossal, change. I still believe in democracy, although this experience has drastically undermined my once idealistic certainty. I, like many other Cantabrians, do not wish to be the victim of my own apathy nor anybody else's. The events that have transpired in the city have for the first time in my life led me to take to the streets of Christchurch in protest – in protest of the way the insurers and the Government are dealing with me and the 'recovery' of Christchurch. What is happening to many citizens of Christchurch should not and need not be happening.

The fiasco (it is not too strong a word) described in this book represents a global tale. As I researched, I quickly discovered that people around the world post-disaster have had similar experiences of insurance company dishonesty and authorities' ineptitudes and have suffered accordingly. Natural disasters such as earthquakes and hurricanes come and go but the suffering goes on and on and on... Much of this suffering would be quickly relieved if there was a better (and necessary) preparedness for disaster events; events that require extraordinary measures. This is not business as usual!

I acknowledge that my own personal experience of this catastrophe may have left me with some prejudice toward certain aspects of the subject matter. I do not feel it necessary to apologise for those prejudices. Rather, I trust my judgement and feelings around what has transpired and believe they represent the experiences of numerous others in the years that have followed the 2010–12 earthquakes.

My intentions in the writing of this book are to affirm to Cantabrians their experiences and suspicions, inform all policyholders (any of whom could quite easily find themselves in the same position tomorrow) about the difficulties that are likely to arise with their insurance policies and insurers during times of disaster and great personal need; and, finally, to offer a solution.

This book considers the response to the unprecedented property damage, the role of central and local government in the recovery phase, the long-term implications of the Earthquake Commission (EQC) and the Government Natural Disaster Fund. It also examines the financial vulnerability of the property insurance industry to mega-catastrophic events and suggests how government could improve New Zealand's ability to mitigate losses and finance large insured losses resulting from catastrophic events. I expose some of the stark realities of the insurance landscape during difficult and large-scale insurance claim times, hoping to stimulate debate around the role of government and the private insurance industry in this country, and to propose an insurance alternative for natural disaster coverage with the object of better preparing the nation for the next, inevitable, catastrophic event.

In light of my own and others' experiences, I must raise the question: do our current catastrophe insurance provisions serve our needs or is it time for a comprehensive review in favour of a system that serves the population more equitably and more efficiently? The only answer to that question that sits with me comfortably is a resounding 'YES' – because the current system has failed many Cantabrians very badly.

It is my hope that we citizens of Christchurch will be able to rebuild a strong and vibrant community and that as a nation we realise that planning for the inevitable must not be left to chance. If we wish to ensure a long-term successful future of Aotearoa New Zealand, we must think and act quickly.

Sarah-Alice Miles

Preface to the Second Edition

The *Insurance Aftershock* is an in-depth analysis of a modern wealthy, westernised City in which there are very high levels of insurance coverage and examines how Christchurch City fared post-disaster. The aftermath of the 2010-2012 Christchurch earthquakes in New Zealand offers the author a rare opportunity to examine the national policies and effectiveness of Government policy, funding and management of catastrophe on a national scale. It is a book intended for a global audience - firstly for the affected homeowner, but also for the policy-maker, the politician, the local-government official, the Treasury official, economist, the disaster recovery policy makers and last but not least, the lawyers and all those who work in the Judiciary. The contents will surely be of interest to business people and to those working in the insurance industry, the reinsurers and persons with an interest in the workings, or otherwise, of democracy in an alleged 'first world nation'. Natural processes become hazards when they impact humanity negatively, yet ironically, it is human behaviour interacting with these processes that determines whether they will become a disaster or worse, a true catastrophe. The slow and confused recovery phase in Christchurch, led the author to examine the manner in which the insurance industry operates under such circumstances - both locally and globally. It is arguable that after the stories of undeniable heroic rescues and selfless assistance and contribution by citizens, the insurance industry has played perhaps the most major role in the City's recovery phase and is undoubtedly, in great measure, responsible for the subsequent suffering and deprivation of the local population, post-earthquakes.

The Christchurch Fiasco (the first edition) provided the reader with an 'on the ground', live case study showing the need for proper preparation for a natural disaster in addition to the exposure of the unconscionable behaviour of the insurance corporates. Had the proper preparations been in place, fewer lives would have been lost, damages to homes, businesses and their contents could have been greatly reduced and the population as a whole could have recovered considerably more quickly.

This second edition builds on those findings. As with the first edition, this is not a book about idealistic sociological concepts. This second edition explores and further reveals the extent of the actual Government administrative failure and financial risk-taking, in concert with the corporate malfeasance that has taken place post-earthquakes. The opportunistic behaviour of the insurance companies (both private and government led), together with the lack of transparency and integrity within these corporations, has been compounded by the failure of corporate watch-dogs, such as the New Zealand Government, the legal system and regulators, all of whom have failed to protect the public interest after the catastrophic events. Research indicates that these are the same insurance battles fought by citizens all over the world following similar catastrophic events. In the background, behind closed doors, lurk the strategic alliances and the networked relationships between Government, corporates, professionals and other major, financial stakeholders, with the nefarious object to mitigate and minimalize possible financial losses while securing or increasing profits. The interests and voices of the policyholders and homeowners are conveniently ignored and the arguably intentional lack of redress is well understood by these demonstrably complicit parties.

In a true democracy, a well-informed citizenry is one of the best guarantees for a population's prosperous future. Armed with deeper insights into the connections and interaction between stakeholders and the community we are better able to ask ourselves the critical questions necessary to make better choices for the future. At a local level this will ultimately mean making better decisions about where and how to best invest our available resources. This book discloses the failures and fallacies of current disaster management strategies, not only in terms of the huge financial implications but also in the way the 'recovery' phase is managed. There is comment on the limited efficacy of Civil Law and associated means of redress, as protection against systematic corporate breach-of-contract and bad-faith. This has been not the case only in New Zealand, but applies to similar situations overseas. Given the increase in adverse events world-wide, the need for fundamental change to current arrangements in disaster management is obvious. The author's findings justify an efficient revision of the means to achieve that objective in a viable form. In the event government was to carry out such a revision, it would help to eliminate the current state of financial risk and susceptibility to corporate subversion.

There is unquestionable urgency in this matter. On a global scale, climate change is presenting countries with more and more climatic challenges. The interaction between human and global environmental processes has never been clearer or greater. Nor has the need for understanding these processes ever been more critical as they begin to affect the lives of millions of people on a daily basis. Mitigation is required to ensure a healthy future of the economy and society. Despite the dangers being known and the need for solutions to be found, we encounter the same conversations repeated over and over again. And so a cycle forms - be it policy makers, journalists or local and central government politicians. It is this human behaviour that amplifies the way in which natural hazards become problematic. This is a book clearly evidencing the need to learn more – how to divine our future, and how we give that future a voice. This is a call to National discussion about policy and the need to respond to its undesirable outcomes with action not rhetoric. For any reader, one thing will stand out, - the preparation here in New Zealand for the next 'big one' will require much better thought-out and better coordinated response. All these matters, forged in the aftermath and experience of the years following the earthquakes, justified the amended second edition of *The Christchurch Fiasco*. The issues revisited and explicitly addressed in this Second Edition are detailed below. The second edition in its present format has benefitted from the effluxion of time. There is nothing quite like hindsight. We have learned much. Because of the extensive nature of these amendments it seemed more focussed to change the title more in-line with the aftermath of this disaster as I have actually experienced it: *The Insurance Aftershock*.

Many of the changes and the comments made reflect the events and developments as they have taken place since the first version of this book was published in December 2012. So what is new?

~*New* is a chapter chronicling the events of 2013 and 2014.

~*New* is the demonstration of how the issue of governance and the relationship with stakeholders has become more and more complex and how it has challenged both citizen recovery and democracy itself.

~*New* is a revision of the issues related to the property assessments by the Earthquake Commission and the private insurance industry.

~*New* is an account of the rise in the numbers of claims reaching the courts and the introduction of class actions and some thoughts on why so many of the victimised population failed to take legal action.

~*New* is the account of the failure of the insurance companies to meet their self-imposed deadlines and how they changed their policies away from repair and rebuild to cash settlement, leaving people underfunded to fix properties themselves.

~*New* is commentary on the discussion about the risks involved in properly future-proofing the infrastructure of the City, including heritage buildings.

~*New* is the discovery of the quick fixes which were essentially shoddy repairs. These have now resulted in repairs of the repairs and reassessment of scopes of work having to be done, despite citizens having pointed out the risks early on - yet authorities failed to heed the call.

~*New* is further comment regarding the use of the Ministry of Building, Innovation and Employment Guidelines and the way this has affected the repair and quality of rebuilds as well as settlements for policyholders, in effect paving the way for necessary structural repairs to be assessed as 'cosmetic' repairs.

~*New* are a series of contributions from key members of the public who have contributed their time and energy in putting forward policyholder's perspectives based on their experiences.

~*New* is an account of the discussion about the conflicts of interest between professionals working for insurers and the wording of individuals' insurance contracts.

~*New* is the 'sum insured' debate, the policy change which led to this measure and what it will ultimately mean for homeowners in the event of another major earthquake.

~*New* is a chapter chronicling the events of 2015.

~*New* is a comprehensive referencing of original materials (Notes) in order to assist the reader and researcher to go to the original source for further detail.

~*New* is a revision of my opinions of the way in which certain events and processes have changed over the course of the past five years.

~New is my finding that there is no evidence of change in regulation or legislation to ensure that insurance timeframes are shortened. Still, five years on, thousands have unresolved claims or claims that will have to be reassessed and repairs that will continue on, well into the future.

~New is a new conclusion with a summation of the issues that have arisen and those that require further reflection by the nation and which should be conducted as an inclusive conversation.

INTRODUCTION

Everyone knows that our current system is kind of like legalised prostitution. The corporate sector completely controls the civic sector.
Peter Coyote, Actor and author[1]

The love of property is well and truly entrenched in this country. Property features strongly in people's retirement plans, many viewing their homes as part of New Zealanders' retirement assets. Around 27 percent of New Zealanders own one residential investment property. Owning a home is said to be very much part of the recommended strategy for a comfortable retirement, and people with investment properties are said to be less likely to find themselves in financial difficulties.[2] Most people consider property to be 'a sure bet' and under normal conditions it does produce reasonable returns on investment. But when 'normal' conditions become 'exceptional', suddenly property can become a risk – even a ball and chain. Yet the fact is that property is for most people their main asset.

Insurance and property go hand in hand – New Zealanders love of property is shared with the insurance industry. This is evidenced in the Insurance Council of New Zealand's figures which state that the Council comprises 28 member companies who write approximately 95 percent of New Zealand's general insurance business. Members currently protect approximately NZD 0.5 trillion of New Zealanders' assets. In addition, natural disasters trigger massive sales of insurance policies and this too has happened in New Zealand after the recent events in Canterbury. Figures released by the Insurance Council show that in the year to the end of December 2012, the total general insurance premiums paid will be NZD 4.12 billion, up from NZD 3.6 billion in the 12 months to the end of September 2011.[3] This is the first time premiums have topped NZD 4 billion and despite, and perhaps because of, the catastrophic events in Christchurch, the insurance industry has once again made huge profits – profits on the backs of many who have experienced an enormous economic and emotional calamity.

The core issue quickly becomes, how can we establish a politically sensible way of planning for a very large but infrequent event, both economically and politically? How will we better ensure the protection and return to normality of the lives of our citizens post-disaster? New Zealand requires a coherent strategy to ensure a sustainable recovery plan from large-scale disaster. These are complex issues and a challenge to us as a nation to work together, regardless of the many differing agendas of key stakeholders and legislators within the private and public sectors in dealing with catastrophic risk. Absence of leadership and conflicting interests in this regard will ultimately lead to unnecessary loss of lives, compromised emotional well-being and economic destruction in physically devastated parts of the country. As a small nation we can ill afford this.

Canterbury's experience has revealed a country-wide undertone of apathy towards disaster preparedness and ways of improving planning for this. The attitude is often a mixture of *'What will be, will be'* and *'It's highly unlikely to happen here'*. People living in high-risk areas may accept the threat philosophically, but the reality presents quite a different challenge. How long has Wellington been waiting for 'the big one'? The recent earthquakes in the North Island in August 2013 were a timely reminder.

This general apathy is reflected in economic restraints and a lack of political activism for disaster preparedness. Even when governmental bodies have adopted goals for disaster preparedness, the resources necessary to accomplish the goals have not always been made available or the funds set aside have been depleted by previous governments for other purposes. As a nation we need to address these inefficiencies quickly. The Canterbury events should be the country's wake-up call; they have provided the opportunity for reassessment of our catastrophe insurance situation in New Zealand as well as reassessment of regulation and legislation. Will the country heed the call? I certainly hope so. With informed choice we should be able to better provide for the needs of our citizens.

Natural disasters and earthquakes kill many people world-wide every year. It is said that approximately 81 percent of the largest earthquakes occur in the Circum-Pacific seismic belt.[4] The history of large earthquakes in New Zealand also makes for salutary reading. In 1931 an earthquake in Hawke's Bay (known as the Napier earthquake) is recorded as having caused the largest loss of life and the most extensive damage of any earthquake in New Zealand's history. The death toll was 256 and hundreds more were injured. The Canterbury earthquake on February 22, 2011, five months after the first shocking quake, killed 185 people[5] and injured more than 6,500 people.[6]

Earthquake losses present unique issues due to the nature of the damage and the policies under which earthquake claims arise. Claims for damage after earthquakes frequently involve other types of damage than that caused by the shaking of the earth itself. Liquefaction during the first major earthquakes may have been the worst to be experienced in a city anywhere in the world.[7] In addition the removal of silt has also caused another set of difficulties, leading to land subsidence and increased flooding risk. Even if earthquakes are covered under the terms of an all-risks policy, other causes of loss may be excluded by the policy language. For example, the connection between the earthquake in Japan in 2011 and the subsequent tsunami, and the Fukushima power plant failures that followed, raised complex questions of legal causation, depending upon policy language and the jurisdiction in which the claim was raised. An alarming example of exclusion in policy terms occurred after Hurricane Katrina (2005) where many homes were washed away by water, and insurers argued that the people's hurricane policies covered only wind and not water. Consequently thousands of homeowners 'not covered' under their policies, were left with no recourse and forced to accept total loss. Similar policy language issues have arisen in Australian and British insurance claims in recent years.

It has been said that *'a people get the government they deserve'*. Certainly, locally this is true. There is ample evidence that much of the failure to recover well from Canterbury's recent disaster can be laid at the foot of vested interests within Local and Central Government and a deliberate failure to address the financial 'rape' of the people and the city by the insurance corporations. This failure is likely to result in extended years of both financial and physical hardship for many, region-wide loss of economic prosperity and population flight from the region. The only winners from this catastrophe are likely to be the Government, the insurers and their shareholders.

Insurance, as most consumers understand it, involves standardised risk-assessment mechanisms that provide for a large degree of price similarity between similarly situated insured parties and operates legally on the basis of 'utmost good faith' contracts. It is subject to regulation and mechanisms that are supposed to guarantee the solvency of the companies writing the insurance. These widely advertised features provide a product that consumers feel is a sound and protective one to buy. Price similarity allows insurance agents and insurance companies to achieve economies of scale. It is often said that insurers need only maps and basic data about homeowners to price their product. The Christchurch experiences have shown that this basic data must be based on sound pricing models. As events become more extreme and less predictable these models will be less able to accurately predict risk. In addition, utmost good faith contracts are assumed by policyholders to relieve them of having to read through and understand the usually dense legal documents, essentially implying that policyholders should be able to trust whatever the insurance brochure declares, supplemented by what their agents and brokers tell them about what is covered under their policy and what is not. As a policyholder, I for one, do not expect to have to go looking for the contractual pitfalls in a policy which is supposedly there to protect me. Post-earthquakes and with the introduction of fixed sum insurance, policyholders must become more conversant with their policies and their risks if they are to ensure future protection.

As we look around the world, insurance markets are experiencing difficulties in sufficiently financing and diversifying their risk. Some insurers are taking on excessive amounts of catastrophe risk, voluntarily or involuntarily, which threatens their viability and potentially that of the economy. Other insurers, while sufficiently funded, have internal business structures that are geared heavily, if not solely, towards profitability.

Insufficient insurance regulation in many 'markets' has hindered insurance market adjustments to efficiently support populations in crisis, or to diversify and finance catastrophe risk adequately. These shortcomings are still largely unrevealed and have not, as yet, prompted public debate about appropriate market responses, regulatory intervention and other possible government actions to alleviate their recurrence at the time of another catastrophe.

This book deals predominantly with homeowner or residential insurance, and in particular with the insurance issues that have plagued policyholders in Canterbury throughout the last five years. These issues have drawn attention to the fact that policyholders have placed too much trust in insurance companies, as their policies now appear to be much less 'water tight' and enforceable than they have assumed or expected. What has become very evident following this catastrophe is a fundamental dichotomy of interests between private insurance and individual and community recovery.

In the past some insurance companies were formed as mutual companies, owned by policyholders for the benefit of those policyholders. The mutual structure has proved in the Canterbury event to produce reasonable results for policyholders. However, in more recent times there has been a shift toward 'for-profit' corporate structures, with insurance companies being owned by shareholders. This would appear to place a corporate insurance company in the position of having to choose whose interests to serve – the shareholder or the policyholder. This creates a permanent tension within the industry, which appears to see itself unable to serve the interests of both parties. Experience around the world has shown that the insurance industry's internal drive for profit has overwhelmed its external obligation to policyholders, and led to a corporate culture that is actually totally at odds with its purpose. Many are currently experiencing the machinations of this culture in Christchurch at great personal cost.

The more cash insurers can keep from reinsurance funding and the premiums they receive, the more they can invest. This pool of assets

– most of which the companies invest in government and corporate bonds – is known as the 'float'. Billionaire Warren Buffett, CEO of Berkshire Hathaway Inc., wrote in his annual letter to shareholders, "*simply put, float is money we hold that is not ours but which we get to invest*".8 Insurance companies are no longer following their mandate to take care of policyholders' money so it can be paid out when needed.

In the background, behind closed doors, is the reinsurance industry. The public know little about the reinsurance industry, and it can be extremely difficult to find information on this massive corporate sector. Reinsurers are essentially providers of insurance for insurance companies. Reinsurance represents a way of insurers spreading risk beyond their company's own client base. All but the smallest private insurance companies try to build portfolios of non-correlated risks. By simultaneously writing insurance for events unlikely to happen at the same time, insurers try to spread risk to ensure sufficient cash availability to pay claims. No insurer manages to achieve this accurately one hundred percent of the time. Nearly all insurers find themselves under- or over-concentrated in one area or another and thus turn to reinsurance companies to transfer that risk. In return for a payment, the reinsurer agrees to pay the insurer for some or all of a claim. Reinsurance typically initiates at reasonably high levels: if a single house burns down, the insured's insurance company will almost always pay claims out of its own reserves. Reinsurance exists to cover the costs of major event claims, such as those arising from floods or earthquakes.

Reinsurance and the capital markets are tightly interrelated and thus if the world experiences more and more natural disasters these two insurance industries develop more and more complex financial instruments in an attempt to mitigate their joint risks. Serious questions are now arising around the stability of these instruments in a global economy which is currently experiencing major financial melt-down. Does the reinsurance industry 'stack-up'? Can we policyholders really rely on our private insurance policies? What is the potential for systemic risk? Does the re/insurance industry amount to a house of cards waiting to topple, come the next gust of wind? In the current global marketplace, the gusts of wind are becoming ever more frequent. In addition, with reinsurance costs jumping to astronomical levels, and these ultimately passed on to the consumer, the question has to be asked whether this sort of catastrophe financing is viable for the future.

Willis Re, one of the large reinsurers, says catastrophe reinsurance prices are set to jump from 80–150 percent in New Zealand. In Australia, reinsurance catastrophe premiums have risen 40–75 percent.9 These increases are of course, passed onto policyholders. Cantabrians can already attest to these increases. Around the world reinsurers have begun to restrict cover, e.g. in low-lying Florida with rising sea-levels, and in earthquake-prone San Francisco. This raises the following policy questions: should insurance be required in certain highly hazard-prone areas? If so, is the private sector the right forum in which to provide this coverage or should some alternative structure be considered? Should there be more land-use regulation to restrict new construction in highly hazard-prone areas? Can building codes be better designed and enforced? What does the cost/benefit equation look like? There is also the equity issue to consider: how should we deal with individuals who have been living in high-hazard areas for some time but cannot afford to pay for higher insurance premiums that reflect the new risk assessment? Answers to these questions are critical in a country where natural disasters and catastrophes are inevitable.

Answers and real, concrete solutions are required in dealing with the many hundreds of thousands of claims that have arisen as a result of the earthquakes. Disgruntled insurance customers find themselves powerless to take on insurance companies through the courts, the costs of the process being prohibitive. The justice system has become the preserve of the very wealthy. Questions also arise around the role of the justice system and the limited potentiality for class action in this country, as well as alternative dispute-resolution mechanisms for handling unsettled claims en-masse after natural disasters.

On closer inspection, one discovers that the complaints-handling institutions in New Zealand also afford little assistance to policyholders seeking solutions and resolution. Consideration must be given to the ways in which other countries around the world have solved these issues during catastrophic circumstances. An examination of the insurance framework and the industry itself shows clearly that the system now favours corporate big business. That the asymmetry in the power relationship with the average person or homeowner has resulted in very little realistic recourse for policyholders. In some parts of the world the insurance industry is changing and there are tighter global regulatory frameworks. New Zealand too has 'new' insurance legislation in the form of the Insurance (Prudential Supervision) Act 2010 and the 'new' Fair Insurance Code (2016), but in light of developments here in Canterbury, I query whether this new legislation goes far enough.

Related to earthquakes and on the same catastrophe spectrum, sits climate change: The World Economic Forum recently stated that climate change is one of the most important global risks that key decision makers will face in the years to come.[10] The argument about whether or not climate change is really occurring is irrelevant here. The fact is that there are clearly more and more climate events which are posing major problems and rising costs to re/insurance industries around the world. Though climate change is not the focus of this book, it does bear consideration from a re/insurance perspective as the same economic issues arise regardless of whether they are caused by flooding, landslip, bushfire, earthquake or hurricane. Any large-scale risk is increasingly likely to be harshly viewed by insurers and to be reflected in premiums or, worse still, excluded from coverage. Consequently another method of protecting our population must be sought.

When a natural disaster takes place in New Zealand, it occurs in a context. The private insurers are only one part of that context. Alongside them stand several other major players, not the least of which are the government of the day, the Earthquake Commission (EQC), local authorities, and affiliated construction industries, such as demolition firms, engineering firms and builders. Also relevant are the media and the legal profession. All play critical roles in communication, protection, recovery of communities, and the rebuilding of a city.

The EQC has performed a large part of the government response to the Canterbury earthquakes. New Zealand presents the highest ratio of insured to economic losses around the world. This is because in New Zealand earthquake insurance is mandatory for home mortgage holders and is administered through the EQC, so the insurance industry has had a much greater role to play in reconstruction efforts. There is no doubt that the EQC's task has been an unenviable one and it is abundantly clear that this organisation was in no way prepared for the scale of what has transpired. This raises many questions around how the EQC should be structured in the future and how large a role the private insurance industry should play in the assessment of claims post-disaster.

New Zealand's second biggest insurer, Vero, is calling for the EQC to have a greater role in the insurance market, including insuring commercial properties. Vero former chief executive Gary Dransfield told a gathering of the Trans-Tasman Business Circle that the Commission should remain pivotal to any earthquake insurance model. He called on the Government and the industry to address the questions of what level of capital the Commission needed to fulfil its role and at what speed that capital should be acquired.11 I agreed with Dransfield and in addition I propose (and cover this in detail in this book) that the EQC extend its coverage further, so that the private insurance industry no longer forms *any part* of property insurance in this country. Apart from the fact that this is economically a much more efficient solution, the government is in a much better position both financially and ideologically to protect the interests of its citizens in dire circumstances. That said, this statement must be tempered by the current Government and the EQC performance in Christchurch.

The role of government and the current legal framework are fundamental in assisting an affected community in times of distress. The shock that follows a natural disaster can be tempered by the political decisions that are made in regard to relief. Government has the ability to spend on both preventive and palliative measures around natural disasters. Much criticism has been directed at the current National Government for its persistent reluctance to become involved in the insurance debate and at its refusal to make hard decisions despite pleas from the affected Canterbury population. There are questions around its top-down structure by which community input is compromised and citizens' voices are not heard. The interrelationship between the Christchurch City Council and Canterbury Earthquake Recovery Authority

(CERA) is one, which from the start, has been plagued with tension. Questions abound over the structure of the body tasked with recovery. For a considerable period it was not even possible to identify clearly what body *was* responsible.

Watching from the side-lines are the media. The media can be a mixed blessing in times of catastrophe. In the early phases of recent Canterbury events they were instrumental in helping inform the local and larger New Zealand community, as well as the world, of immediate events and then developments. The *Christchurch Press*, the local newspaper, provided a stellar service in that respect, and it has been and is a good forum for local and national views. Its website, *stuff.co.nz* (see 'Christchurch Earthquake'), has been a tremendous source of interactive instant news on events taking place in Christchurch. Many of those articles are referenced in the pages of this book. In addition, the comments that people add to the news items make for lively local input and actually have represented the only way in which local views have been able to be expressed to any large 'audience'. Even today, more than five years after the first quake, the local paper contains information relating to the earthquakes and issues surrounding the recovery process. And it is abundantly clear from the reporting that all is not well in Christchurch.

There is no doubt that from the journalistic point of view, a natural disaster has all the ingredients of the perfect media event, particularly in the modern electronic age. Such an event can be brief, spectacular, action-based, and easily expose human suffering and courage. Yet, should we not be asking – is it not also the traditional and vital role of the press to act as watchdog over government and big business? Does this not go back to the very foundation of democracy? Though the *Christchurch Press* has performed admirably, still more could and should have been done in this respect. Arguably, the media have actually moderated their adversarial posture towards the very organisations they should be holding to account. Is it likely that due to the extreme nature of the catastrophic circumstances the media have also cooperated with requests by officials to hold back information that might have an adverse effect on the public? It could also be more sinister if there has been no such request; that information has been withheld on the media's own initiative when it was felt to be harmful, or in the interests of the 'process'. Local reporters have a stake in cultivating and maintaining good contacts with local officials, who are often a reliable source of daily news.

No doubt local reporters also have some sensitivity towards the needs of the community. Yet, as time has gone on, their unwillingness to take issues 'by the horns' and hone-in on contentious subject matter has been evident. The first evidence of media involvement in the insurance struggle came on January 11, 2011 four months after the initial major earthquake, and even then there was no mention in the article of the deficient insurer by name although there was a picture of the affected homeowner holding up a letter from his insurer. There has been a slowness and obvious reluctance in many sectors, including the media, to tackle the insurance industry head-on – to recognise that this must happen to enable Christchurch City to get back on its feet and its citizens to return to their former habits and daily routines. Without the media's critical eye we are a population at sea without a captain.

The experience for many residents here in Christchurch has not been as it is portrayed in the media – many consider it a city of two halves, where many are still living in very difficult conditions, others face unpalatable land offers they do not fully comprehend from the Government. While the other, not greatly affected half, is more and more critical of their 'ingratitude' and 'moaning' to the country's taxpayers, who will fund the Government's contribution to the recovery. For that half, life goes on much as usual. In addition, throughout much of the rest of the country there appears to be an almost complete lack of awareness or comprehension of the tensions and frustrations being experienced by many Cantabrians. Of course these tensions must be tempered by the many kind words offered and assistance that other New Zealanders have contributed, but as time has gone on there is more evidence of diminished compassion for the Canterbury situation and its affected residents. Yet now is the time that those still affected require most support. Imagine having your life disrupted for five long years with as yet no end in sight. For many there remain no solutions or relief. Their situation has materially declined, and there is a very real sense of desperation. These are not battles to be fought alone.

New Zealand is said to have comprehensive disaster planning and response arrangements in place. The initial response to a disaster can greatly influence a community's recovery, but the Christchurch experience has shown that New Zealand still has a long way to go toward learning about how to prepare for reconstruction and recovery. To many it appears that the 'authorities' have been making the rules as they go. This flies in the face of the international literature, which promotes that preparedness and recovery have to be clearly thought-out, well organised and efficiently implementable, well in advance of any event. Christchurch, five years after the first quake, is currently only in the very early phases of what is likely to be a very long recovery journey. In this instance 'response' was the sprint, and the recovery has become the unplanned marathon.

In light of New Zealand's vulnerability to earthquakes it is vital that greater consideration is given to ensuring that individuals, communities and institutions are more resilient to future events. And it is important that as a nation we gain a better understanding of what has transpired in Christchurch so that we can ensure that we are better prepared to manage the next major and inevitable catastrophic event.

This book offers a baseline of information and a contextual framework to assist the general public in making informed choices about insurance and the need to diminish catastrophic event outcomes. Society's choices (private and public) with respect to managing catastrophe risk have significant implications for the severity of losses (both economic and emotional) from natural disasters and who pays for those losses. As vulnerable citizens, it is important that we do not allow an unacceptable insurance situation to become the status quo. The insurance 'good faith' contract has had a good airing over the past five years and has been found to be seriously wanting. In order to reduce vulnerability for all property owners, efficient, transparent and robust mechanisms must be put in place to protect them. It is my strong belief that the days of self-regulation of insurance in this country should come to an end. It is not in the policyholders' interest nor in the country's interest.

CHAPTER 1

THE SEQUENCE OF EVENTS 2010-2012: THE YEARS OF AFTERSHOCKS AND CONFUSION

- -

Farewell 2011, you won't be missed.

Neil Irwin, Christchurch resident[1]

In order to review the insurance industry's performance after the events in Canterbury, we have to look at the context. The following pages provide an account of the initial insurance landscape between September 4, 2010 to the end of 2012.

At 4.35 am on Saturday, September 4, 2010 the first of a series of major earthquakes struck the Canterbury region of New Zealand's South Island. It released 2.8 quadrillion joules of energy.[2] This quake measured 7.1 on the Richter scale and is said to have lasted only 30 seconds. The experience itself felt much longer. The quake was centred a shallow 5 kilometres underground and was felt as far north as New Plymouth in the North Island. No lives were lost, though in part this outcome was sheer good fortune: it was a Saturday morning, people were at home, in bed, which meant that masonry fell into the empty streets below. The earthquake was centred in the small rural township of Kirwee (37 km from Christchurch), not far from Darfield.

Massive disruption followed: power outages, damaged roads, water contamination, sewage spillage and the general destruction of sanitation systems. Within 30 seconds the Canterbury region was brought to a stark new reality for which it was woefully unprepared. A series of major aftershocks followed: 127 further shakes on the first day, some as large as 5.4 on the Richter scale. The population of Canterbury was left on edge and in utter confusion; the unimaginable had happened. As of 9.00pm on Friday September 24, Cantabrians had experienced an extraordinary 749 seismic shocks in week one, 186 in week two and 83 in week three.

In the immediate days after the earthquakes there was an outpouring of sympathy and empathy from around the country and the world. The support people within the community demonstrated towards each other was exceptional; strangers helped each other out in a time of great need. There were harrowing tales of survival. Christchurch was a city facing its worst times yet producing its best efforts.

By October 15 the Earthquake Commission (EQC) had received the following claims: Christchurch City 78,248 claims, Selwyn 7,873, Waimakariri 6,126, Timaru 2,440, Ashburton 1,931 and 1,710 from other places, bringing the total number of claims to 98,328. By October 29 this figure had risen to 106,041 claims. The types of damage to property reported included: interior walls and doors, external walls, ceilings, foundations, chimneys, rooves, land, drainage and sewage, hot-water cylinders, basins, sinks and baths, toilets and swimming pools. The population was informed that there would be little building activity until March or April 2011.

The aftershocks kept coming and the EQC claim numbers kept rising. By November 14, 2010 the total number of claims was 165,203. ECQ found it necessary to recruit many more staff. It was clear from the outset that this was a much larger event than even they were prepared for. On September 3, 2010 the EQC payroll was 22; by the November 27, 2010 the staff number had swollen to 1,150 at a cost of NZD 2.1 million a week. Staff were made up of call-centre workers, loss adjustors, risk assessors, police personnel and claims managers. Most of these staff did not possess the skills required for the task they were sent to carry out. Progress was experienced as desperately slow and discontent amongst the population was beginning to grow. Behind the groundswell of dissatisfaction were distressed people, large-scale property damage and enormous personal problems.

Fletcher Building, a large construction firm, was contracted to manage the earthquake rebuild on behalf of the EQC. Some 1,500 registered builders and tradesmen signed up to the government scheme registering them to work on earthquake recovery projects. Even so, homeowners and builders started to get frustrated about the lack of speed and progress with claims assessment and began to blame Fletcher Building, who claimed that it was protecting the industry from 'construction cowboys', and the ongoing aftershocks were predicted to slow work further. In fact by October 2010 the Canterbury (re) construction industry had essentially ground to a halt. The first signs of trouble were becoming apparent. In December 2010 it was reported that most, probably thousands, of Cantabrians would not be able to return to their homes for years.[3]

At around the same time the second of the Earthquake Recovery Commission land reports was released, dividing the city into three zones: Zone 'A' (100,000-plus houses) allowed for immediate repair of properties; Zone 'B' (5,500 homes) involved immediate repair plus some simple land remediation work; and Zone 'C' (3,300 properties) was made up of severely damaged properties where work would be delayed due to the infrastructure requirements necessary before property remediation could begin. At about this time the idea of constructing ring-fenced underground dams was floated in order to mitigate the liquefaction issues. This was clearly a very major project and many of the homeowners in the zones to which this proposition applied had already been renting since the September 4, 2010 earthquake and for those who had managed to obtain it, their insurance policy cover for accommodation had started to run out.

Fears began to surface about the real possibility of bankruptcy for many. How were people to continue repaying mortgages on top of costs for alternative accommodation? Affected citizens were beginning to realise that more should be done to assist them. By mid-December 2010 there was a surge of reports of business people fearing the demise of the once-thriving business community. House prices begin to fall in areas where there had been severe quake damage. At this time the local business population began showing the first signs of growing discontent over the way in which private insurers were/were not processing their insurance claims. This led to a call for the Insurance Ombudsman to oversee the claims.[4] The Ombudsman declared that there was no need for any additional support in Christchurch as the claims could be dealt with from Wellington. The population was incensed, believing bureaucracy had no idea of what was taking place at ground level. As a first peep under the rug with respect to the insurance debacle, Christchurch Mayor Bob Parker acknowledged that *"there are too many cases of people who are caught between what they believed their policy can deliver and what it does deliver"*.[5]

Then, on Boxing Day 2010, more than two dozen earthquakes, including another large 4.9 quake, shook the city. This earthquake not only hit retailers on their busiest day, but was also very destructive, forcing the closure of many more buildings and generating an additional 3,483 claims. The Reserve Bank made the assumption at this time that most rebuilding would occur over 2011 and 2012 and that 85 percent of essential infrastructure would be repaired by June 2012. Experts around this time were predicting that the aftershocks could be over in three or four months and that after a month or so, residents of the area would hardly feel any of them. Christchurch citizens remained hopeful but sceptical.

By the end of December 2010 there were louder calls for Insurance Ombudsman representation in the city. The New Zealand Insurance Council chief executive, Chris Ryan, declared that the insurance industry 'would change its approach as a result of the earthquakes'.

The EQC revised the cost of the earthquakes up to NZD 3.5 billion from its initial estimates of NZD 1 to NZD 2 billion in late September 2010. There is, as of September 4, NZD 5.6 billion in the EQC fund, with a further NZD 8 billion of reinsurance. There were suggestions that insurance claims might take more than two years to be paid out.

The Year 2011

By January 14, 2011 the number of claims had risen to 168,731....

On January 20, at 6.03am, another shake – magnitude 5.1 was felt. It was considered a new incident and by mid-afternoon 53 claims of damage had been received by the EQC. By January 25 this figure had reached 173,599. Then on February 4, at 7.32 am, the town of Oxford was shaken by a 4.5 tremor. There was another on February 5. Christchurch was now in a near-permanent state of apprehension.

On February 7, the Canterbury Employers Chamber of Commerce stated that about 150 businesses would fail as a result of the quake and its multiple aftershocks, while others suggested 2,000 to be a more accurate figure[6] ... and then private insurers began their insidious argument that any drop in trade was not the direct result of the earthquake but rather a consequence of 'depopulation' of the central city... and businesses were consequently not entitled to business-interruption insurance. This strategic piece of reasoning attracted great criticism and growing cynicism toward the insurance industry.

Suggestions began to emerge that the Government had abandoned the central city and, as a result, thousands of businesses would collapse. Simultaneously reports emerged that the earthquake damage would be likely to create thousands of jobs, peaking to around 14,500 by the middle of 2012.[7]

By February 8, 2011, 60 percent of the EQC claims had been assessed and the EQC had now paid out NZD 720.29 million. The EQC claims were separated into three categories – those with less than NZD 10,000 worth of damage, who receive a commission pay-out; those with more than NZD 100,000 damage, who receive the maximum pay-out and then have to negotiate with their insurance companies; and those with between NZD 10,000 and NZD 100,000 damage. Various building firms were appointed to manage the official repairs to homes over the NZD 100,000 EQC cap. The mammoth fix for the city's infrastructure was given an optimistic completion target of 2013.

Discrepancies between the EQC reports and values and, lower insurance company values were becoming depressingly common and disconcerting for local residents. This was coupled with the perceived tardiness becoming unacceptable and frustrating to claimants, while suppliers and contractors caused additional trauma for many with shoddy work and poor service. More and more complaints emerged about the lack of definite answers, the lack of clarity around the process and lack of information available. This led to discussion about holding monthly briefings on quake-recovery work. At that point City Councillor Tim Carter began to push for the establishment of a specialist committee to oversee the city's earthquake recovery, stating that the rebuild should not be seen as 'business as usual' and ought to be the City Council's major focus.[8] This approach produced an immediate rift within the Council.

On February 21, 2011 the Minister for Earthquake Recovery, Gerry Brownlee, announced a NZD 26 million package to assist those who had been forced to leave their homes and whose insurance cover for rental had expired. There were 505 EQC claims from people with no insurance, and the Government declined their claims. Minster Gerry Brownlee stated that the *"Government has no plans to help uninsured homeowners, as any interference in the form of a programme would diminish the insurance responsibility for the rest of the country."*[9]

A 'summit' to be made up of Members of Parliament, councillors, community board members, Environment Canterbury commissioners, Earthquake Commission and Ngai Tahu representatives, together with officials from the police, fire service, and City Care, amongst others, was then called for to report on progress since the September 4 earthquake. Cross-sectorial action and collaborative leadership was called for.[10] The summit format received mixed reviews and there was a general feeling of an absence of engagement by the community. The community desperately indicated that it wanted to be involved. With winter on its way, fears were growing for many that heating might not be restored, and the prospect of a cold bleak winter was another stress to cope with.

Then, the *coup de grâce* – a second major earthquake struck, at 12.51pm on February 22, 2011, measuring 6.3 on the Richter scale. It was said to be among the ten strongest recorded in New Zealand. Considerable damage was caused, crippling the city and some suburbs. It struck close to the heart of the city, in the middle of the day when people were at work. Many buildings, already weakened by the previous quake, collapsed. Liquefaction immediately posed huge challenges for access and remedial work. This event cost 185 people their lives (half of all deaths occurring at the collapsed CTV building), with many more injured. The search for survivors began straight away but the lack of a plan and inadequate or inappropriate equipment caused delays that likely cost some their lives.

This earthquake received worldwide media attention. It triggered a national state of emergency, which was to remain in place for 10 weeks. As result of it, 61,000 new insurance claims were lodged with EQC and an estimated 70,000 people left the city, some for a break from the chaos and others permanently. For most the new reality was very difficult to grasp – Christchurch would never be the same again. What was already going badly had suddenly become much worse.

~~~

I have purposefully written the following section in the present tense, giving the reader a better sense of the pace and dislocation that was experienced by Cantabrians at the time.

After the initial shock subsides, overwhelming questions arise – how to build, what to build and where to build? Plans begin for a temporary Central Business District as it is thought that the heart of the city is likely to be off limits for months. After the September 4 earthquake the plan was to reduce the cordon in the central city, but the February 22 quake has laid those plans to waste – a very different proposition now exists. The scientific community warns the citizens of Canterbury that they can expect aftershocks to continue for many more months.

Census 2011 is cancelled due to the displacement of the population. It is thought likely that 10,000 people will require re-housing and temporary accommodation. Plans for the building of 2,500 temporary modular homes in Christchurch get under way, 150 campervans are made available for temporary housing and another 300 are on standby. Meanwhile people leave the city in droves, assisted by Air New Zealand's NZD 50 flights.

The Insurance Council chief executive, Chris Ryan, encourages people not to abandon their homes as they are likely to suffer financially. Yes, their insurance policy will cover the replacement value of the property but it would be less than the value of the property if that property was repaired and sold with the land. The EQC insurance does not cover vacant land.

There are now many families who simply want to leave, as the barriers they face are considerable. Those with sufficient money can simply go, as can those without any capital investment. It is the group in the middle who are facing the challenging choice of either leaving to begin again or remaining to preserve their hard-earned investment in homes, further complicated by mortgage debt which will follow them if they do decide to leave.

By 26 February 113 people have been confirmed dead... there are 223 people still missing... 600 Search and Rescue staff from all over the world are valiantly working away and there are 12,000 people booked on flights out of the region. The aftershocks continue... and serious questions are being asked around whether or not some suburbs should be rebuilt at all. EQC prepares itself to receive another 130,000 insurance claims. Homeowners are feeling desperate, as the EQC expects that all of the 182,000 insurance claims from the September 4 earthquake already assessed are likely to have to be reassessed in light of the latest earthquake. Even more people will be recruited to perform this mammoth task and the EQC will have to look to Australia and further afield to fill the substantial staffing gaps.

In early March, Roger Sutton, Orion New Zealand Limited chief executive, is named as the preferred candidate to 'rebuild Christchurch'. He is appointed chief executive of the Christchurch Earthquake Recovery Authority (CERA) on May 13, 2011. At this point, Treasury forecasts that the rebuild will run past 2015, with the cost estimated at around NZD 15 billion. Banks begin to slash their fixed-interest rates. The city finally comes to the realisation that the work that will be required is beyond the resources of Christchurch alone and that it will have to look to others for support.

The people of Christchurch begin to honour and bury their dead and there are fears that the death toll is likely to reach 200. March 18 is announced as a public holiday and the day when Cantabrians join together with dignitaries to commemorate their lost citizens.

Another 100,000 homes are thought to have been seriously damaged in the February 22 quake. On March 8 the front page of the *Christchurch Press* reads, "*10,000 homes may be lost*". There is an acknowledgement that the bill to rebuild the city will run into many billions of dollars. A housing crisis looms. 158,000 people are still without access to sanitation. An urgent search for enough portable toilets to service the community is under way. Five thousand portable toilets arrive in the city and a further 20,000 are ordered.

At this point it is predicted that in the Central Business District 755 buildings are likely to be demolished.[11] Commercial property owners begin to get very frustrated at not being given access to their properties in the cordoned-off 'red zone', despite the fact that some of the properties within the cordon were not damaged. Concerns are raised that if the city centre is cordoned for too long it will have a devastating effect on businesses. There are also fears that there will be commercial property owner casualties, especially for those with only indemnity insurance, which will likely only cover the cost of demolishing a building.

Talk of large-scale movement of housing begins and the property developers start vying for position. Government then launches a proposal to buy out the homeowners in the worst-affected areas, given the cost and impracticality of remedial work, and affected residents are offered cash settlements or told of the possibility of their acquiring a section and building plan in a new suburb. Discussions begin around whether or not to spend the millions on repairing the Cathedral, which is considered by many as 'the' symbol of the city. Demolition or repair? The people of the city are divided over the issue. Discussion also begins around the sensitivity of holding a Rugby World Cup in a city which has been so devastated. But by mid-March hopes of World Cup games hosted in Canterbury are dashed.

On March 10 another significant 4.5 earthquake hits the city, striking 10km east at a depth of 10km. Growing discontent at what is perceived to be neglect of the eastern suburbs gathers momentum. Then, on Saturday, March 11, 2011 the first reports of a devastating earthquake and tsunami in Japan are released, followed shortly after by reports of nuclear meltdown. This quickly puts the Christchurch disaster into some perspective. Tsunami alerts resulting from the Japanese event follow in New Zealand, and people are urged to stay off beaches.

There are now reports of buildings in the city being knocked down without some owners being notified and others given only three hours to retrieve what they can. This greatly agitates many business owners. In utter frustration some breach the inner-city cordon to retrieve essential items. Eventually a registration process for recovery of belongings emerges, but only items which are essential for the daily running of people's businesses can be retrieved. Inner-city firms begin to let workers go and the calls for the need for a united vision for the city ring out.

Discussions arise around who will pick up the cost of paying for repairs to damaged hillsides after the state of emergency is over. One private insurer quickly states that any natural hazard that poses a risk to a dwelling following a disaster falls under the EQC's remit. From this point on the EQC's remit continues to grow – to the benefit of the private insurance industry.

By this time the Government has spent NZD 73 million on government job-loss payments and a six-week support package. Inner-city firms and some governmental departments have moved to the outskirts of the city. There are fears of large insolvency numbers, with small to medium enterprises most at risk. Others are still trying to recover financial records lost in the February 22 earthquake. Thirty percent of businesses have closed or are unable to operate as a result of the February 22 earthquake... 9,000 businesses have been approved for subsidy payments for 45,000 employees... 62,000 Christchurch people have received job loss cover from the Government in the form of a payroll subsidy totalling NZD 145 million, which has amounted to between NZD 300–500 a week for each of them for six weeks.[12] This is more than ten times the amount paid out after the September 4, 2010 earthquake.

Towards the end of March 2011 there are reports of tension between the EQC and the Insurance Council and debates around who is going to be responsible for what in terms of payment. Complications are arising from the fact that one party treats the February earthquake as a new event; the other does not. Discussion follows as to whether the EQC should pay an additional NZD 100,000 to homeowners who have suffered further substantial damage in the second major earthquake. If insurance cover rolled over between September 2010 and February 2011, the EQC cover was reset. However, those homeowners who had been severely affected by the September 4 earthquake but not yet assessed by the EQC would only be entitled to one lump-sum payment of NZD 100,000, leaving private insurers to foot more of the total cost of repairs. There is a feeling that there needed to be some leniency around the strict interpretation of these rules.

Also around this time inflows of reinsurance money from the September 2010 earthquake reduce the New Zealand annual current account deficit to a 10-year low. The account was NZD 2.8 billion in deficit in the December quarter, seasonally adjusted, after a NZD 1.7 billion surplus in the September quarter which incorporated NZD 3.6 billion in reinsurance claims on foreign reinsurers. Goldman Sachs economist Philip Borkin states that, *"it is highly likely that New Zealand will, uncharacteristically, experience current account surpluses over 2011"*.[13] The arrival of reinsurance funds for the February 2011 earthquake are less easy to trace!

Feelings of doom and gloom surrounding Christchurch and its future give rise to a pledge by citizens to stay in Christchurch.[14] During the last week of March 2011, Prime Minister John Key arrives in the city to announce the new governance structure, which is seen to have enormous powers to act quickly. A rates relief package is considered by the Christchurch City Council and then the Canterbury Earthquake Recovery Authority emerges (with no neighbourhood consultation) as a government department with a top-heavy command and control structure.

It is at about this time that criticism of EQC begins in earnest. Citizens find it hard to believe that after 60 years of preparation for a major disaster the current Christchurch situation is 'as good as it gets'. Reports emerge of EQC assessors' extravagance to ensure that no one is disgruntled about their assessments. There is concern over the way resources are being so liberally spent. Now that thousands of properties are condemned, whole streets abandoned and damaged hillsides being assessed, questions are being asked: what is the extent of government's responsibility for the costs of the disaster? How is it going to work in terms of compensation? How much 'say' will residents have over where they relocate, particularly when it is the Government that is providing new building sites?

Meanwhile people's lives remain on hold. There are whisperings that entire areas will not be rebuilt on. The Government tries to reassure increasingly nervous homeowners that they will not be left out of pocket. Compensation powers – based on 'current market value' – have been written into the Earthquake Recovery Act passed in Parliament in mid-April. Geotechnical reports are apparently being prepared.

It is not long before the first reports of massive increases in insurance premiums begin. The Consumers Institute warns of a 20 percent increase. Estimates from insurers and financial analysts now estimate the cost of damage as high as NZD 16 billion. There is speculation that insurance companies are taking a very cautious approach in terms of new business and the rebuild settlements, using the aftershocks as justification. The Earthquake Recovery Minister is told by the insurance industry that they will not sign up any new business for 20–30 days after a magnitude-4.0 or larger earthquake. Canterbury is still experiencing at least one magnitude-4.0 earthquake every week.

On April 7, 2011 it becomes clear that the insurance company AMI is in difficulty. The Government announces it will make NZD 500 million available. It may have to inject up to NZD 1 billion into AMI to help cover claims for the February 22, 6.3 magnitude earthquake. AMI is the second-biggest residential insurer in New Zealand. It had 485,000 policyholders, with 1.2 million policies, 51,000 of them in Christchurch. AMI had more than a 30 percent market-share of the fire and general insurance market in Canterbury. If the Government does not bail out AMI there would be chaos within the insurance industry, massive confusion amongst policyholders and further delays in the Christchurch rebuild. Insurance Australia Group (IAG) agrees to purchase AMI, which the Government says is to *"strengthen the Canterbury insurance market and reduce the Crown's liability"*. This sparks serious questions around AMI and its responsibilities toward its policyholders. AMI has failed to inform policyholders of its intention to sell, stating that it has set up a holding company and in so doing skirted around its legal obligations to inform them of its decision to sell the business.

Western Pacific Insurance Limited then collapses as well, unable to meet its obligations. While the company had reinsurance, it could not meet the NZD 1 million excess on each of the policies covering 2010 and 2011. After a court case, 183 residential and commercial property owners share part of NZD 33 million in reinsurance monies received by the failed Queenstown insurer.

Building progress within the region again slows to a crawl. This is put down to the need for geotechnical reports. The Earthquake Recovery Minister states that he is happy with the speed and efficiency of the insurers. The local population, however, is experiencing enormous frustration and anxiety.

Business owners are told they must bring their premises up to modern code standards and although there may be some tax relief on the cost of doing so, the figures and costs are still more than most can swallow. Some believe that the very people who are capable of pulling the economy out of the rubble are being denied a voice by officialdom and insurers.

On April 14, 2011 the Earthquake Recovery Bill is passed into law. The Christchurch City Council is concerned that it was not given sufficient warning about this legislation and that it was not furnished with a copy of the Draft Bill. In addition concerns are raised over the possibility of CERA forcing Canterbury local authorities to sell assets. The Hon. Gerry Brownlee, denies this intention.

Then on April 16 a 5.3 aftershock causes more damage, including 150 new rockfalls and many damaged water pipes. New layers of silt emerge. By April 27 the EQC claims total has reached 302,440. The EQC has paid out NZD 840 million. The February quake is considered to have created its own set of complications, and there is confusion as to which quake was responsible for what damage? Each major event constitutes a new insurance claim. Most of the privately insured losses, it is reported, are to be borne by global reinsurance companies. The Government, along with the EQC contributions, is to carry the remaining losses to uninsured public infrastructure and government buildings. Fears begin to grow that more private insurers might fail and the EQC funds are stretched to the limit.

An article appears on May 14, 2011 in the *Christchurch Press* stating that if homeowners do not seek legal advice they could lose out financially. People are shocked to hear that they may have to spend their savings to protect themselves from their insurers!

As if all of this is not enough, another strong 5.8 earthquake hits New Zealand's South Island at 1.01pm on June 13, destroying buildings already weakened by the two previous major earthquakes. This is followed by another series of quakes. GNS scientists warn that this seismic activity will likely trigger new aftershocks. Prime Minister John Key says the latest earthquakes will probably be treated as new events for insurance purposes. According to EQECAT (which provides catastrophe risk models, software, data products and consulting for insurance and reinsurance industries), the 6.0 magnitude event is estimated to have caused losses of between USD 3 billion and USD 5 billion. And the media fill in the gaps – the City of Christchurch has taken the brunt of the shaking... The City's citizens are at their wits' end... Dozens of people have been injured by falling debris...

On June 13, the Prime Minister confirms that thousands of homes will have to be abandoned but declines to specify which areas will be affected, saying homeowners will be told when negotiations with insurers are complete. The city is divided into red, green, orange and white zones and the Government announces it will buy red zone houses at 2007 Rateable Values. The buy-outs produce 'winners and losers', with equity losses of up to NZD 150,000 for some. Designated 'red zone', large swathes of Bexley, Avonside, Avondale, Burwood, Kaipoi and Brooklands receive the death knell. The Port Hills properties are zoned differently, due to their rockfall hazards, and 500 of those homes are deemed to be too unsafe to occupy, regardless of the fact that many are not damaged.

In July the insurance freeze put brakes on the Canterbury economy. Canterbury Employers' Chamber of Commerce chief executive Peter Townsend says the insurance market in Christchurch is *"broken"*, with a halt called on new business policies and higher premiums for existing customers. He adds, *"if we don't have a free-flowing insurance market, we can't make real progress.*"[15] More than 850 Kaiapoi houses are now officially red zoned. The Arts Centre fails to secure insurance.

In August the rebuild draft for Christchurch is revealed.

In September 2011 Ansvar Insurance, which specialises in insuring churches and education and heritage buildings, withdraws from New Zealand completely, stating that it had NZD 700 million in claims and only NZD 35 million in premiums and is unable to find affordable reinsurance. This raises questions around the capital adequacy aspect of the Insurance (Prudential Supervision) Act 2010. Existing policies were cancelled on December 31, 2011 leaving customers without insurance. It had 2,100 commercial customers and 8,900 domestic customers. Ansvar had reached a deal with Bridges Insurance Services, which is underwritten by Lumley Insurance, to take on some of its customers and its direct customers would be able to get interim insurance with Ansvar Australia. The Government has no plans to help Ansvar Insurance customers caught short by their provider's exit from the New Zealand market. Many policyholders thought that Ansvar would arrange for continued insurance elsewhere, but are left to find solutions themselves. Even though homeowners' policies are expiring, the Hon. Gerry Brownlee states that the Government has no intention of intervening. Community Law Canterbury managing solicitor Kevin Campbell says these newly uninsured but badly damaged or written-off properties could place their owners in a challenging legal quandary.

By October, many citizens feel that the Earthquake Recovery Minister is down-playing the seriousness of the insurance problem for Canterbury home and business owners as the call for government intervention falls on deaf ears. Problems arise around earthquake insurance being unobtainable; those wanting to buy existing homes or build new homes are finding it very difficult to secure insurance. The failure to obtain insurance will ultimately cost Christchurch productive citizens and much investment on which a healthy city depends to survive. Stories of disgruntled owners and their dealings with various private insurers increase in the *Christchurch Press,* 13 months after the first major earthquake! The problem is so bad that businesses look for alternative solutions. Some builders decide to sidestep insurers by arranging their own insurance. If their customers cannot obtain insurance, they are unable to pay builders. Building companies begin to blame insurers for the delays in payments and red tape that are strangling the rebuilding process; repair work is put on hold or cannot be begun. Builders around Christchurch begin laying-off staff. There is a genuine concern amongst the building fraternity that if the insurance industry continues to delay payments, builders will simply leave the region.

There is talk that the EQC levy will treble in February 2012 (which it did). This increase is due to the depleted Natural Disaster Fund reserves and as homeowners are the Fund's primary beneficiaries it needs to be replenished in order to run its day-to-day operating costs and to be available for claims over the next 30 years. The increase is likely to boost EQC revenue from NZD 86 million to NZD 260 million a year.[16] The new EQC earthquake levy comes on top of a series of other massive premium increases from private insurers. Due to mortgage-rate increases as a result of bank rating-agency downgrades, homeowners feel financial pressure tightening from every direction.

October also sees the beginning of protests in Christchurch: people – angry at the Government for the lack of information regarding the fate of their homes and communities – protest against private insurers and their lack of response and blatant delay with pay-outs on valid claims. The Minister for Earthquake Recovery and the CERA chief executive decline to attend. The population is demonstrating that it is tired of promises not being kept. There are protestors occupying Hagley Park, Christchurch's main park, protesting against corporate greed alongside earthquake related protests. Ironically, the protestors have the insurance corporates in common.

People are beginning to feel that the insurance market is neither honest nor fulfilling their needs. There is a suggestion by the New Zealand First candidate Denis O'Rourke, in Letters to the Editor of the *Christchurch Press*, that New Zealand should once again have its own insurance company, backed by the Government. We have a Kiwi Bank, why not Kiwi Insurance? There are more calls for the Government to intervene in the insurance market, which is increasingly viewed to be failing its policyholders.

Reports of the likelihood of further massive increases in home insurance premiums emerge from the Insurance Council. Suggested excesses of NZD 30–50,000 would possibly price many out of the market and leave them with no cover at all. The chief executive of Lumley Insurance, John Lyon, admits that the future of full earthquake insurance in New Zealand is unclear. Home insurance premiums are "expected to jump 150 percent in the next year".[17] EQC is also to go through a full review. The insurance landscape begins to reshape itself and the role of private insurance in the future is now uncertain. The *Christchurch Press* continues to report stories about disgruntled insurance policyholders and celebrates several small victories for claimants.[18] However, tens of thousands of people are still waiting for settlement of their claim. Where are they positioned in the claims queue? Each insurer indicates that it has a clear process in place for making fair triage decisions.[19] Those wanting to sell their properties are held up by the insurance industry because buyers are unable to secure insurance. This does not, however, prevent an increase in property values.[20]

Now Fletcher Building reports that it does not expect the Christchurch rebuild to start in earnest until the second half of 2012 – again the start date is pushed out. In the meantime, builders in the city are desperate for work and the insurers are blamed for their woes. One building company owner states that when he drives to his premises each day he can see enough work to keep his company busy for five years within a one-hundred-metre stretch. One street would keep him busy for 20 years.[21] The reality of the situation begins to hit home – the rebuild is no longer a five-year project, and could easily stretch to well over a decade.

On October 8, Christchurch City Councillor Tim Carter calls for investigation around the insurance of city assets and the potential conflict of interest that the chief executive, Tony Marryatt,[22] may have in relation to a decision to change from one insurer (New Zealand Insurance) to Civic Assurance. Marryatt is a director of Civic Assurance (see Chapter 2, The Politics). Later it is revealed that the city's assets have been significantly underinsured, leaving the city's taxpayers having to foot these losses. The population expresses its disbelief.

A group of 100 protestors meets in the Botanic Gardens on October 16, 2011 to voice their anger at the Government and insurers for the lack of information regarding the fate of their earthquake-damaged land.[23] This is the first of many protests. They call for transparency and clarity. Labour spokespeople Clayton Cosgrove and Lianne Dalziel state that the *"clear message we've got from communities is 'Give it to us, warts and all' ".*[24] The Christchurch community feels it is being left out of the 'loop'.

In early November another colour category is added to the list – 'blue'. This allows people to rebuild or repair on potentially liquefaction-prone land using stronger foundations. Each property would require its own geotechnical assessment report. This new category affects 6,000 homes. New building activity will remain on hold until the new foundation standards are released. People are understandably frustrated. Questions are asked about who will pay the additional costs for the stronger foundations, and the insurance term 'betterment' begins to be bandied around.

A broker predicts *"pain for people whose insurance policy cover ends next February"* as business people's interruption insurance ends.[25] It is thought that this will lead to additional job losses, bankruptcies, mortgagee sales and liquidations as people cannot run businesses without insurance. In the interim the Government has brought in changes to the tax rules around depreciation in an attempt to stop property developers from abandoning the area and to encourage reinvestment in the city. Owners of demolished buildings will not immediately have to pay depreciation claimed earlier. Normally, an insurance pay-out would be treated as a sale, and instantly trigger a bill for depreciation. Owners can now choose to roll over the depreciation into new premises as long as it is in one of the allocated districts, i.e. Selwyn, Waimakariri or Christchurch. Christchurch residents are told by the EQC that they may have to wait years for their land damage to be repaired.

On 18 November 2011, the EQC reports a shortfall of NZD 7.1 billion after the earthquakes.[26] In the year to June 30, the EQC had liabilities of NZD 11.4 billion from earthquake claims, partially offset by NZD 4.2 billion in reinsurance. Its Natural Disaster Fund has been wiped out and it has a deficit of NZD 1.5 billion. In addition, it has sold NZD 1.49 billion of investment assets from the fund to pay NZD 1.2 billion to Cantabrians. As a result, Treasury, somewhat belatedly, decides to apply more oversight to EQC's costings and claims management.[27]

Australia supplies staff to EQC, charging at least a 10 percent margin for international staff,[28] and a Wellington company supplying staff is making NZD 10.00 each hour worked by an EQC staff member supplied by them. Assessors were said not to need any special building knowledge: all that was required was that they be *"experienced and competent in communicating effectively and empathically with a wide range of people, often in stressed situations."*[29] Many property owners and policyholders strongly disagree about the skills needed. For the 2012 year EQC has chosen 132 people from outside Christchurch to inspect Canterbury houses. An EQC assessor employed on a year's contract will receive NZD 105,000 plus NZD 400.00 a week living allowance and those who choose to relocate to Christchurch will receive a relocation allowance. Reports later come in that the EQC is providing *"jobs for the boys and girls"*, after employing the daughter of a claims manager at NZD 75.00 an hour. The EQC chief executive retorts that the organisation is still going through a recruitment process and consequently is not prepared to talk about individual cases but that there is a conflict of interest policy in place.[30] Figures released to the *Christchurch Press* reveals 30 EQC management and field staff have close family relationships with other EQC staff. It later transpires that all those staff who are related to employees come from outside Christchurch and are entitled to food and accommodation allowance on top of their salaries and are said to be having a *"pretty good go on the gravy train already"*.[31] In addition, couples working as field staff have been able to claim separate living allowances. However, the Commission remains adamant that its appointment process is beyond reproach.[32] Local citizens caught up in the Christchurch earthquakes cannot help but find the comparison between support offered to families and that offered to the Commission staff tough to swallow. In early 2012, documents from LSI (a consultancy firm) released under the Official Information Act show that the EQC identified significant gaps in its ability to measure the performance of its claims management personnel.[33] Cantabrians are not at all surprised by the findings.

Another 417 properties are relegated to the red zone. The announcement *"basically obliterated a whole suburb"*.[34] Yet the same Brooklands residents who were left on condemned land are given the go-ahead to rebuild on the land after the February earthquake. For Port Hills residents, life is no easier – those who refuse to leave their earthquake-damaged homes are told they will be evicted.[35] Initially the Council uses the Building Act to try to evict citizens, but without success. It threatens that a court injunction will be sought in 2012 if the notices continue to be ignored.[36] Five hundred homes were issued notices prohibiting entry after the February 22 earthquake because of rockfall, cliff collapse or landslide damage. There is a rumour that a private investigator has been employed to monitor the homes which are supposed to be vacant. The Council admits that indeed it has used a private investigator in some cases to determine evidence of occupancy. Let us not forget that some people have limited insurance, some have no insurance at all, others have accommodation insurance that has nearly run out and many have lost jobs. Their options are very limited.

Towards the end of November 2011 Christchurch residents march to the CERA headquarters calling for an independent body to be set up to hear grievances. The feeling is that an advocacy commission is vital for fair outcomes. Crosses of many colours, representing the various land-zoning categories, are laid at CERA's door. These are removed from sight within the hour.

Also in November, IAG officially purchases AMI for NZD 380 million, subject to regulatory approval (given in March 2012). Residents now state that they feel it is unfair to have to pay rates and insurance premiums for uninhabitable homes.[37] It is announced that the first homes in the red zone are to be demolished in February of 2012, one year after the devastating earthquakes. Private insurers and the Government are expected to take two years to clear large swathes of Christchurch and Kaiapoi. At this point in time, 60 percent of homes in the red zone are still occupied. There is still no decision as to what will happen to the land after it is cleared.[38]

The finger of blame starts searching for somewhere to point. There is some suggestion that perhaps earthquake scientists and civil defence managers should be prosecuted for failing to predict the effects of large earthquakes and it is declared that they should be prosecuted if they fall below an acceptable standard.[39] Six Italian scientists and an ex-government official were sentenced to six years in prison over the deadly earthquake in L'Aquila. Structural engineers also come under fire. The Canterbury Earthquakes Royal Commission hears evidence[40] from tenants relating to the failure of buildings during the earthquakes, in particular from tenants in respect of the failure of the Pyne Gould Corporation building, the collapse of which killed 18 in the February 22, 2011 earthquake.

Meanwhile the people of Christchurch wait and wait…

The New Zealand Institute of Economic Research's principal economist, Shamubeel Eaqub, says that Christchurch's economic recovery will be stunted if the earthquake rebuild does not speed up. He calls for CERA and the Government to push ahead more strongly. There have been 26,800 job losses in the year to September 30, 2011. The longer the city waits, the more businesses and people leave.

An American insurance expert declares that insurance companies have a vested interest in delaying payment as long as they can to collect interest on their funds.[41] The New Zealand Insurance Council chief executive dismisses his comments as 'self-serving'!

On Saturday, December 3, 2011, Wellington experiences a 5.7 magnitude quake that originates 60 km deep and 30 km east of Picton. One of the capital's largest and newest buildings sustains damage, reminding New Zealanders that it can happen anywhere.

On December 22, 2011 an article appears in the *Christchurch Press* stating that 36,000 workers will be required to rebuild Christchurch; 23,900 tradespeople are needed and a further 12,000 required to support the rebuild, based on the need to rebuild 10,000 homes and repair 105,500 homes. The Earthquake Commission and Fletcher Earthquake Recovery announce their targets for the repair of about 100,000 earthquake-damaged homes in the Canterbury Home Repair Programme. EQC General Manager Customer Services, Bruce Emson, says the main target for the Canterbury Home Repair Programme is 80 percent of homes in the managed repair programme completed by 2014.[42] These are the properties with damage falling under the NZD 100,000 cap. People with more serious damage will have to await their insurers...

Citizens are told that the rebuild has 'kicked off'. Peak reconstruction is projected to be the third quarter of 2013.[43] The rebuild date continues to slide forward into the future. The Canterbury Employers' Chamber of Commerce chief executive, Peter Townsend, says the survey points to 2012 as being the year when *"the big wheels of economic recovery are going to start cranking"* and there will be an unprecedented demand on resources and labour.

By mid-December 2011 a poll shows that central city businesses are split over whether to return to Christchurch. Their decision is likely to be determined by factors such as the form the development of the central business district takes, insurance pay-outs, business support mechanisms, building regulations and the quality of information available for business owners.[44]

On Thursday, December 15, 2011 the Council adopts the Central City Plan, which will guide the redevelopment of the city. Mayor Bob Parker states that the process *"has been a balancing act for the council"*, but will enable people to rebuild and redevelop the city centre. There is a call for the plan to *"deliver on the hopes and aspirations of those who we lost"*.[45]

The AMI mutual then concludes the sale of its customer base, minus liabilities (which the Government is to fund) to IAG without consulting its 500,000 policyholders – a perfect sleight of hand. AMI's explanation for its underhand decision is that because it had created a holding company it did not need the vote of the trustee or the members for the sale. Many question why, once again, taxpayers pick up the tab of a mismanaged company like AMI? Shades of the USA – too big to fail?

On December 23, 2011 Christchurch experiences another two earthquakes 90 minutes apart: of magnitudes 5.8 and 6.0. In the central city panicked shoppers flee city malls. Other parts of the city are affected by rockfall and liquefaction. Offshore faults are said to be to blame for the latest bout of quakes.[46] More than 26,000 homes are without power.[47]

The enormity of the potential consequences begins to set in. What is the insurance industry going to make of these latest events? How much more delay will it cause? How many more claims will there be? How many more people will leave the area? Will people be able to sell property? When can they leave? It is only two days before Christmas and Christchurch citizens are reminded of the Boxing Day earthquake of 2010, almost exactly one year ago to the day, and here in Christchurch the shaking continues. This has occurred after six months of relative seismic calm. Ambulance staff treat 60 people for earthquake related injuries, including falls and heart problems. The airport closes for inspection, causing major disruption for Christmas travellers.

Yet again it is the eastern suburbs that sustain the most damage and yet again many areas are flooded because of liquefaction. Parklands residents demand that the Government write off the hundreds of homes that were initially deemed habitable. Residents declare that they have lost faith in the Government's land decisions – *"you can dig down as far as you like but you won't get anything but silt"*.[48]

Then, after Christmas, there is some speculation that Earthquake Recovery Minister Gerry Brownlee may be replaced by Steven Joyce, but Gerry Brownlee retains his mandate. It is thought (and hoped by many) that his presence will be diminished in light of the now-functioning government department CERA.

The Year 2012

On January 2, 2012 the city is initially shaken awake at 1.27am with a 5.1 magnitude earthquake, again centred 20km north of Lyttelton. Just four minutes later there is a 4.3 at a depth of 12km and then a 3.5 at 2.20am and a 3.8 at 5.03am. These are all 20km north-east of Christchurch and at depths of 12km, 20km and 8km respectively. These quakes cause significant new liquefaction in eastern Christchurch, on a scale similar to those on June 13, 2011. They will cost the Earthquake Commission an extra NZD1.1 billion, according to Treasury. Insurers say they do not expect to take a large financial hit, with many claims likely to be under

NZD 100,000, meaning the costs will fall yet again to the EQC.[49] The Hon. Gerry Brownlee says that the latest earthquakes have vindicated the Government's decisions on land, as much of the damage has occurred in already red zoned areas.

Meanwhile, claims are further delayed as a result of differences of opinion between EQC and private insurers over damage costs. The feeling for many is that apportionment for each event is little more than guess-work and an excuse for further delay. There are at least 100,000 EQC claims yet to be settled. This figure does not take into account the private insurers' claims. Stories begin to emerge of EQC reassessing properties and cutting initial claims by as much as NZD 250,000, together with demands to recover from property owners their previously paid-out funds! This is an unbelievable twist of events. EQC is now further under the spotlight, in relation to releasing land remediation reports, and delays in claim settlements. Meanwhile local businesses begin to secure construction insurance from Lloyds of London because local insurers refuse to take on additional risk. Their new premiums are said to be four times pre-quake prices.

Towards the end of January, the Prime Minister again reiterates that the Christchurch rebuild is at the top of his priority list for the next three years,[50] but many Christchurch citizens feel they have been abandoned by their government and Prime Minister.

On 1 February, angry residents in their thousands gather outside the Council's offices demanding that Christchurch City Council chief executive Tony Marryat resign and hand back his NZD 68,000 pay rise. There is also renewed talk of a 'rates revolt'[51] and a reorganisation of the City Council.

This is followed by distressing news to homeowners – that the private insurers and EQC are to join forces and make property assessments together. Suddenly any impartiality that may have existed between the EQC and the private insurers disappears. The exasperation of policyholders is palpable; there now seems to be no one to protect their interests, no one whose opinion is trustworthy. The joining of forces is said to be an attempt to overcome differences that have seen the two sides not completely aligned.[52]

Many view the move as an attempt by EQC and the Government to stem the haemorrhaging financial losses of EQC. Seven hundred properties are likely to be reassessed. In addition, EQC officials are urging property owners to have reassessments done on buildings after the December 23 earthquakes as the cumulative effects of all the earthquakes might be enough to put buildings into the 'dangerous' category.[53] In a series of briefings to Cabinet Ministers, EQC states that it wants to make some changes to its business practices and would like these reviewed. It also notes concern at Canterbury's lack of skilled builders and carpenters, estimating that an additional 20–30,000 will be required.

Meanwhile the Waimakariri District Mayor asks why parts of Waimakariri have been red zoned, as residents feel that this designation is a mistaken judgement call. Other 'red zoners' around the city feel 'cut-off' as mail delivery stops and their neighbours move out. A year after the February 22 quakes, many people in Avonside are still awaiting answers around zoning decisions. In mid-February another 213 properties are transferred to the red zone. Parts of Christchurch are declared unlikely ever to be built on again. Newly red zoned homeowners express anger about the deadline they have been given to vacate their homes. They are expected to have left their properties by April 2013. Many have not yet begun to settle with insurers. Insurers had previously stated that they would not decide the cost of rebuilds until the final zoning was known.

The first week of February 2012 also sees the official earthquake death toll increased to 184 people...[54]

There are questions now about the level of liability for the Christchurch City Council in relation to the more than NZD 100 million emergency repair bill resulting from the February 22, 2011 earthquakes. Council is suggesting that the overall bill is probably somewhere in the vicinity of NZD 110 million and thus far only NZD 6 million in funds has been identified. The Civil Defence Minister, Hon. Chris Tremain, stated that the complexity of the claims means the Department and the Council will interpret differently how the reimbursement policy should apply and which costs should be funded by the Crown.[55]

The Property Council of New Zealand declares that the redrafted city plan is likely to put the rebuild and economy at risk, suggesting that the scheme is 'ideological' and favours a green city over an economically viable one. The Property Council's president goes on to say that the plans infringed people's common law rights for owners to replace what they have lost and will make reinvesting in the city very difficult. It was likely that the plans would cause developers to take their cash elsewhere. Meanwhile, commercial property owners who do receive their cheques, *do* begin to take their funds and buy property elsewhere. Auckland real estate agents state that they are receiving many calls from Christchurch buyers.[56]

On February 6, 2012 a small article in the *Christchurch Press* notes that the rebuild of Christchurch has again been delayed another six months due to the ongoing earthquakes and should begin to gain some momentum by the end of 2012.[57] There is speculation that continuing difficulties between CERA and the Christchurch City Council relate to the Government putting pressure on the Council to raise rates and sell off assets such as the airport, port and electricity company worth approximately NZD 1.5 billion. These assets have been responsible for returns of NZD 980 million in dividends over the past 16 years, money which the ratepayer has not been required to find.

The EQC has 100,000 homes to fix. As of February 11, they have fixed only 8,200, and have carried out 90,000 emergency repairs.[58] At this rate the repairs will take 12 years to complete, and this does not take into account those properties that have sustained more than NZD 100,000 worth of damage.

Meanwhile Christchurch's Lyttelton Port is frustrated by the delays of 'pay-as-you-go' payments by its insurers. The Port claim is likely to be the biggest single claim in the Southern Hemisphere. Three extra staff were employed to simply deal with the insurance issues and this was thought to have to rise to between six and 12 extra staff.[59] The Port is considering legal action after their insurers, Vero, disputed a NZD 20 million progress payment for repairs. Vero has paid NZD 35.7 million toward repairs but the Port has paid more than NZD 10 million of its own money for earthquake repairs because the insurers had stalled.[60]

Local firms are not taking on extra staff because as yet there are no signs of a rebuild commencing and local business people report little evidence of work coming their way, although supposedly, recruitment firms are busy recruiting trade staff in Britain and Ireland.

~~~

On February 22 a memorial service is held in Hagley Park to commemorate all those who lost their lives. It takes almost 13 minutes to read out the names of 185 people. It is a sobering reminder to all of how fragile and precious life is and how unexpectedly it can be taken away.

~~~

On March 23 another 251 homes in Christchurch are zoned 'red'. All insured residential properties in the newly red zoned areas are to be subject to the Government offer of purchase. Christchurch Port Hills residents (2,100 homes) await the decision on the fate of their homes.[61]

The Canterbury Communities' Earthquake Recovery Network (CanCern), which represents 38 residents' groups, suggest solutions designed to streamline insurance and the EQC settlements, including that the Government instruct the EQC to align its interpretation of 'replacement value' in homeowner insurance policies. In addition it suggests that the Government mediate an agreement between the EQC and insurers to allow a homeowner to be paid out the agreed total damage figure without having to wait for internal disputes to be reconciled. They also suggest the creation of a working group to develop Canterbury-specific standardised repair methods and cost ranges.

This month also sees the Hon. Gerry Brownlee overrule a CERA statement that 200 Christchurch residential properties be transferred from red to green zone, which has the consequence of further delaying property owners' ability to repair or rebuild.[62] This leads to residents complaining of a lack of transparency and sharing of information. A NZD 600 million village is approved for Belfast with between 1,300 and 2,000 homes but work will not commence on the project until the end of 2012.[63] By March 9, the EQC has received 2,738 formal complaints. It admits to errors, but fails to provide solutions for the shortcomings. The EQC's slowness to settle is said to be due to its duty to protect the taxpayer.

Now concern over the risks associated with 'fracking' are raised. Does this extraction process have the ability to trigger earthquakes? Fracking, or hydraulic fracturing, is the process of extracting natural gas from shale rock layers deep within the earth. Cantabrians are urged to wake up to the dangers of this.[64]

A township on the outskirts of Christchurch, Rangiora, has its main street cordoned off due to a series of earthquake-induced building closures. Insurers begin to suggest cash settlement, stating that it is likely to take four years to fix some earthquake-damaged homes. This is of course a cheaper option for them. It is likely that this will see a large amount of the city's housing stock inadequately repaired or not repaired at all because cash settlement pay-outs will not be adequate to complete the repairs and contract works insurance will be unavailable for some time, which will create a hopeless situation for policyholders. This would also likely force many owners of structurally damaged homes to avoid consented and professionally managed remediation of their homes and instead adopt a more cosmetic, less costly and random repair strategy. Local authorities are rather quiet on their resolve to ensure that repair standards are thorough!

Policyholders are told to be patient and 'play the insurance game' to retain equity in their properties.[65] However, playing the game costs much time and money, and many Cantabrians do not have these additional resources? The city begins to see the arrival of international assessors 'working for' property owners. Community boards are seeking to have a larger role in the earthquake recovery. Again suggestions are made that communication between the boards, council staff and organisations such as CERA require address. Later on in the month, during a meeting with business leaders, the chief executive of CERA, Roger Sutton, again urges patience.[66] After two years people are running out of patience....

Discussion begins over the possibility of rates relief for earthquake-affected residents. Until now the Council could only set rates based on the status of a property at July 1 each year, which meant that owners of properties demolished after that date would have to continue to pay rates until the following July. The Council would also be unable to levy rates for a house built after that date.[67] Christchurch ratepayers are then told that they are to face a 7.47 percent rates rise to help fund the city's earthquake recovery and the rebuilding of facilities. The proposed rates hike to cover a NZD 330 million repair and rebuild bill, it is said, will provide the city with world-class facilities.[68] Paul Anderson, the Council Corporate Services general manager had stated the estimated cost of repairing and rebuilding the facilities was NZD 767 million, with insurance proceeds covering NZD 367 million. Christchurch citizens express their anger at money being spent on convention centres and stadia when people are still without homes. Others state that they are currently struggling and cannot afford to pay the 7.47 percent increase on top of mortgages for homes they are unable to live in and accommodation rental, while they wait for EQC and insurers to fulfil their contractual obligations. Their desperation is increasing.

It transpires that the Council's insurer, the Local Authority Protection Programme (LAPP), has not obtained enough reinsurance to cover the Council's share of the bill; that reinsurance values were based on the 'best estimates at the time',[69] and the scale of the disaster is greater than expected. Mayor Bob Parker goes on to defend the shortfall, saying the Council had taken the 'best advice available' at the time. Mayor Bob Parker also defends the insurance cover, saying the Council had taken *"all of the appropriate professional steps"* to ensure its infrastructure was adequately covered. A Christchurch City councillor, Tim Carter, has alleged Christchurch's public infrastructure was *"grossly underinsured"* at the time of the city's devastating earthquake. He has previously criticised the city's insurance arrangements, stating that the Council's next rates rise would be a 'legacy' of the organisation's insurance problems.[70] Let this be a warning to other councils around the country!

Now the second-largest general insurer in New Zealand, Vero, steps forward and urges the Government and the EQC to tackle the continuing problem of the impasse with insurers over Canterbury claims values resulting from the differences in the way the EQC and insurers assess damage. These differences lead to sometimes wildly different assessments of the value of damage.

By early April 2012 there are reports of difficulties facing the Mayor's Welfare Earthquake Relief Fund, which provides assistance to Christchurch residents experiencing financial hardship as a result of the earthquakes. It had received more than 1,300 requests for help since January 2011 and due to the large number of requests the trust has suspended applications.[71] Meanwhile the Science and Innovation Minister, Steven Joyce, announces plans by the Government to invest NZD1.8 million in an information technology hub in central Christchurch, the Enterprise Precinct and Innovation Campus (EPIC). The 'big business first' strategy is incomprehensible to residents who are still living in hardship and chaos.

Around mid-April, IAG's New Zealand chief executive, Jacki Johnson, states that the company now has 40 percent of the New Zealand insurance market. It will be raising average property premiums by up to 30 percent and is also looking at new risk-sharing models to reduce its exposure in future catastrophic events. *"We're looking at business owners taking on a certain percentage of earthquake claims and the insurance covering the rest"*.[72] This is the start of the slippery slope of massive increases in premiums.

Also at this time the first letters containing an offer for the purchase by the Government / CERA of properties in the red zone are received by these residents. Their agreements to sell these properties are to be lodged by May 19, 2012 and they are informed that if they do not return the agreement in time, they will forfeit the Government's offer to buy their land.[73]

On April 12, another earthquake rattles the city. GeoNet reported that the 4.6 earthquake was located 10 kilometres deep and centred 10 kilometres northeast of the city and struck at 12 noon. It was felt across the city but there were no immediate reports of damage.[74] The whispers around the city are almost audible – what does this mean for the insurance situation now? A series of major earthquakes also take place around the world, including one off the west coast of northern Sumatra which registered as a magnitude of 8.6, followed by an 8.2 earthquake with numerous aftershocks of magnitude 5.0 or greater.[75] In Mexico City a magnitude 7.0 earthquake is registered.[76] The future of affordable insurance everywhere begins to looks shaky.

Ongoing discussion rages about insurers using underestimated or 'fictional' completed repair costs to justify smaller pay-outs for residents in the red zone. By classifying red zone homes as 'repairable', insurers are able to greatly reduce the amount they will have to pay homeowners. It is suggested that this will provide savings for the Government and insurers of hundreds of millions of dollars.[77]

Quietly in the background, by Order in Council under the Canterbury Earthquake Recovery Act legislation, the law is changed to exempt the EQC from the one-year settlement deadline in section 29(4) of the Earthquake Commission Act 1993 (while retaining the requirement that the claims be settled as soon as reasonably practicable), allowing the Commission to enter into agreements with, or invoice, claimants to recover excesses due to the Commission.[78]

Around the city the rental and housing crisis worsens. The Hon. Gerry Brownlee states that *"this is a problem, I'll accept that, but I don't think this is a crisis,"* adding that the steep increase in rent was *"not a problem that has been brought to my attention"*. The Government will not intervene in the issue, leaving it 'to the market', despite clamours from citizens for assistance.[79] Robin Clements, a senior economist with research and investment house UBS, says the Government must intervene in Christchurch's rental housing crisis and assess the level of crisis rather than leave it to the market.[80] This is followed by a public protest on 26 May. The Human Rights Commission begins to take an interest in Christchurch.

Then on April 18, the Hon. Gerry Brownlee announces a new Christchurch Central Development Unit, saying it will be given 100 days to prepare a 'Blueprint for Action', *"the plan is the basis for the way forward because it has such widespread community support"*. He says that the creation of the unit does not represent the Government taking over the Council's responsibilities, and the new group will work alongside the local authority. The unit is to be headed by Warwick Isaacs, who was the general manager of operations for CERA.[81] Brownlee states that it is time for action and the city needs a clear direction for its central rebuild.[82] Mayor Bob Parker says that the new unit will offer a 'true partnership' between the Council and the Government and is the best way to manage the rebuild of the central area. Many Cantabrians feel that it simply adds another layer of bureaucracy. One Christchurch Councillor states that the Government was telling them, an elected council, what was happening and was not involving them in any serious discussion about what they thought should happen. Still there is no published plan for the repair of the city. Is this the beginning of a better future for Christchurch or simply more of the same, which will further slowdown the Christchurch recovery?

The Government anticipates spending more than NZD 2 billion on earthquake recovery in 2012, including the rising number of red zone pay-outs. It states that its guarantee of the EQC claims could run to *"a few billion"*, much higher than the NZD 800 million estimated in late August 2011. The Minister of Finance, Bill English, states that while the Government was making a NZD 13 billion commitment towards the earthquake recovery, the region needed to show it was *"open for business"* to attract essential outside investment and new people. English said the NZD 13 billion was fully funded through budget provisions, which included ongoing revenue raising such as bond issues and state-asset sales.[83] The Government has raised NZD 26.6 million towards the costs of rebuilding Christchurch through an Earthquake Kiwi Bond, but investors are not seeing much reward for their support as the rate on the bond has dropped from 4 percent to 2.75 percent per annum since its launch.[84] In an attempt to find further funding the Government has also moved offshore to Asian sovereign wealth funds. Investment is also sought from Australia, and a new government agency has been set up, Invest Christchurch, to encourage the private sector to contribute billions of dollars towards Christchurch's rebuild.[85]

As the Government develops a new blueprint for the City the threat of compulsory acquisition of private property begins to loom. Reconstruction will require the amalgamation of some current property titles.[86] Property owners begin to accuse the Government of bullying tactics. Lisle Hood, co-owner of properties around Poplar Street, said, *"It's a land grab. They are nationalising private property and stomping all over our property rights… They are buying up all this land and they will flog it off to the big corporates and make a huge killing on it."*[87]

Canterbury is now (at the time of the first publication) early in the third year since the first major earthquake, and the housing shortage remains of considerable concern to many. Housing Minister Phil Heatley uses public interest as justification for *"blacking out 95 percent"* of reports released under the Official Information Act on housing issues in Christchurch. Labour Member of Parliament Annette King declares her outrage on discovering that virtually the entire report had been blacked out, stating that *"It is unacceptable for the Government not to be upfront and straightforward about the problem."*[88] Christchurch residents are stunned by these events – what is happening to their democratic rights?

Meanwhile tenants' advocates call for the provision of temporary villages for earthquake refugees needing short-term housing.[89] A leading building business, David Reid, states that a significant law change needs to be introduced that will accelerate an urgent residential rebuild, *"as an industry we do have the ability to react but the frustrations of having our hands tied is taking its toll. We have had so many false starts…We have people leaving red zoned or red stickered homes with nowhere to go. We need to bring in outside labour and again nowhere to house them."*[90]

Towards the end of May 2012 a group of white zoned (land classified with complex geotechnical issues relating to land slip and rock fall requiring further assessment) Christchurch residents take to the street, angry that they are still in limbo.[91] They have now been barred from their homes for almost 15 months. A protest organised by Occupy Christchurch to highlight the issues of housing shortage and homelessness in the city is organised. The group wants the building of social housing to be a priority as well as a rent-freeze on both social and private housing and a democratic process for people's housing concerns to be raised.[92] On top of the already existing housing issues, the chief executive of the Built Alliance Training Environment, Philip Aldridge, forecasts that 40,000 workers will be needed by the end of 2012, which is an 84 percent increase on the current size of the workforce in Christchurch. Where are these people going to live? No one seems to have answers.

The effects of the Christchurch earthquake are beginning to affect other parts of the country. For instance, the Dunedin Catholic diocese reports increased insurance premiums in the region of an extra NZD 200,000.[93] The fallout from the Canterbury events is increasing residential rental prices in Auckland and Wellington; and in the commercial rental environment, the rise in earthquake insurance levies is pushing up operating costs and lowering net rental returns in a market dominated by net leases, according to the commercial real estate (CBRE) report.[94] In the Manawatu, councils are considering opting out of a local government collective insurance scheme and have given notice of withdrawal from the Local Authority Protection Programme fund. Horizons Regional Council has also considered withdrawing this year amid concerns about its exposure to risk as premiums are being driven up by the earthquake reinsurance fallout.[95] The creeping effects will continue to be seen throughout the rest of New Zealand.

There are also fresh calls for mid-term council elections, with many feeling that the Council's performance has not improved since February despite the appointment of a Crown observer, and rates increases for the city remains a hot topic.[96] A rates rise of 7.5 percent is proposed by the Council. (This figure eventually increases to 7.8 percent). It is felt by many that the Council should find alternatives to borrowing and increasing rates to raise required funds.[97] Again discussion around the sale of City Council assets is raised. Historically, the dividends paid by these entities have been instrumental in keeping Christchurch City rates as some of the lowest in the country, and some feel that the revenue stream they provide is now more important than ever.[98] The Government is now strongly encouraging the Christchurch City Council to partially sell its assets, with Local Government Minister David Carter suggesting the Council sell some of its shares in the Christchurch airport and the Port of Lyttelton to fund the rebuild. Again views are mixed and feelings are running high;[99] many citizens feel that a rates revolt of some sort is the only solution.

And still the process of recovery is moving at a snail's pace. Hundreds of insurance assessments of earthquake damaged residential property have to be reviewed again as they are considered inadequate and yet others have to be revisited because of subsequent earthquakes. Several loss adjusting companies engaged to do the assessments are now considered to have done an insufficient job.

Insurance companies and the Earthquake Commission are urged to *"stop mucking around"* after talks between the EQC and private insurers on collaborative drilling break down.[100] On May 19, Minister Gerry

Brownlee declares that he has met the Insurance Council representatives and the board of the EQC and the issue of who covers what has been sorted out and claims can now be settled more quickly.[101]

Three hundred and eighty homeowners have been surveyed and responded to questions about the status of their properties and the service they had received from their insurance companies. One hundred and fifty two were insured with IAG, either directly or through its subsidiaries Lantern, State and NZI. Of these, 53 said they were still waiting for IAG to complete an on-site assessment some 18 months later. More than 80 percent of the IAG customers in the survey rated the progress in handling their claims as *"poor to awful"*.[102] Legal action against IAG begins to be discussed as an option by a Christchurch group frustrated by inaction on earthquake claims – a class action against State Insurance, one of IAG's subsidiaries. The suggestion is that the insurer had been *"improperly delaying"* action on claims and that this could result in a class action being taken.[103] Commercial earthquake claims are said to be being settled faster than residential claims.

The insurance 'cat and mouse game' is driving residents onto the street. More and more people are losing patience and feeling desperate about the lack of progress with their private insurers.[104] Hundreds of elderly Christchurch residents vent their anger at the insurance industry, declaring that they are too old to keep *"boxing with shadows"*. A crowd of some 300 challenge senior managers from IAG, Lumley, AA Insurance, Vero and Southern Response and the chief executive of the Insurance Council.

Then in early August a series of smaller quakes are felt. Disgruntled technical category 3 (TC3 – land with moderate to significant damage with future liquefaction possible) residents brave the rain and wind to picket the Christchurch offices of the EQC and IAG to again express their anger and frustration at delays.[105]

Vero announces it will spread repairs and rebuilding in Christchurch over three years, with some customers facing a potential start date in 2015. IAG indicates that it has settled almost 50 percent of its 13,000 commercial claims and Vero one third, but these are only material damage claims.[106] Then there are reports that IAG is to pay around NZD 3 million to underpaid Christchurch policyholders. The Australian owned insurance company says it *"undercalculated"* the sum it paid out in 643 earthquake related claims.

Jessica Mutch interviews Earthquake Minister Gerry Brownlee and asks him which of the insurance companies he is referring to in relation to slow claims handling. He skirts around the question, declaring, *"I don't think that's helpful. I mean, it's the old story – if you start blaming, everybody loses. I think what I'm saying is, 'Come on. As an industry, you've got a challenge here which I think has been picked up reasonably well, but we've had probably a few too many months not being able to get any clarity about the go-forward,' and I think that's the problem at the moment"*.[107] Not surprisingly, the insurance industry disputes Hon. Gerry Brownlee's claims that it is dragging its feet in settling claims. Later on in the year the Minister asserts: *"Now the private sector needs to do the sort of things that the private sector claims it can do so particularly well. I've lost my patience."*[108]

The Christchurch City Council now asks the Minister to take urgent steps to help homeowners locked in disputes with their insurers. The Council voted unanimously to request that he urgently set up an insurance tribunal and advocacy service based in Christchurch.[109] However, Insurance Ombudsman Karen Stevens states that she has yet to be convinced of the need for a tribunal.[110] Christchurch citizens wonder just how bad things have to get before they can expect assistance?

Meanwhile insurers' profits rise. Tower's net profit is shown to have jumped by 82 percent in the first half, to March 31, compared with the previous first half, with net profit reaching NZD 23.6 million, paying an interim un-imputed dividend of 5 cents per share. Earthquake claims were said to affect the bottom line by only NZD 4 million in the latest period! The insurance business has almost doubled net profit to NZD 12.4 million in the six months compared with NZD 6.3 million in the equivalent period in 2011.[111] Tower says earthquake related claims will mean its annual net profit will be only NZD 9.4 million, below market expectations. The market had been looking at a net profit of about NZD 50.1 million for the 2011–12 financial year, so a figure of around NZD 40.7 million now looks likely.[112] IAG (NZ), the nation's largest general insurer, reports an AUD 103 million annual profit, reflecting a 27 percent increase in gross written premiums. Overall, the New Zealand business produced an insurance margin of 10.4 percent for the full year and 13 percent in the second half. Rate increases and the contribution of AMI produced a net earned premium of 40 percent in the second half of the 2012 financial year. IAG's integration with AMI is said to be well advanced and likely to produce cost synergies of NZD 30 million in two years.[113] This is thanks to the New Zealand Government's extraordinary decision to take over the AMI Christchurch earthquake liabilities to facilitate the sale of AMI to IAG.

As time marches on, dissatisfaction with the Government's handling of the Christchurch earthquake is growing. The *Christchurch Press* reports that a survey of more than 2,000 Fairfax newspaper readers across the country shows that almost two-thirds of them believe the Government has not done enough. In Christchurch, among the *Christchurch Press* readers, 87 percent think the Government should have done more.[114]

Red zone residents aggrieved by the Government's '2007 valuation' offers take their plight to the United Nations in the belief that the buyout offer breaches their human rights. Their pleas for intervention at the local and national level have gone unheeded and so the decision is taken to *"go international"*.[115] In addition, nearly 300 uninsured Christchurch property owners in the red zone are threatening legal action if the Government does not make an offer on their homes. The group is said to represent those people who had been told to leave their properties with no government offer. The Government 'offers' to buy uninsured and vacant land in the residential red zone at half its rateable value. Unsurprisingly, uninsured red zoners plan legal action against the Government over the Crown offer.[116] The Government orders new valuations for red zoned homes, but refuses to reveal them to homeowners or 'top-up' those who have been short changed. The Canterbury Earthquake Recovery Authority is to 'independently' value the properties so it can 'negotiate' with insurance companies over settlements on properties it has bought at 2007 rating valuations. Many have been paid out considerably less than market value.[117] The Government states that it is unlikely to hold on to the land it buys in earthquake-hit central Christchurch for long; rather the land acquired will probably be sold to private investors. Does anyone imagine that it will be sold to these private investors at half its rateable value? An expert in public policy and governance, Sacha McMeeking, states that the *"command and control"* approach that the Government is using in Christchurch is no longer appropriate. She believes that rather than imposing *"pre-packaged solutions"* on Christchurch the Government should be taking a deliberative approach to decision making in the city and engaging more with the community.

On September 1 another 300 people attend an insurance protest in the city.

Ironically, Aon New Zealand, New Zealand's largest insurance broker and an American insurance subsidiary, has become one of the first companies to open doors on a new office space in Christchurch since the February 2011 earthquake. The newly built Aon House was officially opened by Prime Minister John Key.[118] Somehow there is something rather cynical about the fact that the first major new business to establish itself in Christchurch is the very industry that is crippling its residents.

In September the insurance industry re-enters the Christchurch market in force. Lumley Insurance, part of Wesfarmers Insurance (one of the largest companies in Australia), states that its response unit will provide faster resolution to all earthquake claims.[119] Westpac is teaming up with Lumley Insurance to offer insurance policies for new Canterbury construction projects and full-replacement home and contents policies.[120] In addition, BNZ in association with IAG (NZ) will offer cover to those wanting to build or purchase a residential property. The bank will also give contents cover for those wanting to rent a home, and give cover for property investors and small business owners.[121] It would appear that Christchurch is once again rapidly becoming an Australian insurers' 'cash-cow'.

Discussions begin between the government and private insurers about a new service which is the insurance industry's response to growing public anger. Details have yet to be released, as insurance company chief executives still need to give their approval.[122] Meanwhile, Earthquake Recovery boss Roger Sutton is calling for better 'triaging' of insurance and EQC claims so those most in need get their homes fixed first.[123]

Mr Jimmy Higgins, the head of Vero Insurance, while speaking to delegates at the New Zealand Insurance Law Association conference in Auckland, states, *"No individual participant such as an insurer or government agency can control the recovery pace nor can they justifiably be held responsible when that pace does not meet customer or community expectations."*[124] *"There is still far too much public criticism by these groups about the performance or shortcomings of others involved in the recovery… That is making the task of clear and consistent communication about the true situation in Christchurch more difficult than it should be."*[125] This rather revealing corporate comment aligns with Vero's stated 2015 commence date for property repairs.

On September 19, the beginning of the third year post-earthquake, the Government announces a review of the Earthquake Commission.[126] The Treasury-led review will consider the types of property the EQC insures, how it prices its insurance, and how it should be financed. The review team is said to include officials from the Reserve Bank, the EQC, the Ministry of Business, Innovation and Employment, and an independent expert.[127]

On September 20 and again on September 22, some 2,000 angry Cantabrians take to the streets, this time to vent their anger at the Government's proposal to shut 13 schools, merge 18 schools into nine, and relocate seven.[128] I can hear the bells of Milton Friedman's disaster capitalism begin to toll. He believed that it was only a crisis that could produce *"real change"*. After Hurricane Katrina (New Orleans 2005) he stated that *"the children are now scattered all over the country. This is a tragedy. It is also an opportunity to radically reform the educational system."* A right-wing think tank seized upon this and converted the schools in New Orleans into 'charter schools'. Within 18 months the public system in New Orleans had been completely replaced with privately run charter schools, just like those proposed for Christchurch. According to Naomi Klein in her book *The Shock Doctrine: The Rise of Disaster Capitalism,* a pattern is seen to develop post crises whereby large chunks of the state are sold to private citizens while the affected population stand-by in shock and quickly the new reforms become permanent.[129] The protesting parents of Christchurch have made their views clear but to no avail. Charter schools are instituted. There is a sense amid those affected that a small group of people are trying to control a national agenda, define issues in their own narrow terms and obfuscate their vested interests and motives. Is education really an area to be run by private 'market forces'? Dame Beverley Wakem (the Chief Ombudsman) warned that proposals to make charter schools exempt from the Official Information Act and Ombudsman Act would detract from public confidence, and remove the fundamental right for an independent review mechanism. Meanwhile staff are also still having to deal with issues in their own homes. Travel times, disruption and the ongoing house repairs all take their toll.

The same side-step can be seen in the foreign investors and the international lenders who have appeared on the scene post- earthquakes. The 'blank canvas' that Christchurch City represents has become an exciting proposition and a perfect environment in which to advance corporate goals and represents the use of *"collective trauma to engage in radical social and economic engineering."* (Naomi Klein: The Shock Doctrine).

By April 28, 2012, IAG had stated that in the past two months it had completed four home rebuilds, 10 house repairs and 851 repairs to driveways, paths and swimming pools not covered by the EQC and that it had 58 rebuilds and another 21 home repairs underway.[130] Its target had been to build 85 new homes a month and to complete 47 major repairs. At that time, IAG would not reveal how many repairs and rebuild claims it had in total. On 5 September, 2012, during an interview with John Campbell of TV3, an IAG spokesperson tells Mr Campbell that in the past two years only 35 houses have been completely rebuilt.[131] The IAG spokesperson states that IAG has 66,000 claims, of which 27,000 are residential and IAG will be responsible for building 70 percent of the new homes in Canterbury. A quick calculation reveals that at this rate it will take IAG decades to complete its residential mandate! Is this the sort of performance New Zealanders want from the country's major private insurer?

~~~

Postscript. At the time of writing the second edition of my book in 2016 the harrowing images have faded, and the regular news updates about this devastated region have dwindled, all that is left are the ongoing out-of-sight battles over matters to do with insurance, housing and infrastructure. Personal economic imperatives soon become the focus. Questions around land values and whether the insurance industry will honour their contractual obligations abound. Differences of opinion emerge between the major players as to what the appropriate repair or reinstatement cost of property should be. Sandwiched in the middle of these debates are the people of Canterbury, awaiting honest and fair solutions to what are possibly the greatest hurdles many of them have ever faced. For those who are able, this will mean action to move past being dependent upon the Government, the Christchurch Earthquake Authority or the City Council, in order to find just solutions to those problems. The corporate erosion of property owner entitlements by the insurance industry is profoundly affecting the financial and social wellbeing of many people of Canterbury and the suffering continues….

CHAPTER 2

THE CHRISTCHURCH FIASCO BUILDS MOMENTUM 2013 & 2014

- -

The Christchurch recovery is New Zealand's greatest human rights challenge.[1]

David Rutherford, Human Rights Commissioner

Though it is currently 2016, I have chosen to recap the following section once again in the present tense, giving a better sense of the high pace of events and the dislocation that was experienced by the population of Canterbury during this period.

In 2013 and 2014, many buildings still lie in ruin, many sites are still strewn with rubble, the roads are still an uneven and ruptured mess and little appears to be happening in the Central City. Despite this, the Canterbury Development Corporation declares that Christchurch's rebuild is soon to peak. Of the residential homes that have been repaired, stories begin to emerge of shoddy repairs, indicating that the next crisis looms and many homeowners believe that we are likely to see another 'leaky home' style debacle in Christchurch.[2] In many instances homes are being resold with substantial price hikes, despite having had very superficial repairs.[3] In a few years' time, when buyers and owners go looking for someone to hold accountable, those organisations and companies responsible will have disappeared. Information emerges that Southern Response is to be wound up, the EQC and its alliance with Fletcher Construction (EQR) are likely to have been dismembered as well, along with many of the private construction firms responsible for repairs and rebuilds. No doubt, escape routes are already being planned.

Human rights abuse claims have spiked in New Zealand as Canterbury residents file claims against insurance and construction companies. People are still affected by the earthquakes in many ways and continue to experience deterioration in standards of living and negative impacts on their quality of life that go well beyond the immediate physical effects of the disaster. Earthquake affected residents resort to the Organisation for Economic Cooperation and Development Guidelines that require companies to respect the human rights of those affected by their activities. The Human Rights Commissioner declares that the Canterbury earthquakes represent one of New Zealand's greatest contemporary human rights challenges.[4]

Peter Townsend of the Chamber of Commerce declares in September 2014 that the City is *"only about 10 percent into the physical rebuild."* The EQC repairs which had begun in 2011 are still not finished and official documents reveal that the EQC cash reserves are beginning to run very thin. The EQC is quick to ensure Cantabrians that all the funding required to meet their obligations in Canterbury will be available, but the pace at which they pay it out suggests otherwise…. The shortfall is now estimated to be at least NZD 650 million.[5] (The EQC fund has been 'raided' by government at least twice in the EQC history in order to top up the Consolidated Fund. This amounts to a misappropriation of funds, as these funds were set aside specifically for a natural disaster sequence).

Meanwhile complaints against the EQC top 20,000. Almost 70,000 homeowners were billed hundreds of dollars for an unpaid excess on their earthquake repairs. The maximum excess is $1150.00.[6] In addition, Christchurch City Council staff state that it is impractical to offer a rates relief or a discount to policyholders who have been out of their homes over the past four years, often still paying mortgages and rent, placing an additional financial burden on earthquake affected families.

It is fair to say that thousands now fear the drawn-out recovery process and more than they did during the initial disaster itself. Unresolved insurance claims are emerging as the biggest impediment to the Christchurch rebuild and there are still many decisions to be made and so much still to be done. Many have come to the conclusion that the insurers are playing a deliberate game of delay tactics or putting pressure on homeowners to cash settle rather than repair or rebuild earthquake damage as cash settlement is invariably cheaper than doing the necessary work, and a way of reducing outgoings for the insurers.

There are reports of more than 66,000 depressed Cantabrians and the Canterbury District Health Board mental health unit is sitting at 90 percent occupancy. Authorities are said to have ignored 70 percent of Maori with a typical pattern emerging in the East. Maori are suffering some of the worst effects of the quakes - stress and poor quality housing as well as loss of income.[7] A survey carried out by the Mental Health Foundation and the Canterbury District Health Board shows that more than 80 percent of those polled state that their lives have significantly changed with most indicating for the worse. The increase in hepatitis is said to indicate how difficult and risk-prone it is for people living in poor quality and overcrowded environments post-earthquakes. There is also an increase in the level of street related crime and disorder.[8] The numbers of suicides related to earthquake stresses soar.[9] Hair loss has become prevalent.[10] Blowing dust from dried liquefaction increases the risk to residents of contracting pneumonia.[11] By the end of 2013 the Canterbury health and welfare agencies are concerned that earthquake related stresses are fuelling increasing alcohol and drug abuse.[12] Overcrowding in Canterbury homes comes with issues of potential epidemics, leaving children vulnerable to abuse and mental health problems. It is reported that a fifth of children beginning school in the worst affected parts of Christchurch are showing signs of post-traumatic stress disorder with signs of anxiety, aggression, withdrawal, and concentration difficulties.[13] The first results are presented at a symposium.[14] There has been a 35 percent increase of new patients since 2011 for psychiatric emergency services, a 40 percent increase for child and youth community mental health services and a 20 percent demand increase for adult community mental health teams. A series of secondary stressors are identified including: insurance woes, living in damaged environments and loss of recreational facilities.[15] The Cabinet considers backing a plan to deal with post-earthquake mental health and relationship issues - the Greater

Christchurch Strategic Psychosocial Plan.[16] The population is warned that the winter ahead is likely to be difficult for those continuing to struggle with anxiety, depression or the continuing aftershocks. In addition, reports appear in the media suggesting that many Cantabrians will be waiting until 2017 before their earthquake damaged homes are repaired.

The elderly have a particularly hard time and quake strain is the catalyst for elder abuse. One resident calls the way his case had been handled as *"state sponsored elder abuse"*. Alf Johnson, a 92 year old from St Martins asks *"why am I still waiting for a new house?"*[17] His insurer, State Insurance (IAG), says the company was aware of Alfred's situation and had prioritised him based on his age and the condition of his home. It transpires that despite the fact that the EQC is supposed to have identified the vulnerable and elderly a large number of them have 'slipped through the cracks'. Toward the end of 2014 it is estimated that there are at least 6000 'vulnerable' insurance customers still waiting for the resolution of their claims. Every month more vulnerable people are identified. There are cases like Mrs Dot Boyd, 85 years of age, who has been living out of boxes while still waiting for repairs to her home, despite her plight having been brought to the attention of authorities eight months earlier.[18] Some of the elderly believe the EQC *"are waiting for us to die"*.[19] Letters to the Press indicate the extent of the problem.[20] One resident described it as *"First we were scared, then we were anxious. But now, we are angry."*[21]

Meanwhile life in the red zone is described as 'unbearable' and two thirds of people believe that the quakes are a convenient way for the National Government to pursue its own agenda in respect of clearing these areas.[22] The Human Rights Commissioner raises concerns about the way property revaluations are carried out in the red zone. The loss of equity for property owners in these areas is very concerning. Some property owners loose NZD 250,000 in value overnight.[23] Many feel that they have glided out of the middle class and the trappings of middle New Zealand life and are now living in unfixed homes and are very cash and asset poor. At the other end of spectrum, a rapid rise in the wealth base is seen amongst contractors, building firms, investors and developers - all doing well out of commercial rebuilds and insurance pay-outs in the central city and starting new developments on the outskirts of the City. There is a remarkable spike in the sale of Maseratis.[24]

As at 30 September 2014, there is an average of 11 cases filed in the High Court a month. 54 cases were filed in 2012. In 2013, 196 new cases are filed. In the nine months ending September 2014 a further 104 new claims are filed. There have been 437 earthquake cases filed since September 2010 and of those, 21 have been appealed. Though these numbers may not seem great, the reality of our justice system is that the courts only provide justice for the very wealthy. For the vast majority of Cantabrians they have had to be sufficient with *"you'll have what we give you"*.[25] Labour launches a bid to help *"sick and tired"* Canterbury voters, promising NZD 2 million to fund test-cases against insurance companies and the EQC.[26] Those sums are unlikely to assist more than a handful of families and the promise dies a slow and total death. Labour also commits to NZD 25 million for full buyout offers across the red zone if it gains power at the forthcoming election. The Earthquake Minister, calls the Labour suggestion a *"reckless"* promise. The suggestion is met with little or no support from the Insurance Council or the Government. The reasons given for the delays in recovery are attributed to the complexity of the issues involved.

Information released under the Official Information Act shows that the EQC has now spent more than NZD 23.5 million on legal costs since the September 2010 earthquakes, which includes NZD 10 million paid to the legal firm Chapman Tripp. A further NZD 1.9 million has been spent on expert advice such as engineering and geotechnical reports. This is taxpayer money spent fighting court battles with Cantabrians, the people they are supposedly protecting and assisting to recover. The EQC contests 230 cases - these costs are also met by taxpayers, the Crown and reinsurers.[27] The EQC staff have called police 90 times in the past two and a half years in response to threatening or distressed clients.[28]

Many people have had multiple 'assessments' completed and still no definitive repair/rebuild determination.[29] This is indicative of the much wider systemic issues at play.[30] There is a sense among the affected that the Christchurch rebuild has stalled.[31] The community constantly hears declarations that the rebuild is about to start in earnest, some four years after the initial event.[32] By mid-2014 the rebuild is said to be slower and flatter with its peak likely to be in 2016 according to an Aecom New Zealand six monthly survey.[33]

A time of crisis can increase markedly the amount of information a population receives about current or incumbent politicians and their governance style and outcomes. Disaster produces a highly informative environment where voters are continually debating and experiencing the performance and merits of the operators in power – be that a Prime Minister or a City Councillor. It is in these high information environments that voters learn enough to enable them to consider taking the decision to replace perceived defective political incumbents. In October 2013 Lianne Dalziel leaves one political arena to join another and becomes Mayor of Christchurch. She calls for public consultation and engagement and heralds the fact that if Council led the recovery process, it could give people the assurance that their views would influence any outcomes. In early 2014 the new Mayor warns politicians against using the post-earthquake struggles for political point scoring.[34] By the end of November though, the honeymoon is over and Earthquake Minister, Gerry Brownlee, is once again threatening to seize control of the city housing rules which control the amount of housing that can be squeezed into the city's existing residential boundaries.[35] As time proceeds it becomes more and more difficult to make an assessment of the relationship between the Council and the Minister of Earthquake Recovery, though it is clear that at times the relationship is strained.[36] Letters reveal that the relationship between the parties is at best 'frosty'. Lianne Dalziel, six months into her new role as mayor writes that the parties have yet to establish the necessary structure and systems to support a collaborative and efficient partnership at a governance level.[37]

Intensive new building is agreed upon in parts of Riccarton, Barrington, Papanui, Merivale, Sydenham, Linwood, Waltham and Richmond. The new rules will form part of the Land Use Recovery Plan (LURP). Developers with between 1500 square metres and one hectare of land will be able to build between 30 and 65 dwellings on their properties. In the outer suburban areas up to 22 houses per hectare are allowed. Long gone is the 'quarter acre section'.[38]

Dame Jenny Shipley, a former National prime minister, is to oversee the transition power from CERA back to local authorities, which would include a board said to provide advice about the transition of functions and powers held by CERA. The board is to exist for one year while the CER Act expires in April 2016. There are concerns raised about CERA's ability to lead Christchurch to the next stage of recovery particularly as CERA is struggling to find 'good' staff.[39]

In addition the awareness amongst residents emerges of some very creative, though highly dubious, solutions from the Ministry of Business, Innovation and Employment's (MBIE) engineering and advisory group. Named the MBIE Guidelines, they produce a guidance document with the specific purpose of standardizing certain repairs carried out, which in turn has the effect of reducing the standard of repair required to damaged homes and ultimately reduces the costs the EQC bears. The private insurance industry is quick to jump on the band wagon, seeing the cost saving potential. Many Cantabrians conclude that a Government of the future will have to accept its own liability for this deregulation experiment inflicted on the building industry and local government. Government will ultimately have to take responsibility for the liability which will undoubtedly be accumulated by the private sector builders, designers, architects and certifiers, most of whom will no doubt become insolvent and be unable to meet their responsibilities to the homeowners of these badly repaired homes. A decided 'sleight of hand', these guidelines also appear to be at odds with the legislated Building Act 2004.

The true cost of the Christchurch rebuild continues to climb. In less than six months it jumps from NZD 30 billion to NZD 40 billion with the Crown's contribution rising from NZD 13 billion to NZD 15 billion and it is not yet over. Migrants pour into the City but there is a continuing ongoing urgent need for unskilled workers. The migrants come predominantly from Ireland, South Africa, and the Philippines.[40] Not everyone is in favour of this solution stating, that the unskilled jobs ought to be being filled by local staff. There are reports of migrant staff being treated badly, living in cramped conditions and in some instances simply not being paid.[41]

Insurance is highlighted by Korda Mentha as the big risk for the City and its infrastructure. Despite this assertion, the Earthquake Recovery

Minister believes that there is only *"a slim possibility"* that the Council's financial position is as weak as Korda Mentha suggests.[42]

The Earthquake Commission's performance continues to amaze and infuriate the local population with countless stories of delay, lack of communication, empty apologies and questionable use of experts. The cries can be heard far and wide *"insurance firms must stop messing with our lives"*,[43] the people of Canterbury really begin to feel the pressure. Homeowners state openly that they have no confidence in the insurance industry's ability or willingness to settle claims before 2016. It is reported that insurance companies in the Christchurch market have been rated the world's slowest to respond to a major disaster. Meanwhile the insurance giants' profits soar.[44] IAG and Suncorp are reporting massive profits which leaves a very sour taste in the mouths of most affected Cantabrians. IAG New Zealand's annual profit was AD115 million, up 11.7 percent on the 2012 year. Gross premiums grew 27 percent in New Zealand dollar terms to NZD1.8 billion, including the 12 month contribution of AMI.[45] Overall premiums collected in New Zealand were AD1.575 billion.[46] IAG's Australian parent posted profits of more than AD1.4 billion, its net profit up 275 percent. An overseas 'captive' reinsurance business is helping Australian insurer IAG, which owns State, NZI, AMI, and Lumley (given the go ahead to buy this entity in May 2014) record tax losses for its businesses here, while reporting profits for the 'New Zealand Division' in its annual report.[47] Despite this it has ranked poorly in customer satisfaction surveys.

Finally a 'multiple quake claim ruling' changes the ball game for the insurers when the courts decide that losses for each earthquake event should be paid to the sum insured. Up until the ruling, insurers had been rejecting multiple claims where a partial loss was followed by a full loss.[48]

In the background, the hardship continues to be felt by many families. They often belong to the most vulnerable groups in society and are now faced with unaffordable rents and are having to compete with each other because of a high demand for accommodation. Accommodation being at crisis point in the City.[49] Thousands of people are still battling the EQC and the private insurance industry. The unconscionable delays are exacting a very heavy toll on the local population. Reports of quake-hit families living in squalor are all too common. People living in garages and tents, sheds or in overcrowded conditions. There is an increase in poverty-related illnesses among Christchurch children.[50] Meanwhile the cost of renting continues to soar.[51] The constant moving between schools and houses leaves children feeling very vulnerable. Local schools experience massive role changes as families living in rentals go in search of homes across the other side of the city.[52]

In 2014 new property valuations come into effect which leaves owners of earthquake damaged homes with another 'hit' to the pocket. The previous valuations were based on 2007 values.[53] Red zoned land took a significant hit and written-off land was treated as 'unsuitable for residential occupation' with most properties valued at less than NZD 50,000. In many cases there was considerable inconsistency in the valuations provided. For instance for one Brooklands 'red zoner' (severe land damage) the value of his property dropped NZD 236,000 and a property two doors down dropped by NZD 154,000 while the 'green zoned' (no land damage) property between the two rose NZD 106,000.[54] Despite this, Christchurch is becoming one of the hottest housing investment markets in New Zealand with more than half the sales being 'as-is-where-is', that is, earthquake damaged properties being sold to landlords. According to the property analyst CoreLink, more than 43 percent of Christchurch homes are snapped up by investors.[55] This will have consequences in the years to come. Property experts begin to raise concerns about the lack of a public record which details the condition of properties because of the risk to unsuspecting house hunters buying quake damaged homes which have been 'written off' by insurers.[56] Wrecked houses are used for rentals, snapped up at bargain prices by savvy investors and then rented out for high returns in a housing-resource strapped city. The insurance industry then supports calls for a public record to be kept of earthquake damaged homes that have been written-off, but nothing eventuates. The Government was warned about these perils in 2013. However, there remains no entity overseeing the quality of housing stock in Canterbury. No one ensuring that a house is reinstated to an insurable condition or insisting that an uneconomic irreparable house be demolished following cash settlement. The surge in 'as-is-where-is' sales continues, as property owners with insufficient funds try to recoup their losses. (It is likely that the Government, CERA and the private insurers have just let the issue ride as it takes the pressure off the insurance industry and they can continue to pay-out less than satisfactory cash offers to homeowners with damaged properties). Adventurous entrepreneurs see the possibilities and the money that can be made and the market becomes something of a feeding frenzy, particularly with the ability to find off-shore finance and insurance. Raising loans from mortgage brokers in the United Kingdom, using the land as collateral for a mortgage, has become not uncommon. However, the big question remains, are these properties safe? Smaller construction companies are accumulating 20 to 30 properties in order to provide a work stream for future remediation projects and to keep their swollen staff quotas occupied. These properties are also appealing to the first home buyer who would otherwise have great difficulty entering the property market. For those not concerned about insurance or problems associated with foundation damage then this is the latest form of equity release.[57] Community leaders call for a rigorous repair review.[58]

The net for compulsory acquisition is slowly widened as the National Government decides on the future use of red zoned land, which will mean that some properties are likely to be compulsorily acquired. This is likely to encompass another 130 homes at least. The new land values are seen by many as evidence of government policy and not as a necessary consequence of the earthquakes. Those who are unable to live in their damaged homes are still having to pay rates and insurance premiums on those properties. On inquiring as to why premiums still have to be paid, the insurers' standard answer is 'you need public liability insurance'. A quick calculation shows that the insurance industry is making millions of dollars a year on homes for which they will not pay-out.

Insurers receive an "F" for their performance in Christchurch. Delays are considered to be "*self-serving*" and the repairs in the red zone seen as "*amoral capitalism at its most naked*".[59] The suggestion is made that perhaps empathy from insurers is missing because the insurers have the seat of their power in other countries, predominantly Australia. Letters to the Editor in the *Christchurch Press* emerge with headings such as "*repugnant insurance companies earn our distrust*"[60] and "*insurance firms must stop messing with our lives*".[61] The chief executive of the New Zealand Insurance Council, Tim Grafton, denies that there is any benefit in withholding payment to policyholders stating that *"the residential recovery of Canterbury is definitely ramping up"*.[62] A leaked report prepared for the Southern Response board and Treasury backs up comments that indeed insurance companies are lagging behind.[63]

In December 2013 around 500 people protest outside Southern Response offices about the unreasonable delays and poor communication with policyholders. Mr Peter Rose, Southern Responses' chief executive, accepts the group's challenge to front again with answers to the individual cases presented. Protestors again stand outside Southern Response offices - this time Mr Peter Rose is flanked by security personnel. He tells media that the company had *"not been as flexible as we could with some of our customers"*.[64] Mr Rose states that the delays and confusions are a result of a *"tentative journey into the unknown"*.[65] The following month a large spread placed by Southern Response appears in the *Christchurch Press* reading *"we've listened and now we are acting"*. The chief executive lists some 'positive development' following feedback about their approach to settling claims. Among these are an extension of the jurisdiction of the Insurance and Savings Ombudsman (ISO) to extend their ability to resolve claims above the currently capped NZD 200,000, even if they are currently under legal action; the provision of mediation services through ISO; and the establishment of internal checks to deal with claim delays.[66] These promises are seen as *"smoke and mirrors"* to simply deflect customer disputes to mediation and not even independent mediation.[67]

Evidence emerges of policyholders reluctantly settling for lower pay-outs because they have neither the time nor the energy left to battle through the claims process. Insurance specialists expect earthquake litigation to grow in the city. Nevertheless legal action is seen as a last resort for most, its cost being prohibitive.[68] One might have expected that the earthquakes rewrite the insurance law landscape,[69] but it emerges that there is a reluctance by the courts to produce precedent and instead claims are dealt with on a case by case basis. This provides little assistance to the many thousands of policyholders still waiting for answers to vexing legal questions. Concerns are also raised by the insurance industry that some of the insurance public adjusters that have popped up in Christchurch such as Risk Worldwide, WorldClaim, Earthquake Services, ProClaim and KSL Audit Services, are making huge commissions on the back of desperate policyholders.[70]

2014 also sees the widespread emergence of social media support groups amid affected policyholders. Facebook is littered with groups such as the EQC Insurance Woes, TC3 Residents, Flood Affected Cantabrians, Christchurch Earthquake Dodgy Repairs, Southern No Response, Save Our Schools, and Empowered Christchurch - all who are battling one insurance issue or another. Blogs also appear – thechristchurchfiasco,[71] Avonside,[72] Rebuilding Christchurch,[73] WeCan, CanCern, The Real Recovery,[74] Empower Christchurch,[75] and Claimants4claimants, all examples of private citizens helping each other through the quagmire that is insurance, sharing information, providing support, organising gatherings and filling in the gaps left by officialdom. In research carried out by Gregory Simons, a Sweden-based New Zealander, it is found that there is a "*significant gap*" between how officials and ministers view the region's recovery and how residents feel about it. He adds "*There is a clear connection between the political mobilisation of these groups based upon the issue of official accountability and transparency, which is seen by many as a failure*".[76] All these groups are created in the knowledge that they are now in the midst of a fiasco and no one is coming to fill in the gaps. On the other side of the fence in the social media world, 'insurance moles' are also tracking the movements of affected property owners. Renee Walker, spokeswoman for IAG is axed from one social media group.[77] It has become 'them and us'. The rest of the country however has little idea of what is taking place and the National media, other than the TV nightly Campbell Live, is seen as content to keep it that way.

Councillor Glenn Livingstone vows to continue to fight for an insurance advocacy service in Christchurch which will operate on residents' behalf. CERA announces plans for a new advisory service with the financial backing of the insurance industry. The independence of this service is questioned by many Cantabrian insurance policyholders.

An advocacy service is approved but the Earthquake Recovery Minister warns that the Christchurch City Council will be *"on its own"* if it's new service incurs major legal costs. The Government service is slammed as a *"total let down"* meanwhile the Earthquake Recovery Minister continually criticises the Christchurch City Council over its decision to fund the separate insurance advocacy service.[78]

Insurers such as IAG and Southern Response continue to assert that they will complete their earthquake claims by December 2015 and 2016 respectively. IAG by this point has only completed 28 percent of its residential claims mid-way through 2014. Southern Response completed only 34 percent. Between them they have 6000 earthquake damaged homes to rebuild. It is taking 70 weeks from the start of settling a 'new home build claim' to completing it! Insurers blame the EQC's slow decision making on land damage and customers 'dragging the chain' on rebuild decisions. IAG buys the insurance business of Lumley Insurance, expanding its dominance and market penetration even further. This will in effect lift IAG's market share to almost 50 percent of the insurance market in the country. The Commerce Commission nevertheless rules that it does not consider this to be monopolistic, despite the public's strong opposition to the purchase. This move increases IAG's ability to destabilize the industry. In addition, IAG now has strong partnerships with several banks, underwriting insurance which is offered by banks to their customers.[79] Insurers generally, begin imposing huge excesses in new policies on some structures, meaning that homeowners will pick up the cost of paying for fixing damage to driveways, paths, swimming pools and fences caused by earthquakes, storms or tsunamis. Vero, for example, increases it excess to NZD 10,000 for pools.[80] It also declares its interest in increasing its share of the national premium pie to above 30 percent over the next five years. Clearly the industry sees that there are profits to be made. In addition, Vero offers a return to total replacement cover for fire and other damage not caused by natural disasters, while the other major insurers opt for 'fixed sum' insurance. Vero also warns that their premiums are likely to rise because of a potentially large reinsurance shortfall for its Australian parent company, Suncorp Group. This will mean that it may well have less reinsurance coverage for the Christchurch earthquakes, though they declare that they have the financial strength to absorb the cost.

Citizens call for insurance regulation and the need for lawyers to provide more cost effective assistance to policyholders. Neither emerges. Frustration builds in the community over the Government's inaction in relation to an insurance advisory service.[81] Razor wire is removed from around one of the EQR's hubs because of concerns about the public perception of this measure.[82] It now emerges that the fortification at some the EQC hubs has been extensive.[83] Meanwhile policyholders begin to take action into their own hands. One man holds a hunger strike outside IAG offices and has his IAG (State Insurance) claim settled before lunch-time.[84] Another threatens to print and deliver toilet rolls with anti-State Insurance (IAG) wording, throughout the country- this too produces a rapid and successful outcome. Others threaten to publish full newspaper anti-insurer advertising and radio advertising, this also works! While some threaten to self-harm, but that produces a less than satisfactory outcome.[85] As time proceeds, the stunts have to become more and more dramatic to attract media attention and ultimately insurer action. Media attention seems to be the only thing that produces immediate action from the insurance corporates. Threats of legal action has a much slower success rate and will cost the policyholder dearly in delay and dollars. The average civil case is not heard for well over a year.

Accommodation issues for incoming labour remains a problem, despite the early predictions of more than 20,000 workers required to complete the rebuild. An unprecedented number of building firms continue to go bust leaving millions owing to creditors who are unlikely to see their money.[86] Some homeowners lose everything.[87] One of the major contractors working for Vero, MWH Mainzeal, goes into receivership leaving sub-contractors out of pocket.[88] Labour calls for Genesis Energy chairwoman Jenny Shipley to stand aside while legal action against her is pursued. The liquidators filed a suit against her and other directors upon Mainzeal's collapse.[89] Mainzeal had also been responsible for two of the largest earthquake projects in the city, leaving sixty local builders among the 200 laid off. Many sub-contractors feel vulnerable, owed money and scramble to retrieve their tools before the receivers step in. At the other end of the spectrum, Fletcher Building's share price soars. Questions are raised in the House about Fletcher's possible involvement in fraud in Christchurch.[90] There is a major push for the 'anchor projects', including a convention centre, a rugby stadium and sports facility, to go ahead. The convention centre is heralded as the catalyst for hotel projects in the city.[91] It is not long though before questions are asked about why the City requires a 2000 seat venue.[92] Some question whether Canterbury is seeing 'disaster capitalism' in progress. Then the AMI stadium becomes a deal clincher for the new Council as it will have a major effect on its financial position. There is an insurance impasse on the stadium, the insurers arguing that the existing stadium can be fixed.[93] Revelations emerge that the insurance money the Council thought was available for a new aquatic centre has been spent. The Mayor, Leanne Dalziel, declares that tough calls will have to be made on what community facilities are to be rebuilt.[94] While people are still living out of their homes, many feel this is an extravagance too early on in the recovery. The public urges restraint on big projects. The council finalizes plans to raise the rates by seven percent in order to help meet their share of the Christchurch rebuild.[95]

Central city property owners are given two months to finalize deals with the government before compulsory acquisition of their properties begins.[96] Nevertheless there are still plenty of landowners unwilling to give up their land. By the end of April 2014 the Christchurch Central Development Unit begins to review its strict approach to the recovery blueprint as it realises that more flexibility is needed to rebuild the central city. 19 properties have been so far compulsorily acquired.[97] The *Christchurch Press* reports that at least one city property owner is being bullied by CERA. CERA is saying, *"if you don't take what we're offering, you'll get nothing and we'll see you in court on our terms"*.[98] Less than three quarters of the land requiring acquisition has been bought by the Crown. Some NZD158 million is earmarked for the anchor projects. The Prime Minister, John Key, suggests that the big ticket projects could be scaled back to take account of the shortfall in funding. It soon becomes clear to the Christchurch Central Development Unit that its strict recovery plan is not flexible enough and will not work in all anchor project areas.

The issue of Council asset sales raises its head yet again. The previous Christchurch Mayor had rejected the idea.[99]

For those who have begun the rebuild process, they are discovering that they incur big rate increases despite the fact that their new homes are 'like-for-like' rebuilds. Rates are levied using a capital value system and are adjusted depending on the value of the land and the improvements. This poses problems for the elderly who are on fixed incomes and in order to maintain their rates at pre earthquake levels they must build smaller homes.[100]

Concerns are raised about the ability to attract businesses back to the centre of Christchurch and frustration mounts over the lack of progress. *"There are hundreds of livelihoods collapsing - it's a crying shame"* said Angus McFarlane, a local property developer.[101] New landlords are warned not to exploit tenants but the warning typically falls on deaf ears. The Deputy Mayor, Vicki Buck, says that the affordable rental housing problem has become massive and the affordability of housing becomes a 'hot topic'.[102] The Council planned to bolster the housing stock but despite the fact that the Council had received some NZD 21 million from the EQC it had only managed to secure a handful of damaged units reopened.[103] The Earthquake Recovery Minister 'slams' the council for inaction.[104] Christchurch lost approximately 10,000 homes as a result of the earthquakes and there are thousands of homes that need to be relocated. The numbers of financially stressed families who are renting is increasing steadily.[105] The Human Rights Commissioner suggests that the Council should be leading a massive door knocking exercise to identify those who are most in need of assistance, saying that it is clear that the psychosocial harm in Christchurch is caused by community dislocation, financial distress, unresolved insurance claims and poor or insecure housing.[106]

The Christchurch City Council finds itself locked in a battle with its own insurers, Civic Assurance, over whether it should get full replacement value for 113 social housing units in the residential red zone.[107] Before the earthquakes, the Council's housing stock stood at 2619 units. In the Long Term Plan the council committed to return the housing stock to 2366 units by 2025.[108] This short-fall will be inadequate to return the housing portfolio to pre earthquake levels and insurance settlements will also be inadequate to return the housing portfolio to pre-earthquake numbers. The issue of underinsurance raises its head again when an AIG Insurance NZ Ltd. annual report on Council assets, discloses a disagreement with Civic Assurance, in which AIG alleges that its liability is only NZD 97.5 million to NZD 145 million short of the amount that Civic Assurance contends it owes. The parties enter arbitration. In addition, Civic Assurance is also in dispute with another insurance company for another NZD 50 million.[109]

The Insurance Council asserts that insurers have been forced to increase premiums to cover sky rocketing reinsurance cover, resulting in the majority of insurers switching from offering total replacement cover to offering fixed sum insurance only. The insurance company Vero, asks the Government to allow private insurers to manage all parts of certain multi-unit and shared property claims to 'speed up the process'. Gary Dransfield of Vero says *"it would also be a useful pilot of the type of innovative thinking and processes needed for any future natural disaster in New Zealand"*. This is the point at which the private insurance industry begins to muscle-in and suggest complete control of the New Zealand insurance industry, claiming that the EQC is 'not up to the task' and that government agencies had unrealistic expectations about the pace of rebuilding. (Throughout the last years we have heard the much repeated cry about Christchurch earthquakes having been an 'unprecedented event'. Yet in the Marsh Risk Management Research Report a comparison is made of the following earthquakes: Chile, February 27, 2010; New Zealand, February 22, 2011 and Japan, March 11, 2011 comparing, coverage elements, policy features, and practical considerations in relation to each event. David Pigot, Chairman of Global Claims Practice (Marsh) states that *"New Zealand was the least prepared of all from an insurance perspective. Although the country was conscious of earthquake risk and had a long-standing insurance scheme run by the Earthquake Commission ..."*.[110]

The Central Christchurch's red zone is said to be on track for reopening mid-2013 and the Prime Minister pledges that he will help with the rebuild stating that they do not intend to 'micro manage' the process. But then in February there are reports that Minister Gerry Brownlee may intervene at the Christchurch City Council. Major investors also pull out of the City stating that private investors could have pulled Christchurch together a year earlier.[111] They describe the central business district as 'closed for business'.[112] Property owners state that 'excessive control' has driven out investment. Delays and the lack of certainty are killing the rejuvenation of the Central Business District. They call for the blue print to be reviewed. There are a lack of tenants to fill new office buildings and developers and investors begin to take their monies elsewhere in the face of high construction costs, reluctant tenants and uncertainty over car parking. In 2013 the Earthquake Recovery Minister begins to threaten to compulsorily acquire central Christchurch land to 'kick-start' the retail development.[113] CERA wishes to acquire central city land for its anchor projects. Landowners state that the Christchurch Central Development Unit is making offers to them that are *"off the planet"*. The offers are said to be below some people's mortgages and well below market value. 92 properties are to be acquired.[114] CERA figures show that they had acquired less than three quarters of the land required for the five ear-marked anchor projects. There are plenty of landowners refusing to sell. Meanwhile engineers and contractors begin to put forward solutions for the underlying soil structures. Different foundation solutions are required for the new conditions. It is expected that the new solutions are likely to add significant sums to insurers' pay-outs.[115]

The courts find that the Earthquake Recovery Minister wrongly used powers granted for the immediate purposes of the recovery to settle a complex and longstanding debate over the future shape of Christchurch by simply rubber stamping city boundary changes. While the Government has given Gerry Brownlee 'war time powers' for a fixed time, there are concerns that there is to be an expansion of governance and CERA's mandate is likely to cause further slowdown in the city. Every decision has Minister Gerry Brownlee's finger prints all over it and still the recovery is said to be 'stalling' with the process becoming bureaucratic, fixated on policies and precedents, and ultimately losing touch with the people who live in the City. The feeling among the population is that the power to take action should be handed as far as it can, back to the people. *"It has been a classic case of over-promising and underperforming, the*

Government has wanted to manage the truth" says Jim Anderton, former Wigram MP.[116] What is very clear to the populace is that Minister Brownlee's only real concern is the implementation of a group of anchor projects, most of which Cantabrians have little interest in. It appears that he has little or no focus on recovery for the population. The focus has been squarely a financial-economic one, centred on restarting business. A survey is carried out by the *Christchurch Press* and the overwhelming view is that Minister of Earthquake Recovery has *"taken over Christchurch"*.[117] The Christchurch City Council is seen to be playing second fiddle to the Government's earthquake rebuild machinery. Ric Stevens of the *Christchurch Press* states that the *"Prime Minister is No 1 on a list which reflects central government's wholesale takeover of the South Island's largest city following the earthquakes"*.[118] Many feel that there has been a general downgrading of the City and regional councils. Wellington government seems unable to trust the regional councillors to come up with the outcomes it wants. Last year it threatened to sack 'dysfunctional elected representatives' on the Christchurch City Council and then decided it would revamp Christchurch schools and in addition, it seeks to control the building consents process and the impact of housing prices. This has fundamentally changed the Christchurch regional power base, leaving many wondering what the ulterior motive is. Minister Gerry Brownlee holds day-to-day power and the final political and executive power rests with the Prime Minister, John Key. The power hierarchy list is a clear indication that there is a need to restore democracy in the City. Yet as time passes the population becomes more resigned to its apparent inability to control the process any longer. Councillors complain that they are left out of the loop in discussions of cost sharing for the city rebuild, including who will pay for the anchor projects. A significant gap emerges in the cost sharing arrangements despite the Government committing to more than NZD 800 million for rebuild work. The Government's overall contribution is NZD 15 billion.[119]

At this point, Southern Response, formerly known as AMI and now better known by many Cantabrians as 'Southern No Response' has about 6700 properties with claims over NZD 100,000 plus GST.[120] The reinsurers agreed on cash settlement because this would speed up the settlement process and provide greater certainty for the reinsurers in what they would be paying rather than having to wait years for houses to be built. The crown-owned insurer offers cash settlements at 'full replacement cost' to customers in certain circumstances. Southern Response expects 400 difficult lengthy disputes over repairs or rebuilds of homes in Canterbury.[121] Its' outgoing public relations specialist is on record as stating that it *"is idiosyncratic and run more as a military campaign or wartime project than a company. But it is effective"*.[122] Many Southern Response policyholders would most likely disagree.

An EQC-leaked spread-sheet containing the details of 98,000 claims from some 83,000 claimants is sent to a former EQC employee, Bryan Staples, owner of the newly established Earthquake Services business, another claims management service. The EQC lays a complaint against Mr Staples (a former EQC employee) stating that other people may have seen the spreadsheet.[123] The Earthquake Recovery Authority then asks the public for assistance in plugging any EQC leaks, the inference is that there is someone on the inside leaking the material. The spreadsheet indicates discrepancies in settlement amounts. In one instance the EQC said the repair work was NZD 55,000 but had cash settled with the policyholder for NZD 30,000 and the EQC had allocated NZD 59,000 for the repairs. In another case a couple was paid NZD 8000.00 when the spread sheet indicated that they had NZD 80,000 worth of damage.[124] Mr. Staples threatens the release of information contained on the spread sheets to affected homeowners. A spokeswoman for the Privacy Commissioner states that people had a legal right to request their own information from a government agency that was holding it and that they should be able to go directly to the EQC and expect to get the information. The EQC panics and serves an injunction on the two parties said to be releasing the information from its leaked email. The EQC publically states that they were not prepared to discuss the purpose of the spreadsheet.[125] The EQC chief executive, Ian Simpson is publically supported by the Earthquake Recovery Minister. Then again in mid-March, the EQC is forced to admit that it has been sending misleading information to homeowners eligible for cash settlement. They state that if homeowners opt-out and take the money rather than have the repairs completed, then their uncosted

Scope of Works will be attached to the Land Information Memorandum (LIM). The intention behind this is so that future purchasers can make an assessment for themselves as to whether the scoped repairs were actually carried out or adequately carried out. The implication though, is that if the repairs are carried out through the EQC, no such Scope of Works will be attached to the LIM.[126] After the privacy breaches, the EQC website, email, database and Twitter account is closed to the public in an attempt to get to the bottom of the breach. A reboot is suggested as a way of getting their systems back on line and public communication re-established. The public law specialist Mai Chen declares that Cantabrians should be lobbying the Minister of Earthquake Recovery if they want to see the EQC claims management system reviewed. Later it emerges that the EQC has overpaid not underpaid earthquake claims by up to NZD 100 million but declares that it will not pursue customers for over payments.[127]

In the wake of earthquake events, the Government orders the EQC to turn itself into a general reconstruction company with Fletcher Building as its project management organisation, with thousands of people and systems and processes to take over the responsibility of undertaking every under-cap repair in Canterbury. Fletcher Earthquake Recovery (EQR) is formed and qualifies almost as a state owned enterprise. So it is no wonder the EQC quietly moved its home repair completion targets forward, originally due to be met by Christmas 2012 stating that it would complete all serious structural repairs and the most vulnerable repairs by Christmas 2013. The criticisms of the way EQR and the EQC are operating, now harden dramatically within the population. Despite the fact that the reasoning behind the Government's decision to give the EQC control of under-cap repairs was to protect the value of Canterbury's housing stock. Assessments consistently underestimate the degree of damage to properties, particularly foundation repairs in marginal land areas, which in turn leads to cosmetic patch-ups and little if anything in the way of real engineering. Few of the staff employed to assess these properties would have ever seen earthquake damage before, most are unqualified in the field and spent their time assessing cracks and warping walls rather than real structural damage. Splits in concrete pads are often considered to be 'pre-existing', plaster cracks on ring foundations passed off as 'superficial' without any further investigation carried out. Many believe that the EQC is systematically turning a blind eye to the serious nature of some of the damage, particularly foundation damage and as a consequence there will be the same general blighting of the housing stock that New Zealand has experienced with the leaky home syndrome. (One wonders whether insurers will soon take hard-line views on insuring patched up properties. The insured public seems to be blind to the reality that if the insurer decides it no longer likes the risk it has taken on a property it can give 14 days-notice that cover is being cancelled).

The general public were, at this stage, under the impression that the EQC natural disaster cover was part of the general replacement value policy they held with their insurers. So in the event of damage they expected that they would receive the same straightforward 'as new' standard of repair. This however proves to be a major bone of contention and the wording set out in the EQC Act 1993 (Schedule 3, clause 9) causes considerable confusion. The problems with the EQC slowly escalate and eventually result in 200 unhappy homeowners registering their interest in a group legal action against the EQC. The proposed action sought is a declaratory judgement from the High Court confirming that the properties must be repaired or reinstated to the condition specified in their insurance policies, that is to a condition 'when new', subject to applicable laws. The complaint is that the commission is relying on the *"reasonably sufficient"* standard as specified in the EQC Act 1993.[128] The matter is currently being tested before the Courts.[129] In line with the EQC's position it refuses to pay for household rewiring in some cases, requiring homeowners to upgrade pre-1970s wiring at their own expense. This policy change emerged when the EQC was hit with wiring bills of NZD 50,000 per property. Legal opinion is that the EQC was obliged to repair to 'as new' and to the current consent standard, which would include upgrading wiring and other components if need be.

Cantabrians also continue to struggle to get access to personal information about individual property claims. The EQC's continued failure to provide policyholders with information about their claims instigates the Ombudsman and the Privacy Commissioner to investigate. The Human Rights Commission releases a joint report[130] on how the EQC has handled Official Information Act (OIA) requests.[131] It comes to light that the EQC was telling staff to flag claimants who were 'television personalities and sports stars'. There were 36 high profile claims. The EQC assures Cantabrians that no specific activity was triggered by the existence of this category, but not too many Cantabrians were convinced by their assurances.

The EQC then delays payment on 14,000 land settlement cases with no timeframes for resolution.[132] Adrian Cowie, a registered cadastral surveyor calls for an EQC audit, claiming that Cantabrians have been deprived of adequate repairs and possible rebuilds.[133] Many of those using laser levels are not qualified to do so and the results are correspondingly inaccurate. He stresses that in many cases a lack of damage is not an indication that floor levels have not undergone change. A third of homeowners are querying the repairs that have already been carried out.[134] The Earthquake Minister defends the EQC's performance once again, but a couple of days later he signals that he is losing confidence in their performance as it comes to light that a survey carried out by the EQC intentionally excluded disgruntled homeowners.[135] A KPMG partner is then asked to investigate into whether in fact the EQC did mislead the Minister and the Auditor-General about its customer satisfaction survey.[136] Unsurprisingly the report clears the Earthquake Commission of any serious performance issues and once again the Minister of Earthquake Recovery has full confidence in the EQC and its' chief executive, Ian Simpson. Cantabrians are not even slightly surprised by this outcome.

Residents begin to report telephone calls received from their banks stating that 'their money is waiting for them' - an EQC cheque for an unexplained amount of some description awaits them. Policyholders come to the conclusion that this is the EQCs way of trying to make their problems disappear quickly.[137] Homeowners can now claim cash in lieu of earthquake repairs after changes to the EQC opt-out scheme. This could, however, mean that homeowners could well find themselves out of pocket when it comes to having the repairs carried out and homeowners will have to pay the difference if the completed work ultimately costs more than the EQC payment.[138] In addition, the EQC land damage pay-outs are also being pocketed by residents rather than spending the money on fixing the damage to the land. Insurers request that the law be changed so that policyholders are obliged to remediate the land. It is anticipated that an EQC review would address this issue in the sense that earthquake land cover would be likely in the future to apply only to situations where homes could not be rebuilt on their original site and owners were forced to buy elsewhere.[139]

The heritage restoration debate is also continuing at this time. The fate of the Christchurch Cathedral[140] continues to stir strong emotions from different factions of the community as does the Majestic Theatre. Some feel that this is the National Government abrogating its responsibility to protect important aspects of local and national culture. Despite this, genuine concern remains around the repopulation of heritage buildings. Many of the heritage sites have yet to have start dates for restoration tabled. Questions are raised about a lack of a heritage plan and many feel that Christchurch residents are being denied a say when it comes to decisions about listed heritage buildings. University of Auckland Professor of Fine Arts, Jonathan Mane Whoeki, warns of a 'shabby future'. *"Bloody cowboys went in and bulldozed a whole lot of stuff that shouldn't have gone such as the Bell's Arcade"*.[141]

There is a general call for a hard-line to be taken in relation to inferior engineering and building practises. Despite Housing Minister, Nick Smith's assertion that he wished to reform the regulatory system for engineers to a 'world-class standard' and despite the fact that regulatory change for commercial structural engineering was recommended in 2003, Cantabrians continue to be incredulous about the ever increasing relaxing of the Ministry of Building, Innovation and Employment Guidelines (MBIE Guidelines). The apparent initial high level of confidence in engineers in Canterbury has taken a nose dive in the past four years particularly with those firms working for the insurers. Those parties with valid complaints quickly discover that the engineering professional body (IPENZ) has little or no power to effectively censure the offenders and it seems that it is also unwilling to do so. A point in case is the designer of the CTV building, which collapsed during the earthquakes, who simply quit his professional body days before a disciplinary hearing, stripping IPENZ of their power to sanction him.[142] In another case, a Napier engineer, Graeme Robinson, who was working for the EQC, faced a disciplinary hearing having carried out more than 2000 assessments. Only after continued complaints from the public was action taken.[143] The EQC's 'top engineer' is later found to be negligent and incompetent and expelled from the Chartered Professional Engineers' register for three years for 'upper level' misconduct. However, a year later he wins an appeal and is pardoned.[144] Builders and engineers face a litany of complaints.

The 'MBIE Guidelines' are published by the Ministry of Business, Innovation and Employment for the repair and reconstruction of houses damaged by the Canterbury earthquakes. (The document was issued as a guidance document under section 175 of the Building Act 2004). MBIE involvement was part of a centralised, standardised strategy to contain the costs of the rebuild while also rolling through a repair programme as quickly as possible. The Government was aware early on that it was cash strapped. Successive governments had raided the EQC coffers and cost minimization was essential. The MBIE Guidelines are 'the elephant in the room' in Christchurch and are arguably the most dubious of policies to emerge post-earthquakes. They are also in large part the cause of much confusion and consternation amongst professionals and policyholders alike. The creation and continual 'updating' of the MBIE Guidelines can only be described as a seismic slight of hand.[145] In this respect, there is purported evidence of collusion behind the scenes with the EQC and the insurance industry being well represented in the actual drawing up and input into the MBIE Guidelines. They endorse a system where damage is presumed not to be of a serious structural nature – penned hastily after the earthquakes. Through a system of exemptions the Council uses them as the authority by which they are able to wash their hands of any liability for the poor quality of assessment and repair work that ensues and no Council oversight is required. Some of these cheap fixes include epoxy filling foundation cracks, under floor expanding foam, jacking and packing, and notching of bearers. Despite the fact that Canterbury is the centre of the world when it comes to the number of foundation crack repairs that are taking place, it has the flimsiest of official repair standards, with no requirement for training or accreditation.

Many feel that by accepting and applying these guidelines the insurance industry and engineering profession have seriously let the region and its population down.

The Earthquakes have caused a raft of other problems other than simply quake damaged houses. Much of the geography of the city has shifted. In large parts of the City the land has sunk up to 50cm causing many properties to become flood prone in areas such as Flockton, Shirley and St Albans. On top of this it is predicted that the sea rise, as a consequence of climate change, is likely to increase one metre over the next century. The result is that many properties will be continually under the threat of flood. Since the earthquakes, much of eastern Christchurch finds itself under water after a big rain. In some areas, the earthquakes have created a shallow bowl where the surrounding streets have lifted and the centre dropped. Flooding only takes a small amount of rain to collect in the centre with no place to drain. Despite this, the land has been deemed to be repairable by authorities. The plight of the 300 families living in these areas has been further complicated because many insurers refuse to remedy property damage until the drainage issues have been resolved and as a consequence solutions for these properties are said to be years away. Affected residents call for the Government to zone these areas 'red' so that they can be compensated and move on with their lives. Since 2011 some have experienced the flooding of their properties on six separate occasions. The Mayor, Lianne Dalziel makes the comment "*If we can't provide wide protection, then we have to have a hard conversation about retreat.*" As yet, that conversation has not taken place. Instead, two camps of thought emerge. On the one hand there are those who see the flood damage as an act of God and therefore it is for the officials and politicians and insurers to fix. On the other side of the debate is the hard-line right wing view that what has happened to the land is simply 'an investment gone wrong' and therefore there is no automatic right to compensation from the State.[146] In the background is the Government, with its view which essentially is that as yet it is still unsure whether the earthquakes were actually responsible for worsening the flood risk in parts of Christchurch. This, despite the fact that a recent Tonkin and Taylor engineering report shows that the city clearly sank after the earthquakes.[147] University of Canterbury coastal science lecturer, Dr Deidre Hart, states that the best course of action is to abandon these affected areas which are under threat from the effects of sea level rise and that suggested temporary engineering fixes are not the way to tackle the rise of sea-levels. The Earthquake Recovery Minister suggests the problem is related to the drainage plan, stating that flooding in areas badly hit had not been *"all that unusual"* over the decades.[148] Warren Lewis, a Chartered Professional Engineer makes the point that Environment Canterbury handed over all drainage issues in the City to the City Council a couple of years ago.[149] The Earthquake Commission's response is that property owners who are at a greater risk of flooding as a result of the quakes will receive money to fix their land, however each individual homeowner will have to find a solution for the remediation of that land.[150] The 'buck passing' begins. It has become clear over the past five years that the need to actively manage 'nature' in the city has become critical and that there is no time to waste. So how do you 'fix' land that has sunk below the flood plain, and add to this a continually rising water table in a city that was originally built on a swamp? The Council invites Dutch experts to examine the feasibility of a tidal flood barrier for the Christchurch's Heathcote River estuary. The project is estimated to cost in the region of NZD 250 million and NZD 300 million.

With a new awareness of the issues relating to climate change and that fact that New Zealand is a seismic country, water management should no longer be a personal problem, nor should it be a local problem. Water management in New Zealand must be addressed nationally. How many catastrophic events must the population endure (such as Manawatu and Aorere) before the country begins to take this issue seriously - a national solution is imperative.

Not surprisingly, the affected property areas are subjected to large drops in land value with some banks reluctant to lend, insurers refusing to cover clients who wish to buy in those areas, or if they do with premiums that are exorbitant.

In East Christchurch, residents find themselves in the unenviable position of battling with insurers once again to replace belongings and repair water-logged homes. The 'once in a hundred year flood' is becoming an all too familiar occurrence post-earthquakes. Then residents in Richmond, St Albans and Mairehau are warned about the overnight flooding potential. The Heathcote River bursts it's banks.[151] These floods again draw attention to the fact that the City needs to make some hard decisions about which areas it intends to protect and which it will need to retreat from. 'Red zoning' is seen as a last resort. Storm battered residents ask why they are having to live in these conditions. Many feel something should have been done after the flooding in 2013 but they have had little assistance. *"Our homes are insured, our land is insured so why after three years are we still living like this?"*[152] It is for the Christchurch City Council to consider these issues carefully. A changing climate is only likely to make matters worse. Yet the council suggests a flooding solution is two years away, as engineers look into how they might protect 400 low lying homes in St Albans / Mairehau area. Some of these residents have been evacuated from their homes four times since 2011.

Citizens Speak

Repairs Upon Repairs: After the earthquakes, we were contacted by AMI / Southern Response. In late 2011 they wanted to complete the repair of our home in 2012. I was not terribly comfortable with the timeline. I had a business, which had lost its premises in the 2010 quakes, my husband worked offshore and I had two young children to manage. I felt that pressure was applied, so we agreed – statements like *"go now, you will get the best contractor, no resource shortages – the contractor is well regarded, you can expect quality all the way, go later – and well who knows"*.

So we agreed, moved out, put our family pets into care. What an undertaking, trying to manage my business and family, children, with my partner working overseas. For me it was massive, stressful and challenging, but I was the lucky one, right? Compared to others whose homes were worse off than mine and we were already actually being repaired. I had no right to complain, or feel hard done by, so I 'manned up'.

Now jump to completion of the repair. The home is given a 'practical completion', a code of compliance from Selwyn District Council, but no quality documentation for the repair was initially provided, and what we were eventually given was agreed later as being rather untruthful.

On returning home the repair looked pretty good to my untrained eye, but I really did not know what to look for back then (I do now). My partner returned to New Zealand, and everything changed. He inspected the property and was horrified by what he discovered. We were fortunate, one of us had the skills to know what to look for – so it turns out all aspects of our NZD 200,000 repair had failed and the repair had resulted in more damage than had been originally caused by the earthquake itself.

Our experience with Southern Response, from the time when we first notified them of the failure of the repair, has been nothing but appalling. It took an enormous emotional toll on me and I often felt we were intentionally road blocked each step of the way.

But, here is the thing, my story is for context only, this is not about me or my home. Yes it was one of the very first repairs and that's what makes it important. One of the first repairs (not even a very complex repair) and yet it was total failure. There appeared to be zero quality processes in place, administrative failings on a massive scale, and I felt that there were lies and dishonest behaviours from the insurer, project-management company and the contractor. If this was what was happening to the so called 'first repair' when there was apparently no skill shortages and light demand on resources, then what would that mean for people with homes in a worse state than mine?

I wrote to Mr Brownlee, I have met with my MP (Amy Adams), I met with the Selwyn District and Christchurch City Councils, and engaged lawyers. The end result is that our NZD 200.000 repair is now estimated by a Quantity Surveyor to cost NZD 490,000 to correct, add other costs for damages and hidden costs and it is likely to cost Southern Response almost NZD 1 million.

So here's the rub! Someone got paid to do the work on our home and some of the directors of those companies, that were very small in 2010, now make it on the 'rich lists' – and that might have been ok, but it is not – because that wealth has been created on poor quality, zero controls and, what in my view is a dishonest system from end to end. It is not good that the people at the top are still in their positions of control and decision making and that no matter how much we try to highlight these issues, and provide suggestions to ensure they do not repeat these mistakes, nothing has changed.

I believe, no, more than that, I know, secondary repairs are going to be one of the biggest challenges to be faced. I had to fight and fight and fight to have our repair failure accepted and acknowledged, and it took a huge personal toll. Many insurers and their contractors will try to avoid this emerging problem with even more vigour than they avoided the issues around the first set of repairs. Throughout all this, I ask myself where are our MP's, those we gave authority to manage this situation, those with the power to effect change? There have been some really dumb decisions made and there is no excuse for this, but there has also been ample time for lesson learning and change to be implemented - but the same mistakes remain often repeated.

So, what is a homeowner to do? Firstly, stand firm. Get the required reports and bear the cost of them. Remember this is purely commercial and always was. By that I mean that the insurers have the finances to do this right and do it right first time. Do not take it on the chin, do not think there is something wrong with ensuring you receive your entitlement, or that you are greedy – you are not! I often use an analogy, if you order a red car and got a blue one, you would expect the car to be replaced? The insurer entered a commercial agreement and they must be held accountable for that.

And then, there is Southern Response with that 'government guarantee' – I believe they will need it and mostly for secondary repairs – as a tax payer this is unacceptable and our MP's are still invisible… five years on, since repair #1.

By Melanie Tobeck.[153]

CHAPTER 3

THE POLITICS

- -

The earthquakes have created an extraordinary situation where successful and expedited recovery depends on the genuine partnership of community, city council and central government. A solo effort by one of them will not serve. Nor will a partnership that is not founded on trust and openness.

Professor John Cookson, University of Canterbury[1]

Is it not reasonable to expect any government of a seismic nation or a nation prone to any particular class of natural disaster to be legislatively prepared and to have an idea of what government leadership might be required in the circumstances of a catastrophe? In exploring the roles of Central and Local Government after the recent Canterbury earthquakes I found myself asking the question: *"What is their role in the disaster recovery/response phase?"* Is it to ensure the immediate assistance and relief required to get essential systems up and running, or is it oversight of the planning and organisation of the city recovery / rebuild? Does the Government's responsibility extend to assisting the local population in post-disaster need?

One would imagine that the economic and residential recovery of the nation's second largest city might be considered of paramount importance, economically, to the Government. So what sort of structure is the best for the 'lead' authority in Canterbury's recovery phase? Is there place for 'political agendas'?

From an onlooker's perspective there appears to be an uncomfortable coupling of roles and responsibilities between Central Government, thinly disguised as the Canterbury Earthquake Recovery Authority (CERA), and Local Government (in the form of the Christchurch City Council), with little or no invited involvement at a grass-roots level from the Canterbury community, despite its desire to be more actively involved.

This coupling on the one hand is said to provide for a more strategic 'umbrella approach' to the recovery of Christchurch. On the other hand it has not been able to promote a harmonious, reliable and efficient reaction on the ground. Surely Central Government should be responsive to the local circumstances of a disaster so as to ensure that all concerned may be confident of a high degree of consistency and effectiveness in that response? Even though the Earthquake Recovery Minister is a citizen of Christchurch, authoritarianism has dominated to the point of the Government assuming total control over the shape and scale of the rebuild of the city in a totally undemocratic fashion. The only thing left for residents of Canterbury to do is to guess what the actual agenda is.

Noticeable in the past five years is the time and effort put into discussion of ethereal debates such as 'what should the new Christchurch look like?', and 'should we rebuild the Cathedral?' Very little focus has been directed to the speedy relief of the tribulations of the population at large. In the worst affected eastern suburbs, clearly in need of a rapid and focused response, people have had to organise themselves into community committees and assist each other as best they can with the limited resources available.

Perhaps one of the problems is that centralised nations such as New Zealand have fewer decision takers and they are placed at a higher level in the response hierarchy. They have a tendency to interfere with the free flow of information and decision making processes. They are slow to act, wanting to take control of all decisions and, yes, they sometimes have external agendas. Herein lies the dilemma. The initial disaster response must be focused at the local level, because of local intimate knowledge of the environment in which the emergency occurs and of the immediate nature of community needs, such as food, shelter and medical attention. Without local level 'buy-in' recovery will be slow.

Governments traditionally provide considerable financial assistance to communities devastated by natural disasters and even though assistance has been provided to Christchurch in the form of temporary accommodation, financial assistance to business and employees, the actual amount of assistance provided has been considerably less than is needed. But should Central Government's role be confined to only short-term financial aid and coordination of emergency services or should it also encompass ongoing financial assistance to help property owners, businesses and local governments to quickly rebuild damaged structures? Should government, in the interests of protecting its citizens, have influence over and power of direction to insurers to carry out policy promises within reasonable timeframes? There are now very strong arguments that it should, for nothing is clearer now than that in the current situation normal political management is not enough!

Disasters by their very nature will change the type and quality of our relationship with the Government. In dire situations the population will expect much more from their representative bodies, local and national, and it becomes critical that government manage its relationship with the affected citizens carefully, ensuring that understanding and a trusting environment is forged. The shameful events that have transpired in this city over the last five years have again and again demanded government intervention, but evident now is a gross failure in this responsibility from a government wedded to market forces and private enterprise. There has been so much focus on big business at the expense of residential property owners in Canterbury.

Many Cantabrians have experienced the Government as constraining disaster assistance by 'standing by' as they struggle in the ongoing profit-driven insurance 'quagmire'. Their calls for assistance with this issue have fallen on deaf ears. With our knowledge of the aftermath of the Haiti earthquakes and Hurricane Katrina in the USA, are we in New Zealand prepared to leave our own distressed populations to struggle with large corporate insurers (more concerned with their 'bottom lines' than settling with their clients), with indifferent and unprepared government and with incompetent local authorities. A reliable insurance market is pivotal to the citizens of Christchurch rebuilding their lives and to the recovery of the region; a government must take action on an issue of this scale.

Ultimately all elected officials and their ministry appointees are subject to the will of the voters. Dr Martin Luther King Jr once said *"there is nothing more powerful to dramatize a social evil than the tramp, tramp of marching feet"*.[2] It is also very surprising that no other political party, except a couple of local Labour Members of Parliament, have taken up the baton of the insurance aftershock and run with it. While it is true that regulating catastrophe risk is a difficult, cumbersome, politically challenging and, by definition, imperfect process as it does not originate in the political sphere, and there are also real challenges in balancing private business behaviour with the public interest in controlling disaster-assistance costs, the preparedness of a government to act after a disaster goes beyond normal political management.

History shows that near election time, electoral aspirations may even influence whether or not in a disaster a national state of emergency will be declared. Governments are not indifferent to disasters – they can be used strategically to strengthen the position of a government over and above its political rivals. We can be thankful for at least the fact that the first major Canterbury earthquake in September 2010 took place shortly before an election, both for central and local government. Canterbury's fate may have been even more tenuous had the present government already been re-elected.

How the confusion developed

When a natural disaster affects a community, in the first instance it is the City Council that is responsible for providing comprehensive and integrated emergency management. This involves preparedness, mitigation, response and recovery. Christchurch City has a strong mayor–council form of government. However, due to the extent of the disaster and damage, local government was quickly superseded by Central Government (CERA). When the civil defence emergency period ended, earthquake response and recovery functions were transitioned out of the Emergency Operations Centre and many of the key roles and responsibilities were then shared between CERA, the Christchurch City Council and other local authorities and agencies. Lines of responsibility were thought to have been clearly delineated. However, in fact they became alarmingly confused.

What led to this confusion? The initial phase went according to plan. Soon after the earthquake on September 4, 2010 a state of local emergency was declared within each of the three affected districts, Selwyn District, Waikamariri District and Christchurch City. The local state of emergency persisted until September 16, 2010.[3] On Monday, 6 September, the Hon. Gerry Brownlee was appointed the Minister responsible for the Canterbury Earthquake Recovery. An ad hoc Cabinet Committee was also established and a process to develop legislation to assist in the management of aspects of response and recovery of this first earthquake was initiated. Parliament enacted the Canterbury Earthquake Response and Recovery Act 2010 on Tuesday, 14 September. On Thursday, 16 September of that same week the declared state of emergency in the three affected territorial authorities was terminated. At this point in time the Government was acting swiftly and the population felt that assistance would be on its way.

It was not long, however, before the cracks began to appear. In the Agenda Order Paper of the Canterbury Civil Defence Emergency Management Group Joint Committee of December 13, 2010 several issues arose in response to the local state of emergency: including the coordination of information management problems at local and regional levels, which were also evident at a national level; and the manner in which the legislated and planned role of the Ministry of Civil Defence Emergency Management was diminished in both response and recovery. In addition it was felt that the new legislation, organisations, processes and roles, although intended to expedite and streamline response and recovery, actually interfered with and undermined arrangements previously put in place. Indeed it seemed that the left hand did not know what the right hand was doing.

The legislation relating to natural disaster and hazards in New Zealand is broad and complex. The Civil Defence Emergency Management

(CDEM) Act specifies how civil defence management is to operate in New Zealand in emergency situations. Civil Defence Emergency Management Groups are a central component of the CDEM Act. Civil Defence Emergency Management Groups comprise members of regional and local councils (there are 16 groups across the country) chaired by a Mayor or by other delegated representatives. These Groups prepare Civil Defence Emergency Management Group Plans. The purpose of the Plans is to inform and involve the community in understanding the hazards and risks they face. The Christchurch City Council Civil Defence Emergency Management Arrangements 2004, slightly abridged in 2008, stated that regarding earthquake risk in the region, *"Christchurch lies on the edge of a technically seismically active region. Consequently, earthquakes are likely to occur at a magnitude that will have major impacts on the City... The most susceptible areas to liquefaction are those with water saturated, loose, well soiled silt, and sand."* The risks were clearly known.

Other earthquakes were to follow the first, and after the large February 22, 2011 quake, a 'national state of emergency' was declared. Prime Minister John Key declared the national emergency when he addressed media at 11.00am on February 23 after meeting with Cabinet.[4] He stated that he had faith in the leadership in Christchurch but national emergency status would give more control to the Government. In practice this would enable the government to direct local, national and international resources to achieve the best possible response in the shortest timeframe. A national state of emergency provides the authority to suspend some normal functions of the executive, legislative and judicial powers, alert citizens to change their normal behaviours, or order government agencies to implement emergency and rapid response plans. This authority would be exercised working in close support of and in cooperation with Mayor Bob Parker and the Christchurch Civil Defence team.[5] At least, that was the idea in theory. This was the first time in New Zealand history (other than during the 1951 waterfront dispute) that a national state of emergency had been declared subsequent to a civil defence emergency event. Reports emerged of a full emergency management structure being in place within two hours, with national coordination operated from the National Crisis Management Centre bunker in the Beehive in Wellington and a regional emergency operations command established in the Christchurch Art Gallery.

In an aide-mémoire the Hon. John Carter stated that the declaration of the national state of emergency "... *demonstrates the Government's commitment to help people in Canterbury to respond to this disaster*". The Hon. Gerry Brownlee's regular portfolios were distributed amongst other Cabinet Ministers so that he could focus solely on earthquake recovery. The national state of emergency remained in place for almost ten weeks.

It is useful to examine the moves and procedures that led to the establishment of the Canterbury Earthquake Recovery Authority (CERA). The Government passed the Canterbury Earthquake Response and Recovery Act (CERRA), assented to under extreme urgency, on September 14, 2010. The Canterbury Earthquake Recovery Commission was also created under CERRA.

The Commission came under severe criticism because it was established as part of the emergency legislation passed under urgency 10 days after the September earthquake. It did not go through the usual regulatory impact analysis process, which meant that its design benefited neither from detailed analysis of recovery best practice, nor from the scrutiny and feedback from experts that consultation would have provided. This exacerbated the confusion about who was meant to be doing what, which in turn unravelled the recovery planning processes already in place.

Some felt that in the five months after the September earthquake the Christchurch City Council completely failed to take over the role of leading the recovery for Christchurch as the Civil Defence and Emergency Management regime required, deciding to operate 'business as usual' processes, which had the effect of stalling the rebuilding effort. Almost nothing happened to advance the city recovery from the moment the Commission was up and running, up until the second major February earthquake. By February 22, 2011, many felt that there was no recovery plan and no one in charge. The Christchurch City Council came under harsh criticism. The Commission was later replaced by the Canterbury Earthquake Recovery Authority.

Initially the CERRA bill received virtually unanimous support from within Parliament, although reservations were almost immediately expressed, from the Green Party primarily, as well as by ACT and Labour Members. Within a fortnight a group of 27 constitutional law experts from all six New Zealand university law faculties had issued an open letter detailing concerns about the breadth of the powers granted under CERRA, calling it "dangerous precedent"[6] because it abandoned established constitutional values and principles. It was said to represent an extraordinarily broad transfer of law making power away from Parliament to the executive branch, with minimal constraints on how that power could be used. The danger was said to be in a poorly framed general power to regulate, with weak legislative oversight and limitations on the review of that power by the courts. CERRA permits the making of Orders in Council, on the recommendation of various Ministers of the Crown, to *"grant an exemption from, or modify, or extend any provision of any enactment"*, with the exception of five constitutional enactments (the Bill of Rights 1688, the Constitution Act 1986, the Electoral Act 1993, the Judicature Amendment Act 1972, and New Zealand Bill of Rights Act 1990). An Order in Council under CERRA has the force of law as if it were a provision of the primary Act. The availability of Judicial Review of such Orders is limited.

CERRA was rushed through Parliament on the basis that it was required to hasten earthquake recovery. It was later repealed by the Canterbury Earthquake Recovery Bill 286-1, 2011.[7] It was felt that there was a need to put in place legislation that would provide a timely and coordinated recovery effort for Christchurch and the greater affected region. The Bill largely carried over the provisions in The Canterbury Earthquake Response and Recovery Act 2010. It put certain checks in place to guard against the inappropriate use of the powers given to the Minister and CERA. The Minister has now also to prepare and present to the House a quarterly report on the operation of this Act.

CERA was established by the Government under the State Sector Act as a public service department the week before the second major earthquake, in February 2011. It is effectively a government department reporting to the Hon. Gerry Brownlee. The Government recognised the enormity of the task and passed legislation to establish the Canterbury Earthquake Recovery Authority to lead and coordinate the recovery efforts. CERA was to lead the Recovery Strategy, policy and planning and be responsible for the coordination and planning of infrastructure. CERA's chief executive was initially sought from the ranks of the civil service. However, in May 2011, Roger Sutton, from the private sector (previously chief executive of the power company Orion), was appointed, possibly as a result of considerable local lobbying.[8] He was painted as something of a 'white knight'. Many subsequently came to see him as having little influence on measures which might genuinely help to alleviate the plight of affected citizens, and it is widely believed that the Hon. Gerry Brownlee actually called the shots. CERA's mandate is to run the greater Christchurch region for the following five years. It has powers over local authorities and although its chief executive is said to have considerable authority to enable it to advance the recovery, evidence of these being exercised is sparse from the point of view of distressed policyholders and citizens.

The Recovery Strategy operates as an overarching document for the more detailed recovery plans and programmes for Canterbury. The Bill provides that only the Recovery Plan for the Central Business District requires consultation with affected communities, with a view to restoring the social, economic, cultural and environmental wellbeing of these communities. The Canterbury Earthquake Recovery Minister is not required to consult with any person about the development of any other Recovery Plans.[9] This places considerable power in the hands of one individual. Underlying all the recovery efforts is said to be the Government's absolute commitment to greater Christchurch and its people. For many Cantabrians this is the point at which CERA has failed most dramatically. There has been virtually no public consultation at all, despite repeated calls from the public for involvement.

CERA's mandate is to work closely with other Central Government agencies to ensure the Government has a coordinated approach to its contribution to the recovery. The authority is to be overseen by an independent four-person review panel, chaired by a retired High Court judge, and will assess all legislative and regulatory changes CERA seeks to make. A cross-party forum of Canterbury Members of Parliament was set up to provide advice and a forum of Canterbury community leaders is to provide input on important local issues. There would be appeal rights against decisions made by the authority, with hearings heard in the High Court. The authority is subject to the Official Information Act. All in all, one might have expected this considerable legislative and administrative push to have effectively kick-started an efficient and rapid rebuild programme, but this has not happened.

The Minister of Earthquake Recovery stated that many of the powers in the CERA legislation were based on those put in place in Queensland to deal with that Australian state's devastating floods in December 2010. He said that it was important that the public have confidence that the powers would be used judiciously and to these ends the appointment of the Canterbury Earthquake Recovery Community Forum was set up. The forum consisted of 38 members from a wide cross-section of the Canterbury community, representing business and ethnic groups as well as residents associations and groups. Since its inception, little has been heard from the Forum.

In summary then, CERA's task was to build on the work already commenced by Civil Defence and local authorities, while the City Council was to lead the planning for the redevelopment of the Central City. This raised questions about how the relationships between CERA and the Minister and the Christchurch City Council were to be managed. Even though each of these bodies had its mandate, the lines were unclear and confusion and suspicion set in. Sandwiched between these parties was a large portion of the population of Christchurch, desperately waiting for some relief, and with a growing sense that decision making was disconnected and overly centralised, leading to a lack of clarity about how the community could best contribute to its own recovery.

The only agent required to report to Parliament is the head of CERA. The Minister may be asked questions in the House, but there is no other formal opportunity for scrutiny and accountability. City Councillors and others engaged with the Council have effectively become CERA employees. Council meetings are often not open to the public and there are real risks of poor accountability practice, important in good governance.

Looking back, it has become overwhelmingly clear that the quality of the interaction between CERA and the Council has had a major impact on the success and efficiency of local recovery. Intergovernmental co-operation creates both problems and opportunities for local strategic choices. Differences arise in priority setting, differences in perception of the importance of certain mitigation efforts as well as the proper organisational process of recovery planning and decision making. Local authorities view their relationship with the Government negatively as a result of their perception that the Government is unable or hesitant to provide the desired technical or financial assistance. When there is urgent heavy local dependence upon governmental financial assistance and local authorities wish to respond rapidly and require ready cash, these difficulties intensify. It is apparent that Central Government policies are useful in the initial phases of a disaster but as the disaster moves to the longer-term recovery phase, the need for site-specific adaptive planning becomes critical.

In New Zealand, responsibilities for immediate disaster and then recovery phases are spread out around both public and private organisations as well as across functional boundaries involving city, region and nation. This results in a situation where no single institution, person, or level of government is perceived as responsible for the whole process. Accordingly, the disaster recovery goals and policies of various agencies are often contradictory or non-existent. Thus the drive to resolve issues and 'get things done' is hampered by a lack of accountability or a confusion of roles and responsibilities. CERA was set-up in an attempt to mitigate these problems.

In March 2012, 18 months after the first quake, a Parliamentary Select Committee stated that emergency management systems were not strong enough to handle the Christchurch earthquake.[10] The system had struggled to respond on the scale needed and it was difficult to coordinate local and central government services. The emergency response systems were simply not designed for such a large-scale event. A rather surprising finding in a country well known for its earthquake risks.

Perhaps applying limited resources to prepare for the 'the big one' is not seen as cost effective. This is partially understandable, but in a seismic nation like New Zealand, it seems obvious that we cannot afford such an approach. EQC's documentation makes consideration of a major disaster as constituting no more than 30,000 to 150,000 claims.[11] The recent Canterbury events involve claim numbers of over 500,000. A disaster of this magnitude was simply never within the scope of this agency and thus is a real wake-up call.

In light of the recent Canterbury experiences it has become clear that inter-organisational coordination is one of the major issues in disaster response. Consequently we might posit that perhaps more funding and time should be spent on resolving operational issues around inter-organisational responsibility and accountability. While it not possible to prepare for every disaster contingency, some problems, such as earthquakes in New Zealand, occur with such regularity that the effects are quite predictable and these should be amenable to planning. Any major disaster will require procedures for the centralised gathering and sharing of information about the circumstances at hand and the required and available resources. When planning is then performed on an inter-governmental basis, it is more likely to result in a well-coordinated response.

Disasters frequently create non-routine tasks for which no organisation has clear-cut responsibility nor accountability. Often these tasks have no counterpart in routine emergency operations, and there are no precedents to assist with the delegation of responsibility, e.g. discussion about what constitutes an 'adequate response' to the disaster – a centralised or decentralised response. When the demands of disaster cannot be met by existing organisations, new organisations have to be created to fill the gap, as was CERA. The 'gap filler' often comes in the form of a coordinating 'committee' or group. However, communication difficulties are often hard to separate from coordination difficulties, and the greatest coordination difficulties stem from inter-organisational communication. No matter how many organisations are set up, if the communication issues are not overcome, the inadequate response will persist and the population will continue to suffer. This tension has been clearly visible in the relationship between the Council and CERA.

It is clear that in the case of Christchurch, many of the communications problems have been and are to do with inter-agency information sharing and the mechanisms for this. Solutions would include formal contracts, joint planning and training, pre-planned agreements for the division of disaster responsibilities, and the use of similar terminology, procedures, and performance criteria. These strategies would assist in the promotion of trust between organisations as well as an understanding of how each organisational component functions. With evidence of these processes, the affected population gains understanding and a sense that someone or an organisation is in control and has a plan, and knows how to implement the plan and see it through, hurdles and all. Many Cantabrians are still waiting and yearning for this plan and surety.

Crown Entity versus Public Service Department

International best practice suggests that CERA-type structures should be run as Crown entities and not as public service (government) departments. Others believe that CERA should be independent of government or at least be a layer of governance between the Authority and the politicians. The lack of independence is seen by some to be CERA's fundamental weakness. Much criticism about the way in which CERA is structured has arisen. There is a sense that the Government has replaced an independent body with no power, with one with lots of government spin which is designed to influence what people outside the affected communities think is happening instead of *"genuine and meaningful engagement with the affected communities…. that the rest of the city and the country cannot see"*[12] (Labour's Member of Parliament, Lianne Dalziel). Indeed, as time has passed CERA has had the flavour of a public-relations machine rather than an entity genuinely concerned with the welfare of its citizens.

The Government is also seen to be inventing its own recipe for recovery without any heed to international experience. Many of the natural disasters in recent years in Australia were managed by independent Crown agencies or their equivalents, not by government departments. A Crown entity is legally separate from the Crown and operates at arm's length from the responsible or shareholding Minister(s), and Crown agencies are included in the annual financial statements of the Government. The reason why a Crown entity is favoured is likely to be to do with the need to be free of 'politicking' and so able to focus on the task at hand. This single factor alone may be the region's greatest impediment to rapid recovery.

In New Zealand, academics, government and local politicians felt that the top-down approach was the right way to manage Christchurch's recovery. However, it was said to tend toward a militaristic command and control model considered inappropriate for the building of an integrated community, where "recovery is bottom up".[13] International experience shows that recovery should be a grassroots process, with the community actively involved in the creation of the plan. Instead, Christchurch is seen to have a model whereby the Government makes decisions through CERA – in fact the Minister does – and announces them through the media to the citizens rather than face-to-face with the affected communities. This has fuelled resentment and caused repercussions that contribute to slowing down the recovery. The disaster is seen to have been politicised. The literature also tells us that the Government – both central and local – must stop thinking of citizens as taxpayers and ratepayers and as consumers of the services they provide. Internationally existing inequalities have been shown to grow in the aftermath of major disasters, Christchurch has shown itself to be no different in that respect.

Community engagement is critical to recovery; it is not a waste of time or something that stands in the way of decision making. Decision-makers who engage with the affected communities and major stakeholders send a powerful message of support and thereby gain respect. The community is entitled to the information, the explanations and alternatives. Communities often produce ideas that are not immediately apparent to those tasked with writing plans and strategies. This strengthens the process and the outcome. 'Citizens actively engaged in their community's future – what a legacy that would be!' The response to the failure of the authorities to engage with the community in meaningful dialogue was evidenced (late September 2012) by the 2000-strong protest against the proposed closure of 13 Christchurch schools and merging of 25 others announced by the Education Ministry together with the introduction of charter schools, for which there was no mandate and considerable public opposition.

The Christchurch City Council

The Christchurch City Council has also come under considerable criticism from both the public and other quarters, for having taken a passive approach to earthquake risk. The Council has provided the drama in the backdrop of this disaster. Immediately after the September 4, 2010 earthquakes it was said that Christchurch City Council was failing to take on the role of leading the recovery. Instead, Civil Defence and the emergency management regime decided to operate on a 'business as usual' basis. This led effectively to stalling the Christchurch rebuild effort. Virtually nothing happened in the Council to advance the recovery from the moment the Earthquake Commission was up and running until the second major earthquake, on February 22, 2011. The strong impression was that there was no recovery plan and no one in charge. It is vital that the Government and the Christchurch City Council learn the lesson of this failure. The clear sentiment on the street was preference for an effective people-led planning style. It was felt at the time that poor leadership and a lack of a long-term vision at the Christchurch City Council could potentially jeopardise the city's recovery.

The report which was prepared by business and community representatives well before the major damage of 22 February, said that the Council had lost momentum and energy after its initial response to the earthquakes. As the earthquakes continued and the recovery response became more complex, the Christchurch City Council was criticised for a total lack of strategy. Councillors understandably became divided.

The compromises and corner-cutting of the past, such as the building of homes on liquefaction-prone land[14] and the laxity surrounding house building consent standards started to 'come home to roost' and led to confusion and growing frustration for the local population.

In the early days after the initial event, Local Government, in the form of the Christchurch City Council, chose a community-based approach. These two opposing mind-sets, community-based on the one hand and authoritarian on the other, created bedlam. The Christchurch City Council became CERA's ball and chain and the local population was happy with neither approach. Expectations for CERA were high with the appointment of a local chief executive. When the expectations were not met, tensions between the parties arose. Christchurch City Council was content to have CERA being more authoritarian and making the 'hard calls' (e.g. on the Cathedral), but then sided somewhat with the community, half-heartedly listening to its citizens. The Council and CERA were perceived to be talking different languages, with a constant string of miscommunications. Then an 'independent' reviewer was brought in to carry out a review of the Council. This would involve discussions with up to 120 people within the Council and the community as well as analysis of the Council's communication materials. It would also involve a public survey of ratepayers. The results of the survey suggested that the main area that residents wanted improved was transparency of decision making.

Some Christchurch City Councillors wanted more involvement in decision making at the beleaguered organisation. Several called for a special meeting in an attempt to start sorting out that organisation's woes, others called to have the Council re-elected or disbanded. Councillor Glenn Livingstone agreed there had been a "loss of confidence" by the public, but he disagreed with Councillor Wells' view that it should be disbanded. In short, the Council engaged in a very public exhibition of political suicide.

The Council is said to still be responsible for regular council-related matters such as water and waste issues; road infrastructure and traffic management; kerbside collections; water conservation and restrictions; and a rodent-management plan. However, effective management in these areas also has visibly been sorely lacking. The Council is also responsible for earthquake-prone building policy; heritage; resource consents; Land Information Memoranda and Property Information Memoranda; Central Business District putrescence cleaning; and flood protection.

In the initial phases, the Government announced that the Christchurch City Council would lead the development of the one mandatory recovery plan – the Recovery Plan for the Christchurch Central Business District in the form of the Central City Plan. The final draft Central City Plan has been unanimously adopted by the City Council after nine months developing it in consultation with the Greater Christchurch community, key stakeholders and partners Te Rūnanga o Ngāi Tahu, CERA and Environment Canterbury. It provided the framework to guide the redevelopment of the Central City, including more than 70 projects and initiatives to be implemented during the next 10 to 20 years.

The direct responsibility for rebuilding Christchurch's battered infrastructure which once upon a time would normally have been core work for the Council – was then delegated to a public–private 'alliance' that included representatives from CERA and the Christchurch City Council, which was then trumped by the Government and CERA's latest creation – the Christchurch Central Development Unit. The 'Blueprint for a new Christchurch' was released on July 30, 2012. It envisaged a more compact central city core, reducing the city from 90 hectares to 40 hectares.

On June 10, 2011 the Christchurch City Council announced plans for a 7.1 percent rates increase in 2011 and predicted a deficit of NZD 73.8 million over the next three years. NZD 2.5 billion of damage to city infrastructure caused by the quake is said to be covered by insurance and government subsidies, but the Council will still be faced with significant costs as there are 'unbudgeted costs' which will have a considerable impact on the Council's activities, major projects and finances. In addition it is faced with significant losses in revenue as a direct result of the earthquake, including: loss of dividends from council-owned companies of NZD 14 million, loss of parking revenue of NZD 6.9 million and loss of income from sports facilities. It was at this time that the suggestion first arose that in order to cover some of these costs, the Christchurch City Council should sell some of its assets in Christchurch City Holdings Limited, the proceeds of which could help fund the estimated NZD 20 billion rebuild of the central business district. Residents were, and many remain, strongly opposed to such a sale, which eventually led to the Earthquake Recovery Minister stating that the idea of selling the city's assets is one he would reject, despite the Act allowing him to "amend or replace" the City's Recovery Plan at any time, and also the dismissal of a proposed Labour amendment that would have protected the Council's strategic assets. By mid-2012 he had indeed changed his view.

Christchurch City Council can only be described as having experienced an internal meltdown, sparked initially by Chief Executive Officer Tony Marryatt's ill-timed acceptance of a NZD 68,000 salary increase. Marryatt came in for increasing criticism throughout the year. His fraught reappointment would not have been out of place in a local authority soap opera. In June 2011, Mayor Bob Parker threatened to resign if Marryatt was not reappointed. The Council's handling of the chief executive's appointment process also lead to one of the most significant and flagrant leaks of confidential information from the council table.[15]

Toward the end of the year Marryatt did indeed receive a NZD 68,000 pay rise, taking his salary to NZD 538,529 per annum. The city was appalled and expressed its discontent by organised protest, while families are still living in damaged homes, with no sign of real relief, many still with 'porta-loo' sanitation, struggling to pay for power and groceries let alone Christmas presents. The inequity and inappropriateness astonished New Zealanders. Peter Beck, the Christchurch Cathedral Dean, asked Marryatt to refuse the pay rise. In letters to the *Christchurch Press* people vented their fury over the issue, and calls for Marryatt to go continued on into 2012. He defended his pay rise, stating *"I've never worked so hard in my life"*. 'No Pay Rise for Tony Marryatt', said the organised protests outside council offices. In the early New Year an 'independent' review of the Council was planned – at a cost of NZD 80,000.[16]

Issues with the City Council came to a head when Sue Wells, a City Councillor, called for the Government to step in.[17] Mayor Bob Parker finally conceded the understatement, *"We're in a bad place"*.[18] The problems within the Council were blamed on 'leakers' who were destroying the trust between councillors.[19] People responded that it was the culture of clandestine, preconceived contentious decisions that was the problem, not the people who leaked them.

The then Local Government Minister, Nick Smith, was called in to assist because of the 'catastrophic failure of trust' and a need for 'ground rules'.[20] By the end of January 2012 Marryatt was making noises about reconsidering his salary raise.[21] The Prime Minister suggested that this was 'probably a clever thing'. Eventually Marryatt rejects part of his pay rise, although he has already received NZD 34,000.[22]

The dysfunction within the Council was cited as eroding confidence in the future of Christchurch.[23] Commissioners are requested as replacements for the Council.[24] The Government is reluctant to do this, though it warns that if things in the Council do not improve it may be forced to take more drastic action. Instead, a Government 'observer' is appointed.[25] An employment law specialist suggests that it is possible that if Marryatt 'goes' it could cost the ratepayers NZD 1.5 million in the form of a constructive dismissal.

On Saturday 28 January 2012, some 400 protestors descended upon the council offices demanding answers, talking of a rates revolt if no action is taken.[26] However, in mid-February 2012 the then Local Government Minister Nick Smith, ruled out the possibility of early council elections as a solution to Christchurch's woes.[27]

By mid-March 2012 more details surfaced around Mayor Bob Parker's request for help from Minister Nick Smith, urging that a new charter be put in place to bring the Council under control.[28] Parker was not prepared to have urgent meetings with councillors until the charter was in place. There were then threats of personal grievance claims against the Council; these could cost that body millions of dollars.

Mayor Bob Parker describes the City Council as standing on the edge of a precipice and says that councillors have to put aside their differences if they want to avoid government intervention. The Council was seen to be increasingly torn apart by internal squabbling between elected members, with the added fuel of the hefty pay increase handed to its chief executive. Public disquiet grew steadily, with repeated calls for the

Council to be disbanded and Commissioners appointed. Hon. Nick Smith reiterates that the Government had no plans to appoint Commissioners to run that body. The Canterbury public responded vocally – that fresh council elections were necessary and a new CEO should be appointed. Much of the public had lost confidence in their council's ability to govern for the benefit of all. 2011, the year of the city's greatest need, was unquestionably a bad year's performance by Christchurch City Council.

The Christchurch City Council under its own steam, has produced a Three Year Plan[29], an Annual Plan[30], Area Plans[31], a Christchurch Transport Strategic Plan[32], and a District Plan review.[33] CERA has drafted a Land Use Recovery Plan[34] including the Blue Print Plan[35] and then there's the Greater Urban Development Strategy.[36] Many of the plans overlap and it is clear that the current reality is far from the future vision. Disconnection abounds. As the writer Peter Robb reported in the Sydney Morning Herald, after a brief visit to Christchurch, *"all I saw of the future city was a rapid slide show of artists' impressions of a series of low slung cuboids"*[37].

Dame Margaret Bazley, the Environment Canterbury chairwoman, wades into the dispute on the issue of public transport delays, calling the Christchurch City Council *"a totally incompetent organisation"*. The Mayor at the time, Bob Parker, responds with a hand written apology. Then the issue of building consents raises its ugly head. It is revealed that Tony Marryatt, the CEO of the Christchurch City Council, failed to let Councillors know that the organisation was about to lose its consenting powers (which are granted by courtesy of International Accreditation New Zealand) as a result of the council's failure to address internal processing issues.[38]

The City Council is later stripped of its accreditation. The Mayor tries to play down the event declaring that he had failed to read the initial report that raised the concerns. The Earthquake Minister uses the opportunity to assert that the Council is failing in fundamental tasks and this is followed up with a team from the Ministry of Business Innovation and Employment (MBIE) sent to 'help' council officers, process consents. Once again, the Government steps in. The Environment Minister then orders an examination of the Council's resource consenting arm.[39]

Tony Marryatt is formally investigated over his actions leading to the council's consenting debacle[40] On his final self-inflicted departure, Tony Marryatt receives a pay-out of NZD 800,000.[41] The shocked and disgusted community requests a full investigation into his employment history.

The now retired ex-Mayor, Bob Parker, graciously bows out of the mayoral race rather than face what would obviously be an absolute rout, citing exhaustion and leaving Labour Member of Parliament, Lianne Dalziel the hot favourite. Lianne Dalziel vows to put the city first. Other candidates such as Vicki Buck (former Christchurch mayor) and Paul Lonsdale throw their hat into the ring too. Cantabrians express their views and the City is once again divided on policy and intention. Bob Parker is later knighted for his somewhat dubious but amazingly media-savvy efforts during his mayoralty.

Developers in the Central City blame inexperience for the development failures in Christchurch's centre. About NZD 150 million of available capital is expected to leave the central city after failed negotiations with the Government.[42]

The exciting vision many Cantabrians had aspired and contributed to, is instead heading for a rather ordinary solution. The Earthquake Recovery Minister continues to be seen as failing to be inclusive and secretive in his sharing of information about the Government's plans for Christchurch. Meanwhile there is a strong sense on the ground that the Hon. Gerry Brownlee's personal involvement in all significant decisions should be reducing as CERA's role is due to end in the next two years. Yet if the Council is to have a greater role in the recovery it must be able to prove its ability to be 'up to the job', which will be defined by the quality of its decision making in the years to come. As it stands the role of local government has become totally subordinate to the role of central government. CERA's primary mandate was to streamline bureaucracy and accelerate decision making - but there is no sign that these objectives have been achieved. Nor is there a sense that the two bodies are easily able to work together. A prime example is CERA's absence from a community forum dealing with the issue of CERA's role in recovery and how CERA would exit Christchurch. All the local district mayors attend but CERA is absent despite them confirming as guests. Hon. Gerry Brownlee makes it publically known that he sees it as too early to talk about CERA leaving the City.[43] CERA continues to expand its numbers while emerging more and more as an essentially Wellington-based bureaucratic government department.

By the end of 2013, asset sales are back on the agenda being seen as the key to fill a *"black hole".[44]* Consultants are hired to review the Council's asset holdings in order to ascertain how the cash-strapped organisation can raise enough money to pay its share of the rebuild costs. Borrowing more money is now out of the question.[45] There is a call for the need for openness in council finances and the Earthquake Recovery Minister, Gerry Brownlee says there are concerns about the fact that no one seems to know what the Council's full insurance situation looks like. It is reported that the Council has almost completely depleted a NZD 225 million fund established post-earthquakes to pay for roading, footpaths and facilities. There is great concern that the shortfall could pose a *"real threat"* to the pace of the rebuild.[46] The depletion appears in part due to the underinsurance of many of their facilities.[47] The new Christchurch City Council is now faced with a dilemma. It had agreed to contribute NZD 1.9 billion toward the rebuild of damaged horizontal infrastructure and the construction of the anchor projects. It did so on the assumption that it would get its full insurance entitlement on the quake damaged facilities. However, at this point it is yet to reach agreement on whether the key facilities are repairs or rebuilds and it becomes clear that the previous council's assumptions about receivable insurance monies were overly optimistic.[48] The Council also battles to find an insurance company willing to take on the risk of insuring publicly owned buildings and assets.

Meanwhile the new Mayor brands the former Council as *"irresponsible"* for signing a cost sharing agreement with the Government and declares that the ex-Mayor led council, had left a *"tragic legacy"* and potentially serious financial predicament in that they had committed to projects the Council simply could not afford.[49] By the end of 2014 that prediction becomes a reality. There are funding shortfalls wherever one cares to look. In turn, Bob Parker, criticises Lianne Dalziel for doubling staff numbers without consulting ratepayers.[50] In the Korda Mentha report into the Council's financial position, a shortfall of NZD 534 million is detailed and this shortfall is said to increase significantly because the Council is unlikely to receive the NZD 1 billion insurance pay-out it had predicted. It seems that the Christchurch City Council is also not immune from major insurance nightmares as it tries to negotiate settlements with both Civic Assurance and the Earthquake Commission. What develops is a trade-off in deciding between spending on 'anchor projects' or making sure that the city's infrastructure is sound. By late 2014 the land available for the anchor projects is reduced by 23 percent and hundreds of damaged community facilities are said to likely have to go unrepaired due to the Council shortfall.[51] The list of things still to be done is eye watering: streamline bureaucracy, fix broken houses, make housing affordable, create alternative housing, build houses for the long term, and decide whether to stabilize or rebuild, build better roads, complete below-ground service repairs, – and the list goes on.

After a couple of knock-backs in the courts over the lack of formal process, (such as consultation) by the Earthquake Minister, CERA is now producing publicly consulted recovery plans to pave the way for their major decisions. Former Canterbury district police commander, Dave Cliff, will lead a team charged with overseeing CERA's final phase.[52] The Earthquake Minister, Gerry Brownlee will continue to retain most of the power under new legislation governing the next five years of Canterbury's earthquake recovery. The Greater Christchurch Regeneration Bill allows for changes to approved recovery plans paving the way for 'rethinks' and potential project abandonment. Under the new legislation the Crown would still have power to compulsorily acquire, subdivide and amalgamate land subject to a few additional safeguards. The Government will continue to have control of the City with a Minister-led future for Christchurch through to 2021. CERA now declares that the recovery phase is likely to take 10 to 20 years.

CERA's special powers are to cease from April 2016, when the five year Canterbury Earthquake Recovery Act expires. The authority is to then be assimilated into the Department of the Prime Minister and Cabinet. The Mayor throws her support behind the Government's new plan but hopes it will not take five years for the council to regain full power. 'Regenerate Christchurch' is the name of the new entity to take the City into the future and a new law is to be introduced to take over the management of the central city rebuild from CERA. The Mayor and Christchurch City Council slowly try to claw back some power and it is agreed that a more collaborative approach is required with the inclusion of the Council's development authority, Development Christchurch.[53] Its mandate is to provide advice to the council on unsolicited development proposals and to look after some of the major capital projects, reporting monthly to council.[54] In July 2015 the Council again sends the Government a strong message that it no longer wants to be a back seat passenger in the city's recovery. *"It is time for a transition back to local leadership and decision making"*.[55] CERA's command and control thinking has not gone down well with the population or the business community. An example of this is CERA's plan to shred quake documents and destroy Official Information Act requests leaving only a shell of administrative records. This, despite the extremely high level of public interest in all documents relating to ministerial notes, correspondence policy documents, minutes and engineer's reports. There is a strong sentiment amongst the population that the central government-managed recovery has 'fallen to pieces'.

The Interrelationships

Disagreements among the various groups were mainly around financing, responsibilities and control. The media reported on inter-governmental disagreement more often than it cited ineffective control. The Earthquake Recovery Minister accused parts of the Christchurch City Council of slowing the earthquake recovery and refused to rule out sacking councillors.[56] Some were outraged by Gerry Brownlee's threats to sack democratically elected city councillors. Others pointed to National's track record, as it had already sacked the democratically elected Environment Canterbury and in 1991 the democratically elected hospital boards. Others argued that both CERA and the Christchurch City Council should have representation but not overall control, warning that if responsibility for the planning and control of the inner-city rebuild is not moved to a new and competent commercial body, incorporated under CERA, Christchurch could be facing tragic circumstances in four to five years. Cantabrians are rapidly approaching those then-distant timeframes and for some this looks likely to be the case regardless of who is in control, as without intervention, the insurers will make it so.

Some called for an organisation between CERA and the Christchurch City Council, to be made up of non-bureaucratic individuals who would be able to drive recovery. In line with this, speculation continued about government intervention in the Council. It was claimed that CERA and the Council are working independently of each other. Christchurch resident and Member of Parliament for Labour, Lianne Dalziel, warned that the Government had plans to seize control of the central-city rebuild and that democracy was rapidly being "discarded". She suggested that Cabinet was set to approve a proposal to create a new unit within the Canterbury Earthquake Recovery Authority (CERA) to manage the rebuild. The Earthquake Recovery Minister's response to this was to suggest that Dalziel was having a "crazy rant".[57] He rejected her claims that there would be a takeover by Central Government. By mid-April a government announcement was said to be likely on the appointment of a new executive to lead the repair of Christchurch's earthquake-damaged infrastructure. Auckland Watercare chief executive Mark Ford, the former executive chairman of the Auckland Transition Agency, was tipped as a possible candidate for a Canterbury Earthquake Recovery Authority role, to lead the rebuild of the central city. This was quickly followed by Christchurch city councillors warning the Government not to encroach on democracy. Councillor Glenn Livingstone stated, *"I think the Government needs to be very careful, so they don't diminish what is the people's plan."*[58] Yet despite the Earthquake Recovery Minister's denial that there would be a takeover, this is exactly what came to pass, although it became Warwick Isaacs, the current general manager of operations at CERA, who was to lead the new crusade. Was this to be simply another layer of bureaucracy or would it help to restore some direction to a rudderless rebuild? Many felt that it would not. There was talk of plans to model the Central Business District on the Beirut Central District, London Docklands Development and Lower Manhattan Development Corporation, and then more talk of American big-business-dominated development and the potentiality of a 'pervasive politics of exclusion' emerging. It was not what Cantabrians wanted. They wanted a city where all citizens mattered. There was a sense amongst a segment of the community that what was currently taking place, using insurance as the conduit, was a calculated culling of city residents.

A Major Issue – The Red Zone

One of the major issues around the Christchurch 'rebuild' has been the Government/CERA 'pay-outs' of properties in the red zones at values based on 2007 Quotable Value figures in Christchurch and environs. These property values, to state the obvious, were five years old! This has produced groups of 'winners and losers'. For many, this package was not sufficiently equitable to allow citizens to buy an equivalent property elsewhere, nor would the package include the cost of moving and re-establishment wherever they eventually choose to go.[59] It was announced that 5,000 red zoned homeowners (that is, land too badly damaged to economically repair) had 'accepted' the Government's offer for their homes.

The Government presented them with two options: Option 1, the Government would purchase *"your land, the buildings and fixtures on your land, your EQC claims for the damage to your land, your EQC and private insurer's claims for any damage to the buildings and fixtures on your land"*; and Option 2 – *"your land, the buildings and fixtures on your land, your EQC claims for the damage to your land."*

Some citizens said that they felt bullied into leaving their homes.[60] Many were unhappy with the offers, declaring that it would leave them out of pocket or force them to leave properties that remain habitable. Constituents have been left with little confidence in the integrity of the government deal and this has led to a real erosion of trust. Many still feel that they have been misled by the original promise that the cost of their home improvements between the 2007 valuation and the 2011 and 2012 pay-outs would be factored into the offer the Government proposed. The

Government/CERA reneged on its offer. Added to this was the fact that it has not offered affordable land or housing options and most residents in these areas will be out of pocket by many thousands of dollars. *"The CERA offer is so well spun it needs unpicking!"*[61] Many see it as a theft of property rights in a supposed democracy and that the Government is undermining citizens' contractual and property rights to appease foreign insurers, saving them from the cost of honouring replacement contracts, EQC land payments and then yielding the Government a huge parcel of land for future development. Talk continues about a covert government agenda. In addition, no geotechnical reports and details are yet available to show how zoning has been determined. There is an expectation that the population will do just as it is told, and the population feels it deserves more explanation. For most, their home represents their greatest asset. To have their equity eroded is a hard pill to swallow.

The Government's line was that the offer was fair because on average, property prices fell by 5 percent from 2007–10. It is difficult to imagine the Government trying this out in a high socioeconomic area such as Fendalton or Parnell. It would appear that the 'powers that be' can categorise and minimise people's losses in any way they see fit, marginalising them further. It just happens too, that the red zone consists of predominantly lower socio-economic groups. These are the people who are more likely to be affected by government and insurance company decisions. The 'average' disguises the reality that confronts many people.

The establishment of a simple dispute-resolution process that would enable any 'material discrepancy' between rating valuations and market valuations to be resolved could have alleviated people's concerns. However, the Government noted in its June Cabinet papers that the suggestion to have such a body had been dropped.[62] On the CERA website there was a warning that if red zone residents did not accept the government offer, their insurance policies could be cancelled or the Council may not install new services and other utility providers may find it unfeasible or impractical to maintain services. There is no complaints authority for citizens to air their concerns, as most such authorities do not have the power to assist in cases where the quantum is above NZD 200,000 plus GST. The situation seems wholly unfair and unjust.

On August 9, 2012, in a Cabinet Committee on Canterbury Earthquake Recovery Minute of Decision, the gross cost of buying out the residential red zone was estimated to be NZD 19,768 million. The net cost of purchasing properties within that area was withheld from the report. What re-zoning has done is to bypass and undermine the insurance that people have. The Government has seemingly arbitrarily zoned areas red, while initially refusing to release the geotechnical data supposedly justifying their decision. Red zoning is seen as an arbitrary ruling by the Government to save Treasury from the embarrassment that EQC has not been managed to properly provide the protection the New Zealand population has paid for since 1944. Red zoning is seen by some as the confiscation of people's property and contractual insurance rights. People feel that if the land is going to be too costly to remediate then they should be paid in accordance with their insurance policy and not a potentially self-serving cost-saving pay-out from the Government. The only losers under the current strategy are the homeowners. An Avonview retirement village owner was told by the Earthquake Recovery Minister, Gerry Brownlee, that despite the owner's protests that the Government offer was not sufficient to pay the equity of the residents of the village: *"the situation is we believe, [that] the 2007 government valuation is fair and we will not be negotiating further"*.[63] This has been the attitude throughout… no need for public consultation… no need for justification. We make the rules… be quiet and accept what you are given. For the elderly, the problem is even more serious; many who prior to the earthquakes were mortgage free, do not have enough income or money to buy elsewhere and are now unable to take on additional debt, even with the remote chance of their being able to get a mortgage. What does the future hold for this group?

A lot of Christchurch 'red zoners' are in disagreement with the government offer. In addition there are many residents in the Brooklands area who have a registered valuation for house and land of only around NZD 250,000 or less. These people cannot afford to go anywhere, and in the absence of any information about what will happen once the government offer expires, they are choosing to stay put. In April 2012, CERA ruled out a review of the residential red zone despite homeowners challenging the decision to write-off their land. Around 100 red zoned property owners formally asked CERA to change their zoning to green in order to enable them to stay on their land to rebuild or repair their homes.

Labour Member of Parliament Lianne Dalziel, whose Bexley home was red zoned last year, quizzed Earthquake Recovery Minister Gerry Brownlee about whether he shared Prime Minister John Key's concerns that some residents would be out of pocket by more than NZD150,000 through the Government's buy-out offers. Brownlee's response was that he was *"deeply troubled"* by the question raised by the Member as she had a *"personal concern about how much she was being paid"* for her land.[64] Well yes, you would, would you not? The quantum you receive for your land, your home, is vital; it determines the landscape of your future.

The families of displaced elderly residents of red zone retirement villages in Christchurch have asked the Earthquake Recovery Minister to explain why such vulnerable people are not being given the same financial help as homeowners, when a sharp spike in death rates suggests that the stress of having to deal with CERA and the negotiation process is killing them. Nearly 200 elderly people need help desperately. But it is not just elderly people who live in retirement villages who are being treated so badly; it is also elderly people who have bought their own 'over-65 units' who were forced (by legislation) to have Body Corporate insurance. After the earthquake, the insurance companies decided they 'could not' honour the full rebuild price that this unfortunate group of people had paid insurance for. Once again the industry moved the goal posts – these people were only insured for a full rebuild if the ground was not damaged and their homes could be rebuilt on the existing land. Low 'market valuations', decided by supposedly 'non-independent' valuers, have been organised by the insurance companies, leaving many of these people seriously out of pocket.

Others believe that because there is a government deadline for settlement, April 2013, private insurers are deliberately delaying settlements with residents, thereby forcing homeowners to accept government offers which are well below what they are entitled to recover. The Government's original position – that people will be forced to leave their homes in April 2013 – was eventually extended by three months. People viewed this as forced eviction and many had literally nowhere to go. What is happening is seen as a compulsory land grab by government, denying landowners their entitlements under insurance contracts and simultaneously taking land titles, with compensation considerably lower than their existing entitlements. When questioned about what might happen if residents were to stay on their land, Mr Brownlee is said to have stated that if the occupier had not left by April 2013 they may be forced off their land and the compensation may be even less than originally offered. This seems both heavy-handed and extortionary.[65]

One Christchurch-based law firm holds the opinion that insurers cannot offer red zoned owners payment for repair costs only. The proper approach for insurers is to accept that properties in the red zone are constructive total losses, regardless of the extent of actual damage which has occurred to the house, on the basis that the houses are no longer able to be occupied. This would appear to be a logical conclusion, even if unpalatable to the insurers, but is likely to require a legal test case to settle the matter.

In mid-April 2012 the insurers brought some red zoned homes 'back from the dead', telling homeowners their 'rebuilds' are now 'repairs'. This change of policy understandably infuriated homeowners – most of them IAG customers in Brooklands. Affected residents accused insurance companies of hiding behind the Government's red zone offer to save money at owners' expense.[66] This single unilateral decision by the insurers, means that many will lose more than NZD 100,000 under the Government's red zone buyout offer. Insurers deny that the switch is a cost-cutting measure, claiming it was the result of the Government 'relaxing guidelines' for quake repairs. Despite IAG providing a quote for repairs, the work will never take place. In the red zone, where land is expected to be abandoned, repairs are hypothetical and merely provide a way for insurers to produce a dollar figure. According to IAG, when they returned for more detailed inspections, the damage was assessed under the new guidelines (introduced late in 2011), resulting in some homes being switched from being rebuilds to 'repair jobs'. The new guidelines permit even larger cracks and tilts in building foundations, meaning many homes in Brooklands now need not be written off. IAG states that the guidelines have been "internationally peer reviewed"– by whom, one wonders? Questioned about who initiated the changes to the guidelines, Ms Walker (a spokesperson for IAG) declared hesitantly that it was the Department of Building and Housing and these new guidelines were then agreed to by the District Councils in the region.[67] Presumably the rest of the country has not agreed to the changes in the building/repair guidelines. More guidelines were to follow. These changes are not only red zone specific but now apply to all earthquake-affected homes and they certainly save the Government and insurers considerable sums of money at the expense of the equity in residents' homes.

It comes to light that Minister Gerry Brownlee disregarded advice from officials to give red zoned Cantabrians a full pay-out for their quake damaged properties and instead offered them only half the rateable value. Without fair compensation it is likely that those affected will experience considerable difficulty re-establishing themselves. Labour's earthquake spokesperson at the time, Lianne Dalziel, stated that the offer was 'outrageous'.[68] The Earthquake Minister Gerry Brownlee later denies this stating that it was incorrect to suggest that the CERA report gave recommendations as to values.[69] There are also questions around whether the Earthquake Recovery Minister has been overly cautious and red zoned too many properties. The Human Rights Commissioner asks the Canterbury Earthquake Recovery Minister to extend the red zone deadline so that those affected have more time to consider the Government's offer. The label 'red zone' has rendered the affected properties almost worthless,[70] and local valuers astutely point out that it is not the earthquakes that have caused loss in value but rather Government policy. Zoning had basically 'stripped' the value of land. Some affected homeowners petition the Government and threaten to fight the decision in court. The Prime Minister provides a 'quick-fire' apology for the threat he makes to *"walk away"* from Christchurch red zoners who are challenging the Crown's buyout. *"Thanks very much, it's been a lot of fun. If you don't want to take the offer, that's where it's at*". Earlier on in the year he had dismissed post-earthquake issues as "*microlevel... hardluck stories*".[71]

The first legal battle over insurance entitlements in the red zone finds its way into the High Court. The O'Loughlin's dispute the repair value offered by their insurer, Tower Insurance. Despite the fact that the case was considered to be a landmark case for the red zone it does not in fact address the issue of red zone land. In the event that the judge had ruled in favour of the O'Loughlin's, declaring all property in the red zone 'written-off', then insurers would have been forced to pay full replacement value for the properties. Justice Asher stopped short of this and avoided a landmark decision. 300 red zoners fail to accept the Crown offer of compensation for their land. The Government offers were designed to coerce acceptance, sidestepping common law and statutory principles.[72] By mid-way through 2013, only 150 property owners have rejected the Crown offer and choose to stay on in largely abandoned neighbourhoods. Those remaining, pay full rates on their properties despite the Crown's stated intention to cut services to their neighbourhoods.

A group of red zoners fight the Government's 'abuse of power' said to be "*oppressive, disproportionate [and] contrary to human rights*".[73] This case marks a test of primary property rights in New Zealand. They seek a judicial review of the Government's compensation policy for red zoned land. The 68 strong group referred to as the Quake Outcasts, seek a declaration of the zoning and the 50 percent buyout offer from the Government to be deemed illegal and for the Christchurch City Council to be ordered to continue to provide services for those who wished to remain where they are. Minister Gerry Brownlee and CERA chief executive Roger Sutton are named as respondents. The Quake Outcasts win their case. Justice Pankhurst rules that the Earthquake Recovery Minister and CERA chief executive should reconsider the 50 percent offers and the new decisions be made 'in accordance with the law'.[74] The Government appeals the judgement [75] and the Earthquake Minister has a 'swipe' at the Judge in the High Court.[76] The Court of Appeal backs Justice Pankhurst's ruling but overturns a finding that the red-zoning process was unlawful. Quake Outcasts file an application to appeal that decision and the Court of Appeal upholds the High Court's ruling stating that the government offer was unlawful but would not go so far as to say that the red zoning process was unlawful. An application is subsequently made to the Supreme Court.[77] *"The harm to [uninsured or uninsurable land] owners has arisen, at least to a degree, because of Government policy of facilitating voluntary withdrawal, rather than their insurance status."* The court finds that it was the Government's red zoning policy that has left landowners potentially out of pocket, not their insurance status. The Court also ruled that the Government had not properly considered the Canterbury Earthquake Recovery Act and its purpose of *"social, economic, cultural and environmental wellbeing"* when making the reduced offer.[78]

There is an extension to the date of departure from their homes for red zoners in New Brighton and Southshore. Yet many feel that the extension of two months is not enough time in light of the difficulties associated with buying other properties or the time required to secure a building consent. It comes to light that CERA planned only limited publicity allowing red zoners possible extensions.[79] Despite calls for more time, CERA refused to budge on the date. Only a few were granted extensions and then for only a very limited time frame. Later on in the year, a group of 270 green zoned properties suddenly become red zoned after a *"zoning review"*. The rezoning throws these families into total chaos. Some residents call for compensation for the unnecessary final loss and stress they have had to undergo. Conversely some red zoners now become green zoned. By December 2014 the red zone demolition is extended by a further six months, there are still some thousand properties that require demolition.

For 132 residents in the Port Hills, the fate of their properties also remained uncertain. These are properties said to be affected by rock fall. Those affected expressed concerns around why it had taken seven months to review the data of 100 properties affecting hundreds of people's lives. After more than two and a half years the residents of 51 green zoned properties are still unable to return home. The Council issued section 124 notices which prohibit entry on 'safety grounds'. 305 red zoned Port Hills homes are subject to s124 notices. Most insurance policies pay-out only if the house is damaged beyond repair. Then the

Earthquake Recovery Minister states that the Christchurch City Council has it terribly wrong, reneging on agreed risk standards and confusion about s124 notices. He calls for the red stickers on properties in the green zoned Port Hills to be removed.[80] The Human Rights Commission then wades into the issue stating that there are *"unconscionable delays"* which are taking a *"heavy toll"* on residents.[81] Two properties in the Port Hills have dropped in value by 97 percent - the total valuation of NZD 13 million for these properties has plummeted to NZD 2.3 million, according to the Spokesperson for Christchurch Earthquake Issues, Denis O'Rourke.[82] It is not until December 2013 that the Port Hills residents are finally given decisions about the status of their land - two and a half years after the earthquake. In a Court of Appeal ruling in 2015 it is confirmed that the insurer does not have to pay full replacement value for these properties because there was no actual *"physical damage"* to the property.

The red zones raise interesting legal questions in light of such precedents as *Invercargill City Council v Hamlin* [1994] 3 NZLR 513,[83] where the plaintiff homeowner found cracks in his home, which were determined to be the result of inadequately constructed foundations. The Council was responsible for inspection and approval of the foundations. The Court of Appeal found that on the basis of New Zealand precedent, a council owed a duty of care to the purchaser in the inspection of the house for the purpose of compliance with building regulations.[84] One wonders whether this might not also be extended to land that has been built upon knowingly, when the Council was aware, based on previous geological reports, that liquefaction was a risk. The case of *Brown v Heathcote County Council* [1986] 1 NZLR 76 (CA), [1987] 1 NZLR 720 (PC) is even more to the point. In this situation the plaintiffs built on a site which unbeknownst to them was subject to flooding. They brought an action against the Council and the Drainage Board for negligence. They succeeded against the Drainage Board on the grounds that the Board should have warned them about the danger of flooding. These findings clearly favour the New Zealand case law precedent for the recovery of damages in negligence for pure economic loss, which is a proposition now firmly established.

A report written by the Enfocus Ltd (policy professionals) stated that when Environment Canterbury decided which land was suitable for urban development, it took the view that the risk of liquefaction and lateral spreading were not reasons to prohibit development. It was believed such risks could be mitigated by the territorial authorities through engineering at the time of subdivision and building, which, generally speaking, did not occur. As a result, it gave much greater consideration to the risks of flooding and sea-level rise than to the risks of liquefaction, yet liquefaction has been the major contributing factor to damage in the eastern suburbs of Christchurch.

In September 2012 discussion around land in the central city became a top topic. The National Government was now seen to be nationalising land. CERA has plans to compulsorily acquire 53 hectares of central Christchurch private property for an estimated NZD 636 million – 880 letters were sent to central city property owners advising them that their property was to be compulsorily acquired under the powers of the Canterbury Earthquake Recovery Act 2011 "once all other options are exhausted" to ensure the retail precinct has the look and feel of the Australian city Melbourne, considered to be one of the most 'liveable' cities in the world. The new rules require retail developments to be planned in 7,500 square-metre lots. There is concern amongst small landowners that this will require complicated negotiations between multiple title-holders. Whether CERA has considered the need for formal bodies for dispute-resolution where disputes arise is not clear.

So where does the insurance industry fit into all of this?

The insurance industry's claim that the insurance market is improving in Christchurch was strange as it became evident that it was very hard to get fresh cover, even for home contents. However, in September 2012 some of the larger insurers re-entered the Christchurch market. A recent survey of Christchurch businesses shows none of the main players in the rebuild of Christchurch had earned a '50 percent pass mark', and insurance companies ranked at the bottom of the list. Insurance companies scored 'poor' or 'very poor' by 55 percent of the 400 respondents and won only a 20 percent rating of 'very good' and 'good'. More than half of the 400 businesses surveyed considered the insurers' performance 'poor'.[85]

The slow progress in recovery is in large part due to the insurance industry and its lack of willingness to process claims within reasonable timeframes. Many citizens have long had the necessary assessments and reports and invasive testing on properties, and believe that they have all the necessary documentation upon which decisions by the insurers can be made and yet they are still waiting on action from their insurers. The financial preoccupation experienced by those worrying about the future of their properties and their ability to negotiate a reasonable settlement with the Government or their private insurer inevitably impedes their recovery. In the process they become socio-economically disenfranchised individuals. The longer they have to wait for resolution the less likely it becomes that they will ultimately stay in the region.

Very much in the background sits the insurance industry, quietly waiting, investing its EQC and reinsurance funds and watching its float bloat to unprecedented levels. It has until recently kept itself under the radar. At first the population's attention was focused on the poor performance of EQC and its dubious assessment criteria, then for the aftershocks to subside, then for geotechnical land reports – finally the excuses have dried up. The people of Canterbury have waited long enough, have had enough of dealing with the delay tactics; many are ready for action. If all else fails, not all the legal avenues for redress have yet been explored by the citizens of Christchurch.

If international experience is anything to go by, the insurance industry is among the top ten political campaign contributors. It begs questions about contributions to political parties here in New Zealand. These are hard to track, but are of great importance as it is at this level that most regulation occurs. Money buys influence. Influence also comes from corporations. The insurance industry and its close association with banking, teems with corporates that influence public policy. In essence there is a revolving door between public officials, public servants and lobbyists. Questions also arise around the influence of reinsurers on government. A nation which is unable to finance its own natural disasters finds itself at the beck and call of the reinsurer, careful not to step out of line for fear of being without catastrophe protection. One can only wonder about the conversations that take place behind closed doors (such as the New Zealand delegation rendezvous in Monte Carlo[86] in September 2011), conversations that ultimately have enormous impact on a nation's citizens.

Conclusion

In Prime Minster John Key's 'state of the economy' address in Auckland on January 26, 2012, he said that 2011 in Canterbury had been about *"dealing with the damage"* caused by the destructive earthquakes. This year, 2012, was about *"starting to rebuild a vibrant, strong city"*. He went on to state that the Government was totally committed to the reconstruction of Canterbury, *"I can assure you that we won't hesitate to use the powers we have to clear blockages in the system"*.[87]

This rhetoric has not been borne out in action; five full years have passed since the first earthquakes. Canterbury has had three years of optimistic statements about the future of Canterbury by the Prime Minister. We hear the words, but thousands of people are still waiting – waiting for government to step in and protect the interests of its citizens. As the whole of the debacle about control and leadership has unfolded, it was noticeable that the insurance industry pocketed its reinsurance pay-outs and kept its head well down while contributing almost nothing to any recovery over the initial two years. Nor was its absence much noted by local or governmental factions while the higher-level infighting and dissent was in focus. The rest of the country's voters have also forgotten and are getting on with their lives. Public demonstrations relating to Local Government salary increases were the start of public displays of dissatisfaction at the way the community has been treated.[88] When the public is badly served they eventually take matters into their own hands.

The role of government is often debated in the context of economics, and private firms seek to limit or eliminate government involvement in the provision of goods and services which, the private sector argues, should be produced by that sector. The current situation brings into focus the relationship of this policy to the provision of insurance cover. As we cast a critical eye over the behaviour of a government committed to 'the market' and the capitalist-oriented world, a consistent general principle emerges: the belief that governments should intervene only in areas where markets fail; that is, where private firms are unable or unwilling to produce a particular good or service. So the question arises, how bad does the situation in Canterbury have to become before the Government is willing to step in and address what many Cantabrians now see as a failing insurance market – market failure not as a result of failing businesses but arguably due to the concerted policy decision within these insurance corporates to manipulate the bases for payments and delay rebuild actions and pay-outs until the last possible moment, in their own financial Interests.

The distinction between a government 'policy' decision and 'operational' decision is basically a legal rationalisation. The key issue is 'duty of care',[89] and when there is 'proximity' (a duty of care is owed).[90] The duty of care is the duty to take care – every person has the legal obligation, or duty, to be careful in what he or she does, or chooses not to do, so as not to cause harm to his or her neighbour. It was originally a duty between private individuals but, with the evolution of case law, it came to apply equally to the Crown, both for the actions of its servants in the conduct of their duties and for the decisions taken in the course of their day-to-day work. It is a reasonable question, in the light of the unfolding of events, to ask if the Government is failing in its duty of care to the citizens of Canterbury? Since Roman times, public safety has been a primary responsibility of governments, illustrated in the Latin phrase *salus populi suprema lex esto*, or *the welfare (safety) of the people is the supreme law*. Today, the protection of citizens remains one of the primary responsibilities of public officials. Where people are unable to protect their civil interests, governments have an obligation to take appropriate action in the public interest. They hold a position of absolute trust.

In a major disaster consistent and formalised central support becomes crucial for effective decision making. The question is how to reconcile the daily operational imperatives of numerous local agencies with the need to provide a common and effective coordinated effort that addresses the central issue of protecting the public, society and the environment from any unnecessary further harm. Up until April 2012, CERA and Christchurch City Council were operating in isolation. CERA was designed to help support the Canterbury region and it took over some of the Christchurch City Council functions, e.g. recovery strategy and policy and planning. And although this is the way the CERA legislation has been crafted, what is required is one overarching strategic process to enable it to connect with community needs. Private and public sectors have to work in unison. With the introduction of the Christchurch Central Development Unit, it is to be hoped that some cohesion will be fostered.

But nor should Council be left to resolve the city's investment strategy entirely on its own, determining what its monetary contribution is to be and how it is to raise that contribution. Without well planned investment strategies there will likely be 'capital flight' from the city. If people are not willing to reinvest in the city, it will die. If people perceive that the city is not being holistically managed, they will not reinvest. From the disaster, opportunity needs to be created. As Labour MP Lianne Dalziel suggests, Christchurch has the potential to be a platform for a recovery process for the rest of New Zealand. A truly integrated strategy is required. This means a joining of forces – Central Government, Local Government, community representatives, the business sector, the insurance and banking sectors – and the development of an overarching and integrated understanding between each of these sectors.

Meanwhile the Government remains reluctant to call to account the insurance industry, which is a basic cause of so much frustration and delay in the recovery process. Nor does the Government openly acknowledge the vital and key role that insurance plays in the speedy and effective re-establishment of the community. Insurance has become the 'elephant in the room'. Without pressure or challenge to that industry from CERA and Government, Christchurch City's recovery has been and will continue to be severely hindered by the deliberate tardiness of the insurers to respond to local need.

The Insurance Council chief executive at the time, Chris Ryan, stated that New Zealand needed to be prepared to join the likes of Japan and California, where natural disaster insurance was limited and expensive. Following their earthquakes, a number of insurers refused to re-insure policyholders. What he did not suggest is that Christchurch may need to be prepared to join the list of other places around the world that have found other methods of protecting their citizens without major private insurer involvement. If a new approach is not found, our citizens are likely to continue to suffer from the poor performance of insurers. This has become the prime reason for continued and long term human distress, delayed restitution and ongoing population displacement following natural disasters around the world. And in Christchurch, insurance is the' bogeyman' among the major rebuild players.

Minister Gerry Brownlee says that a huge taxpayer-backed financial guarantee is among options being considered to break the insurance deadlock delaying the rebuilding of Christchurch. However, he feels that the 'best option' is for reinsurers to resume giving cover, and that the Government *"would be very cautious about entering a market like that"*. Naturally Mr Ryan, the then Insurance Council chief executive, said his organisation would prefer the Government to stay out of the reinsurance and insurance markets. *"We are doing everything here as an industry to make sure the reinsurers return,"*[92] he said. Government involvement was not necessary. This stance is not surprising, as the moment Government is seen to step in, it becomes clear for all to see that the private insurance industry has again failed its policyholders and the spectre of 'market failure' arises. Seemingly sympathetic to their cause, the Hon. Gerry Brownlee stated that he was *"firmly in the camp of having the private market participate"* in insuring Christchurch and that a bigger government role was not favoured, but he went onto say that *"Even the most extreme right-winger would look for quick solutions."*[93]

The National Government's legacy will in large part be determined by how well it is perceived to have handled the Canterbury catastrophe. Thus far its effectiveness in terms of actually aiding and reducing the suffering of many Christchurch people has been highly questionable. In the initial phase after the September 4, 2010 earthquake (far less damaging than that of 22 February 2011) it responded with speed and urgency. As time has passed, its efforts seem to have slowed, become ineffective and at times misguided and heavy handed and many view the recovery period to date as compromised and unsuccessful.

When will the Government fulfil its statute mandated duty toward Canterbury's victims?

Citizens Speak

When Sarah-Alice invited me to contribute to a short piece on my personal experience of the insurance recovery in Canterbury five years on, two words immediately sprang to mind: Greed and Power.

Before the earthquakes, as today, there is no external regulation to police the settlement of a claim for damage within an insurance contract.

Hence Canterbury is the laisse-faire, Wild West for insurance claims.

And when the earthquakes hit, the Gold Rush was on.

Those that arrived first sought the largest claims.

A newly created Sheriff, in the form of the Minister of Canterbury Earthquake Recovery, was created, his official powers unprecedented and vast, but like all good Wild West Sheriffs, the law was often a secondary method to dispense justice. Either deliberately or foolishly, the Sheriff was immediately given control over the Earthquake Commission, with its NZD 6 billion Natural Disaster Fund. He was heavily armed. His posse of Insurance companies (including EQC) immediately realised they had nowhere nearly enough reinsurance to fulfil the promises they had made to their policyholders for decades.

They realised were going to need to minimise damage assessments by watering down the law. This recovery was going to be one that would be won on paper, not with hammers and nails. The greedy and powerful are never ones to waste a good disaster, and so important decisions were made at a time when the townsfolk were just picking themselves up off the ground. Land Zones were announced, cost sharing agreements signed, buildings torn down, budgets for replacements hastily agreed, most of this with only token consultation.

Legions of so called 'expert' firms of Project Managers, Engineers, Surveyors and alike, eagerly took any instructions they were given from the Sheriff and his Posse, so long as cash was attached. And once these Wild West experts were ensured that the Sheriff wasn't going to interfere, they had free rein. Building Codes and other standards were played with endlessly. The infrastructure of the town was assessed and then standards were relaxed, then assessed again and again until the damage matched the money 'available' to repair it, a practice repeated by many different organisations. Timelines and budget promises were broken almost as quickly as they were made. Those that disagreed with the Sheriff and his posse were delayed, given the run around, ostracised and thrown in the stocks of isolation.

Sadly, many of the posse, those that have done so much damage to this town by aiding and abetting the Sheriff and his Posse, are not even aware of their participation, which allows many to sleep freely. So, five years on – is there hope?

I believe so.

Many are now aware of how and why early decisions were made, and more importantly some are even starting to understand those decisions made, were not in their or their town's best interests. Many who were either intimidated or frustrated by the Posse have left town.

Those that stayed I believe, are truly passionate about our region and our future. They will not leave and they will not simply agree with what the Sheriff and his posse say is best for them anymore. They are wiser. As am I. We are stronger for our shared experiences.

The gold is starting to run dry, a sure sign that the Sheriff and his Posse will move on soon.

Whether it will be under a blaze of gun fire, is yet to be determined.

By Cam Preston[94]

CHAPTER 4

EQC AND EARTHQUAKE INSURANCE

The series of 'multiple events' complicated both our assessment programme, and the way we apportion costs across claims. In most cases this has meant multiple visits to houses from our teams. We know that this has been frustrating for some of our customers, and at times confusing.

Bruce Emson, General Manager Customer Services, EQC[1]

There is a trend both domestically and abroad towards increased public expectation of government to ensure that there will be greater engagement and assistance by its agencies in the event of a catastrophe. There is no doubt that the Earthquake Commission has had the lion's share of claims during the months following the Canterbury earthquakes of 2010–12. There is also no doubt that the degree of disappointment of treatment toward policyholders at the hands of the EQC is thoroughly disheartening.

Before the earthquakes of 2010 and 2011, the EQC did not participate in the emergency response to disasters. It did not evacuate people; assess buildings for health and safety, either before or after repairs; carry out inspections of houses for damage; provide, or pay for, temporary or transitional housing; purchase or stockpile construction materials; employ building tradespeople or arrange for their relocation to the disaster area; delegate claims assessments to insurance companies; or share resources and provide local authorities with details of claims received. However, after the Canterbury earthquakes, the EQC's operating environment changed markedly and it now has the responsibility for many of these functions.

The EQC stated that it expected 182,000 claims from the September earthquake and a further 130,000 claims from the February 22 event. As of January 19, 2016 there have been 68,772 homes in the Canterbury Home Repair Programme, 167,357 properties with a building claim, 187,188 contents claims and 80,169 properties to be assessed for land damage, and 8960 properties to be assessed for increased liquefaction vulnerability (ILV).[2] The earthquakes have had a significant impact on both the EQC and private insurer resources. On February 23, 2011, AIR Worldwide, who provide risk-modelling software and consultancy services, released the first industry insured loss estimates for the Canterbury events of between NZD 5 billion and NZD 11.5 billion. AIR said that these estimates account for insured physical damage to property (residential, commercial, and industrial) for structures and contents, and direct business interruption losses. The Insurance Council of New Zealand stated that the cost of the September 4, 2010 earthquake was at that time unknown but that the vast majority of claims payments would be made from reinsurance payments. By November 2011 the cost of the earthquakes had reached approximately NZD 20 billion (10 percent of GDP), as firms picked up the tab for interrupted business, temporary accommodation, inflation and other adjustments. By April 2013 these figures had ballooned to NZD 40 billion and predictions are that it will continue to rise.

~~~

By the mid-nineteenth century, insurance was a mature industry in Europe. However, there is no evidence of earthquake insurance being a purchasable commodity in New Zealand at that time. The first insurer, the New Zealand Insurance Company, was established in New Zealand in 1859. Prior to that, early settlers were left to resolve their own losses. Individuals carried the risk of hazardous events themselves. In practical terms this would have meant either funding a repair or rebuild themselves if they could afford to do so, or leaving the region or country in search of new beginnings. Despite frequent seismic events throughout New

Zealand, the net population of Wellington and other centres continued to grow and there was an acceptance by the population that seismic events formed part and parcel of life in the country. It was not until the 1940s that insurance became a commodity. The Murchison earthquake of 1929, the Hawke's Bay earthquakes of 1931, Pahiatua in 1934 and the two Wairarapa events of 1942 demonstrated New Zealand's vulnerability to earthquakes and subsequent events like the Abbotsford landslide in 1979 reinforced the need for a government entity to provide access to affordable insurance. These seismic events also provided the first incentives towards officially revising certain improvements to existing building standards. But it was not until the Masterton earthquake in 1942 that insurance became an accepted commodity on the New Zealand business scene. Both the community and government were in agreement that a provision was necessary to ensure that the enduring scenes of rubble and unrepaired buildings became a thing of the past.

In 1942 a War Damage Commission was set up. Through this scheme, people who had insured their property against fire were now also covered through the State Fire Department for damage resulting from war related acts. The Government later took a decision to extend war damage cover to earthquakes and formed the Earthquake and War Damage Commission in 1945. If citizens had purchased fire insurance, then earthquake cover was automatic. The Government reforms of the 1980s saw the State Fire Department change from a corporation to a state owned enterprise, which was then sold in the early 90s. The Government retained the Earthquake and War Damage Commission and reformed it significantly. War damage cover was eventually abolished and the name was shortened to the Earthquake Commission (EQC or 'the Commission'). The Earthquake Commission Act 1993 restricted the new EQC scheme to residential property, leaving commercial property owners outside the scheme and forced to make their own decisions about insurance protection, which they continue to do today. Prior to the Canterbury earthquakes, many policies were based on replacement cost rather than indemnity value, i.e. market value or present day value. In 2013 there was a move to fixed sum insurance, sometimes referred to as 'sum insured' or 'nominated value'. This requires homeowners to now calculate their own rebuild costs thereby shifting the burden and responsibility of underinsurance to the homeowner.

EQC produced its first disaster plan in 1993. It began very simply by means of an 'all hands on deck' policy; commissioners and staff would be 'on call' to man the phones and take claims themselves. Arrangements were also made to use rented office space in Manukau City in the event that the current allocated space in Wellington became unusable.

In 1994 the Government carried out a series of overseas studies and follow-up visits to acquire knowledge of best practice catastrophe response arrangements. The Northridge (California, USA) earthquake of 1944 provided a timely scenario upon which to base their findings. State Farm, a large American domestic insurer based in Illinois, provided what at the time, was considered the best model to follow. However, State Farm, unlike EQC, was a large private organisation of some 65,000 employees which meant that mobilising the necessary staff and resources to meet the many thousands of claims they received each year posed no significant difficulty. Both people and materials could be sourced from within the company. In the event of a major incident in New Zealand, the EQC simply could not emulate that kind of response with only 14 staff. Despite this limitation, the basic business model and field processes that State Farm were using were employed as the preferred blueprint and subsequent benchmark upon which the EQC based its own programme. By 1955, arrangements were in place for a single-site disaster centre, Castrol House (a high rise building!) in Wellington.[3] This 'set-up' eventually became the basis and location of the EQC business continuity plan. Those arrangements still exist today. But the real challenge lay in the design and implementation of a programme for handling multiple claims, both in the field and in the office. This still remains the challenge – how to extend the resources available to the EQC without having to pay excessive retainers for people or storage of equipment that may rarely be required.

In 1997 the plan for managing large scale earthquake damage was agreed upon and implemented and the contractual arrangements required to ensure the plan's success were put in place. The EQC now had not only a catastrophe plan but a catastrophe response programme as well.

During a claim-generating event, the EQC is required to continue with the normal activities of running its office functions, paying staff and taxes, managing the investments of the Natural Disaster Fund (see below), complying with relevant legislation and directives, providing public education and a research programme, as well as the many other routine activities that must be carried out on a daily basis. These functions alone would be enough to tax the small team of permanent EQC staff. In the event of a major catastrophe, on top of this work load, the receipt of many thousands of claims needing resolution is far beyond the small team's capability.

In the wake of several severe storms and floods since 2004, the Government ordered a review of the insurance coverage available to homeowners. This review, despite the recommended reforms, did not result in any changes being made to its existing general policy. It was not until the devastating events of the recent Canterbury earthquakes that the National Government of the day suddenly saw the necessity of major operational and legislative modifications in the form of CERRA legislation (see Chapter 3, The Politics).

The present EQC is a Crown Entity as defined by the Crown Entities Act 2004 and is governed by a board of eight Commissioners who are responsible to the Canterbury Earthquake Recovery Minister.[4] Just before the Canterbury earthquakes, the EQC had 22 permanent staff, all based at the Commission's office in Wellington. The Hon. Bill English is the Minister in charge of the Earthquake Commission in addition to his Finance Portfolio. The Commission's primary objectives are to administer insurance against natural disaster damage as provided for under the Earthquake Commission Act 1993, to facilitate research and educate the nation about matters relevant to natural disaster damage, to manage the Natural Disaster Fund, and arrange reinsurance (see Chapter 8, The Reinsurance Industry). It designates itself as a public benefit entity and constitutes one of the Crown Financial Institutions which manage large funds at arm's length from Government – in this case the Natural Disaster Fund. Any deficiency in the Natural Disaster Fund to meet the liabilities of the Commission is to be made up by the Government by way of a grant or advance. The viability of the Natural Disaster Fund is critical for the effectiveness of the EQC. Since the Canterbury earthquakes, questions concerning its viability have been raised. If the EQC scheme were to be extended, further consideration would have to be given as to how the EQC would best appropriate monies for the Natural Disaster Fund and how it would best invest those funds for the future benefit of the nation and its citizens in the event of a catastrophe. The EQC must invest the Fund on a prudent, commercial basis and must manage and administer the Fund consistent with best practice portfolio management – maximising return without undue risk to the Fund as a whole, and 'avoiding prejudice to New Zealand's reputation as a responsible member of the world community'. The EQC considers responsible investment to be part of an evolving best practice. Until 2001 the Natural Disaster Fund was invested in New Zealand fixed interest securities such as government stock. The Fund had accumulated to a value of NZD 5.9 billion at the beginning of 2010-2011 financial year. Since the earthquakes the EQC has been drawing down on the Fund to meet claims. In the process the Fund's global equities had been entirely liquidated by May 2012 and a portion of Government stock holding were also sold. Since that time the Fund is made up of only New Zealand Government stock and bank securities. The EQC received its first payment from reinsurers in 2012 and these will continue until such time as the reinsurers' contractual obligations have been met. The Fund had been invested in global equities by several fund managers and investments limited to those companies in the Morgan Stanley Capital Investment World Index. The MSCI World Index is a stock market index of over 1,600 'world' stocks. It is maintained by MSCI Inc., formerly Morgan Stanley Capital International, and is often used as a common benchmark for 'world' or 'global' stock funds. The objective of this was to ensure the Commission holds assets outside the region that will not be directly affected by a major natural disaster. That is no longer the case. In the event the Fund is fully exhausted the Crown Guarantee will be activated and the Government will meet the remaining claims. As the Fund gets closer to being exhausted the remaining claims in Christchurch become more difficult for policyholders to settle - resources have become very 'tight'.

On the strength of the Government's guarantee (the Crown Fee), the rating agency Standard and Poor provides the EQC with a claims-paying ability rating of AAA (the highest possible). The Government currently requires the EQC to pay NZD 10 million per annum for this guarantee. Standard and Poor stated that the New Zealand Government is 'almost certain' to provide any extra support the disaster funding agency needs if there is extra shortfall, even though the EQC's standalone creditworthiness has materially deteriorated since the Canterbury earthquakes. So the EQC already functions as a national insurance scheme to cover a major catastrophe.

In light of the recent events in Canterbury the EQC has begun to re-evaluate its function and consider ways of improving its structure. The private Insurance industry has called for a complete overhaul of the EQC Act. Meanwhile the Earthquake Recovery Minister suggests that there are likely to be only 'minor changes', by, for instance removal of the allocated NZD 20,000 contents insurance cover, re-examining the policy rationale of land cover, introducing variable premiums, depending on house size or hazards risk, introducing automatic adjustment of premiums and pay-out caps and increasing the excess on claims. There is also consideration being given to the possibility of the EQC scrapping its operational work altogether and instead becoming purely a financial re-insurer to stand behind private insurance companies.

Currently the EQC insures land and will pay the value of the damaged land at the time of the natural disaster or the repair cost, whichever is lower. The EQC currently insures homes, land and personal belongings (though this is likely to change in the future) against earthquakes, landslips, tsunami, volcanic eruption, hydrothermal activity, storm or flood damage, as well as fire following any of the above. The EQC insures homes for their replacement value, up to NZD 100,000.00 + Goods and Service Tax (GST, which is 15 percent), known as 'the cap', for every new insurable event that occurs. Also covered are services that the property owner owns (e.g. gas and water pipes). The EQC also insures personal belongings (this is to be removed) up to NZD 20,000 + GST per insurable event. The EQC cover therefore effectively operates as a 'first layer', with the upper layer, i.e. damage that exceeds the cap, covered by the private insurer.

Prior to 2010 the EQC cover cost five cents for every NZD 100 insured (0.05 percent). The current maximum is NZD 50.00 + GST for cover of NZD 100,000 on the dwelling and NZD 10.00 + GST for cover of NZD 20,000 on personal belongings. Cover for land is included at no cost. Since that time the EQC levies have been increased. The EQC cover costs 15 cents + GST for every NZD 100 of home or contents fire insurance that the homeowner has. The most paid per year for one home and its contents is NZD 180+GST.[5] In the future the premium paid could be tagged to the value of the associated land as produced by Quotable Value. QV Rating is New Zealand's largest and most experienced supplier of rating valuation services to local government, operating in a contestable market since 1998. A more valuable piece of land might attract a higher premium. This would ensure that small property stakeholders would not be unduly levied. This also circumvents the 'poor subsidising the wealthy' objection.

A premium is collected on behalf of the Commission by insurance companies via the fire insurance policies they issue or renew. The Commission must invest the Fund with the objectives of achieving an average rate of return of at least one percent per annum over the Crown's cost of borrowing over a rolling ten year period (where the Crown's cost of borrowing is measured by the change in the Credit Suisse First Boston New Zealand Government Stock Gross Index). The EQC must ensure that the Fund is subjected to no more than one chance in four that in any ten year period the annual rate of return will be less than the Crown's cost of borrowing and also ensure that there is no more than one chance in thirty of the Fund incurring a return of less than negative two percent (a loss) in any single financial year.

Given the turmoil that still grips the financial markets at the start of 2016, the question arises as to whether further involvement in the financial markets strengthens the EQC's position or actually weakens it. The continual invention of new capital market devices and more and more interrelationships created between the various financial institutions and markets, coupled with increasing global financial uncertainty leads to a potential undermining of the stability of the EQC and its ultimate ability to support the New Zealand population in times of natural disaster (see Chapter 8, The Reinsurance Industry).

So what is a sustainable size for the Natural Disaster Fund and what is the appropriate suite of investments? Prior to 2010–11 the Natural Disaster Fund was NZD 5.6 billion.[6] EQC has investigated what the Fund balance would have to be to achieve this sustainability and determine the effect this might have on the Commission's reinsurance and investment strategies. Such a determination is of course highly dependent upon the disaster-scale scenario which the EQC decides to 'adopt', presumably based on its research and modelling findings. The task is not an easy one, requiring consideration of a large number of factors, including escalating costs, inflation, building costs, and the effect of major demand on labour supply during the recovery and rebuilding phases, though the historical data on the Canterbury quakes will be very useful. What has become very clear is that the current Natural Disaster Fund is inadequate to address losses of the scale recently experienced in Canterbury. A considerable increase of the Fund to a much higher minimum is required. To date the Christchurch events have cost in the region of NZD 30 billion. The current funding criteria, based on computer modelling, using an annual average claims cost that takes into account the 'quiet' seismic period that New Zealand has experienced for the past sixty-six years, equates to costs of NZD 45 million. An additional NZD 5.9 billion was factored in, being the cost of a one in 600-year earthquake on the Wellington fault-line. The Fund has also calculated cost increases over time which had been set at five percent per annum, as well as meeting any loss when it occurred and an ability to meet that loss again within a ten year timeframe. The growth factor applies to construction costs, which have exceeded consumer price index inflation in recent years. Included in this calculation is NZD 5.8 billion for the cost of a repeat round of the six major earthquakes that occurred in New Zealand between 1929 and 1942, a span of fourteen years.

Reinsurance is essential for the EQC to mitigate its liabilities. Without reinsurance, the Natural Disaster Fund size would need to be around NZD 10.75 billion (between NZD 9.5 and NZD 12 billion). Reinsurance purchase by the EQC of NZD 2.5 billion reduces the net funding requirement to NZD 6.9 billion. The leverage arises out of the reduced balance needed in order to seed fund growth for future pay-outs (NZD 2.5 billion of reinsurance saving more than equivalent capital needs). The EQC payed an excess per natural disaster of NZD 1.5 billion under the reinsurance programme, prior to the earthquake, and the quantum of this excess also has a direct bearing on the cost of reinsurance.

Should a disaster occur leading to EQC pay-outs in excess of its cash reserves (NZD 250 million), the EQC must consult with the Minister before liquidating any of the Fund's investment portfolio other than the holdings of New Zealand bank bills. In addition, the EQC would have to come to an understanding with Treasury as to which of its investments would be sold first.

Before the Canterbury earthquakes, the EQC Board had recommended there should be several reforms to the insurance scheme. The first of these recommendations related to the maximum amounts payable (the 'caps') for damage and loss to contents and homes. These had last been revised in 1993. The EQC argues that inflation in the domestic construction industry would indicate that to regain parity, the cap on a dwelling should now be doubled to NZD 200,000 from the previous NZD 100,000. An argument supporting this adjustment is that property values disadvantage the owners of modest properties and favour the owners of more valuable homes. The claim is that the poor are subsidising the rich as the rich have more to lose and therefore tend to have higher claims. For example, a NZD 500,000 home is much more likely to sustain a higher dollar value of damage in an earthquake than is a NZD 150,000 home. Yet both get the same cover from EQC and both pay the same premium. It follows that the higher the cap, the less pronounced the subsidy.

In addition, increased construction costs since 1993 have driven up the cost of repair and rebuilding following a disaster. Holding the lower cap reduces the EQC's ability to provide for a community's recovery. For example, a NZD 30,000 claim in 1993 was equivalent to a NZD 60,000 claim in 2012, yet the EQC is receiving the same premium on a dwelling insured for at least NZD 100,000 that it was receiving in 1993. So capping the EQC coverage sums limits premium income but fails to account for increases in property values. An increase in the levy[7] seems reasonable in order to meet the EQC's operating costs and to replenish the rapidly diminishing Natural Disaster Fund. However, these recommendations are not based on an actuarial assessment of future liabilities. That assessment is intended to be carried out as part of a wider review of the EQC in the future. The Government believes that the now increased EQC premium is a prudent interim step given the EQC's increased costs. A review of the Act began in 2012 (and completed in 2015). The review suggested that content cover should be left to insurers as this would eliminate any uncertainties for claimants between the EQC and private insurer content claims. Also proposed is that earthquake land cover apply only to situations where homes could not be rebuilt on their original site and owners were forced to buy elsewhere. This would see the EQC build cover increase to NZD 200,000 plus GST, from NZD 100,000 plus GST. Claimants would lodge their claims directly through their private insurer and no longer through the EQC. One of the concerns, if this policy is implemented is that homeowners are unlikely to have access to the EQC funds to assist them to prove their claim. Instead the EQC funds are likely to be syphoned directly to the private insurer concerned. The reforms are said to be designed to ensure that the EQC scheme remains focussed on insuring homes and negating the difficulties experienced in Canterbury with the interaction between building and land cover. But do such reforms go far enough?

The Government view is that it is better for insured homeowners, who directly benefit from the EQC's cover, to pay those costs through a levy rather than raising income tax, which would have a negative effect on economic growth. Although it is the EQC's intention to operate within the limits of its annual premium income, each year, expenses increase and the amount for claims pay-outs also increases. So, although every year the Fund grows, so do expenses and inflationary pressures, meaning that it will become increasingly difficult for the EQC to operate within its premium income, forcing it to utilise investment income on an ever more regular basis in order to cover claims. Another major disaster within the next thirty years has the potential to devastate the EQC's projected financial recovery unless a solution for raising funds is found quickly.

The Government's original argument against raising caps was that there was no market failure in the insurance sector for the government to have to address. The citizens of Christchurch disagreed. In addition, the recent failures and exit of insurers AMI and Western Pacific as well as Ansvar's withdrawal from the New Zealand marketplace, made it a mistaken premise. Some argue that insurance companies would not reduce their premiums despite the transfer of risk from them to the EQC and, consequently, raising the caps would result, in the public perception, as an increase in government levies. The EQC disagrees with this stance and believes that neither the industry nor the public would oppose an increase in the caps. If the people of Canterbury felt they would be better served, the cap increase would be unlikely to be an issue. In the event, this has proved to be the case.

The EQC's land insurance is unique and its provisions show up some inequalities which, it has been suggested, should be revised. The EQC's exposure to payments for land damage continues to escalate and this is reflected in the increased average land claim amount. The estimated value of all land under the EQC scheme grew from NZD 65.6 billion in 2003 to NZD 207.6 billion in 2007, a period during which the EQC's premium income rose by 9.25 percent. Land is not rated for the EQC premium, so the only method by which this increase can be matched under the current system is by increasing the charge on the dwelling by way of either the rate factor of .05 percent of the sum insured or the capped sum insured.

There is an emerging consensus amongst the affected population in Canterbury that the first priority after a natural disaster should be the re-establishment of communities: keeping as many people in the affected area as is possible, followed quickly by a return into homes, with the provision of temporary or transitional accommodation if required. The current EQC scheme, as a contribution to the cost of rebuilding, is simply not able to meet the above objectives. The Canterbury experience also suggests that a good many of the private insurers are also unable or unwilling to achieve these objectives in a timely fashion, in part because they await the outcomes of the EQC assessments and because they are private and often foreign owned operations with a primary focus on their profitability and their shareholders, with considerable financial benefit accruing to them through delay of pay-outs.

The Commission has been required to take into account the different levels of damage (both property and land) in the various suburbs together with government policy in respect of land rehabilitation or re-zoning options; coordinate with Canterbury Earthquake Recovery Authority, the local authorities and also incorporate the claims settlement activities of the private insurers. The EQC's mandate has now been greatly expanded. As well, the Commission must contribute to wider policy work with information and advice, aligning itself with the Government's overall recovery plan for Canterbury. This wider policy work must also include identifying legislative and operational changes that would help improve the EQC's response to future large-scale events; advice, in conjunction with Treasury, on the ongoing size, structure and investment profile of the Natural Disaster Fund; and identifying lessons learned from the EQC's response and their potential applicability to other government entities and functions.

The intention here is not to hail the EQC as the saviour of the day. The EQC throughout the last five years has rightly come under increasingly harsh criticism. The *Christchurch Press* noted *"EQC*'s persistent line has been that its procedures are as good as can be, its settlement of claims as speedy as possible and fair, and any problems it does have are being put right – and all that in the face of a civil emergency unprecedented in New Zealand's history".[8] Since the Canterbury earthquakes of 2010–12 the EQC claims system is at capacity and under stress. That stress has manifested its presence in the last five years in the following ways:

Assessment Discrepancies between EQC and Private Insurers

Under the rules applicable at the time of the disaster, if the damage was deemed to fall below NZD 100,000, the EQC would foot the bill. If the property damage was above NZD 100,000, the EQC would contribute NZD 100,000 and private insurers bear the cost of the remaining shortfall and use their own 'assessors' to make a re-assessment of that damage.[9] Many discrepancies have arisen between assessments made by the EQC and those made by private insurers. In the early phase, immediately after the September 4, 2010 earthquake, the EQC sent out permanent staff members to carry out assessments. Some of these staff members had twenty years' experience and their assessments were thorough and comprehensive. As the earthquakes continued and damage became more widespread and extensive, the EQC chose to employ less experienced staff to carry out the ever increasing numbers of assessments. The quality of the assessments declined dramatically. There was much public criticism of the new staff, many of whom were seen not to have the skills required to carry out the level of technical assessments required and it was widely believed that they were recruited for their ability to 'deal with the public'.[10] No formal qualification is required in law for loss adjusters; instead, the new EQC workers attended three-day induction courses covering stress management, process, communication and safety. There are many accounts of the assessment gaps of between NZD 200,000 and NZD 500,000 and more. The ever increasing numbers of shoddy repairs is testament to this problem.

Issues with staff escalated, two EQC assessors faced drug-smuggling charges,[11] while accusations of nepotism were made as some highly remunerated employees were found to be related to other senior EQC staff family members.[12] Towards the end of the assessment process, people who knew nothing about buildings or building were being sent to make assessments of damage. Meanwhile the private insurance companies also began to send contracted 'loss adjustors' to damaged properties, with varying degrees of know-how and experience. This has led to numerous massive discrepancies in assessments of damage and the values associated with the damage. Because of these discrepancies, homeowners have been left feeling vulnerable. Those who can afford to do so, employ independent structural engineers, quantity surveyors, registered property valuers and/or lawyers at their own expense in order to ensure that their interests are protected. At one point in the process, government figures indicated that only eleven of the ninety five EQC staff from abroad had trade or property related qualifications. Could this perhaps account for some of the discrepancies? EQC recruited its staff from outside the city, paying accommodation and food allowances, while some skilled assessors left Christchurch, as a result of a lack of employment opportunities.

Finally, seventeen months into the process, it was agreed that insurance companies would work with the EQC to jointly assess some quake-damaged properties in an attempt to overcome differences that have seen the two sides *"not completely aligned"*.[13] Many problems have arisen where one of the parties classified the damage as a 'repair job' and the other considered it 'a rebuild'. AMI Insurance (Southern Response) earthquake recovery executive manager Peter Rose stated:

Our policy says we will reinstate the property 'as new'. There's not much wriggle room there. [The EQC Act] says 'substantially the same as when new'. 'Substantially the same as when new' isn't the same as 'as new' ... We are talking about humans who are making assessments and ... it's possible they simply have a difference of opinion.[14]

However, this 'difference of opinion' is invariably to the detriment of the homeowner; it introduces more uncertainty, massive delays and is the cause of considerable additional stress.

Delays Caused by the EQC Revisiting Payments Apportionment

As a result of the February 2011 quake, the EQC pay-outs from the September 2010 quake were revised, from over the NZD 100,000 EQC cap downward. Some people with multiple quake claims were subjected to an 'apportionment' process which complicated the cost split between insurers and the EQC and often led to disputes.[15] The question became which of the five 'official' earthquakes was responsible for which degree of damage. Customers were notified about changes to assessments only when they were settled. This usually involved talks between the EQC and the private insurer on liability, leading to massive delays for homeowners who were often not informed of the discrepancies. Sometimes this reassessment led to discovery of an alleged over-payment by the EQC.

In some cases, the over-payment was not recovered as the payment had been made 'in good faith' more than a year earlier. The EQC often assessed properties as 'over cap' then revised that to 'under cap' after the ruling on how it was to be apportioned. Many had multiple visits from the EQC. Others tell stories of the EQC assessors removing visibly damaged items from the list of the September 4, 2010 assessment. Many who had houses that were originally deemed a total rebuild, suddenly discovered that their homes were 'able to be repaired'. For those who did not obtain and pay for their own independent engineer's report, the outcomes were bleak.

Windfalls

In the early phases after the September 2010 earthquake, reports emerged of the EQC assessors going to great lengths to ensure that no one was disgruntled about their assessments. Typically, people with minor cracks in walls, who would have been content with funds to buy paint and plaster, were told that their entire rooms should be re-gibed and painted – a considerable cost.

There needs to be concern over the way the EQC resources were initially so liberally spent. For those with damage over the EQC NZD 100,000 cap, battles with private insurers down to the last dollar have been fought. The process has been very inequitable.

Insurers Not Paying Tradespeople and Professionals in a Timely Fashion

Many complained about the EQC's and their private insurers' failure to pay tradespeople and engineers promptly for the work they had carried out. In some cases payment was not made for several months. Many recount stories of tradespeople in Christchurch in serious debt because of the outstanding payment of invoices, by the EQC in particular.

Poor Workmanship

The Earthquake Commission has received over 20,000 complaints from Christchurch residents unhappy with the work contractors have done to fix their houses, leading to accusations that *"Mickey Mouse"* operators are fleecing the system.[16] The major themes being the poor professionalism of contractors, the low standard of emergency repairs, poor heating work and shoddy work quality.[17] A typical comment was:

> *I have heard mostly good things about contractor repair work... however, the little old lady across the road whose house needed to be done inside and out was definitely given a raw deal.. she had to move out for five weeks while ceilings and walls were repaired inside... the contractors didn't even make holes in the ceilings for the wiring... so when the electrician came he had to find the places and create the holes... then the holes in the walls for the power points were cut incorrectly and the wall behind the fireplace wasn't even fitted properly.. In the end they asked her to sign off so the men could be paid... she did [be]cause she felt she had to... now of course Fletchers will say that she approved their work by signing it off... I wonder how many other elderly people will have had the same issues... and there were many more issues as well... they turned off the power and left it off when they knew there was a freezer full of food in the garage... all of it went off. She's not likely to complain either, not wanting to make waves.[18]*

Other stories tell of painting contractors painting round beds and other furniture rather than moving these items. More than a quarter of the active complaints lodged with the EQC have been open for at least six months with some dating back years.

Claims Apportioned Over the Numbers of Claims Lodged

Where a house is a 'rebuild' or requires major repairs and the claim does not reach the cap of NZD 100,000, the claim cannot be passed to the private insurer. As a consequence, the EQC becomes responsible for the rebuild or repairs. The following, which focuses on rebuilds, is specifically about those in the red zone, but the underlying EQC issue also affects many in the green zones. The Crown Offer policy documents were drawn up before the apportionment matter went before the High Court in Wellington. The Declaratory Judgement makes no decision (or comment) on how apportionment is to be carried out, nor on the effect it is to have on insurance policies. Apportionment has become a very contentious issue in Canterbury.

Changes to the Degree of Damage and the MBIE Guidelines

Prior to the September 2010 earthquake the Building Code was the standard by which damage was measured. Soon after, the Department of Building and Housing issued a set of guidelines which could be used by builders, assessors and engineers when qualifying and quantifying earthquake damage. This was later followed by the *'Revised guidance on repairing and rebuilding houses affected by the Canterbury earthquake sequences (November 2011)'*,[19] indicating what would be considered acceptable levels of damage and since that time these *'acceptable levels have been changing'*. Then, from March 1, 2012 *'Restricted Building Work'* came into effect. This means that if residential building work is structural and/or affects the weather-tightness of the building, then it may be restricted building work, requiring a Licenced Building Practitioner to be employed to design and undertake that work.[20]

As the goal posts for acceptable levels of damage continue to move, the EQC and private insurers' reassessments of property are also changing, their financial liability inevitably trending in a downward direction. The MBIE Guidance document has enabled Fletcher EQR to maintain tight control on subcontractors by having a rates-ceiling manual and a list of some 800 repair solutions that have been priced and which are easily ticked off a spreadsheet, providing an easy and rapid pricing mechanism. This is said to have kept the average price of building work down. However, the MBIE Guidelines provide 'guidance' on repair and replacement of not only foundations but chimneys, roof structures, wall structures, roof and wall claddings and outbuildings as well. It must be noted that the methods and solutions presented in the Guidelines are not mandatory and as the guidelines indicate, must be considered in light of any private insurance contract between the homeowner and an insurer. Therefore, although the guidelines may be indicative of possible solutions to damaged dwellings, they cannot and do not override the provisions of any insurance policy where damage is deemed to be above the quantum covered by the EQC. Nor can they override the requirements of the New Zealand Building Act 2004 and codes. The EQC Act clearly states that the insurance of any residential building, residential land, or personal property under Section 22 (i.e. voluntary insurance against natural disaster damage) shall be subject to the conditions set out in Schedule 3, unless as *"otherwise provided in the contract of insurance". Schedule 3 of the EQC Act (s9, Replacement of Property), states that the EQC does not have a responsibility to replace or reinstate exactly or completely, but "only as circumstances permit and in a reasonably sufficient manner" unless the property is insured against natural disaster damage for its replacement value to a specified replacement sum which exceeds the EQC cover in which case, "the property will be treated as though it had never been insured under the EQC Act". Hence the EQC Act makes it clear that any property insured above the EQC cap is to be dealt with under the auspices of the applicable private insurance contract. Based on the EQC Act, one concludes that it was never the intention of the legislation to extend the use of 'MBIE Guidelines' to private insurance contracts that exceed the EQC cover limits. It could be argued and is likely that they were instigated purely to save the EQC money.*

Unsurprisingly, the private insurance industry jumped on the bandwagon and also extensively used the Guidelines and the tolerances set out within the guidelines as justification and standards for repairs which, in their view, do not require consents, and which become repairs which do not fall within the Building Code and which ultimately save the insurance industry hundreds of millions of dollars at the expense of the integrity of building structures and ultimately, the equity inherent in policyholders' homes. Since the initial introduction of the Guidelines, they have undergone several revisions – and all of the revisions have led to an incremental lowering of the level and standard of repairs and a lowering of the ultimate estimate of repair costs. This has had a twofold effect. Firstly it has enabled the EQC and the insurance industry to keep down the cost of repairs which are under the EQC cap (i.e. <NZD 100,000) and furthermore it has introduced standards which are lower than those set out in the Building Code. The private insurance industry has conveniently, mistakenly or negligently (or all three) extended the use of these Guidelines to all insured properties. Most, if not all, engineers working for the insurance industry have and are knowingly using the MBIE Guidelines to diminish the cost and standard of repairs as a means to lower costs for their employers, declaring that they have no obligation to take cognisance of anything other than the instructions given to them by the person paying their fees, despite the fact that the guidelines are not the 'policy standard'. Consequently their assessments have added to the significant delays in the settlement of earthquake claims. In addition, this has led to homes with significant damage, which have been badly repaired or not repaired at all. Instead, what has emerged is an ethical and professional failure prevalent throughout the professionals associated with earthquake recovery. At times, one wonders why insurance policy wording even exists. Despite public outcry, the Ministry of Business, Innovation and Employment continues to run trials in search of cheaper repair solutions, greater tolerances and questionable engineering solutions. *"Cantabrians are being asked to wear second-best fixes because anything else is too expensive"*.[21] Curious is the fact that the Courts have used the MBIE Guidelines as the means for property assessment too. But one wonders whether the Judges are aware of the legal basis for the MBIE Guidelines. East v Medical Assurance Society New Zealand Limited [2014] NZHC 3399 [22 December 2014] judgement is a

case in point and to this date, no case to decide the legality of the use of the MBIE Guidelines has been heard.

As a result of the continual downgrading of repairs, the future integrity of the housing stock in Christchurch has been and continues to be seriously compromised. It is rather ironic that post-disaster in other countries, the building code and repair standard goes up, not down - in Christchurch, quite the opposite has taken place. In a report carried out by Emeritus Professor of Surveying, John Hannah, it was stated that there was clear evidence of *"at least some"* poor or incorrect assessments because of failure to consider a wider suite of assessment criteria *'and incorrect or inadequate floor levels being obtained'*.[22] These issues raise real questions about the true status of damaged and repaired post-earthquake Christchurch properties despite the CEO of IAG, Jacki Johnson, declaring that Christchurch will become *"one of the most insurable cities in the world"*. It is common to see repair strategies (for example, re-levelling a concrete slab) that propose a method of repair with no reference to the standard outlined in the legal contract, and no 'standard of repair' provided by the insurer. Without these standards explicitly stated, the repair proposal could be to any standard, and not the standard required as the legal contract requires. The argument commonly floated is that an assessor (be it structural engineer, geotechnical engineer, builder, or surveyor) cannot assess to the standard outlined in the legal contract as they are not legal professionals and therefore the assessor should 'just do' an assessment and repair strategy, and the insurance company (or their legal team) will then determine compliance with the standard in the legal contract. This approach leads to a host of problems and more often than not a homeowner is left with a property that has been inaccurately assessed. Thousands of homes throughout the Canterbury region have been subject to damage assessments and reinstatement strategies by people not properly qualified to carry them out or professionals unable to understand the standard to which they were assessing and reinstating.

The new guidelines advise assessors or builders working for insurers or the EQC to tolerate larger cracks and a greater slope in foundations before recommending repairs.[23] Some building industry sources have expressed concern about the changes, claiming they could leave homes with obvious quake damage while saving the Government and insurers money. One Canterbury builder said relaxing standards and the push to speed up repairs meant that the city would face a problem similar to the 'leaky homes' saga in ten to fifteen years' time, with many homeowners eventually discovering hidden quake damage when it causes a problem.[24] One Cantabrian, Brent Cairns stated, in a Letter to the Editor in The Press:

> The government relaxing the guidelines for repairing quake damaged homes, benefits one party, insurance companies.... All of these decisions are about saving the insurance companies money, to the detriment of us.... The Government are licking the boots of the insurance companies, saving the companies millions. Brownlee and CERA you shouldn't be bowing your heads to the insurance companies, you should bow your heads in shame.[25]

Stories of Poor Assessments by the EQC Staff and Private Insurance Loss Adjustors Abound

A builder with 25 years' experience spent some time as an estimator working for EQC. Some of the discrepancies he found were:

> A Linwood house built around 1950 was assessed by EQC as needing plastering and painting work and some pile jacking. I found the house was out of level by 100mm and suggested an engineer look at the house. He found gib bracing had failed and the house needed to be completely re-piled. A Cashmere house built around 1945 was assessed without checking the roof or foundation. A structural engineer found significant damage to roof framing. A Redwood house built around 1980 was assessed as needing plastering and painting but I found a 45mm fall. An engineer found the land was not capable

of bearing weight down to 1.5m. A 1950 piled house with brick veneer was repaired by Fletcher but the owner felt uneasy. An inspection revealed the chimney had sunk significantly, dragging the floor and roof structure down with it.[26]

And the list stretches on.

Reassessment of Claims

The need to reassess claims undermines confidence in the claims settlement process and impacts on the efficiency of claims processing by, in effect, increasing claim handling costs through rework. This was one of the problems that arose after the February 22, 2011 earthquake. The EQC felt that it would have to retrace its steps and reassess the many thousands of properties assessed after the September 4, 2010 earthquake. The EQC General Manager of Customer Services Bruce Emson said Canterbury's multiple earthquakes had created a unique situation for the EQC and the insurance industry in which the multiple events complicated both their assessment programme and the way they apportioned costs across claims. It meant that teams made multiple visits to the same properties.

Then there is the Issue and Confusion as to who pays for Additional Work

EQC is required to restore the land to the condition it was in prior to the earthquakes, but any improvements have to be paid by the insurers. In some zones new foundation designs are now required to cope with the potential for liquefaction of the land. Confusion has arisen about where private insurer's liability ends and the EQC's obligations commence and the discussions around 'who has responsibility for what' has led to long delays, well over a year in many cases.

Preferred Contractor

The EQC chose Fletcher Construction, for work up to the EQC cap, and to run the EQC's Canterbury earthquake project management office. They are required to manage the repair of approximately 50,000 properties moderately or seriously damaged. People have the right to opt out of the Fletcher scheme if they wish. Issues raised relating to Fletchers include: their management of repairs on properties damaged well above the 'cap' rather than passing them onto private insurers; their declaration that retrofitting insulation was not allowed was in contradiction of recent 'warm-homes' initiatives and owners' rights; and the use of pressure tactics to encourage owners into signing off on work despite its quality being unsatisfactory to the homeowner.

Repairs Carried Out without Building Consents

When a building is constructed new, it is required to have a building consent and a Code Compliance Certificate which indicates that there has been testing and inspection by the territorial authority to provide a third party with some assurance that the building code has been met. When repairing or reinstating a house to 'as new' or 'when new', a building consent should also be obtained. Only 1 percent of the 66,769 earthquake repairs carried out by the EQC have been done under a building consent or an exemption. In light of the fact that we experienced a series of large earthquakes and considerable structural damage resulted, the number of consents is very low and in future will go toward explaining the very high volume of defective repairs which will eventually come to light. Christchurch City Council had issued 332 building consents and 325 exemptions for the EQC repairs between June 2013 and August 2015. This means that in the main there is an overwhelming reliance on the repairer. As we know, many of the repairers/contractors will have vanished when the homeowner goes looking for someone to hold to account. The question must be asked - How can a home be repaired to an 'as new' state without having a building consent, inspections, and a code compliance certificate, when it did have these when it was new?

The EQC Foundation Repairs

The EQC is to review all properties in its managed repair programme where structural repairs were carried out without building consents, equating to thousands of properties.[28] Independent experts in the City have raised their concerns with the EQC and MBIE about foundation repairs over the previous five years. Their concerns were ignored,[29] MBIE launched a review in 2015 checking workmanship at 14 properties which revealed quality and building code issues at 13 of these properties. The foundation repair issue is a ticking time bomb.[30]

The EQC Imposed Home Repair Deadlines

In April 2015 the EQC announced that homeowners had less than two months to join the EQC home repair programme, involving several hundred people who were not in agreement with the EQC's repair scope or repair strategy. Those who were undecided or who could not be contacted would simply be cash settled.

Mould

Mould has also played a significant role post-earthquakes. The earthquakes and aftershocks caused burst water tanks and pipes, roofs to leak, repeated flooding, and 'liquefaction' of soil under homes. A 100-square metre home could have up to 100 tonnes of silt removed from under the floor cavity. Experience from the USA, after Hurricane Sandy's 'mould legacy' suggests a high failure rate of remediation attempts where mould is present. It was found that mould remediation is difficult, potentially expensive, and easy to do incorrectly. In Christchurch also, mould contamination has become another reason a home may be deemed beyond repair and the longer homes have had to wait for remediation, the worse the problem has become. Many policyholders have been faced with the invocation of the insurer exclusion 'hidden gradual damage' clause in an attempt to avoid this liability.[31]

Failure to Manage Asbestos Risks

Concerns have also become a 'health landmine' with an estimated forty three thousand homes supposedly containing asbestos. Workers complaining of asbestos exposure have increased some 350 percent following the earthquakes.[32] Amazingly though, asbestos is not covered by health and safety notification laws and therefore companies are not obligated to report it. Nor is it accounted for in the EQC cash pay-outs, often leaving homeowners out of pocket. Asbestos is a known carcinogen causing mesothelioma, a rare fatal cancer of the lining of lungs or the abdominal cavity, lung cancer or scarring of the lung tissue.[33] There is a suggestion that any asbestos found should simply be 'encased' rather than removed. A medical officer from the Canterbury District Health Board expresses his concern *"we have an opportunity to make sure houses are safe. They should just take it all out"*. The landfills are triple lined and asbestos is said to be buried at an average of four meters deep.[34] The EQC home repair programme manager, Reid Stiven, defends the policy.[35] More than 32,000 tonnes of asbestos contaminated waste is buried deep within North Canterbury which makes up 1.5 percent of the 2.32 million tonnes of waste disposed of, at Kate Valley landfill since opening in 2005. Worksafe New Zealand released findings from an investigation into the EQC's home repair programme but only ten homes had been tested as part of the investigation up to 2012, despite the fact that some 9000 homes are likely to be affected.[36] Experts declare that the risks associated with work being carried out in earthquake damaged homes was *"unlikely to cause any asbestos-related deaths."* This 'independent research' was commissioned by Fletcher EQR...

Failure to Provide Information to Policyholders

Involving the failure by the EQC to keep customers informed and the failure to provide clients with information regarding their property in the EQC files and a failure to meet OIA requests. There has also been inconsistency in the information provided to the homeowners about the scope of works and any variations to the scope of works.

As-Is-Where-Is Sales

A market quickly emerged of houses which are sold 'as-is-where-is' and this market continues unabated to 2016. It has become the city's new gold mine.[37] There is a very brisk market in the sales of these often uninsured and uninsurable homes. This market creates a second tier market for repaired or insured homes that suit investors with the right skill set. Buyers will often pay little more than land value for the damaged homes whose sellers have taken insurance pay-outs. These sales lead to questions about the nature of repairs that have taken place and lead to some interesting questions around the cost of repairs, the requirement to strengthen buildings, future insurance cover, the availability of bank funding and the assignment of existing claims. This also leads to some sellers being accused of 'pocketing' earthquake pay-outs for claims they are not disclosing to buyers. Other residents complain that the sale of nearby homes in 'as-is-where-is' condition is bringing down the value of property in their neighbourhoods. A moral argument arises – should money paid out for repairs be spent on repairs? It's a difficult question to answer when you consider that some people have waited five years for resolution of their claim. To then have to spend another year undergoing a major repair and all that entails is perhaps asking too much. Then there is the issue of uninsured homes as a social risk. During the 'leaky building syndrome' fiasco, the issue of pre-purchase property inspection arose where the Courts took the view that where a purchaser failed to obtain a pre purchase inspection and then later tried to make a claim against the vendor - they were held to be contributorily negligent. The same may well apply to earthquake damaged properties in the future. Suddenly, purchasing pre-earthquake property stock becomes considerably more complex.[38] In December 2013 the City Council's Land Use Recovery Plan (LURP) clears the way for the development of up to 40,000 residential sections over the next fifteen years. Thousands of homes have been lost in greater Christchurch as well as significant population shifts which have affected economic and transportation patterns.

Demand Surge

Is defined as the demand for products and services exceeding the regional capacity to efficiently supply them.[39] Demand surge is a function of the size of the catastrophe: the larger the disaster and damage to property, the greater the magnitude of demand surge. The critical element here is how economically can reconstruction materials, labour, equipment and financing be brought to the affected area? The cost of building materials, availability of materials and labour will physically affect the repair and rebuilding of Christchurch. If demand for labour exceeds supply then the labour force can and will command higher wages.[40] In addition, the total amount of repair work in the region will define the demand surge and the local building codes should determine the level of repairs required and the necessary skill of the labour force required to effect those repairs.[41] The heightened wages and labour shortages have a knock-on effect and create a long waiting list for repairs which not only causes severe hardship for owners but increases the loss at the property (due to deterioration over time, or further damage - of which mould is an example). This scenario is now playing out in Christchurch. Without a strong mechanism for the control of construction quality, materials and labour pricing, residents face a frustrating time ahead. This leads to an examination of New Zealand's building materials cost which is found to be generally out of step with the rest of the world. Australia's building costs alone are 15 to 25 percent cheaper than New Zealand's. After the Newcastle earthquake in Australia, rebuilding costs were said to increase by 35 percent. After Cyclone Tracey in Darwin, building costs increased by 75 percent. Preliminary reports following Cyclone Larry in Queensland indicate that there was a significant increase in local building costs after the disaster; with insurers estimating building costs increasing by at least 50 percent immediately after the disaster.[42] Insurers have to battle with the uncertainty of demand surge on claim costs following disasters. They see themselves as having a legitimate right to pay only the portion of the loss for which they have calculated and charged a premium despite the time that has elapsed between the event and the eventual repair. On the other hand, policyholders have to ensure that these demand price surges are factored into their final claim settlement, otherwise they will be considerably out of pocket and find themselves potentially in a situation of being unable to afford to replace what they have lost. This too is fuelling the 'as-is-where-is market. One such home sold for NZD 1.13 million.[43] The efforts of local and national government also affect the timing of reconstruction. By April 2013 house build costs in Canterbury skyrocketed and the price of a new house was up 12.2 percent on the same time a year earlier. In 2014 house build costs were still on the rise, ahead of the national new house inflation of 5.1 percent.[44]

It also becomes clear that insurers with their pricing models, did not adequately account for changes in the building code requirements post-earthquakes, particularly in relation to the need for strengthened foundations for TC2 and TC3 land, when determining the quantum for replacement of property. Depending on the new foundation design, the repair bill may have ballooned by several hundred thousand dollars.

Flooding

In 2014, the EQC sought a declaratory judgement on 'complex legal issues' including whether or not it is liable to settle claims on the basis of long term loss of land value. The outcome will affect the entitlements for homeowners. Their modus operandi is to determine how much the land has dropped in value since the earthquakes and settle claims based on that figure. It is likely that 9000 properties will be affected by the outcome of the declaratory judgement which is still pending.[45]

It becomes clear that in Christchurch's post-earthquake damage repair strategies, flood modelling was not included in many parts of the City (such as Fitzgerald Avenue) and this has led to a heightened flood risk.[46] Yet the Government continues to rule out red zoning of the Flockton Basin area as the *"criteria for red-zoning was not based on flooding. It was based on the potential of the land to support a building".*[47] An incredibly convenient and short sighted view, which at the least, failed to take all conditions into account.

The Building Act and Building Code both address the flood risk. A council is unable to issue a consent if the land is likely to be subject to natural hazards, of which flooding is one. The Building Code states that a building should be designed and constructed in such a way that the likelihood of water entering buildings is not greater than 2 percent in any one year (i.e. a one-in-50 year event). If the house is unable to obtain a consent then it must be redesigned in a way which complies with the District Plan. The question arises as to whether the floor level allowance ought to match the latest international projections of sea level rise projected over the next century. The EQC pledges to assist the Christchurch City Council to speed up mitigation work by making a financial contribution to the council-led flood mitigation as part of its role in settling residential land damage claims.

Insurers are responsible for properties and foundations but not the land they sit on and though the EQC recognises higher flood risks due to subsidence as a form of land damage, an insurer will not pay for a property's floor level to be raised if that is not required as part of the earthquake remediation. It is estimated that there are 45,000 properties in flood-prone areas in the City. In a decision released by the courts, it is stated that the increased flood vulnerability is a kind of natural disaster damage to land which the EQC should compensate for by remediation or payment and that where a house has subsided with the land and the land and building has become vulnerable to flooding this is damage to the land but not to the building. Sometimes, but not always, the EQC can compensate by paying the loss in the value of the land, rather than reinstating the land.[48]

As yet, the Flood Management Area rules have not taken into account the way in which land has dropped since the earthquakes. Despite this, the MBIE guidelines continue to allow a considerable degree of house and foundation repair without consideration of the likely current or future flood risks. This enables insurers to repair homes to existing floor levels despite the fact that those homes have sunk since the earthquakes and are now a known flood risk. In essence, meaning that any future risk and liability will fall squarely on the homeowner. In addition, the City Council can issue hazard notices on properties which result in insurance cover being withdrawn and any outstanding mortgage on the property immediately payable. If there are unconsented repairs, and thanks to the MBIE guidelines, there are many, then the Council would also have no Building Act liabilities and the poor homeowner will be left with no legal recourse. Some homeowners affected by the sinking of land have been told by their insurers that if they want their homes lifted, then they will have to cover the costs themselves. Essentially this will mean that every affected property owner in these areas will have to fight individual legal battles in order to get what they are actually entitled to. But who's looking and who cares? CERA's people argue that many of these properties were below flood management height well before the earthquakes. CERA states that there is no obligation on the insurer's part to future proof a house against likely flooding as a result of climate change unless a full rebuild is required. And while the insurance industry cannot be considered responsible for properties now considered to be a future flood risk, solutions must therefore come from the EQC. The flooding issues pushed city rates up 7.96 percent.[49] Rising sea levels will place some suburban areas of coastal Christchurch, such as South New Brighton, South Shore, Sumner, Brooklands and parts of Linwood, under water within the next 100 years.[50] In reports by both the Intergovernmental Panel on Climate Change and also a Tonkin and Taylor report, it is stated that a worst case scenario will see the sea rise by 2m by 2100.[51] They warn that large parts of the City could be submerged by rising sea levels - the storms producing a combination of rain and tide causing widespread inundation, only to be compounded by the broken storm water systems. In other parts of the country, councils are already beginning to use zoning rules as a way of ensuring people do not develop property in future potentially risky areas.

So which organisation is to be responsible for footing the bill to raise the large chunks of land that have sunk since the earthquakes? Insurers have agreed in some circumstances to raise floor levels for new builds, but will not do so for repairs. The EQC will not raise floor levels if the work is not required under a consent. The local populous calls for the Christchurch City Council to refuse to consent quake repairs that do not address the flood risk.[52] Councillors vote unanimously that residents should be consulted on the options. The residents express concerns about the ongoing costs associated with insurance in the area. Meanwhile flood affected Sumner and Heathcote River residents are concerned that the Council has ignored their flooding plight. The recent floodings have exemplified the existence of institutionally entrenched inadequacies with the current regulatory regime. If insurers worked with council and government to assist with mitigation by helping owners to understand and prepare for floods, they ultimately reduce the cost to their industry. Meanwhile, residents have been told that their land does not meet the EQC's criteria for increased flood risk. This will mean continuing to pay mortgages on homes that families cannot live in and are very unlikely to be able to sell easily.[53] *"What we are seeing in parts of Christchurch is almost a fast-forward of the future with climate change, sea-level rises." says Tim Grafton.*[54] Excesses for flooding have risen to NZD 10,000 for some customers. It is reminiscent of Queensland, Australia, where flood insurance has become unaffordable. Political pressure will build on the government to buy Flockton Basin homes that have been repeatedly hit by flooding, yet the Minister of Earthquake Recovery, insists that this is the City Council's responsibility. Is his decision based on advice from his ministry? The Greens advocate a 'blue zone' where the Government would offer to buy flood prone homes if people wished to move, a sensible solution. At the end of 2014, the Christchurch City Council settles on a NZD 48 million solution for the Flockton Basin including waterway improvements. Work was said to commence in April 2015, however, who is to foot the bill is as yet unclear. This serious and ever-pressing issue remains unresolved.

Fixed Sum Insurance

The insurance corporates have begun implementing major changes to the way the private insurance industry structures its' premiums - 'fixed sum insurance' commonly referred to as 'sum insured' or 'nominated replacement' has been introduced over the course of the past two years. This is the cost to rebuild a home to the same size with similar materials at today's rates. The insurers argue that with a sum insured policy the customer has control of establishing the value of the home and ensuring that value is kept up-to-date. Prior to the introduction of fixed sum insurance many policies were total replacement policies – i.e. whatever it cost to rebuild the home, essentially 'like for like' using current building materials. A large number of properties were underinsured and the foundation repair strategies for properties on TC2[55] and TC3[56] land have had to be specially and expensively engineered, adding additional costs to the final repair bill. So 'fixed sum insurance' is the insurance industry's answer to capping insurer liability. Ultimately, this will have the effect of the homeowner having to carry the burden of any cost overruns in the event of serious damage in another earthquake. Few policyholders understand the true implications of realistic costing of this new insurance regime and many will suffer the serious consequences in the next event. Despite the huge shortfalls likely for the policyholder, the insurance industry contends that this method will provide swift and certain resolution to claims. Moving from a square meterage methodology to a sum insured methodology will allow homeowners to know upfront the '*most their insurer will spend to rebuild their home in the event it does need to be rebuilt*'.[57] This statement is accurate, but it will in no way provide peace of mind to a policyholder imagining that their insurance cover will protect them from loss. The marketing hype serves well to obscure the reality of fixed sum insurance. In addition, the vast majority of homeowners will have simply accepted default calculations suggested by insurers using on-line calculators. These are intended to provide a free, easy-to-use way of estimating the potential cost of rebuilding a home. They provide only a minimal estimated rebuilding cost and they are at best only a guide, they are not a substitute for a detailed quantity surveyor's report, nor do they factor in the type of land upon which the property is built. Homeowners throughout the Canterbury region are able to attest to the fact that the real cost of repair and rebuild could well be several times greater. It is not until the damage to a property has occurred and been assessed by an engineer that the true costs of remedying the damage come to light. Nor will the fixed sum amount account for the demand surge or increase in building costs associated with long time frames for resolution of claims following a major event. Under a fixed insurance policy, where demand surge can cause the costs of rebuild to potentially escalate by up to 70 percent over their original value, policyholders will be seriously disadvantaged. Great for insurers and devastating for policyholders. Unless your property is a clear rebuild, expect that the insurer will dispute every aspect of the claim, as they currently do, and only that percentage of the sum insured value which equates to the percentage of damage to the home, will be paid to the policyholder. In this way the insurance industry passes liability back to the homeowner while maintaining shareholder profit. If a fixed sum policy is to be the norm, then it is absolutely critical that there is a legislated requirement that an insurer settle a policyholder's claim within a very limited and fixed time frame, three to six months, otherwise the fixed sum will in no way accurately reflect the true costs of replacement, even if it was accurately calculated at the outset of the policy cover. Some of the claims in Christchurch will not be settled for 7 or 8 years or more, post-earthquakes. Surveyors, valuers and economists agree that much of the country's housing stock is underinsured. Mitigation for homeowners has just become critical. Land in liquefaction prone or flood prone areas is likely to require additional foundation strengthening in the event of an earthquake – this should be factored into premiums or this land should be avoided.

Since the Canterbury earthquakes of 2010 and 2011, the EQC claims system is at capacity and under some stress. This highlights the need to ensure resilience of the system, but how this is to be done has not yet been detailed by the Government or the EQC. A further consideration is the fact that EQC will have to account for the costs of four major Canterbury earthquake events in a way that satisfies their reinsurers as well as accounting for the expenditure of large sums of public money to a standard which satisfies both Parliament and the public. Due to the current demands on the EQC infrastructure, there is an ongoing need to fill positions in the EQC structure to support what has become, since the Canterbury earthquakes, a markedly different organisation, with much wider responsibilities from those it had prior to September 4, 2010.

EQC maintains that it will be able to point to success in claims handling if all claimants are able to lodge claims with the EQC within the statutory period and if claims are determined and settled within a timeframe acceptable to the public (how is this to be determined?) in accordance with the Act. Claims also need to be settled to standards of individual and overall fairness acceptable to the public and reinsurers in accordance with the Act. It is also important that essential office services are maintained at a level commensurate with a standard of operational honesty and efficiency acceptable to the Board of Commissioners.

In light of the recent Canterbury earthquakes, the EQC outlines its priority for the next three or more years as becoming more efficient in management and settlement of claims. The EQC maintains, however, that the length of time required to settle claims varies from a few days to years.

We now know that a single major catastrophe can generate hundreds of thousands of EQC claims. The rate of settlement of claims following a natural event is dependent upon the resources that can be marshalled to investigate and handle them. Factors causing further delays include the availability of specialists such as engineers, the ability to deal with legal or regulatory issues, and the need for time to elapse to allow land to become sufficiently stable to be worked on.

In 15 months, the EQC had assessed a total of 447,943 properties, made up of 81,775 full inspections before February 22 2011, 182,838 rapid assessments post-February 22 2011, 196,468 full assessments post-February 22, with a total of 461,081 inspections and these numbers have continued to rise. To date this represents the lion's share of the claims-assessment task. The EQC initially also paid out on many claims within a reasonable timeframe but those happy days have long since gone. In its place are the thousands of disgruntled policyholders who on a daily basis battle to be heard. In an EQC Customer Interaction Review carried out in February 2015 the EQC organisational structure was found to be *"Suboptimal"* and its time management *"substandard"* with customer interactions becoming secondary.

The EQC Reinsurance

New Zealand's Earthquake Commission paid the first layer of claims from the recent Christchurch Earthquake using funds from the sale of stocks and bonds in order to raise enough cash to cover these. The Government has now sold some of the assets that it holds in order to quickly make good its claims obligations.

This highlights New Zealand's vulnerability in the event of another major natural disaster. Does the EQC have sufficient assets remaining to cover future claims and how efficiently is the EQC's reinsurance cover structured? Is the EQC considering the use of parametric products which are triggered by an 'event' itself. A parametric insurance product can be defined as an insurance contract where the ultimate payment or contract settlement is determined by a weather or geological observation or index, such as average temperature or rainfall over a given period or the intensity of an earthquake or wind storm. Parametric insurance pay-outs are determined according to the measurement of a highly correlated index but there is the potential for a mismatch between parametric insurance claims settlement and the actual losses of the insured.

It has been postulated that robust risk transfer and capital markets protection could be achieved by the use of catastrophe (CAT) bonds (see Chapter 7), contingent facilities or parametric products, ensuring claims can be paid promptly in emergencies. The argument is that developing access to capital markets and post-event bonding capability will allow the EQC to offer more affordable, higher-value coverage – and will strengthen the sustainability of the organisation. Undoubtedly the EQC will be looking to re-establish its reserves, as soon as possible. In light of recent events, now is a good time for the EQC to reconsider its cover generally and to review what needs to be restructured to most efficiently cover the costs of a future major catastrophe. Whether CAT bonds as a coverage mechanism is the best option, is debatable (see Chapter 8, The Reinsurance Industry).

Currently, the EQC places a large reinsurance programme with Lloyd's syndicates and other reinsurers. This cover supposedly protects the Natural Disaster Fund against a pay-out that would threaten its viability following a major natural disaster. The programme is placed through, and with advice from, reinsurance brokers. The EQC manages the Natural Disaster Fund in an environment characterised by a number of risks and challenges over which it has little or no control. Limitations on allowable asset classes and the ratio of onshore to offshore balances are also constraints. These are set by ministerial direction after consultation with the EQC.

The EQC maintains that its success in meeting the requirements of the Earthquake Commission Act 1993, Insurance Scheme and management of the Natural Disaster Fund is ultimately evidenced in a reduction of the pricing of New Zealand risk by global reinsurance companies. It is vitally important for the EQC's investment performance to achieve the targets set in the Statement of Investment Policies, Standards and Procedures and that the EQC's investment management costs are in line with its peers. The EQC's current goal is to continue to be able to renew its reinsurance programme (together with the Natural Disaster Fund assets) so as to meet the maximum probable loss in a catastrophic event. If New Zealand were to have another major event tomorrow this would be simply unachievable. As has previously been mentioned, the recent flurry of natural disasters around the globe (including the Canterbury earthquakes), along with the ongoing international financial crisis and increasing global geoseismic activity has resulted in considerable uncertainty about the pricing of risk. The EQC states in its Statement of Intent June 2011 – June 2014 that it will continue to be able to,

> … access sufficient reinsurance capacity but that there
> is likely to be a change to the pricing and structure of

EQC's current reinsurance programme. This must be done in an efficient and fair manner in accordance with the [Earthquake Commission 1993] Act. Efficient claims handing and settlement minimises the costs faced by levy payers and by international reinsurers. Fair claims handling and settlement in accordance with the Act ensures that claimants and the general public have confidence in the scheme and its administration and that third parties who also have a financial interest in the claim (for example mortgage holders, private insurers, international reinsurers) can have certainty about their costs and risks – and price this accordingly.

Despite the EQC assertions, EQC failed to renew any of its multi-year (originally a three-yearly renewal term) reinsurance contracts and has replaced them initially with annual contracts. This is considerably more costly. Prior to the Christchurch events, the EQC had several sets of reinsurance cover: one on an annual basis and renewed yearly, and the other three were multi-year reinsurance agreements, each lasting three years and expiring in three successive years. Staggering it in this way ensured that the EQC did not have to negotiate all renewals at once and the structure assisted in smoothing out any volatility in premium increases. Multi-year cover allows the reinsured to access cover at a predictable cost over a number of years. Currently EQC is at the mercy of renewals and rate rises on an annual basis and will have to factor these increases into its funding strategy in the future. The question arises – could this lack of predictability force them to consider CAT bonds as a replacement for some of their reinsurance cover? Some financial commentators suggest that it is likely that the EQC would be attracted to the multi-year, fixed-cost and collateralised nature of a CAT-bond transaction as a CAT bond has the potential to provide a layer of multi-year cover. By all accounts there are CAT bond investors willing to take on New Zealand earthquake risk under the right premium conditions. The problem of the cost of issuance for the poorly capitalised EQC remains. Perhaps EQCs reinsurers will consider this option for themselves? But are CAT bonds really the answer in an ever-uncertain financial market place? (see Chapter 8, The Reinsurance Industry).

Conclusion

"The starting point is: Do you want to have an EQC, and has it worked well? I think the answer overwhelmingly to that is yes, we do want one and yes, it has worked well", the Hon. Gerry Brownlee.[58]

In light of the daunting task that the poorly prepared EQC faced since the Canterbury earthquakes, the EQC has actually performed dubiously and has consequently sustained a well-deserved degree of criticism from the wider community. There have been repeated requests for a royal commission of inquiry into the EQC handling of claims and shoddy repairs but this has fallen largely on deaf ears.[59] In order to achieve the EQC's current mandate, it has had its scope of functions widely extended to include not simply claims handling but also project management, the design and supervision of additional land remediation activities, provision of engineering advice to the Government, as well as a social assistance component to the recovery. These are functions that pertain essentially only to a government department; they are not functions that the private insurance industry is involved with. In light of the extension of the EQC's role and new-found experience gained in the management of a major natural disaster, it would seem a natural and desirable progression for the EQC to retain and further extend its capabilities to become the insurer of last resort in the event of a catastrophe. With its structure already in place, *notwithstanding the admission that it would need major overhaul*, extending this to a more comprehensive and formalised catastrophe scheme would not require too much more funding or implementation. The 'bones' for a more comprehensive scheme are already in place; all that is required is some fleshing out and an overhaul of its management structure. This would mean that communities in future would not be at the mercy of the private insurance industry.

In the future, the Natural Disaster Fund needs to achieve a sustainable balance and in the event of a natural disaster the reinsurance policies need to be able to adapt from focusing on fund growth to the maintenance of the Fund, as well as the protection of a substantial minimum fund size. Any alterations to the Act's insurance coverage will affect the liability profile of the EQC and the sustainable size of the Natural Disaster Fund. Due to the way in which the cover is constructed, any additional cap increases would increase the EQC's premium income by a higher proportion than the growth of its liabilities. For instance, in the event that the property cap was to be doubled, this would double the premium income, yet the liability would increase by only about 30 percent. The EQC should further increase its reserves, and constantly seek new ways of growing and protecting those reserves to ensure that there are sufficient funds to deal with a major event at some time in the future, which could be tomorrow. Legislation will be required to back such a programme, and additional incentives for action are needed.

The EQC national insurance scheme for natural catastrophe losses also has considerable potential to stimulate mitigation activity. The success of any central government action will also depend equally on the development in society of a 'participatory culture' in which citizens both understand the risks they face and the necessity of organising a national body to oversee those actions that need to take place in the event of a major catastrophic event and citizens should be prepared to participate in the management of them.

Though the EQC has come under harsh criticism, and for good reason, it remains the natural choice, (after restructuring and careful management), as the institution best equipped to provide the citizens of New Zealand with protection against the devastating effects of natural disaster (see Chapter 7, Catastrophe Insurance).

Citizens speak

A City of Silos: Five years on from the first earthquake and the majority of our city are moving on. Many residents however, still await their own recovery as their homes remain damaged, and they are 'stuck' as firmly as if it were the day after the September 4th earthquake 2010. It is hard to comprehend how a first world country with incredible resources can leave its people in a situation as complex and devastating as post-earthquake Christchurch.

It appears that for many Christchurch people, this is as a result of the Agencies tasked with the recovery, working in isolation. Instead of viewing issues in a holistic manner, instead of working with other agencies to find real solutions that allow affected people to move forward, the agencies have worked in isolation and have not included the residents in their planning. Many people have been left in dire circumstances. What makes this outcome even more difficult is that many people do not have the skills or financial resources to mitigate their situation.

An example of an agency with this disconnection is the EQC which provides cover for contents, homes and land. The EQC have chosen to address each type of claim separately for reasons of expedience. This was sensible for contents. However, to assess a house in isolation from the land on which it stands is, in retrospect, foolish. These flawed separate house and land assessments, led to inadequate scopes of work, and inappropriate repair strategies. A perfect illustration of silos within silos leaving a legacy of failed repairs. A subsequent review into the quality of Canterbury repairs is called a 'whitewash' after it comes to light that the Government allowed insurers to choose which homes could be looked at for assessment. 100 homes were sampled and the purpose of the review was to identify whether the work which had been completed complied with the Building Code and Building Act.[60]

For Flockton residents and others affected by post-earthquake flooding, EQC has decided that a Diminution of Value Payment calculated on convoluted criteria that they have created, is an appropriate outcome for damaged land. All this has done is to leave people at great risk of flooding, with land and homes that can flood, and not enough money to put it right. The land cover New Zealanders' thought they had, does not actually exist.

In Flockton people remain stuck with homes that are damp and with land that is at risk of flooding. Some houses are unliveable and have been left derelict, other residents have homes that they are unable to sell, and so are unable to move on. The Christchurch City Council (CCC) continues to work towards drainage repairs that are still years away. Despite this, because of a fear of setting a precedent for other flooding areas, no one is brave enough to make a decision that will allow the homeowners of Flockton options and a future.

CCC has the legal responsibility for drainage across the city post-earthquake. With input from residents, CCC provided an excellent model for community engagement. They communicated transparently and honestly with the community and told them the truth, even when it was very bad news. They consulted with them and tried to remove barriers. The CCC developed joint newsletters from all agencies at residents' request - informing them about flooding issues. The Mayoral Taskforce, which included all agencies, was led by the CCC and looked at flooding and drainage issues across the city. This model could be adopted by other agencies.

As many vulnerable residents face yet another winter in damaged homes, our country needs to look at those things that have gone well in Christchurch and use this learning to help those who are still stuck.

By Jo Byrne[61]

CHAPTER 5

'GOOD FAITH': THE INSURANCE INDUSTRY AND CATASTROPHE

- -

... Tell you what, you decision-makers come and live in some of these homes, pay your mortgage and rates, try and not get a fright when a truck passes your home (up to 60 a day go past my home now), live with constant choking dust, and intermittent sewers, see how you like it – sick and tired of these excuses. Stop changing the goalposts because it suits you. It doesn't suit me or my neighbours, we are stressed beyond belief, stop lollygagging, having bloody meetings and get on with it!

J123, Canterbury Resident, February 20, 2012

A second major disaster has taken place in Christchurch – the insurance aftershock, in which tens of thousands of people are currently being cynically exploited by the local insurance industry.

During the 'good times' and bad, insurance companies spend considerable funds shaping the public's perception of their business through sympathetic marketing and advertising. However, the industry as a whole proves very unwilling to disclose information about its internal workings, particularly information relating to failure to deliver to their policyholders. The fact is that there is simply very little information about the insurance industry and its performance, on either the internet or in libraries and the press. In addition, the internal structure of insurance organisations is carefully devised so that the bottom layers have no idea what the top layer strategies seek to achieve. Such information is held very closely. Much effort is expended on limiting the information produced and endeavouring to keep that which is produced out of the hands of policyholders. It is for that reason in the light of experience of the behaviour of the industry, that this information is made public.

Insurance policies are sequential and contingent.[1] This means that the policyholder pays the premium now and the insurance company must later pay a claim, if one is made. Under the Fair Insurance Code, insurers are required to settle valid claims 'quickly and fairly' (2015) and under the new revised Code 'as quickly as possible' (2016), which means they must act promptly after the policyholder has supplied the relevant information. Because insurance policies concern a raft of potential risks, they have a tendency to incorporate abstract language which leaves insurers significant contractual discretion and inevitably leads to a temptation for insurers to adopt overly aggressive claims-handling practises. Every dollar that an insurer avoids paying in claims adds to their profit margins. Arguably, in some cases that temptation has become policy. Consumers purchase insurance as a way of protecting themselves from significant financial risk. When those risks arise, they are often in an ill-equipped position to 'battle' their insurer to obtain what they have paid for, and if they do, they find themselves in a very unequal contest.

Yes, it is true that Christchurch has not had only one event, but a series of earthquakes and aftershocks. However this, I believe, has been used as a convenient excuse for insurers simply to sit and wait. True, it has been a major event, but again, this was excessively over-used as one of the excuses in their armoury of delay tactics. Insurers well understand the risk profile in New Zealand. The risk was defined and priced by the insurer, the price paid and the risk then transferred from the policyholder to the insurer. All that is legitimately and contractually left to be done by the insurer is to settle the claim on the basis of 'good faith'. In theory, and according to the concept of 'good faith', the insurer must not place its own financial interests above those of the policyholder. Since September 4, 2010 there has been anything from poor sequential performance, to non-performance by the private insurers.

Not every insurance company should be tarred with the same brush. There are a few, generally smaller insurers (usually mutuals), who are performing their contractual obligations as best they are able, in contrast to the larger players such as IAG and its subsidiaries such as State Insurance and NZI, which show very different results and behaviours (evidenced in a television interview with John Campbell on TV3 on September 5, 2012). Contributing to the current difficulties is the fact that IAG holds the major contingent of the policies in Christchurch. Unfortunately when the Commerce Commission was taking the decision to allow IAG to purchase AMI's client base and Lumley, it chose not to regard what essentially amounts to a monopoly, as a problem.

So why the delays? The answer is simple – generally, an insurance company will pool the premiums paid by policyholders to pay losses and expenses, not simply banking the money locally until they need to pay-out, but rather reinvesting the premiums and reinsurance payments, often offshore and in a variety of financial instruments. The time between taking in premiums and paying out claims is known as the 'float'. The subsequent income earned from such investment is a major source of insurer profit. There is absolutely no incentive for insurers to break these term investments. That is a major reason why the population of Christchurch still waits and waits for the insurance industry to carry out its contractual obligations. In this way, insurers mitigate their own liabilities and inflate profits. Simply put, Cantabrians have become the faceless victims of insurers' corporate profit strategy.

Without their insurance pay-outs many homeowners are unable to repair the damage to their homes and move forward with their lives. The quick settlement of each individual insured's claims would serve the region as a whole by mitigating economic disaster in the affected area. Now, as the sixth year since the September 4 earthquake is under way, Canterbury has seen the effects of slow insurance settlement as businesses fail, jobs are lost and disillusioned residents have moved on to greener pastures, or simply still remain trapped and helpless through a complete loss of options.

Imagine the following scene. A recently widowed older woman in her late 70s has just experienced the series of devastating Canterbury earthquakes. She has also recently lost her husband, who died from a heart attack shortly after one of the earthquakes. She lives in one of the badly affected parts of eastern Christchurch. Her home has suffered substantial damage and is deemed a 'complete loss' by the EQC. Her private insurance company, on the other hand, is trying to tell her that with some minimal repairs the house will be habitable again within a few weeks. She has little education beyond high school and her home is all she owns; it represents her equity. She is currently renting and her limited accommodation funds from her insurer are rapidly diminishing. She is concerned about her future and her ability to 'save' her home and her ability to support herself. She is totally dependent upon obtaining sound advice and money from her insurer in order to rebuild her life. The insurance claims 'case manager' or loss adjustor sitting across from her is experienced in the art of negotiation and knows immediately that he is dealing with a person with little understanding of the insurance industry, the building industry or the negotiation process, and that she is desperate to have her problem resolved and is expecting her insurer to take care of her. There are some insurers that will. The evidence is, however, that many will not and did not. There are thousands of such people in Canterbury today, still waiting in the wings for those all-important conversations with private insurers. As a society are we prepared to watch them being thrown to the wolves with little possibility of recourse to justice, some five years after the event?

Consumer impressions of insurers are formed on the whole by advertising and word-of-mouth rather than on actual hard fact and identifiable results. Insurance advertising tends to focus on abstract unverifiable promises e.g. "love your stuff", or "we'll take care of that problem". Most people who are insured will never test the most critical element of their insurance policy – that of the low-probability, high-cost loss. This premise is, of course, how insurance works. However, in Canterbury, between 2010–16, many thousands of policyholders are still testing just that. It is also the case that when consumers do have these experiences they are not well equipped to make judgements about the performance of their cover provider as they have little with which to make comparison.

The major question on the lips of most owners of damaged property in Canterbury was/is *"Why is my insurance company taking so long to do anything effective about my damage?"* No matter how well you held up your end of the bargain, extensive delays continue throughout the claims process, and these delays to their repairs or rebuilds are causing real suffering for many as their accommodation allowance has run out or is rapidly running out and they are having to also pay mortgage payments and rates on properties that are often uninhabitable. The insurers provide a variety of reasons for these delays, and the expected timescale for resolution of a settlement remains a mystery.

There are also rather more sinister corporate forces at work. Canterbury is not alone in experiencing great difficulties with insurers in the aftermath of major catastrophe. Not paying out or paying out less than their entitlement to victims of catastrophes has helped produce record profits for the insurance industry. In the past 15 years, insurance company net income has soared – even in the wake of Hurricane Katrina, which was the worst natural disaster in US history, Property/Casualty insurers reported their highest-ever profit of USD 73 billion in 2007, up 49 percent from USD 49 billion in 2005. Have Cantabrians become major contributors to such insurance industry profit statistics?

There are plenty of stories of American insurers, giving rewards (such as portable fridges) to employees who quash valid claims or use a 'boxing gloves' approach to policyholders who refuse to accept 'lowball' offers. When units of the American International Group (AIG) lost money, former Chief Executive Officer Maurice Greenberg was reported to have put in place new teams of staff to systematically reject thousands of valid claims, according to the American Association of Justice.[2] The AAJ went on to say that State Farm, another major US insurer, went so far as to engage in fraud to deny claims. After the 1994 Northridge earthquake in California, which caused an estimated USD 33.8 billion in damage, company officials forged signatures on waivers of earthquake coverage to avoid paying earthquake related claims. Incredibly, internal documents used by Allstate featured an alligator motif and the caption *'sit and wait'*[3] – a clear reference to their delaying of claims to increase the likelihood that a claimant would give up. There is good evidence that similar tactics have been are being employed in Canterbury. If you think this could not possibly happen in New Zealand, recent lobbying and talk of class action against IAG and the need for an insurance tribunal is proof enough that it is.

Insurance companies are often prepared to back their conviction that in the asymmetric power relationship which exists between company and policyholder, the client will lack the means to litigate or use other means to obtain a fair resolution. They also have gained confidence from the fact that the cost of seeking justice in the courts is now so high that few people have the means to use that avenue. If policyholders do litigate, the insurers are masters of delay and use every means open to them to delay trial, often for years. Having had the financial benefit of huge delay, insurers rarely go through the courtroom door, preferring to 'settle on the steps of the courtroom' before trial. The fact is that the industry has been raking in spectacular profits while increasing the use of more and more audacious tactics towards their customers. You may well be thinking, 'well that's the USA, not New Zealand'. In the aftermath of the Australian Cyclone Yasi and in the wake of the New Zealand earthquakes, staff from some of the same American companies,[4] have in fact, also been working in the Canterbury area.

Good faith…

The first thing to learn about insurance contracts is that they are different from other contracts. An insurance contract is a contract of utmost good faith. This is the standard on which the courts judge performance by insurers. There is also a duty of disclosure by policyholders in insurance contracts, which is about the duty of openness and honesty. Good faith between parties is said to underlie the entire contract. There is also a recognised duty of good faith in relation to the insurer's handling of claims. As Neil Campbell (Senior Lecturer in Law, University of Auckland) writes in *Claims for Damages Against Insurers in New Zealand*: "An insurer who fails to indemnify the insured for a valid claim breaches the contract of insurance."[5]

What has repeatedly happened in Christchurch, and is still happening five years out from the earthquakes is that many insurers are still denying and reducing policyholders' claims, routinely refusing to pay market prices for homes and replacement of contents, using 'low-pitched' computer programmes to cut pay-outs, making changes to policy coverage with no clear explanation, ignoring or altering engineering reports, and sometimes asking their adjusters to slow down claim progress or lie to customers. Then the insurers make low offers, or refuse to pay at all. They stall until claimants are so desperate that they are then prepared, or forced by circumstances, to accept what the insurer offers them. Customers who try to take a harder line with them are subjected to even more delay and are then offered a 'take-it or leave-it' deal. This does not sound like 'good faith'.

This is by no means a definitive list of the insurance issues suffered by the residents of Canterbury. It is simply the beginning of a long process of uncovering the true nature of the problem. The insurance issues will continue to escalate and those still waiting will begin to get more and more desperate for action and answers. Several public demonstrations in Christchurch have already pointed to this outcome as has the initiation of several class actions.

In addition, good faith is seen to be lacking in the unwillingness of insurers to provide case files to policyholders. Many people reported that despite their repeated requests for their client files (even when formally requested under the Privacy Act 1993, Privacy Principles 3 and 6), private insurers often delay providing files to policyholders, which are then found to be incomplete or heavily redacted. In some cases it has taken months for policyholders to receive files and vital missing documents are claimed by the insurer as 'legally privileged', despite the fact that an insured's lawyer could successfully bring an action to compel the insurer to provide the material. Statements from insurance staff such as, "*I am not going to release anything that may be prejudicial to the ongoing investigation of the claim,*" are used to withhold all manner of information, including quantity surveyor reports, loss adjustor reports and engineering reports.

Other 'bad faith' behaviour includes the failure to explain the true coverage available to policyholders: e.g. the need to rebuild to legally mandated standards and for payments for rental or temporary living quarters, reduction of payments for alleged depreciation, reducing a settlement amount without explaining why, as well as failure to properly investigate claims. In addition, there are reports of insurers discouraging professionals being present at meetings, be they lawyers, engineers or builders. Often the 'professionals' they employ to prepare reports are 'captive', understanding well that their job in the process is to ensure that the lowest costs are achieved, not the best solution. This enhances the power asymmetry between the parties, so that the insurer is likely to achieve a settlement for less than the policyholder is justifiably owed.

A lack of good faith is also evident in the continued delay of payment of claims. Although an Australian court found in the case of *Oakland Investments (Aust.) Ltd v Certain Underwriters at Lloyds* [2012] QSC 6 that if an insured is able to prove greater losses as a result of late payment, then insurers will be exposed to those losses. The Court also ordered them to pay interest on those damages. This case should serve as a warning to insurers to pay on time or risk paying more. In New Zealand, the Judicature Act 1908 serves the same purpose and sets the interest rate applicable to such damages.[6] The current rate is 5 percent, which was amended in 2010 downward from 7.5 percent. However, insurers know that delays have an effect of both 'wearing down' claimant resolve to be treated fairly and to improve investment income. The insurer-invested premiums which are temporally due, even before any repairs are made or costs actually incurred, as well as their investment earnings from reinsurance payments etc., add up to significant returns when an insurance company has thousands of claims and the longer the delay, the greater the probability that the insured will settle for less.

Further evidence of exercise of a lack of good faith by insurers is the excessive investigation of claims – another tactic which has emerged as common in the Canterbury context. Insurers request more and more reports and information which often seem unnecessary in resolving the claim. This has the effect of dragging the process out and again can cause the insured to lose resolve to hold the insurer to the letter of the contract.

Vast amounts of paper and documentation are involved and generated and the whole estimation process loses any semblance of efficiency. This is deliberate and confusing for uninitiated claimants. Many people have reported having to participate in the protracted generation of between 6 to 15 reports of various kinds, involving visits by numerous 'experts', on the same issue(s).

Other evidence of a lack of good faith on the part of the insurer is the 'low-balling' of claims and the 'stonewalling' which Cantabrians are encountering continually. This refers to the strategy of offering a depressingly minimal settlement, which signals that the insurance company is willing to fight the claim in order to lower the claimant's expectations. Stonewalling is the tactic whereby the insurer simply refuses to negotiate a settlement because they know a claimant has limited financial resources or mounting legal costs; this can place considerable psychological and financial pressure on claimants. Insurers also often resort to unreasonable interpretations of policy terms or add (by interpretation) 'surprise' conditions or interpretations which are not stated in the residential policy, for example, the notion of 'betterment'.

There are numerous reports of incidents where the EQC assessors and private insurance assessors have been adamant that massive cracks in foundations or major distortion to structures 'were there prior to the earthquakes' or that walls were originally 'built on a lean'. Such judgements conveniently overlook the fact that the local authority inspector would have signed off the building as 'compliant' when it was constructed. These tactics are essentially to minimise damage and cost to the insurers. Often insurers will just 'try it on' by minimisation and denial of the cost of damage, based on dubious expert reports – for example, one insurer's quantity survey in a reported case was NZD 800,000 less than a professional and independent survey. There have been many reports of even bigger discrepancies since 2012. People are beginning to suspect that the low-balling and stonewalling was achieved in part through the use of 'biased' computer software and low square-meterage costs used to value damage. Errors in estimating the scope of damages would naturally produce inaccurate estimates. The software produces an estimate of repair costs, but an estimate will rarely be the same as a final price. Finding local contractors to do repairs for software-estimated prices is difficult, as the software is usually set to under-price. One builder stated, after working for some time with the EQC, that some of the software was an excellent data-collection tool but a poor tool for scoping a repair strategy as it has limited options and led to unrealistic repair strategies. The American experience shows that the system is often fed with price lists that are old, and are intentionally well below fair market value. Insurers are known to have failed to update their price lists to account for cost increases associated with the damage sustained, and failed to ensure that their staff are properly trained to keep the price lists current. This fact alone is of considerable concern given the rapidly rising costs of building in Canterbury, which have steadily risen over the past six years. In the USA, insurance companies recognise that information regarding the use of claims-handling software may be damaging to them and have sought to keep such information from discovery and use at trial. Bloomberg, a former Insurance Commissioner of Texas, stated that these programmes are *"designed to systematically underpay policyholders without adequately examining the validity of each individual claim"*.[7]

Further examples of 'bad faith' practices include some private insurers' insistence that policyholders pre-fund their losses, that is, that the insured spend their own funds before being compensated for any loss suffered (related to either contents claims or accommodation and storage fees). This is at odds with the sequential nature of insurance contracts.

Insurers will try to tell you that 'there has been no loss until you have spent it' – which is a direct violation, as they are contractually obliged to provide the funds sequentially, if damage from the insured event occurs. Many people were told that they had to *spend* the EQC's contents cap of NZD 20,000 before the insurer would pay any balance on their contents claim. The psychological impact of an earthquake leaves people wondering about the 'value of items' and whether or not they want to replace what they have lost. This does not mean, though, that they are not contractually entitled to receive the monetary compensation for their loss. Many people are not in a position to spend hundreds or thousands of dollars pre-paying for items and services that they may, or may not, recoup from their insurers. Their lives may not be sufficiently settled for several years and they may not wish to immediately replace lost or broken items.

Another unscrupulous insurer 'bad faith' practice includes the use of other professionals to deflect claims. Claimants report that often insurance companies hire professionals, who are used inefficiently, as a means of further delay. Engineering firms are used widely for this purpose. An engineer is identified by the insurers, time passes, the engineer arrives and inspects the property, and declares that more invasive testing will be required. Often months pass before another engineer or two arrive to carry out invasive testing. A report has to be written, more time passes and eventually a report will be filed. This can take as long as the insurers make it take; many cases have taken 4 years. The engineering firm does not drive the process, nor is the engineering report binding on the insurance company and by that I mean that they often choose to ignore the engineer's findings if the report does not suit their strategy or they think that they can settle on a cheaper 'fix'.

Policyholders have been refused cash payments. Some home insurers were settling claims with vouchers from retailers rather than paying out in cash. In many instances this made it impossible for policyholders to get like-for-like replacements, yet voucher payment options are not even mentioned in policy 'terms and conditions'. It is unlikely that insurers would take premium payments in the form of luncheon vouchers, so why should they issue policyholders vouchers instead of cash? This would be a 'no-brainer' in court.

Various functions within the insurance industry are deliberately specialised and compartmentalised for supposed efficiency. This is an effective way to train and supervise employees, so that when a team has a specific job, that job becomes easier and more efficient. It also means that no one person is likely to develop a 'conscience' in respect of unfair transactions and start to question them. This methodology also tends to sever the ties with the client and often leads to a breakdown in communication between the insured and the insurer.

The use and abuse of 'experts' in the claims-handling process is also often bad faith. This despite the fact that the professionals are key actors in making Important contributions to improve, simplify and shorten the disaster mitigation, rehabilitation and reconstruction phase. In order to maximise value to their shareholders, insurance companies engage the services of consulting firms as they have proven to be an effective tool in increasing efficiency and cost reduction and permit the employment of fewer permanent staff. However, they can often be over-relied upon or even abused, resulting in unfair claims handling. Not only must insurance companies know when to listen to their experts, they need to know when they have hired an unreliable/incompetent source. When insurance companies hire experts to evaluate various parts of a claim they must properly consider the information that is provided. When companies choose to ignore their own experts, courts may find that they have breached the duty of good faith. There is also the issue of the 'instructions' insurers provide to their consultants/experts, which in most cases appears to 'tie' the consultants/experts ability to produce an unbiased finding. This issue has arisen consistently with the use of the MBIE Guidelines. (See Chapter 4).

An insurance company has the duty of performing its contractual obligations to a policyholder in good faith and not take advantage of vulnerabilities created by the sequential character of contract performance. Mutual good faith is implied in every contract; courts (especially in the USA) have viewed the insurers' requirements as one-sided and found in the policyholders' favour.

In smaller centres there is also the 'moral hazard' risk that in the event of a major event there will not be sufficient 'professionals' to meet the assessment needs of the area. Certainly this has been the case in Canterbury. During normal times, many of these professionals obtain substantial work from the insurance industry, which is a significant client. They cannot afford to be 'offside' with the insurance industry and will often yield to covert pressure from insurers to keep their estimates low or use doubtful assessment standards. As a result of the poor supply, professionals may be working for both an insurance company and their own clients in a 'conflict of interest' situation which is never disclosed. There is substantial evidence that this has been the case in Canterbury and many homeowners report that their privately commissioned assessments by 'out-of-town professionals' were substantially higher than those produced by 'local experts' acting for them or for their insurer. Following Hurricane Katrina, the Mississippi Attorney General sued at least five major insurance companies in relation to their claims handling, stating that the claim-adjustment practices kept millions of dollars out of the pockets of the homeowners, according to *USA Today*. There were more than 6,600 suits filed in the federal courts in New Orleans alone following Hurricane Katrina. In the book *Delay, Deny, Defend: Why Insurance Companies Don't Pay Claims*, Jay Feinman[8] states that people complained to the Louisiana Department of Insurance at the rate of 20,000 a month. Unfortunately here in New Zealand we do not have such a body. There is clear evidence that the underlying insurance dishonesty scenario is the same in New Zealand but continues to be ignored by government and regulators.

Some of the other general insurance issues that have arisen in Christchurch relate to the perceived 'red-tape'. Some business owners have indicated a high degree of frustration with what is perceived as an extreme level of 'red-tape' and bureaucracy from authorities which, in their view, has hampered business recovery efforts. Business owners looked to authorities to meet them halfway, in order to ensure that all parties were working together for the benefit of the city. In the publication *New Beginnings Christchurch Central Business District: Evolution from an Earthquake* by The Field Connection (Brenda Snook and Toni Hannah)[9] the authors were repeatedly told by business owners that there is too much emphasis on unnecessary red-tape when what was most required was flexibility and a commitment by authorities to assist business owners to move quickly toward economic recovery and stability. The research findings by the Field Connection make for interesting reading for those people who are specifically interested in commercial/business insurance claims.

People have also experienced changes in policy as underhand. After the September 2010 quake, assessors would ask homeowners to sign a form to show their agreement when they had finished a house assessment. After the February and June quakes of 2011, they stopped this practice and kept homeowners at arm's length in the assessment process. That clear change of policy enabled them to minimise damage, which led to people losing trust.

Many expressed their concerns around the use of 'preferred contractors' by private insurance companies, for example Fletcher Construction, Arrow International, Hawkins Construction or Maxim Projects amongst others. These companies carry out the estimating and perform or project-manage the work of repair for the estimated price. They receive payment from the insurance company and offer a limited guarantee on the work performed. If the homeowner chooses to work with someone other than with these contractors, then some insurers require the policyholder to assume 'all the risk'. In reality, even if one does work with the building contractor, the risk is still carried by the insured, as contracts are written to carefully exclude insurance company liability and in effect the insured contracts directly with the contractor and has no legal contractual come-back on the insurance company. There is always great asymmetry in such a contractual arrangement, which is, arguably, quite deliberate.

Other concerns relate to the lack of expertise of loss adjustors and estimators. Very few insurance estimators at the outset of the earthquakes had experience in estimating earthquake damage, which is largely the province of engineering professionals. In the days following the initial earthquake, many insurance assessors were determining the value of damage without the expertise to do so. This can cost an insured party hundreds of thousands of dollars and, at the least, predisposes the negotiation of cost to be based on a very low initial threshold, giving the insured the costly burden of proving that the damage cost is actually much higher. Many of the assessors quickly employed from other parts of the country had no connection to the building industry. One participant reported that his training involved one visit to an earthquake-damaged house in Mt Pleasant. Those who did have building experience, had next to no experience with earthquake damage.

There has been a general sense that the delayed scoping of repairs required to properties has led to inaccurate assessments and hence the minimising of damage results. Two years after an event, properties tend to 'settle' and what was obviously 'new damage' can more easily be minimised. Six years after the event properties look very different.

The inability to obtain earthquake insurance for new situations alarmed many. Some wanting to buy existing homes and people wishing to build new homes found it very difficult, if not impossible, to secure insurance. Some builders decided to sidestep insurers and arrange insurance for new buildings for their customers, who then secure finance and move in without delays. If people cannot get insurance, they cannot obtain mortgages and are usually unable to pay builders. Building companies are still blaming insurers and red tape for strangling the rebuilding process. Delays in insurance payments also mean that work remains on hold. Repair work and new building work cannot take place until insurance settlements start to come through. Builders around Christchurch have laid off staff, and many in the building trades have left the city for greener pastures. It was estimated that more than 15–40,000 tradespeople would need to be available to keep the rebuild moving at anything like a reasonable pace. There was concern amongst the building fraternity that if the insurance industry continues to delay, more builders will leave the region and there will be an enormous future shortage. By any assessment, there is no doubt that the rate of rebuild and recovery never met estimates by either the City Council or the Government.

Another issue also arose – that of private insurers trying to access the EQC funds from personal bank accounts without authority. Insurers have attempted, and no doubt in some cases been successful, in accessing the EQC funds from claimants, well before they have begun work on the property concerned. The EQC payments are paid to the policyholder or their mortgagor as a result of their EQC policy. These funds do not at any time belong to the insurer until agreement exists to put them towards costs of an agreed repair or rebuild exceeding NZD 100,000. These funds often enable policyholders to obtain the professional reports required to prove their loss. Without access to those funds they are often at the mercy of the insurers' assessments. There are accounts of IAG policyholders receiving phone calls from their bank saying that the bank has received a letter from a private insurer asking to access their account and remove the NZD 100,000 EQC payment. This in spite of the fact that work was unlikely to occur on their properties for at least a year and no discussion had been held with the policyholder! Some banks, for example KiwiBank, have allowed people to put this payment towards mortgage repayment while they wait for their insurance company to begin work. Those without mortgages can accumulate interest until such time as work commences on their properties. Private insurers try, even illegally, to access those funds, as they can benefit from denying the policyholder the financial ability to prove their claim, pooling the funds, reinvesting or simply profiting from large interest payments. It doesn't take a great leap of the imagination to guess that after five years, many of the EQC funds acquired have been reinvested by insurers and put toward minimising the private insurers' liabilities without any reconstruction or repair work having been commenced.

Some large insurers appear to judge clients who bring professional representation with them as adversarial and immediately close ranks. The fact that you choose to be represented and protect your interests with either your engineer or lawyer, for example, is viewed very dimly. Insurers' usual move has been to stipulate that your lawyer is only to communicate with their lawyer. The immediate result is that timeframes extend greatly and costs for the homeowner escalate dramatically. However, with many policyholders' financial security at stake, it is entirely reasonable that they seek to protect themselves, particularly in light of the power imbalance between the parties.

Another common scenario is that private insurers attempt to affirm 'non-compliance' with current building codes or a lack of compliance with codes related to the date of original construction of the building, regardless of the fact that a consent was issued and the City Council signed off on the construction. They use this as an argument to compel the homeowner to contribute up to sometimes 50 percent of the repair costs. Any house built prior to today's date is likely to fall short of current compliance requirements and modern building standards and codes. Some policies exclude the cost of fixing faulty design or faulty construction by todays' building standards. This provides the insurer with the excuse to go looking for those defects. A house built 25 years ago would have been built in a time when the construction standards were different. Insurers agreed to insure these properties in full knowledge of these facts, so their argument of non-compliance is simply another instance of bad faith. Nevertheless, in some cases, insurers send builders to properties to look at the building from a 'date of build' perspective. Reports are then written about the structures in terms of their non-compliant aspects and the private insurer attempts to bully the homeowner into accepting financial responsibility for the alleged non-compliance. A new house or present-day repairs must be built to modern standards, using modern construction methods and codes, and the cost of meeting these usually exceeds the cost of repairing or rebuilding to a 25-year-old standard. Insurers are regularly heard to say there is to be 'no betterment' in the work carried out. Clearly 'betterment' is unavoidable in these situations and usually required by law if the codes are to be met. This is not imposed by the property owner (although it is their contractual right to do so) but by the present building regulations.

Despite the fact that each insured has a primary exclusive contractual relationship with their insurer, the majority of the private insurers have hired the services of a major construction company to front their repair operations. Some insurers have then presented 'Project Management Agreements' (PMAs) to policyholders prior to the commencement of any repair or rebuild work, with the inference that it was a requirement for policyholders to sign the agreement. The Project Manager of the designated contracting firms typically arrives at the doorstep with the PMA in one hand and a packet of biscuits in the other. (Apparently this assists public relations – and the homeowner has to make the tea)! Many homeowners, including the author, who held an IAG/State policy, were told that if they did not sign the PMA then work simply would not commence or we "might find ourselves at the bottom of the list". The PMAs contained many onerous clauses, legally severed the homeowner completely from the insurer and established a contract only between the builder/repairer and the policyholder, with no redress back to the insurer in the case that the work was not satisfactory. This move left unsuspecting homeowners in a vulnerable position vis-à-vis their contractual rights and few really understood what they were signing. A Christchurch solicitor warned that insured homeowners were at risk of being hit with onerous legal clauses for the rebuild of their quake-damaged houses. Labour Member of Parliament Clayton Cosgrove said there were significant issues with IAG's contracts, particularly over indemnity and altering an agreed work plan. He told the companies that quake victims, who were "going through the mill", should not have to pay lawyers to keep insurance companies honest. Time and money was spent clarifying the justified reasons for not signing the project-management agreements until finally it was agreed that some of the private insurers were enforcing onerous additional terms on policyholders. These agreements were then simplified, but with the same object in mind, before being scrapped altogether when the general public became more aware of the insurance company agendas.

Insurers have 'preferred contractors' because they are simply cost-effective from the insurance company's viewpoint. They will often negotiate low rates and shift the contractual relationship insurers have with the policyholder to the builder. From the homeowner's viewpoint, preferred contractors have the potential to cause considerable complications. The insurer may send contractors who ask the homeowner to sign their paperwork and that they will then handle everything. This would likely give the impression that the contractor is operating for the insurance company, which is not the case. The contractor is contracted with and working for the person who signs and consequently that person (homeowner) is going to be responsible for resolving the various problems that may arise. Any oversight is deemed to be the homeowner's responsibility. This is far from an ideal position to be in.

It is not uncommon for private insurers to offer what appear to be very generous replacement terms in their policies, often without a sum-insured limit. They might promise to rebuild or repair your house to an 'as new' condition or pay the cost of rebuilding your house as new in the same or similar construction and style. However, some companies attempt to convince or 'encourage' claimants to take much less than actual full replacement. Policies often contain clauses limiting the obligation to replace using "commonly available materials" – rather disappointing if your rimu villa is destroyed. Sometimes the policies contain clauses that say that the insurance company does not have to replace 'exactly' what was. Once an insurance company agrees to replace a house, it cannot force the owner to accept something of a lesser quality, though there are stories of people settling for a smaller-square-metre rebuild in order to simply move on. If a house had wooden window frames, that is what should be installed, and cedar tongue-and-groove flooring likewise, even if it costs more. The insurance company cannot and should not force a policyholder to take aluminium window frames or particle-board floors because it is cheaper for the insurance company.

Homeowners usually purchase 'replacement cost' insurance, which is supposed to meet the full cost of repairing or replacing an item even if that cost is currently greater than the item's current value. For example, under a policy of this sort, the homeowner should get a new heat pump rather than having to make up the difference between the actual depreciated cash value of the old heat pump and the price of a new one. The discrepancies between the way in which the various insurers calculate the sums involved, are enormous. State (IAG), for instance, does not pay all professional costs for a rebuild as a matter of course; it will pay them only if they are necessary and with a 'package home' they are often not essential. Nor will they include the cost of project management fees by their mandated and preferred contracting firms in the replacement value.

After six years, it now appears that insurance companies are less and less prepared to honour the financial burden of massive damage despite having collected Cantabrians' premiums to do just that. This is further evidenced by the need for and outcome of the High Court Decision (Wellington CIV-2011-485-1137), which declared that the EQC is responsible for the first NZD 100,000 of every 'new event' earthquake. As a result of that Decision, the private insurers minimised their liability and the Government will pay a large chunk of the losses sustained by the Canterbury region. In addition, a large proportion of the losses are borne by the homeowners themselves through low-ball pay-outs. The insurance company profits continue to rise. Subtracting the amount insurers paid in claims, from the net amount they earned in premiums, insurers made NZD 1.56 billion in 2014. This is 17 percent more than they made in 2013, and 54 percent more than they made in the year prior to the Canterbury earthquakes (2009).[10]

The examples given above are only a smattering of the long list of issues that have arisen and there is no doubt that the list will continue to grow. Due to space constraints I have not included all the issues around commercial property, though one of the major issues which has emerged relates to Contingent Business Interruption Coverage (CBI). While business-interruption coverage is designed to indemnify an insured for business income losses sustained due to damage or destruction of the insured's own property, contingent business-interruption coverage provides indemnity for business income losses that the insured sustains due to damage or destruction of another's property. Many businesses in today's global economy are contingent or dependent on other business entities, such as customers or suppliers.

CBI coverage protects a company whose income is largely derived from these dependent properties. Typically, coverage is provided to an insured under CBI insurance when a supplier or customer suffers a direct physical loss that interrupts the insured's own business, resulting in a loss of earnings. A related category of coverage to CBI coverage is *contingent extra expense* coverage, which generally provides coverage for the extra expenses or increases in costs that the insured incurs as a result of the physical loss or damage to a supplier or customer. The perils insured against are those covered by the insured's own policy, not by any policies purchased by the insured's customers and suppliers. In Christchurch, issues have developed around policy cover not being sufficient. Problems arose when, for example, Civil Defence informed business owners that they could not have access to their business premises for a period of six months as they were within the central city cordoned red zone. As a consequence, small business owners began to experience real difficulties with their insurers over claims for stock 'irretrievable' from business premises they were not allowed to access. The word 'irretrievable' is defined by one insurance company (State) as unable to access or sell stock or retrieve contents. Irretrievability is considered on a case-by-case basis according to the insurer. Legal opinion suggests that if a building has been red-stickered (was unsafe and was to be demolished) and a business owner is unable to legally access it and retrieve the stock, this constitutes irretrievability. However, where stock is not damaged and the building is not going to be demolished it would be unlikely that a claim could be made for lost stock. Business owners unable to access their stock in a building that was not going to be demolished found themselves in a very precarious situation, with their capital tied up and threatening the viability of their business. Further problems then arose around definitions of 'inaccessibility' and where that becomes 'irretrievability'.

For those who had not taken business-interruption insurance the future looked bleak, as they were also uninsured for the February 22 earthquake. In the event that the insurer agreed to pay-out on contents claims, if the stock was later retrievable, the stock would become the property of that particular insurer. Delays to progress were further hampered around the city due to the hold-up created while insurance assessors approved the removal costs associated with removal of rubble. An estimated 4.5 million tonnes of rubble needed to be moved.

The February earthquake had an enormous impact on the business community. On February 22, 2012, many of those policyholders reached the end of their Business Interruption and Contingent Business Interruption insurance, which caused another wave of businesses to go into receivership and business owners to leave the central city or relocate to its periphery. It became unaffordable for them to do anything else. The list of problems for businesses is still enormous. Of those who left for the perimeter, or moved West, how many are likely to return after six years of more?

'What about the public's involvement in insurance fraud' I hear the insurers cry? Insurers have expended much effort to paint themselves as continual victims of fraud by the public, to persuade the public and regulators that the only real insurance fraud that takes place is fraud against them. It is well past the time that insurance fraud perpetrated by insurance companies should also be readily prosecuted and the insurers punished appropriately by the use of substantial exemplary damages. The American courts have been ruthless in their use of exemplary damages against dishonest insurers. Unfortunately, either by government design or poor legislation, the New Zealand courts have not until recently been economically accessible to the general public for class actions (see Chapter 6, Policyholder Protection) against insurance corporations and this fact, well known to the insurers, has emboldened many of them to the point where they deal with claimants with dishonesty and impunity. That scenario is still working its way out in Christchurch and will lead to many years of grief and will ensure slow recovery for the Garden City.

Conclusion

The Canterbury experience has taught many of us that the insurance companies are not our friends. They do not have policyholder interests at heart. Their systems are not designed to make friends, but to maximise profits. The pictures they paint of themselves are in stark contrast to who they actually are. The worst insurers will of course, quickly acquire a reputation for failing to pay claims and as a consequence are likely to have a harder time attracting customers. The risk is that a few major players, such as IAG, will obtain a major hold on the market, leaving policy purchasers with little choice but to fall victim to their ever-reducing standards of protection. The Commerce Commission and the Financial Regulatory Authority appears to be looking the other way and allowing this to occur. In the meantime, policyholders must protect themselves where they can by thoroughly checking everything their insurers tell them – particularly about repair costs and the extent of damage and if at all possible, avoid doing business with companies that have a track record of anti-consumer behaviour. Gary Dransfield, former chief executive of Vero Insurance, stated:

> The thing that's most exciting about insurance is it's one
> of those few industries where you get to help people at
> their time of greatest need.[11]

Yeah, right, Mr Dransfield! In 'normal times' successive governments have done little to contribute to the benefits and have sought to limit the large costs associated with consumer protection in the insurance domain, despite the fact that they could legitimately have done so in a seismic country such as New Zealand. The result has been that commercial asymmetries and 'sharp practice' have come to favour the insurance corporations, many of whom are foreign-owned and have no allegiance to the people of New Zealand. Consequently, in the interests of retaining some semblance of 'action on behalf of the people', it is in Government's interests to speed up the Class Action Bill at the very least. In exceptional times, such as those we continue to experience in Canterbury, justice and fair-dealing for those with legitimate grievances are made even more difficult when government becomes complicit in mandating rules which further disadvantage policyholders; for example, buying private property for diminished values and relaxing requirements associated with acceptable building standards (foundation damage tolerances in Canterbury have now been successively relaxed three times since the September 2010 quake) to the financial advantage of insurers. The ability for owners to assert their property rights quickly becomes compromised and anyone could be forgiven for holding the view that government itself is complicit in the insurance corporates' disregard for fair-dealing and their contribution to the slowness of the recovery of Christchurch and the misery of its citizens.

Citizens Speak

Their Finest Hour? I was quoted on Facebook in relation to my view on what the insurance industry should be post-earthquake; *"it should be their finest hour"* is what I said.

Well, the hours have become days, the days weeks and the weeks years. Houses remain broken and health for the majority of Cantabrians has deteriorated over the last half decade. It has been saddening that fellow Cantabrians have suffered because of the actions, processes and lack of commitment from the EQC and Insurers. The EQC and Insurers have been comfortable to provide reasons why they couldn't do more; but sometimes YOU HAVE TO do more, be better, get stronger, climb Everest, sail in a Waka across a vast ocean, and win a Rugby World Cup... This was an opportunity for an industry that I know well and understand, to shine and demonstrate why it is a critical and needed component of any financial economy; and to deliver the promises that they freely made.

Without the surety and guarantees that Insurance provides, our economy would fail; indeed it wouldn't exist *"as we know it Jim"*. Much has been written over the centuries about the benefits of insurance and you may want to read further on that, if it perks your interest; the Yangtze River and Fire of London are 'time stamped' moments in insurance history.

My expectations were high - some will call me foolish but I still 'believe' and sincerely hope that the New Zealand Insurance industry finds a way to crawl out of the huge hole they have dug for themselves because of their behaviour. Expectations were high, because that is what was advertised, sold and promised by Insurers. In the late 1980's NZI (IAG) promised you would never have to have *'half-a-pyramid'* when you bought Peace of Mind cover and a decade or so later they sold insurance with the help of Dickens - *'it was the epoch of belief, it was the epoch of incredulity…'*. It was a great campaign and NZI were rightly proud of it. I worked for them at this time and we were taught the significance and relationship to insurance of what Dickens wrote. Well where the bloody hell are the actions that fully and unreservedly meet those words now?

Insurance works! Scott and Rebecca moved into their house just a few days ago and we shared a few beers and pizza to celebrate. It was the first time their daughter had ever had her own home because she was born not long after the February earthquake of 2011.

Insurance works! Stella and The China Kitchen kept their reputation intact and showed love and caring to their customers that has allowed their business to be healthy and fully recovered within a year of the earthquake.

However, like Mr & Mrs Scott, Bernie, Fiona, Craig, Rose, Rob and thousands more Scott, Rebecca and Stella's had to drive their insurance claim and overcome tears, anger, uncertainty and the possibility of potential financial ruin before they received the indemnity that their insurance cover provided; what it promised!!

I am angry, upset, frustrated on a daily basis because I'm human! But like all 'good' Cantabrians and fellow New Zealanders I've tried to lift myself above those feelings to recover. Recover personally, recover in Christchurch, recover as a Nation, recover as one of the larger insured events in history.

Solutions are presented to the EQC and Insurers on an hourly basis; I continue in the hope that some 'good' insurance people will be brave enough and caring enough to change. It should be their finest hour.

By Dean Lester.[12]

CHAPTER 6

POLICYHOLDER PROTECTION

- -

Justice and costs cannot be pitted against one another: justice must be considered on its own terms and cost must be borne by the state that wishes to call itself just.

Zoe Williams[1]

When it became clear that the difficulties I was having with my insurer, IAG (State Insurance), were not being resolved, I began to look into avenues that might assist in helping me to resolve those issues, for instance their continuing refusal after almost 20 months to provide us with an accommodation allowance despite the fact that we were unable to live in our home. I was quickly to discover that in the event of difficulties with an insurer there are few places a person can go that will assist in protecting their contractual rights. I was shocked to discover how 'on our own' we policyholders really are. It appears that, on the whole, complaints authorities work only for 'business-as-usual situations', where the sums at stake are not large. In cases of catastrophe, where total loss is common, most of these authorities are not in a position to hear the complaint and can provide only limited assistance to the insured in insurance disputes.

An insurer's ability to sell insurance is based on the policyholder's belief that in the event they suffer loss, the insurer will make good on the contract. However, insurers' reputations and marketing representations do not often accurately reflect the true nature of their claims-handling practices. As well, it is extremely difficult to find evidence of their 'track records' in relation to claims complaints made by policyholders.

Most complaint schemes have the capacity to hear only disputes of up to NZD 200,000 plus GST and many of the complaints authorities concern themselves only with registered participants, which most of the major insurers are not. As the recent Christchurch experience indicates, ruined property, and claims discrepancies are often higher than NZD 200,000 plus GST. Bear in mind that the average house price in Christchurch is now approximately NZD 482,000. The only option unhappy claimants with disputes over NZD 200,000 have, is to refer the case to the High Court. This is a very time-consuming (a case may not be heard for a year or two) and expensive exercise with uncertain outcomes. Very few people are in a position to risk tens or hundreds of thousands of dollars on the chance that they may win the case against their insurer. Litigation tends to be too slow, too costly and too stressful for those who have recently suffered major financial loss. Insurers can only be well aware of this fact.

The cost of justice today informs the cost of justice in the future in New Zealand. The cost of justice is no longer a debate around the provision of legal aid for the poor, it has now become a debate around legal aid for the middle classes. The reality of the situation where one is faced with a legal dispute has become one of having to risk perhaps even your home if you are to seek court redress as costs are now unpredictable and may be out of all proportion to the value of the dispute. I attribute the blame to the Government, the Judiciary and to the legal profession. I am reminded that while searching for legal counsel to represent us in the High Court, a well-known insurance lawyer told us that *"justice is no longer for the middle class"*, followed by the statement that it would cost NZD 800,000 to represent us and that *"we simply weren't wealthy enough"* to have our day in court. So why has this situation developed? One reason is that the judiciary's Rules Committee has expanded the technical, detailed and prescriptive procedural requirements which have increased the costs of litigation. What we have seen transpire in the court process is that when there are disagreements between the two contesting parties' expert engineers or quantity surveyors for example, the court sends the experts off to 'come to an agreement'. More often than not, agreement cannot be reached, usually because the parties are working on the basis of two different repair standards - the insurance policy standard (the homeowners policy) and the insurers 'adopted' standard (the MBIE Guidelines in the Christchurch scenario). Rarely do the parties reach agreement. In the interim the homeowner is being charged tens of thousands of dollars in legal and professional fees while this process takes place. Involved is the production of extensive written reports and briefs and the need for mandatory filing of prior written submissions and memoranda. In order to prove their case, homeowners usually have to bear the upfront costs associated with this work. In addition, there are what can only be described as exorbitant lawyers' fees, from many lawyers who charge on an hourly basis at rates in excess of NZD 360.00 an hour. This is the real reason litigation is unaffordable - lawyers are paid by the hour, without an upper limit and regardless of the outcome. A very comfortable earning machine which also rewards inefficiency! Lawyers are justly deserving of the criticism that often comes their way. In addition there are also those lawyers who charge fees based on the amount at stake in the litigation. On examination of the situation in Christchurch, it is clear that there has been a failure, purposeful or otherwise, to tailor court processes to suit insurance cases and the impact that has, by way of high and unnecessary costs for the policyholder, is enormous. Then there are the common issues around delays in the delivery of Judgements and the appeal process, which once again cost the litigants both financially and emotionally. This also casts doubt on the efficiency of the processes and the efficacy of the hearings. There is a particular focus on excessive use of expert witnesses who actually duplicate the lawyer's job of presenting submissions. There is also the issue of intolerable court congestion. Homeowners on the current 'earthquake' court list will be waiting upwards of a year for their case to be heard - this after an already five year wait! The Earthquake List was set up in May 2012 to manage litigation arising from the earthquakes. As at 30 September 2015, 61 percent of general proceedings in the Courts deals with earthquake cases. Since the list was established 437 earthquake related proceedings have been filed and placed on the list. There are currently 227 active cases.[2] Many of those cases will not be heard for another two or more years.

So what other options are there? Most complaints schemes also require that an insured's insurance company is a signed-up member before an insured is able to utilise the scheme – examples include the Financial Dispute Resolution (the reserve scheme) and Financial Services Complaints Ltd. It would appear that most of the larger insurers are not listed in these schemes, and it does not require much imagination to determine why this might be the case!

Insurance internal disputes departments often have inadequate resources to meaningfully review claims and the reviews they conduct tend to be biased in favour of the insurers. Prior to invoking external review, insurers typically require that the complainant exhaust the insurer's internal review process. This is also an effective way of keeping the insurers 'dirty laundry' from the public gaze and inevitably greatly extends the timeframe, to the insurer's total advantage. All documents, information and correspondence which are generated as a result of that process are likely to form part of any record which later goes to an external review body.

The main dispute-resolution organisations in New Zealand for insurance matters are those covered in the paragraphs below, but it is evident that not enough is available and accessible to deal with the innate power imbalance between the insured and the corporate insurer.

Insurance and Savings Ombudsman (ISO): A number of insurance and savings companies participate in the Insurance and Savings Ombudsman scheme, including members of the Insurance Council of New Zealand, Health Funds Association of New Zealand, and the Investment Savings and Insurance Association of New Zealand. The ISO is the most common scheme utilised by insurers. Membership fees are either based on the company's gross written premium or number of contracts. There is no joining fee. The scheme has a jurisdictional limit of NZD 200,000 (i.e. NZD 200,000 + GST, GST does apply to the rebuilding and repair of homes, so the limit is actually NZD 230,000) and can only exceed that sum by agreement from both parties to the dispute. It is not in the interests of the insurance company to agree to this, as forcing a claimant to seek legal advice and forcing them to go to the High Court can strengthen an insurer's position. The scheme currently charges a flat fee of NZD 1,000 plus GST for each complaint investigated.[3] The Insurance and Savings Ombudsman is reputed to be an 'independent' authority; however, it is in actuality a joint venture among insurers. Is this really independence? Like many such services in New Zealand (e.g. the Banking Ombudsman), the service is funded by the industry itself. This surely is in need of revision; many would argue that 'self-regulation' is biased and amounts to no regulation at all.

The ISO considers complaints regarding all types of personal and domestic insurances, and savings services. The scheme is free of charge for insured people, and the Ombudsman's decision is binding upon the insurance company involved in the dispute.

If the Ombudsman recommends the insurance company should make a payment to the complainant, the complainant may only accept the payment if they agree not to take any further action on the matter without the insurance company's consent. This is usually referred to as 'full and final settlement'. If the complainant agrees to the Ombudsman's recommendation the Ombudsman may make an award of money against the insurance company.

The Ombudsman will not consider complaints that would be better dealt with by a court or other body; or where the complainant has not brought the matter to the attention of the insurance company concerned; or where a dispute has been previously considered (unless new evidence is available). Nor will they consider an issue that has already been considered by a court or any other body; or where the issue at hand is considered to be being pursued in a trivial, frivolous or vexatious manner or in bad faith; or one that relates to an insurance company's commercial judgement; nor matters relating to methods or procedures for determining prices or premiums payable; nor matters that relate to an insurance company's decision to impose conditions or limitations on a policy, or terminate or refuse cover under an existing policy or agreement as a result of alleged material non-disclosure. There are clearly many impediments to assistance! Anecdotal evidence suggests that insurers do not like going to the Ombudsman, so they tend to try to settle before an issue goes that far.

While member companies must accept the Ombudsman's ruling, claimants have the right to take their case through to the disputes tribunal (for disputes under NZD 15,000) or the courts should the Ombudsman not provide an acceptable ruling and if the matter falls within the jurisdiction of those bodies.

The Insurance and Savings Ombudsman's website states that in 2010 there were 1,985 inquiries made and that 334 of these complaints could not be heard as they were outside the Ombudsman's jurisdiction. Only 284 of the complaints were investigated and it took 96 days on average to settle a complaint. One has to ask is the Ombudsman's service providing the kind of service people need? The website further states that in 2010, 67 percent of people lost their case with their insurer; 16 percent of people settled with their insurer before the hearing and 14 percent of people 'won' against their insurer. Three percent of people 'partly won' their case. As of 17 November, 2011 there had been 350 inquiries from Canterbury related to the earthquake; of those, 14 had gone through as formal complaints. As of February 2014 their *"dedicated Canterbury Earthquake Response Team has dealt with over 1300 compliant enquiries"*. Of the complaints made, 40 percent have had positive outcomes for consumers. People using the Ombudsmen's service have claimed that it is a slow and stressful process. In addition, the premise upon which the Ombudsman works places a burden of proof on the claimant to show that the insurance company involved is operating outside the policy wording. Given the 'abstract' policy wording present in many policies, proof can be an elusive target!

The courts: The District Court can hear cases under NZD 200,000. Anything above NZD 200,000 is heard in the High Court. Insurance law has a list of remedies that are available to successful claimants that include award of lawyers' fees, and emotional distress damages. Punitive or exemplary damages are still unclear in relation to insurance. This, too, needs a test case, as in New Zealand, unlike in the USA, it is still undecided. So it is as yet not possible to receive punitive/exemplary damages for a 'bad faith' or overtly dishonest handling of a claim as it is in the USA, where the courts take these matters very seriously.[4] In many cases insurance companies have paid a very high price for their underhand dealings. In addition, the New Zealand courts often stop short of finding that insurers acted in breach of their duty of good faith in order to avoid becoming embroiled in the murky waters of the good-faith debate.

So insurance litigation arguably provides poor compensation for most aggrieved policyholders not because the remedies available are inadequate, but more because litigation is slow, costly and unpredictable, while policyholders generally require compensation quickly to relieve them of their current circumstances. Damages available include compensatory damages for breaches of the insurance contract and pecuniary losses (such as where the insurer's failure to indemnify has caused the insured to incur costs in renting alternative accommodation or where the insurer's failure has caused the insured to default on loans and incur penalty interest). Damages are also available for non-pecuniary losses (such as physical inconvenience and mental distress).

The cost of court hearings is now so high in New Zealand that few ordinary citizens have either the emotional or financial resources to devote to litigation. In other countries, where there is large-scale discontent, often after natural disasters, 'class actions' become commonplace and after Hurricane Katrina in the USA, they were used extensively to good effect.[5] Class actions spread the cost of legal fees across a group of people. In New Zealand, however, class actions are structured less favourably than in the USA. For instance, in New Zealand there are higher upfront costs and more 'downside risks' for plaintiffs, which explains the more restrained use of class actions here. It requires a significant number of class members to agree to share upfront costs and the downside exposure in order to attain any real cost-spreading benefit. Another complication that arises is whether the questions to be tried are considered common to the class or group of people as opposed to requiring proof on an individual basis. If person-by-person proof is needed (as is often the case with insurance), it is unlikely that a class action claim will succeed.

On the whole, litigation is considered by most as 'risky' and people in New Zealand tend to be risk adverse. So insurers generally hold the upper hand in settlement negotiations and know it. As a result, litigants often settle with their insurer for considerably less than they are entitled to. As well, unsuccessful class action plaintiffs must pay a portion of the defendant's legal bill. It is also the case that insurers artificially delay the litigation process, sometimes by years, to exploit their strategic advantage. A parliamentary report into finance company failures[6] has recommended fast tracking a draft Class Action Bill (on the agenda since 2009), making it easier for out-of-pocket investors to take class actions.[7] As Helen Macfarlane, a Senior Associate of Hesketh Henry, states:

> Class actions certainly further worthwhile objectives – they promote efficient use of the courts by avoiding the need to try multiple individual actions and reduce the likelihood of inconsistent findings in different individual cases. They can also serve to level the playing field by allowing a group of less affluent individuals to call more wealthy institutions to account, something that the difference in means between the parties might otherwise preclude.[8]

The Ministry of Justice was to prepare a report to the Minister of Justice, the Attorney-General, and the Minister for Courts, providing information on the Rules Committee's proposal, outlining a proposed work programme, and seeking an indication of the Minister who will lead this reform. That was in July 2009 - seven years ago! There seems no reason why the Bill should not extend to cover insurance actions. Why is it that the Class Actions Bill is still languishing in the shadows? Perhaps the fingers of corporatism are extending into government again?

In Christchurch, the District Court has also established a little-publicized procedure. It can be downloaded from www.justice.govt.nz/courts/civil/forms#1, filled in and delivered (two copies) to 100 Orchard Road near the Christchurch airport. The fee is NZD 170.00. This has the effect of forcing EQC and/or insurers to face a judge who can hear the insurance contract issue and decide upon remedies. If the complaints claim is accepted by the Court, the respondent, i.e. the insurer, must respond within ten days. But, again, the claim must fall under NZD 200,000.

Disputes tribunals: These are informal as there are no lawyers or judges. A referee hears a dispute. Any ruling they make is binding and will, if necessary, be enforced by the courts. A claim can only be NZD 15,000 or less (or NZD 20,000 if both parties agree), so this provides very limited recourse. The procedure is designed to be 'quick and dirty' and is often short on legal rigour.

Arbitration and mediation: The Arbitration and Mediation Institute of New Zealand (AMINZ) originated as a branch of the Chartered Institute of Arbitrators (UK) in 1979 and became the Arbitrators' Institute of New Zealand in 1987. In 1996 it merged with the Mediators Institute of New Zealand to become AMINZ. It is New Zealand's professional association for those practising in dispute resolution, including arbitrators, adjudicators, mediators, conciliators and facilitators.[9]

Mediation has been used successfully in other countries after natural disasters as a way of coping with many thousands of disgruntled claimants. Mediations too, have proven to be only a partial solution or alternative to the court process and have often resulted in lawyers settling for less than the homeowner's entitlement and to homeowners often being gently pressurized into acceptance and moving on. The unprincipled conduct which often prevails in mediation, will often lead to an unjust settlement that the policyholder is pressured to accept. Mediation like other alternative dispute-resolution processes, is not a closely policed process. The unregulated practice of mediation does present some risk of abuse by those who use it. Mediation may be abused by businesses that use it for purposes other than the resolution of disputes. Some argue that the mediation process can be or is used to stall litigation or to reduce legitimate obligations to pay. Parties sometimes also use mediation to conduct 'fishing expeditions' to discover how prepared the other side is for a full trial. Mediations have also been found to be frequently unsuccessful at convincing insurers to compromise.

In New Zealand currently, an insurer would have to agree to join a mediation or arbitration forum. In post-earthquake Christchurch an advisory service was set up to assist homeowners facing challenges in getting their home repaired or rebuilt. ICNZ members contributed NZD 300,000 for the Residential Advisory Service (RAS)[10]. In addition, insurers have been invited to fund a new service called Breakthrough which is said to be a free facilitation service to help homeowners and insurers in the resolution of their insurance claims, setup in association with Southern Response. With major Insurance funding one must question the 'independence' of these services. A trust, the Canterbury Insurance Assistance Service (CIAS) was also set up to assist victims resolve problems associated with the earthquakes.[11] There is evidence from other countries that in times of need, particularly after natural disasters, governments have insisted insurers take part in alternative dispute-resolution processes, for example Hurricanes Katrina, Rita and Ivan as well as claims for asbestos injuries, and bankruptcies in the USA. Insurers around the world are being held to greater account, e.g. in Australia the Queensland Floods Commission of Inquiry was required to examine the performance of private insurers in meeting their claims responsibilities. This involved an inquiry into the performance of private insurers in processing and deciding flood-related claims, including timeliness of processing claims; the adequacy of the assessment process; the adequacy of communication between the insurer and the insured; the adequacy of the complaints processes about the claims; and whether any potential claimants have been inappropriately dissuaded from lodging or pursuing a claim. The House of Representatives Standing Committee on Social Policy and Legal Affairs in Australia examined the performance of the insurance industry in assessing claims following the 2010/2011 extreme weather events. The Parliamentary Committee also inquired into the insurance-related matters arising out of Cyclone Yasi and other non-flood-related disaster events.[12] Australia would appear to be having the same problems with their insurance industry – and after all, the insurance corporates involved there are the same companies operating in Canterbury. All around the world people are finding the industry, in times of catastrophe, to be fundamentally flawed and often dishonest.

It did not take long before international 'disaster insurance recovery' organisations (public adjusters) such as Risk Worldwide and WorldClaim entered the scene in Canterbury. A public adjuster is an insurance claims adjuster (or company) who advocates for the policyholder in appraising and negotiating a claimant's insurance claim directly with the insurer. When the American public adjusters first swung into town not long after the earthquakes, many people were very sceptical about their presence – me included. In fact, my view was that they were little more than vultures, coming to feed on the misfortunes of homeowners, whilst simultaneously making 'big bucks' from the pickings. But as time went by and I met with these groups and learned about their processes and the bottlenecks, I came to the understanding that there are very few insurance specialists in Christchurch who know the 'ins and outs' of the insurance business and the nature of the corporate games. The public adjusters demonstrated a consummate knowledge of the business we were dealing with and the dishonest tactics by the insurers that required serious expertise to address the problems. Few local lawyers could come close in expertise. What is not so well known is that public adjusters are usually able to secure a far better settlement than most professionals doing similar work would be able to achieve. Primarily, they are experts in appraising the damage, preparing estimates and other claims documentation, reading the policy of insurance to determine coverage, and negotiating with the insurance company's claims handler or lawyers.

The emergence of such companies is in itself clear evidence that private insurance is not working for people. These events also lead one to question what is the government's fiduciary responsibility toward its citizens in respect of such exploitation? As research around the world shows, New Zealand is behind the times in terms of ensuring its citizens are protected post-disaster.

Complaints authorities could be vastly improved with the implementation of a truly independent government entity, the sole function of which would be to resolve consumers' disputes with financial service providers generally, including insurers. Consumers should be able to lodge complaints with such a body against their financial service providers, free of charge and without representation if so desired. The public identity of this body would allow it to manage decision-maker bias, while at the same time its independence from insurers and regulators would counteract the problems of perceived and actual bias.

Natural disasters tend to produce very large numbers of claimants, resulting in large numbers of disputes. It is clear from evidence around the globe that natural disasters produce considerable tensions between private insurers and locally affected populations. Neither private insurers nor complaints-handling authorities are equipped to cope with and manage effectively the numbers of disputes involved. Instead, other mechanisms are required to assist in cases where there are many hundreds, or thousands, of disaffected claimants. Without such a change, policyholders have few realistic options for challenging an insurer's adverse coverage determination.

After the natural disasters of recent times in the USA, state-sponsored mediation programmes were arranged to assist with the massive number of claims and the ever-rising backlog that emerged as a result of deliberate slow settlement by insurance companies. After the Florida storms of 2004 and 2005 there was an 86 percent settlement rate and 14 percent impasse; after the 2004 storms 90 percent settled and a 10 percent impasse settlement; after the 2005 storms 81 percent settled and a 19 percent impasse settlement. More than 25,000 mediation requests resulted.[13] The average settlement was USD 23,058 and the settlement range was between USD 50 to USD 1.5 million. In addition the estimated settlement amounts as of May 2007 totalled USD 374 million.[14] After Hurricane Katrina, insurers agreed, with some 'government encouragement', to take part in dispute resolution. On December 20, 2005, Mississippi instituted Emergency Rule 2005-2. The programme resulted in over 3,400 insured's claims disputes being resolved and saw an 83 percent successful resolution of all insurance claims that participated in this Mississippi Insurance Department, Hurricane Katrina Mediation Programme. For those claimants who were already in legal proceedings with their insurers, the Commissioner of Insurance went on to adopt Insurance Department Regulation 2006-4, which enabled the Court to order any party in litigation to participate in the Mississippi Department of Insurance Hurricane Katrina Mediation Programme. This programme also achieved an approximately 50 percent success rate. This was subsequently followed by Emergency Regulation 2007-3, which established a non-binding arbitration programme for 'personal lines' residential insurance claims arising from Hurricane Katrina.[15] One would have to question why mediation and arbitration action on such a large scale was necessary. Naturally these methods of resolving policyholders' claims did not hold favour with the insurance industry.

On December 22, 2005, Louisiana promulgated Emergency Rule 22[16] which also established a hurricane mediation programme.[17] Both programmes named the American Arbitration Association as programme administrator, and both stated the conditions for mediating and the procedures to be followed. Both rules required the mediator to satisfy its state criteria for mediators in terms of experience and education and called for the insurers to pay all costs associated with the mediation. Private insurers were required to participate. All cases were handled without counsel on either side, but legal representatives from the Attorney General's office were on hand to respond to legal and procedural questions. The Hurricane Andrew programme[18] had an arbitration option as well, if agreed upon by both the claimant and the insurer. Within one year more than 1,900 cases had been handled by the American Arbitration Association[19] with a 92 percent settlement rate. During 1996, approximately 2,400 claims had been handled.[20] The programmes are often conducted by external organisations with which the department has a standing agreement and show much better rates of claim resolution than ordinary regulatory mediation. As of December 25, 2008, more than 730,000 insurance claims had been filed for damages sustained from Hurricane Ike.[21]

Issues that were considered appropriate for mediation included: scope of loss; mandated building code upgrades; dwelling versus other structures; pre-existing damage versus proximate cause; additional living expense; asbestos abatement; earthquake versus aftershock; hidden damages; and proof of loss and other personal property issues. Issues considered inappropriate for mediation included coverage issues (e.g., the absence of earthquake coverage, and other underwriting issues involving under-insurance, failure to insure, cancellation, non-renewal and rating issues); legal interpretations of policy provisions and terms; the statute of limitations and contractual limitations on filing periods; claims in excess of policy limits in the absence of Full Replacement Coverage; allegations of bad faith, and other demands for extra contractual payments, including under-insurance.

The programmes in the USA have since been extended to cover commercial claims, though somewhat modified as a consequence of a number of factors not present in the residential programme. In many of the commercial cases, lawyers were present. In many other cases, public adjusters (an insurance claims adjuster who is an advocate for the policyholder in appraising and negotiating a first party insurance claim) appear on behalf of the insured or with the insured. Interestingly, payment was made immediately if the parties reached a settlement. The insurance representative was required to appear with a blank cheque in hand. If not immediate, payment would have to be made within a few days. Any issues relating to the power-imbalance problem between the insurer and insured were addressed in some of these programmes by the inclusion of a government staff attorney in the mediation process. No doubt there is an appreciable effect on the mediation process when the government insurance regulator is sitting in the room.

The insurance mediation process has proved that is has the potential to be a valuable tool for homeowners pursuing resolution with their insurer or trying to break deadlocks. As longer settlement timeframes favour the industry, resolution requires both the support and understanding from government and the judiciary, remembering that pressure is on the insured parties to resolve their claim, because in many instances, claimants will depend on those funds to repair not just their property, but also their lives.

The major advantage of mediation to the insured would be the speed of settlement. In the context of a property claim, this can be particularly important to the insured, who likely needs every dollar of the settlement to effect repairs to their property or to make alternative living arrangements. In addition, development of an alternative dispute-resolution programme would have to be implemented rapidly. New Zealand is fortunate in that it has a good number of trained mediators and there would seem to be no impediment in the form of lack of suitable personnel to operate such a programme. This would also ensure that the already clogged judicial system would not be further inundated with a large number of unresolved homeowner insurance claims gathering dust, and more interest for insurers. As of November 1, 2012 the EQC Mediation Service was administered by AMINZ.[22]

Obviously the legal system could never reasonably be expected to complete the incredible volume of proceedings resulting from disputes from a disaster of the size of the Canterbury earthquakes within reasonable timeframes, even if citizens could afford to use that system. The Christchurch District Court system was facing a backlog of around 5,000 cases as a result of the earthquake damage to buildings. In addition, the courts lack the basic tools required to deal with plaintiffs' often difficult circumstances. Litigation does not have the prospective ability to assist the affected citizens regain balance and recreate their future. If the full benefits of mediation are to be realised in times of major disaster, programmes should be set up in advance, plans for staffing must be in place, and constant improvements need to be sought to provide and maintain a level playing field on which the parties can negotiate. One thing of which seismic New Zealand can be certain is that there will be further major events and the lessons of Christchurch need to be learned and solutions found and implemented.

So what is the solution? A 'public adjuster? In hindsight I believe that a policyholder is better served using the services of public adjusters, where there is little experience of insurance law by professionals – as in Christchurch. Public adjusters know how to play the game and generally achieve a much better result for home owners than a general practice lawyer. Most public adjusters are paid based on a percentage of the total settlement. Some charge a flat percentage, while others use a regressive scale. For example, 25 percent of the first NZD 100,000, 15 percent between NZD 100,001 and NZD 200,000, and 10 percent of any amount beyond that. Regardless of the fee structure, the fee may be offset by their ability to produce an increase in the settlement amount. But like any profit orientated venture, they are only as good as the people working for them.

All of the above methods of possible settlement have their limitations. My method of choice for large numbers of affected policyholders is the class or group action. Class action litigation allows individuals access to the courts by pooling a large number of claims which would not have been financially viable for the claimants individually and very importantly it holds the promise of a more level playing field on which powerful defendants (such as the Government, private insurers and banks) can be held to account. Class, group or representative actions ('class action') have flourished in the USA and Canada and are also on the rise in Australia after the Federal Court of Australia Act was amended in 1992 to introduce 'representative proceedings'. I fervently believe that a class action regime must emerge in New Zealand and quickly, unless we are to believe some government agenda to be the continued delay. Class actions have the potential to effect massive and much needed social change in an environment increasingly shifting in favour of corporate interests, by improving access to justice, improving judicial and court efficiency, producing stronger corporate regulation and providing for an alternative funding mechanism for legal proceedings (including access to legal aid). Clearly there is little political will to correct the inequalities. The courts have begun to recognise and take into account that the current costs of litigation may make bringing a claim to court out of reach for the majority of individuals. As with group litigation, courts have been increasingly more flexible and willing to allow third party litigation-funding to further the objectives of the High Court Rules and increase access to justice. Litigation funding usually takes the form whereby a private funder will fund the costs of the litigation for a share of the award (if the litigant wins) on a no-win, no-fee basis. Currently there are at least five 'litigation funders' operating in New Zealand. There have been several of these actions filed in Christchurch such as the Quake Outcasts group action run by GCA lawyers.[23] This group had good success all the way to the Supreme Court, where it was found that the Government had treated uninsured and vacant section owners unlawfully. Sixty-eight of the 'outcasts' were initially offered *no* pay-out post-quake for their uninsured or uninsurable land in the red zone. In addition there is also a group of 150 Canterbury homeowners known as the EQC Action Group have also filed legal proceeding in the High Court against the Earthquake Commission (EQC).[24] They are seeking declarations from the court to define the extent of the EQC's liability when the EQC elects to settle by payment, replacement or reinstatement. In addition, they argue that the EQC's liabilities are not met merely by compliance with MBIE guidance or the guidelines. There is also a group action of some 47 homeowners against the government insurer,

Southern Response. The proceedings allege that Southern Response misrepresented the terms of the Policy.[25] *"Southern Response is only meeting 40 to 50 percent of the amounts claimed based on its own inadequate building reports. This is not an organisation concerned with its policyholders. This is an organisation concerned with limiting its own financial exposure,"* says class action specialist Grant Cameron. He is inviting over 3000 unsettled Southern Response policyholders to join in a united effort to force Southern Response to meet its contractual obligations.[26] Further actions could follow.

There are also other legal professionals from other parts of the country who, recognising the legal travesty taking place in Christchurch are also interested in pursuing the litigation funding opportunities which are increasingly presenting themselves in Christchurch as time passes. It is clear that information of the plight of the Canterbury people has now seeped through to those of experience who can genuinely make a difference to large numbers of claimants simultaneously. People are more likely to participate in movement activities when they believe that this will help to redress their grievances at affordable costs and limited risk.

For the remaining affected citizens of Canterbury – time is running out. The Limitations Act 2010, which specifies that legal actions must be filed within six years of the date of the act or omission on which the claim is based will shortly begin to come into effect. After five years, there will be pressures on policy holders' finances and a limit on the number of feasible means of settling their insurance claims. Christchurch citizens are now heading into the sixth year post-earthquakes and the time has come for those remaining unresolved insurance claimants to carefully consider their dwindling options.

To my great bemusement, despite the massive policyholder disenchantment, there is a genuine reticence amongst those affected, to join group actions, notwithstanding the fact that their risk is limited. Perhaps this has to do with a lack of understanding about the process and a misguided sense that they will 'do better' and resolve the matter more quickly if they tackle the insurer individually.

One of the issues that has also puzzled me greatly, is why is it that a City with so many badly affected citizens has not been more vocal and communally active to the point of angry demonstration. Instead, social media platforms have sprung up across the internet and while social platforms have a positive impact on the ability of residents to organise and communicate and console each other, those same platforms also prevent protest groups from becoming as cohesive and robust as they would need to be in order to bring about mass movement. They do however, help to promote creativity and help people in need to find others with similar problems. The political movements of old often took many years to develop. There is no doubt in my mind that the insurers will have done their research on the impact and formation of the group dynamics of catastrophe and the community's general unwillingness to 'take them on'. I have witnessed much fear in the community, fear that if you 'make a fuss' then you may be further penalized in the process of settling your claim. In my experience this is an unfounded fear. They need to be taken on - head on! As early as possible.

An interesting social phenomena is worth recalling - we were able to organise meetings at the Transitional Cathedral (called information sessions) and pack the room with some 600 or so people. But if you were to call the event a protest, then after the first two or three years, post-earthquakes, rarely would more than a handful of people present themselves. Clearly, one would think that people are more likely to participate in movement activities when they believe this will help redress their grievances but even though it became clear early on that no one was listening – not the Government nor the private insurance industry, these movements never really cohered. The relationship is straightforward: the more effective an individual believes protest participation is, the more likely she or he is to participate. The question is: were people left/abandoned to solve their problems alone or did they choose to do so? There is the makings of an excellent PhD research paper here. Either way, it suited the insurance corporates beautifully!

Conclusion

It should be remembered that modern insurance was born of a desire to provide catastrophe insurance – the 'mutual' was where it had its beginnings; its configuration provided protection for the benefit of the policyholder not for the benefit of the shareholder.

My belief is that in the current New Zealand situation the Government should consider implementing an independent permanent mediation programme for the resolution of insurance claims; a system that contains the following as a minimum: residential claims only; minimum claim of NZD 10,000 and a minimum difference in position of the parties of at least NZD 2000, although both parties may agree on a lower threshold. Participation would be voluntary participation on the part of the insured, with costs to be borne by the insurer.

In addition there should be further amendments to ensure that the Fair Insurance Code entitles consumers to more information on the claims-handling process and to ensure that timeframes and standards are adhered to during disaster events. Timeframes should be set regarding communications with insured parties as to the progress of their claims following natural disasters. This will necessitate further amendments to the Fair Insurance Code. In addition there should be a mechanism to 'name and shame' insurance companies which breach the Fair Insurance Code. While insurers have agreed to a small fine of up to NZD 100,000 for serious breaches to the Code, there are numerous steps that have to be taken before an insurer has to part with its money. Legislation should also be enacted to make a breach of the duty of utmost good faith a breach of the insurance legislation, and the regulation of insurance claims handling should be implemented. Regulations should be amended to oblige general insurers to provide clear and comprehensive information about both internal and external dispute-resolution processes to policyholders at the time of claim lodgement, and to prohibit multi-tiered, time-wasting models of internal dispute resolution.

For the times when life is more normal, consideration should be given to the way in which the Insurance and Savings Ombudsman service is structured and the perceived lack of 'true independence' from the insurance industry, as well as a review of the caps under which it operates. With the average home in New Zealand now costing approximately NZD 558,000, according to Quotable Value (2015), an independent complaints body should be able to adjudicate larger sums than only NZD 200,000 plus GST, particularly in light of the costs of litigation. An independent complaints body with a mediation service as its basis could provide New Zealanders with a means of settling their claims in a fair and reasonable manner without having to go to the unnecessary expense and emotional trauma that is often associated with litigation.

Generally speaking, the redress for insurance clients is very limited, possibly by design, and there is a genuine need to redress the imbalance. Regulation of the insurance industry in light of the recent Canterbury earthquakes has shown that more safety-nets should be in place to ensure that into the future we do not see reoccurrences of difficulties and failures among our insurers on whom the personal welfare and financial futures of large portions of the New Zealand population may rest, together with the speed of restitution of the city.

Failure by government and ministers to address the grievous situation which has arisen in respect of the performance of insurance contracts in a timely manner in the City of Christchurch will be a self-condemning indication that the Government is more complicit in ensuring corporate profits than it is in protecting the rules of law and commerce in New Zealand. And the people and world are watching...

Citizens Speak

Human rights in Canterbury: A time bomb just waiting to happen? The couple were sitting opposite, telling me on camera of their earthquake housing claim dealings with the EQC and their insurance company and how it had impacted their lives. The husband talked of stress and mental health challenges, and giving up his job, when suddenly he began to talk about a suicide attempt. Sadly, his story is not unique. As David Rutherford, the Chief Human Rights Commissioner reported, Canterbury has become New Zealand's greatest contemporary human rights challenge.

In 2013, WeCAN, a community earthquake advocacy group, became aware of numerous vulnerable people in the community suffering as a result of the actions of the EQC, Insurance and construction companies. After setting up an online form to collect information from these victims, WeCAN approached the University of Canterbury, School of Law, to form a human rights law clinic project in order to hold the EQC and the private insurance companies to account. Based upon international human rights law, and using the little known Organisation for Economic Co-operation and Development Guidelines for multinational enterprises, law interns worked over the summer of 2014/2015, collecting evidence of human rights violations and formulating individual statements of claims.

Read together, these claims showed an alleged pattern of conduct by construction and insurance companies which had a devastating effect on people living with unresolved housing insurance claims, or inadequately repaired dwellings. Substantiated by evidence, they demonstrated a wide variety of alleged human rights abuses including, violations of health, adequate housing, dignity, work, discrimination, interference in the family and home, women's rights, and protection of children.

Which begs the question - how could this happen in a country which claims to take human rights seriously? New Zealand was, after all, the first country to give women the vote and we have just taken a seat on the United Nations Security Council.

At a baseline level, it's debatable whether there is in fact any domestic legal protection in New Zealand for these alleged breaches. In 1978, New Zealand ratified the International Covenant on Civil and Political Rights (ICCPR), covering rights such as freedom of speech, and not being arbitrarily detained. It also ratified at the same time, the International Covenant on Economic, Social and Cultural Rights (ICESCR), covering rights such as adequate housing and highest attainable health. However, only civil and political rights were given effect under domestic law through the New Zealand Bill of Rights Act (NZBORA).

Then there is the issue of the Government response. In spite of mass protest in one form or another over the years, by thousands of citizens living in broken homes, the Government has continued with its 'laisse fair' political ideology, having decided upon a 'let the market decide' approach.

Whilst such an approach might be acceptable under normal market place conditions, in a natural disaster, with a stressed and vulnerable citizenry, it would appear to violate the very treaties New Zealand signed, and international law. They require the State to extend special protective measures to vulnerable groups within society and ensure a degree of priority consideration. In other words, to become actively involved in protecting its citizens.

Therefore, with successive governments showing no interest in giving economic, social and cultural rights domestic legal protection, and a hands-off market place approach to governance and regulation, the Canterbury earthquakes have exposed a massive sinkhole in our legislative framework of human rights protection.

By Stephen Patterson.[27]

CHAPTER 7

CATASTROPHE INSURANCE: WHY THE GOVERNMENT SHOULD PROVIDE IT

Better to be the architect of something you can endorse than the placard waving protagonist standing in the rain.

Tim Woods, Communications Consultant[1]

My experience over the last five years has left me with the opinion that we need to seriously rethink insurance coverage for catastrophe in this country. The failure of the current private insurance systems to alleviate the distress and recovery of Christchurch citizens and government's failure to meet obligations toward the people of Canterbury, is a clear indication of the need for New Zealand to develop an innovative programme for reducing future losses from disasters, a programme that involves both the public and private sectors, with the public sector taking on the entire responsibility for catastrophe insurance. What has become increasingly evident is that the current system has failed to protect New Zealand property owners in a catastrophe.

The problem of catastrophe risk was well highlighted by the Canterbury earthquakes. These events have provided an unexpected opportunity to study the interface of economics and politics in relation to the private and government insurance markets, and to consider a sustainable and economically feasible public policy.

The provision of catastrophe relief is one of the principal functions and core responsibilities of government. Under normal circumstances the government's function is not to dictate market outcomes, but in times of major catastrophe a different approach is required. We have seen that government policies can be either supportive or contribute to market problems and distortions. A government standing aloof from damaged communities will create confusion and frustration about roles and responsibilities among those affected or otherwise involved. I would argue that the current situation is showing the signs of distortion, further confused by 'spasmodic' dictates from government without appropriate consultation.

A time of crisis is not the time to be 'leaving it to the market'. When you hear phrases such as 'leave it to the market', in times of crisis, you know that the population is 'on its own' and in for a rough ride. The Government and CERA have suggested that the housing crisis would be best left to the market. As rents rocketed in 2013, more people found themselves homeless, looking for inadequate or unavailable solutions which were likely to lead to illness and possibly death for elderly and other vulnerable groups.

Let us consider the concept of insurability and examine a standard insurance policy whereby premiums are paid at the start of a given time period to cover possible damage and/or losses during this interval. Two conditions must generally be met before insurance providers are willing to offer coverage. The first is that the provider must be able to identify, quantify and estimate the chances of the insured event/s occurring and also the extent of losses which might be incurred. The second condition is that the insurer must be able to rationally generate the price (premium) for each potential customer or class of customers. If these conditions are satisfied, a risk is considered to be insurable. However, the risk cannot be guaranteed to be profitable. It may be difficult, if not impossible, to specify a rate for which there is sufficient demand by clients and sufficient incoming revenue to cover the development, marketing, operating, claims and claims-processing costs of the insurer and still yield a net positive profit over a pre-specified time period. When this risk seems too great, the insurer will usually opt to not offer cover against this risk.

In 2012 the insurers began to opt out of the insurance market in Canterbury. They were less likely to provide cover in areas where land, liquefaction and structural damage had occurred. The most difficult areas in which to obtain home and contents insurance were the Red Zone, TC3 and Port Hill areas particularly where properties had structural, liquefaction or land damage. Slowly the market has restored with the introduction of fixed sum insurance. Insurer capital represents the net worth of a company (assets minus liabilities) and this capital must be able to facilitate the payment of losses by the insurer above those losses that were predicted. So if we disregard reinsurance, this capital serves as one 'last ditch' safety net to underwrite the risk an insurer takes and supposedly provide certainty that the insurer will be able to honour its contractual obligations. In thus doing, the provider is supposed to be able to provide a 'promise of restoration to their original position' to homeowners, business owners, workers and others who rely on the good faith of insurers to provide financial compensation to rebuild lives and businesses. Insurer capital is one of several essential components supporting the insurance promise. The required capital sums will vary as a function of the risk an insurer assumes. The more risk assumed by the insurer the more capital required to support that risk. Insurance regulators and rating agencies must devote significant effort toward evaluating the adequacy of the insurer capital relative to the amount and types of risk they assume.

Catastrophe insurance for the insurance industry, is about smoothing out large losses over time. Yet in property liability insurance, accounting practices prevent insurance companies from earmarking capital surplus in order to fund future catastrophes, despite the fact that a catastrophe may be highly likely. In a seismic nation such as New Zealand, this is a given. Less spoken about is the fact that capital excesses do not sit well with dividend-hungry shareholders.

Conventional catastrophe literature suggests that government should facilitate the development of private-market insurance by reducing regulatory barriers. New Zealand is already considered to be 'lightly' regulated in this regard, for which Cantabrians paid a high price. Canterbury's spate of earthquakes has shown the need for further regulatory measures or interventions by government to prevent the failure of the private-insurance property market. Some private insurers' failure to be adequately capitalised (AMI, Western Pacific and Ansvar) and the failure of insurance companies to act within reasonable timeframes indicates that reducing regulatory barriers further would be highly inadvisable.

The insurance industry has failed the Canterbury population badly; the evidence is overwhelming that this current private system does not provide the protection it claims. An alternative strategy would be that the New Zealand Government consider modifying and improving the already operative, if deeply flawed EQC, to provide full cover for catastrophe insurance and property insurance (both commercial and residential) generally, leaving the private insurers to insure contents only.

So what is the appropriate role of government in financing and managing catastrophe risk? What are the appropriate disaster risk-management strategies that a government should pursue, particularly with regard to the growing population density and concentration of economic resources and, as some assert, indeterminate complications due to climate change? How should the major financial implications be handled?

Financing is a critical part of managing catastrophe risk. It will not be feasible to reconstruct Canterbury without major financial inputs. If sufficient capacity can be directed to financing catastrophe risk through the access of capital by government, why would government *not* finance catastrophe risk?

Questions to be asked involve: will reinsurance and securitisation be enough to maintain insurance company solvency after a mega-catastrophe or major earthquake? How can the various funding sources available for catastrophe insurance be expanded and refined to cope with catastrophic earthquakes? Is the government able to do a 'better' job than the private insurers? The last question is clearly dependent upon how one defines 'better'. If the present performance of the majority of the large private insurers in Christchurch is typical, suggesting that another catastrophe would result in similar insurer behaviours, the answer can only unequivocally support moving to a government-funded and managed system.

Insurers claim that they have been impeded in their efforts to increase prices and manage their catastrophe risk exposure by regulatory constraints and limits on the ability and willingness of reinsurance and financial markets to fully absorb higher levels of catastrophe risk. The conclusion to be drawn from this assertion, if true, is that the insurers are in the wrong business anyway! The losses from the Canterbury earthquakes ripple throughout the local and national economy. Some portion of this loss is borne by the owners and shareholders of the insurers and reinsurers. However, government mechanisms *also* distribute a significant portion of unfunded losses in the form of welfare payments and financial assistance to business owners and, to insurance policyholders and taxpayers, throughout the country.

In the normal course of events insurers need to be able to develop reasonably accurate estimates of their future losses in order to set appropriate policy prices and to be able to structure their investments efficiently, to manage their cash flows. This is undeniably very difficult to do with low-probability, high-consequence events which can be affected by a range of factors and subject to considerable uncertainty. The failure of Western Pacific and the poor performance of AMI and Ansvar to deliver on promises confirms this, and these failures further support the need for the Government (and consequently the taxpayer) to become the insurer of last resort. Government has already financed the burden of private insurance failure and liabilities anyway.

Also, the New Zealand government could well provide the most *effective* insurance instrument for our society. As the single provider, the government has the potential to be far superior to private insurers in its capacity to reduce risk through aggregation, while at the same time providing more cost-effective pricing than private insurers. As a starting point, the fact that Government would have one hundred percent geographical coverage would give it a clear advantage over any private insurer in respect of diversification of risk. Private insurers are not able to aggregate effectively when they have only small market shares and specific market sectors (e.g. 'church' and 'heritage' insurance). Nor do all insurers work in all geographic areas of New Zealand.

It is not yet known whether the insurers presently involved will be able to pay all the Canterbury earthquake claims without triggering further insurer insolvency or market disruption. Some argue that the huge delays in settlements suggest that there are some marginal operations amongst them, or that re/insurers are 'dragging the chain'. It is also noticeable that published estimates of timeframes for recovery have been steadily extending and the Canterbury insurance industry's financial capacity to underwrite the disaster must remain in question despite 'assurances' from the Government. While it is clear that completion of insurance pay-outs will depend in part on whether there are more damaging earthquakes, it is also clear that the local insurance industry does not, in the course of its normal business cycle, have sufficient capital to fund more mega-disasters. This warns of the critical need for change.

In addition, the Government is likely to find it costly and challenging to meet long term disaster-related costs under the current private/public regime. Private insurers will continue to be reluctant to cover properties in high-risk areas which will ultimately lead to high prices for disaster insurance. The geological reality in New Zealand is that nowhere is exempt from catastrophe exposure. The Christchurch events lead to the conclusion that re/insurance due diligence has been poor. Now that liquefaction, flooding and business interruption insurance can be accurately figured into the industry's pricing equations, New Zealand is likely to see a steady increase in premiums as pricing factors are recalculated throughout the country. No doubt inaccurate insurance pricing is also prevalent in other New Zealand cities liable to experience liquefaction, of which there are several.

Insurer pay-outs, together with settlements and disaster assistance, are critical to the flow of funds, without which the region is likely to slowly die. It is because insurance plays such a vital role in the economy that instability in the availability and price of coverage, generally leads to pressure for government intervention in insurance markets, but we have seen little or no pressure exerted on private insurers to perform their contracts.

According to research by the Field Connection (*New Beginnings Christchurch Central Business District: Evolution from an Earthquake*), 16 months after the first event only 14 percent of claims had been settled amongst the business community.[2] The damage to local business and the deterrent to a speedy economic, if not domestic recovery, is obvious. Small business cannot sustain itself for long under these conditions. Some firms have funded their own repairs and redevelopment rather than wait for disputes with insurers to be resolved, as have much larger businesses, e.g. Lyttelton Harbour and some of the supermarket chains.

The democratic ideal is that governments are elected by their populations to carry out the will of the people and govern in their best interests. If democracy were functional and politics honest, it would be a fair assumption that governments of the day would move to correct situational perpetuities which were not in the interests of the welfare of the citizens. Some such issues transcend party politics in the mind of the populace and should do likewise in the thinking of governments of any persuasion. Effective disaster recovery management must be one such issue. Regardless of voters' political colours, it is in everyone's interest to ensure that disasters are managed effectively and equitably. The Christchurch experience highlights a substantial conflict of interest between the public, the Government and private insurance corporations.

The larger insurance corporations can, and do, profit both in 'normal' times and in times of catastrophe. How do they do this? An example is the speed with which the global reinsurance industry carried out its initial assessment of Christchurch after the September 4, 2010 earthquake. This was followed reasonably quickly by reinsurance flowing into the country and the shrinking of New Zealand's current account deficit in one month by NZD 800 million in the 2010 year compared with 2009 – leaving the country with its smallest deficit in a decade. Since that time, billions of dollars in reinsurance have been passed on to the insurers involved in the Christchurch events. For many months there was not a sign of use of these funds to relieve the distress of the people (policyholders) of Christchurch, due to the fact that after investing their reinsurance pay-outs most of the bigger insurers have strategically only trickled out settlements to affected residents, and have sat quietly behind local politics as it tore itself to pieces in indecision regarding direction.

There are also questions to be asked and answered regarding the *declared losses* of the insurers, which led to their reinsurance pay-outs and the *actual losses* they incurred in Christchurch. Whether they will ever pay-out the full value of their reinsurance compensations is a moot point. This question will be worthy of further research. I am aware that the reinsurers have employed firms to carry out due diligence on their behalf. It is now clear that after five years, the true cost to insurers can be determined to a reasonably high level of accuracy. If true investigative journalism were still alive, this would probably make quite a story...

The EQC, with so few permanent staff, seemed immediately after the September 4, 2010 earthquake, to be much more efficient in its crisis management (though this quickly ended after the February 22, 2011 quake). Throughout this process the insurance industry claimed that it could do little until the EQC had made its assessments and settlements. This is, however, untrue; the private insurance industry could have systematically followed the EQC, making settlements at more or less the same pace. There is no evidence that this was done effectively and many of the bigger insurers indulged then (and are still indulging) in time-consuming delay tactics – sending countless inspectors, loss adjusters and engineers, together with months of delay between such visits to damaged properties.

The whole fiasco demonstrates very clearly that catastrophe insurance is too important to be left to private insurers. It represents a major conflict of ideologies. Corporate entities are about profit and returns to shareholders. It is a mistaken premise to think that insurance companies will act either altruistically or with compassion. Privately owned, profit-based corporations are not philosophically oriented to look after the welfare of a community confronted with a disaster on the scale of the Christchurch earthquakes. Insurers will always give priority to their financial bottom-line and seek to maximise profits and strategize to minimise payments to policyholders. The Christchurch experience demonstrates that 'good faith' is nothing more than a slogan.

Countries around the globe have found various ways of financing catastrophe risk. In the USA, after Hurricane Andrew for example, the Florida state legislature worked with insurers and regulators to create a state-run reinsurance fund designed to mitigate losses to the insurance industry and prevent insurers from withdrawing from the Florida insurance market. In effect, they sought to combine the interests of insurers and populace. This is a questionable approach, as it appears that the populace is underwriting private corporations. In that situation, the Florida Hurricane Catastrophe Fund was created as a reinsurance-like entity funded by a portion of insurance premiums and managed by the Florida State Board of Administration. It was created to provide additional claims-paying capacity. Florida implemented percentage deductibles tied to the value of homes instead of a dollar amount, such as USD 500 per claim. It follows that insurers writing residential and commercial property insurance in Florida are required to purchase reinsurance from the Florida Hurricane Catastrophe Fund based on their exposure to hurricane losses in the state. The Florida Hurricane Catastrophe Fund does not have state financial backing but it is operated as a state agency, is exempt from federal income taxes and does not have to pay dividends. This enables it to accumulate funds more rapidly than private insurers. In addition, the fund has the authority to assess member insurers within limits, to meet the case where premiums and reserve funds might be insufficient and it also has the ability to issue tax-exempt bonds. Florida effectively created a state regulated insurer of last resort to provide insurance when no company was willing to underwrite disaster risk. These measures are credited with saving the property insurance industry from financial disaster after the four major hurricanes in 2004 and 2005.[3] Given that the people were funding much of this, the question remains as to why there is any need to support private disaster insurance at all. If a state can do it, a government can do it.

New Zealand and several other countries have established government insurance programmes to provide partial coverage for natural disasters. As a general pattern, these governments collect premiums in return for the coverage, and private insurers generally market the policies and handle claims settlement and other administrative details. A European example is Consorcio de Compensacion de Seguros, established by the Spanish Government in 1954. This is a public corporation that provides insurance for 'extraordinary risks', for both natural catastrophes and terrorism. The extraordinary risks coverage is mandatory and is provided as an add-on to private-market property insurance policies. A premium is collected for the coverage, which is passed along to Consorcio de Compensacion de Seguros by the private insurers.[4] This approach is also used in countries such as Australia, Denmark, Mexico, the Netherlands, Norway and Poland.

In France, a mandatory homeowners' policy covers a number of different potential natural disasters, as well as terrorism risk. The main difference appears at the reinsurance level, which is partially provided by a publicly owned reinsurer, the Caisse Centrale de Reassurance, for flood, earthquakes and droughts, and by an insurance pool, Gareat, with unlimited government guarantee for terrorism claims.

Switzerland also has a mandatory insurance system, where policies cover both damage from fire and natural disasters (though it does not include earthquakes). Property owners in 19 of the 26 cantons in the country are legally obligated to purchase this coverage from a cantonal insurance monopoly. Inhabitants of the remaining seven cantons can obtain property insurance only from private companies.[5]

Another example of a government as reinsurer is provided by the Japan Earthquake Reinsurance Company, which reinsures natural hazards such as earthquakes and tsunamis. All earthquake insurance written by private insurers in this highly earthquake-prone country is reinsured with the Japan Earthquake Reinsurance Company. Reinsurance coverage is based on a layering approach, such that 100 percent of the loss in the lowest-loss layer (up to 75 billion yen), is borne by private insurers; the loss is split evenly between private insurers and the government if the loss is between 75 billion and 1.0774 trillion yen; and 95 percent of the loss is paid by the government when the loss is between 1.0774 and 4.5 trillion yen.[6] In 1995, after the Kobe earthquake, the earthquake insurance programme was modified to provide economic incentives to encourage the building of earthquake-resistant residences. This was done by introducing discounted premium rates based on a building's earthquake resistance, with discounts based on a housing performance indication system under Japan's Housing Quality Guarantee Law. The premiums are based on the estimates of the likelihood of occurrence and the expected damages of an earthquake. These estimates are computed at the geographical level of prefectures, and each prefecture is classified into one of the four rating zones (rank 1 'safest' to rank 4, 'riskiest'). The premiums are based on the government's regulations, not on private-sector calculations.[7]

In Australia, the states and territories largely assume responsibility for managing natural disasters. The states are supported by the Federal Government through the Natural Disaster Relief and Recovery Arrangements. This assistance involves a partial reimbursement of costs to the states once the state's expenditure exceeds a certain threshold. These arrangements only apply to certain events, for instance drought is not included, and only for certain types of assistance. In addition to the Natural Disaster Relief and Recovery Arrangements, the Federal Government also provides an Australian Government Disaster Recovery Payment in some cases, which is administered by Centrelink, the Australian Government Department for Human Services.[8] This provides short-term financial assistance to people adversely affected by a major or widespread disaster. The payment is AUD 1,000 per adult and AUD 400 per child. The Christchurch experience would indicate that sums of this magnitude are too small to be of any significant assistance when urgent relief is required.

In Germany, before the European Union Non-life Directive[9] many of the states had compulsory monopoly schemes covering fire and storm. Since the directive, there has been a transition to private insurance with consequential large increases in premium rates.

In the United Kingdom, private insurers provide insurance for flood risk. The cover is currently provided under a 'Statement of Principles' issued by the Association of British Insurers. The insurance industry provides flood insurance to most properties on the condition that the United Kingdom Government takes action to mitigate flood risk.

In New Zealand the Government compels private insurers to provide disaster-related insurance as an element of coverage. Given such a compulsion, the calculus for the insurer becomes more complicated – no longer is the question: is it possible to offer coverage and to whom and where? but rather, are we more likely to profit with or without the line of homeowners' coverage? The existence of governmental relief funds further complicates this decision. Where there is no government coverage the decision is a clean one. Where the level of government response to a disaster is uncertain, the calculus changes drastically. An insurer who may become insolvent now evaluates its position in the market knowing that there is the potential for the government to shoulder the losses itself.[10] So this half-way solution of part governmental and part private insurance bailouts creates needless complexity, and the population suffers both poor service and uncertainty as a consequence. One body waits to see what the other intends to do, while the affected population is kept 'hostage' between the two. The outcomes of this policy have caused needless suffering in Canterbury. In 2015 it was proposed that this change and that the private insurance industry alone will be responsible for the assessment of property and contents.[11]

Whether this will result in more efficiency is yet to be tested, but based on recent experiencees, it certainly will not result in more honesty.

The current laissez faire position, which the present right-wing government appears to favour, maintains that any market-based equilibrium, however imperfect, provides a more efficient allocation of resources within the economy than an equilibrium involving government intervention. The Government therefore, apart from frequent 'directives without consultation', stands aside and leaves the local community to struggle with private insurance corporations, and instead occupies itself with big business and the 'central city development' in the form of anchor projects, which are still beset with indecision and Inaction, five years later.

With community and industry calling for government protection against catastrophic risk and a failed private insurance response, the government needs to formally and publicly recognise the responsibility it has in times of crisis and acknowledge the asymmetric relationship between individuals and corporations. At the least, government should ensure private insurers act responsibly and within reasonable timeframes.

The Alternative

There are several possible policy regimes: total reliance on private markets and private choice; government regulation and insurance; or a mixed system of private markets and limited government intervention. The latter is the regime currently in place in New Zealand and it has proven to provide only limited protection for its citizens.

Proponents of the second of these – a community and public interest view – believe that in the case of a major event it is government's responsibility to regulate the market and fund disaster costs, thereby ensuring protection and providing the necessary recovery resources. The public-interest view suggests that regulation is supplied in response to the demand of the public for the correction of inefficient or inequitable market practices. Regulation is assumed initially to benefit society as a whole, rather than particular vested interests.

A government-funded system has the ability to provide coverage for all natural perils and can be made compulsory for all property owners, thereby ensuring complete coverage. This also provides the ability to remove the risk of underinsurance as opposed to limiting funding to 'sum insured' amounts. Arguments against this funding mechanism include the fact that there are no disincentives to reduce risk or that there is also a potential risk to the Government's credit rating in the form of a downgrade if it takes on too much risk. These factors can, however, be addressed.

The public-interest view of regulation suggests that market failures can lead to suboptimal allocation of resources and that government intervention addressing market failures can improve welfare. This implies that in catastrophic situations, the government can improve upon the market equilibrium by substituting all of the private-sector input. The information asymmetries and taxpayer bankruptcy costs associated with 'the market' for catastrophe insurance, suggest a major justification for this government role in New Zealand and also around the world.

And why leave it there? The same shortcomings and failures strongly suggest government regulation in the public interest of the whole property insurance market – both commercial and residential. Governments need to tighten constraints on insurers and to find other ways to lower the now rapidly increasing costs and expand the availability of coverage. In New Zealand this would involve extending the EQC's remit considerably. Naturally, it is essential that the population does not pay two premiums – one for catastrophe cover and one for private insurance coverage. For this reason and for financial efficiency, the Government, by way of EQC, should cover all building (commercial and residential) insurance, thus making the EQC sole property insurer – for both catastrophic and non-catastrophic events. This would also ensure that there are adequate numbers and suitably trained staff throughout the country in the event of a major disaster. Though it may appear to be a very dramatic measure, it can easily be shown that if it is profitable for the private sector, and run efficiently by the public sector without the abstraction of profits, a Natural Disaster Fund would rapidly accumulate sufficient resources to face even the largest catastrophe. Particularly as wider coverage would provide a larger national premium base, thus increasing financial resilience. In this way the Government could ensure efficiency and transparency in a scheme run on a sound actuarial basis. In the years between disasters, the fund would regain its strength by means of the total and nationally diversified structure with the ability to spend an annual proportion of the fund on projects solely with the purpose of disaster mitigation e.g. in flood zone regions, or red zoning particular regions with a view to future mitigation.

The EQC legislation to cover such a development would need careful consideration. Due attention would need to be given to preventing any government from again siphoning funds for any other purpose. When the Fund is sufficiently large, the mutualisation of the scheme could commence, with either a reduction of a premium or payment of a dividend. Substantial investment by the Natural Disaster Fund within New Zealand could provide a much-needed boost to national industry and agriculture. To allay concerns that public entities are often inefficiently run, the Natural Disaster Fund could operate as a Crown Entity and function as a corporation reporting to a Minister as sole shareholder, with guidelines set or agreed by Parliament. This entity should be above political tinkering so that no matter which party was in 'power', the EQC's mandate would be clear, its efficiencies regularly audited and It's assets out of the reach of government tinkering. It Is also worth noting that no 'profits' would be removed from New Zealand.

It should not be forgotten that as matters currently stand, the Natural Disaster Fund has been depleted by *one single event*. If there was another major event tomorrow, the government of the day would be picking up the 'tab'. Building a Natural Disaster Fund in the way suggested here represents a solid, low-risk option where the need to use risky financial instruments such as Catastrophe (CAT) bonds is no longer required. Regardless of the actions of the insurance industry players, whether they remain in New Zealand or whether they move out of the market, New Zealand remains a seismic nation and will continue to need to protect its citizens from inevitable seismic events. One can fully expect that after the Canterbury earthquakes some private insurers will leave the residential insurance market, at least in part, or will continue to raise the price of insurance above tolerable values, as has occurred elsewhere after major catastrophes (e.g. Florida and New Orleans). The nation needs to be prepared and to have a long term plan. Five years on and we see little or no evidence of such planning.

Recent governments have misjudged the potential magnitude of modern losses resulting from increasing property values, construction costs and population densities. Nevertheless, even if an event produces losses far above those expected, these incremental losses can still be multiplied by very small probabilities and a suitable small upward revision of national levies should be sufficient to maintain profitability and financial security. This would enable governments to underwrite the risk. With the increasing sophistication of catastrophe-loss modelling it should be a straightforward exercise to justify an increase in levies to the population to cover revised estimates of expected losses.

By extending the EQC's remit and cover, (after substantial overhaul of its present form), New Zealand could enhance its current catastrophe funding system; make property insurance more available and affordable; promote the funding of research (that is, earthquake science, actuarial science, economics, and finance) relating to disaster insurance issues; and expand New Zealand's knowledge and understanding of the scientific and financial aspects of natural hazards and begin to mitigate likely future problem areas.

A government programme should mimic the operational structure of the private market as much as possible, without the same profit-driven goals. There is some evidence from events around the globe that some private insurers are moving away from catastrophe insurance, declaring that such increasingly frequent events are 'uninsurable'. If the New Zealand Government takes on this role of 'disaster proofing' the nation, it will in the long run minimise the costs it has to bear for disaster relief and relieve the large social costs that natural disasters inevitably impose on the private sector.

For insurance policyholders, the obvious advantage of long term insurance contracts is that it provides them with stability and an assurance that their property is protected for as long as they own it. By establishing mandatory 'all-hazards' insurance through the payment of property levies, all New Zealand property owners would be protected following disaster, and be provided with the financial resources needed for recovery. Such a system would also reduce the need for unquantified liberal disaster assistance as well as the unnecessary and unethical delays associated with most private insurance companies, based on the Christchurch experience.

Catastrophe levies and property premiums, tagged to local authority property rating values, would be paid directly to the EQC, or its improved replacement entity, leaving the private insurers to cover contents claims only. This should lead to repricing of property insurance coverage by the EQC – downward. An all-hazards property policy should also be attractive to both the government and levy payers because it also avoids the costly and time-consuming process of having adjusters determine whether the damage was caused by wind or water, fire or earthquake. It seems reasonable that catastrophic property insurance for the long term, should be tied to the property concerned, that is, pegged to Quotable Value assessments,[12] rather than to the owner's assessment of value and could be potentially collected with local authority rates on behalf of the EQC. Quotable Value (QV) produces rating valuations. These are compiled by statute, under the Rating Valuations Act 1998, mainly as a uniform basis for levying local authority and regional council rates. Rating valuations also serve as a useful guide for property owners and other interested parties, as they are impartial and independently assessed. In this way private-sector 'profits and dividends' will be eliminated, making the proposal more efficient. There is no reason for property owners to be concerned that premiums would be higher – in a worst-case scenario the cost of premiums for contributions to the public system would not be any higher than they are currently under a private insurance policy.

In order to achieve this enormous change to catastrophe and property insurance risk generally, major reforms are required. In response to the unprecedented scale of these events, the Government has made a number of policy decisions that change the EQC environment and which will have major impact on the EQC's activities, roles and functions. These include: the transfer from the Minister of Finance (as the Minister Responsible for the Earthquake Commission Authority) to the Minister for Canterbury Earthquake Recovery of powers, functions and responsibilities in relation to the EQC's earthquake recovery work in Canterbury, including, where necessary, directions to the EQC to extend its functions.[13] The combined effect of these decisions took place in a very short space of time (a few months) and had the effect of expanding the EQC's role from solely a Crown financial institution, geared to cash settling natural disaster claims, to one that now also includes:

- the establishment of a project management office to manage residential repairs;

- designing and supervising additional land remediation activities;

- providing key engineering advice to the government;

- a social assistance component through to identification of vulnerable households; and

- the Chimney Replacement Programme.

Private insurers do not undertake any of these crucial activities.

Currently the EQC levy is like an earthquake 'mini-policy' designed by government to provide less extensive coverage than that provided by private insurers. Without the current EQC pre-funding, it is highly probable that the private insurers will not agree to further cover earthquake risk. Any EQC coverage provided must have sound actuarial pricing; it is arguable that the current EQC Natural Disaster Fund is not actuarially sound, as it has been unable to cope with the huge numbers of claims resulting from the Canterbury earthquakes and is currently selling assets to fund the shortfall. The funds collected through the payment of levies only represent a fraction of expected costs, also contributing to the EQC's present shortfall. The Natural Disaster Fund also has to pay significant amounts of money to repair or replace 'repetitive-loss properties', that is, properties that receive loss payments of thousands of dollars, at least twice over a 10-year period, as is the case throughout the Canterbury region and particularly in the eastern suburbs of Christchurch, where residents will have made double and triple claims. Flood-prone areas typically produce these claims. Such multiple claims have the effect of driving a wedge between the EQC and the private insurers, the EQC unwilling to increase its liability from a diminishing pool of resource and the private insurers pushing for the EQC to be responsible for an additional sum, which leads to more profit for the private insurers. It is estimated that such properties, which represent considerably less than 10 percent of covered properties in New Zealand, will account for a large percentage of all loss payments from the Natural Disaster Fund.[14]

Proponents of an EQC-type national reinsurance programme cite the Government's advantage in diversifying inter-temporal risk, that is, the ability to absorb large losses early in a programme, losses that could be recovered over an acceptable timeframe from the continued receipt of premium and interest income from a national client base. In order to reform the programme, the EQC could continue to provide catastrophe insurance but charge levies sufficient to cover both claims and programme expenses to cover all property-insurance-related claims, both commercial and residential, in order to build up reserves during low-loss years, which would reduce the need for government borrowing when catastrophes occur. Additional adjustments would be made for inflation and to reflect the current purchasing power of the dollar. Adjustments for real growth in property values would also be required, as these have for many years increased by more than inflation. The accuracy of the QV valuing process would need review on an ongoing basis to ensure accurate real values of residential and commercial property.

Factors such as vulnerable properties and different risk values, for example coastal properties, will need to be taken into account. Currently government levies do not make a distinction between low and high risk, nor do they make a distinction between low or high-value properties. An average levy is charged to all insured parties. This requires address, as it is principally because of this that the Natural Disaster Fund faces severe budgetary problems. The criticism by experts with experience of government-run insurance programmes, is that the scheme is inadequately capitalised to handle mega-catastrophic events. However, the 'actuarial' view is that catastrophe risk is insurable and often at a surprisingly low price. Moreover, insurance markets have not moved to a sustainable equilibrium in terms of catastrophe risk assumption and pricing, which implies that prices will continue to rise and other forms of risk diversification will be extended before the market in New Zealand is stabilised.

In summary then, if the EQC or its improved successor became the dominant national provider of disaster insurance and general commercial and residential insurance in the public sector, operating as a Crown Entity, this would provide a framework and consultancy to reduce the physical risks and provide cover for high-risk catastrophes. This would be in addition to regulation of the market for other risks, such as having tighter control of the private insurance industry. The private sector would be left to provide consultancy and administrative services for all sectors and to offer coverage for contents and other non-realty property insurance. Further questions that will need consideration include: what cover would be provided for what premiums, and what are the mechanisms for attaching this to a property? How might the premium vary between different regions, if it varies at all? How would capital requirements for the Natural Disaster Fund differ under different government reinsurance arrangements? How will the government restructure its reinsurance arrangements?

Opponents to the use of the EQC as primary disaster/non-disaster insurer, having observed the EQC's dismal performance and governance over the last five years, naturally argue that inefficiencies can arise from government insurance programmes. Some suggest government insurance may create resource allocation problems, such as the overbuilding of building types and locations that are relatively vulnerable to natural disasters. This can be avoided by stricter building codes and more regional council input into appropriate ground allocation for development purposes. Others argue that because government programmes are determined by politics rather than the operation of markets, they are not likely to represent the most efficient solution. While some of these objections may be valid, the current Christchurch situation suggests that the private sector and free-market proponents are in no position to criticise 'efficiencies'.

In the recent past the Government has bailed out several large financial institutions, e.g. South Canterbury Finance[15] and AMI Insurance. These actions will cost taxpayers money for many years to come. The Government also runs an 'insolvency fund' to bail out policyholders should their insurance company become bankrupt. In addition, when disasters occur, the Government provides disaster aid.[16] In light of these already existing government measures, expanding the role of the current EQC system appears to be the solution likely to serve the public interest best. It comes without the 'profit tension' inherent in private insurance and is less easy to manipulate for private gain at the public expense.

To recap, the numerous reasons to justify the EQC becoming the insurer of last resort include:

- the uncertainty of the capital markets in the current global environment and the potential for systemic risk;

- diminished insurance costs for property owners as the government would not have to factor in profit margins and added to this is the potential for dividend returns to property owners. This would operate as a mutual structure for the benefit of policyholders. The 'shareholder dividend' would be retained in the system, i.e. year-on-year dividends add to the cost of the private system as they are extracted from what would otherwise be 'capital';

- government and hence taxpayers would not have to bail out undercapitalised failing private insurers;

- the re-establishment of the now depleted Natural Disaster Fund would be immediate, as all premiums/levies would go directly to the Fund. During times of 'normality' a portion of the Fund could be operated as a 'float' for additional government income creation;

- New Zealand is better able to calculate its risk than international reinsurers and the chosen risk transference structures would be more transparent as there would be accountability to policyholders, ensuring that there are no off-balance-sheet transactions taking place, nor is a lack of 'international reach' likely to cause problems for the government, as it can with private insurers;

- avoids the danger and impact of major reinsurer failure from the primary insurance industry and the economy due to the complexity and opacity of reinsurance. A comprehensive government reinsurance programme could be established on a sound financial basis by utilising insurance industry 'best practice'. The need for reinsurance would diminish as the value of the Fund grew.

- avoids the considerable pressure reinsurers place on primary insurers and the government, for instance if reinsurance is not available or only available at very high prices. The reinsurance market is a very influential force in the primary insurance market. The primary insurer may not obtain client premium increases that will sufficiently cover the increased cost of the reinsurance premium;

- avoids the necessity of investing in CAT bonds and other high-risk dubious financial market products;

- the population would be able to rely on a long term, multi-term relationship with the elected governments of the day and trust such a relationship without catastrophe insurance becoming a 'political football' at election time, which is a typical aspect of New Zealand politics and its three-year electoral term;

- would be more likely to lead to expeditious payments to policyholders. Generally, consumers experience a sharp decrease in their wealth immediately after a natural disaster. They therefore place the highest marginal value on reimbursement from their insurer precisely when the damage to their property is greatest. Prompt payments to homeowners would likely increase their willingness to pay for protection, particularly from a body they perceived to have integrity;

- mitigate the risk associated with the documented increase in severe weather events or seismic activity which may eventually lead to re/insurers refusal to cover such events or result in unaffordable premiums;

- collecting money nationally for the purposes of potential catastrophes also helps to make the population more aware of the social cost of community decisions, thus limiting the moral hazard problem (for example, by discouraging excessive building or rebuilding on areas prone to liquefaction or flooding);

- structuring a national insurance system in this way circumvents the likelihood of future funding problems. (For example, the UK Government decided to provide terrorism insurance following the breakdown of insurance and reinsurance markets when the bombings in London began in 1992. High-risk homeowners' pools in the USA are typically established when premiums that the private insurance market attempt to charge are above the levels that are socially viable or acceptable);

- splitting liability between land (the EQC) and buildings (private insurers) creates unnecessary complexity.

- in conjunction with the EQC programme as proposed, there is also the opportunity to set up a national safety scheme to protect citizens from the effects of large natural disasters related to rising sea levels and flooding for instance. Decision making relative to where the funds would be spent would be based on solid research and funded through the proposed EQC scheme.

There are suggestions that having the EQC as insurer of last resort would lead to insurance becoming politicised. This would be no bad thing as it would ensure that whichever party was in government at the time of a catastrophic event would have to perform well, or it would likely see the end of its term. Others argue that the Government would be taking on added risk, which is true – but as the insurance market is currently failing to perform, the risk is likely to be less in actuality.

Conclusion

A permanent government catastrophe insurance programme which is able to provide an adequate lower-cost public substitute for a notably larger national client base, should crowd out and eventually legislate out the private-market alternative. When catastrophe risk is free to be priced as accurately as possible and assuming that creative financial engineers are able to find ways to raise the capital necessary to fund losses, there is no reason why government should not be able to provide this product. When government programmes are required, they should mimic as far as possible the operational structure of the private market so as to maximise return on capital, but without focus on 'profit' or the sharp/dishonest practices utilised by the private sector to maximise gains.

If private insurers, even with the guarantee of instant access to capital at market rates, refuse to write catastrophe lines, we are faced with the need to structure a public alternative anyway. We cannot afford to leave the choice to private insurers. Any government insurance programme would be required to have premiums/levies which reflect the underlying risks (no matter how large) and such a programme must operate with a strategy which would make it unnecessary to appeal to Treasury for a bailout except on a most exceptional basis.

Around the world there appears to be general agreement that much more can and needs to be done to mitigate catastrophe risk and that many investments in risk mitigation can be cost-effective from a long term perspective. Such risk mitigation as applied to New Zealand should encompass several new measures or improvements. For a comprehensive risk-management programme to work it would need to incorporate the following elements:

- By increasing the mandate and functions of a modified EQC, the Government increases disaster assistance, in particular, for property. Private residential or commercial property catastrophe or general insurance would no longer be necessary.

- Additional actuarial adjustments should account for inflation, real growth in property values, and the growth in coastal properties, which, by their location, are at greater risk.

- To bring damaged structures to current earthquake standards, an increase of tax subsidies for rebuilding and an upgrade of these structures would be necessary, although any subsidies could be of a temporary measure until the work necessary is completed.

- Premiums/levies applied to properties must be local-authority rateable-value linked in order to provide a fair measure of financial assistance and equity to low-income homeowners.

- A reassessment of pre-disaster planning on all levels of government, central as well as local, would be imperative to enhance catastrophe preparedness. Integrated into this model should be the EQC efforts necessary to speed up the recovery process.

- Special attention should be given to how best to involve the local community from the moment a catastrophe occurs. An assessment of existing community-focused programmes would be required. Present public information will need to be scrutinised and updated. Educational efforts should be aimed at optimising catastrophe risk management in cooperation with community, private, public and governmental organisations to create an effective and reliable partnership.

- Present mechanisms in managing the Natural Disaster Fund would need to be reassessed and made financially sound. In the initial phase, the EQC may need to build on its current reinsurance programme in order to carry out its responsibilities until the fund has built to a self-sustainable level.

- Insurance requirements for home mortgages would continue to be imposed on homeowners via the EQC. The EQC premiums or levies would be best pegged to property rating values from local authorities.

- The EQC's 'contents insurance' caps would be scrapped, leaving optional content insurance the sole responsibility of the homeowner and private insurers.

- Private insurers would only be involved in insurance for contents and chattels insurance.

- A move away from reliance on the same financial models as the banks. A lack of diversification in modelling increases systemic risk within an organisation. It is well recognised that the main problems in the last financial crisis were founded in banking, investment banking and 'shadow banking'. However, the insurance industry was not an entirely innocent bystander. The crisis demonstrates the scope for further improvements in insurance business models and is a reminder that there are limitations to the predictive ability of internal models.

Also included is the need for land-use management and regulation; enforcement of adequate building codes relative to new construction and retrofitting existing structures to be more resistant to structural damage from earthquakes. Each of these measures imposes certain costs on the particular groups involved and consequently those parties may be disinclined to invest in mitigation and oppose government attempts to compel them to do so. There are also issues with respect to public subsidies of mitigation investments and there is a clear need for public education about the benefits of mitigation. Regulation may be appropriate in some areas, such as land-use management and building code enforcement, but voluntary mitigation could be encouraged if private homeowner incentives (e.g. tax deductions) existed to encourage investment in mitigation.

Unlike the private insurers, only the EQC is, or could be, equipped to carry out all these functions on a national basis as they constitute a wider public interest. The EQC should be seen as the protector of the people's interests, a government 'crown entity' overseen, but not managed by the government of the day, representative of the people of the country and administered on their behalf for their common good. The investment of portions of the fund locally, would serve to reinforce the scheme as a public good.

In the event of a major catastrophe, for the EQC to discharge its responsibilities to claimants either through cash settlement or managed repair, will require the orderly sell down of Natural Disaster Fund assets. As the EQC makes increasing payments to claimants, this will necessitate the EQC sale of the EQC's holdings of government bonds which are deemed 'non-market'. These are sold back to the New Zealand Debt Management Office (NZD MO) in order that the Office can manage any resulting refinancing as part of the Crown's overall debt requirements. The sale of bonds to the NZD MO reduces both debt (liability) and the cash (asset) holdings of the NZD MO.

In addition the EQC must maintain a 'business as usual' focus, as other communities are also likely to be affected by natural hazard events. The severe weather events of April/May 2011 which led to flooding and large-scale landslips in Hawke's Bay and the December 2011 Nelson and Golden Bay floods are reminders that EQC needs to maintain the capability and flexibility to respond efficiently and effectively to other natural hazard events even whilst dealing with the aftermath of major seismic damage. It follows that the recent Canterbury events will continue to play a principal role in the current and future Commission activity for several years to come.

Change is required. The country cannot afford another repeat of the Canterbury experience – neither socially nor economically.

Citizens Speak

After the quake hit at 12.50pm on Tuesday (February 22nd, 2011) I ran to the car and drove through every back street and shortcut I could think of, desperate to get home. What usually took 20 minutes took me over four hours. I arrived on the east of Christchurch to mindboggling disaster. Roads cracked in half, streets covered in sand, houses cracked down the middle. Down Avonside Drive a young mother cried uncontrollably as her 4 by 4 had two wheels stuck in the middle of a large crack in the road, she was desperate to pick up her pre-schooler. I got home to discover my wife had fallen up to her shoulders in liquefaction on River

Road. My son, carrying our daughter, had also fallen into the road cracks covered by liquefied water after the quake. The quakes were hideous and traumatising for thousands in this City. We would later discover 185 people died in the disaster.

Our only consolation, or so we thought, was that we and nearly everyone else in the city, were covered by insurance. We live in a western country where our taxes are supposed to ensure our Government would back us and be there for us in any disaster, especially one of this magnitude. I was wrong. I spent the next three years after the quakes trying to explain to New Zealand that the Government was backing Insurance Companies over and above its own taxpaying citizens. Few believed or wanted to believe. They loved this Government. They loved John Key. He is a man of the people. Why and how could he do such a thing? What made me most upset has been the willingness of our Government to sit back and allow insurance companies and its own governmental policies around land issues, to stress and create emotional devastation for thousands of Cantabrians. The media also backed the Government.

As part of the Wider Earthquake Communities Action Network (WeCan) we understood a meeting was held between the Government and Insurance Companies leading into the June 2011, red zone announcement. We also understand John Key was present at that meeting. It strongly appears that a deal was struck with Insurance Companies. If there wasn't a deal, the actions of the Government after this time show a clear backing for Insurance Companies. The problem they had was that over 95 percent of all the houses affected had insurance cover.

Much of the red zone (and some TC3 land) was unstable, foundations were badly damaged and unstable. It would cost billions for the EQC to remediate this land and billions for the Insurance Companies to pay-out 'as new' replacement costs. Both the Government and the Insurance Companies were stuck.

Deal Number One: the red zone. The government chose affected areas where rateable values of homes and land were low and offered to pay them out. There were areas in Fendalton, Redcliffs and Parklands which had just as badly affected land as the red zone but their Rateable values (RV) were too high. In the end it was a win-win for the Government and the corporates. No land remediation was needed and insurance companies didn't need to pay for new builds. If people don't like their offer then they could take RV. Red zoners were 'thrown to the wolves'. If they wanted to fight their Insurance Companies that was up to them. After the June 2011 red zone announcement we heard many red zone properties which had originally been total losses now deemed 'repairable'. Often the repair bill came just under the RV or the rebuild costings were so low that you might as well accept the 2007 RV price being offered. I talked to elderly couples who were offered NZD 800 per square metre to rebuild their homes. The industry average at the time was NZD 1770.

To add to the red zoners' woes the Government placed a time frame by which you had to decide whether to accept the offer and leave your home. The pressure was too much. If you didn't accept the offer, the small print on my copy, stated that they could compulsory acquire the land and property at the values, post-quake. Meanwhile, the Government crowed that they were bailing out Cantabrians and paying them out. All were winners. Instead they not only limited overall pay-outs but walked away as the owners of other people's land, right across the city.

Property valuers' explained to the Government that every third red zone homeowner would lose money using the rateable value equation. The house close to us was bought for NZD 420,000 prior to the earthquakes but had an RV of NZD 285,000. In essence the owners had NZD 120,000 stolen from them by the Government. RV took no account of any improvements to the property. In the end the Government created the great escape. Neither the Government nor the Insurance Companies would have to deal with the real loss incurred from the quakes of the most affected homes. Those with no insurance and owning land were even worse off. The Government red zoned their land and offered 50 percent of their RV, these offers were later deemed to be illegal by the Supreme Court. However the Government has totally ignored the highest court in the land and has refused to pay-out fair values to these homeowners.

The Government's second deal was the use of the Earthquake Commission (the EQC). Throughout the city there were homes that were obviously total losses and needed to be rebuilt. Instead they were poorly assessed by the EQC as only requiring repairs under NZD 100,000. One house I was advocating for was assessed by the EQC as needing only NZD 76,000 repairs. The outer walls of this house had imploded on the inside. I remember my engineer would not go into specific parts of this house as it was unsafe. Their insurance company had assessed a NZD 396,000 rebuild for this large two story house! The discrepancy was staggering and I've since heard of worse cases. Advocacy was the only way of achieving a fairer result. The policy of keeping people artificially under cap resulted in the EQC preventing thousands of claims from being handled by Insurance Companies. Over the years they have trickled through. The result, however, was the EQC, using Fletcher Construction, was able to get repairs done cheaply, especially sub floor repairs where they used poor building practises such as jacking and packing and epoxy injection. The Government orchestrated this by changing the building code allowing in the end, repairs to be completed more cheaply. The result - people's 'as new' replacement policies were not honoured.

The 'deal' worked as the Government/ EQC would not have to pay nearly as many over cap NZD 115,000 payments to the Insurance Companies protecting its own governmental books and Insurance Companies would not have to pay-out for full rebuilds.

In the end the Government is elected to protect its citizens. This National Government did everything in its power to protect Insurance Companies and its own drive to budget surplus, one of its key goals at the election. They refused to oversee Insurance Companies to enforce a mechanism that would ensure they acted fairly and in a timely fashion. They refused to enact legislation or any kind of rules to ensure these corporates would act responsibly and adhere to their own 'Fair Insurance Code'.

The Government refused to act against the EQC, its own agency, even when thousands of Cantabrians were crying out about ill treatment. They sat back as they knew this was exactly what they had commissioned this organisation to do. I find the fact that they allowed changes to building regulations so the EQC could repair up to a poorer standard and save millions - deplorable.

Our Earthquake Minister, Mr Brownlee, had a stock phrase when referring to the struggles of so many, "*The market will fix it.*" Even as the property prices skyrocketed across the city, the government did little to alleviate the pain of so many. In the end the least affected were able to sell their homes at exorbitant prices to the most affected. Few red zoners built homes - they instead had to buy existing homes at these inflated prices.

The biggest treachery for me has been the Governments use of the media. They have sold the country a lie and created the Great Escape. They convinced the rest of New Zealand all was well. Yes there are a few losers but on the whole 'we have backed Canterbury'. The media have generally taken this on and backed the Government. Few of the media outlets did any investigative reporting on what is really happening in our city. Our Earthquake Minister continues to have no real critique by our local paper The *Christchurch Press*.

As so many have said to me. It was not the earthquake itself that has destroyed my life it is dealing with the organisations that existed to protect my livelihood. They were complicit in covering themselves at the expense of the people who had paid their taxes and insurance premiums.

By Rev. Mike Coleman [17]

CHAPTER 8
THE REINSURANCE INDUSTRY

- -

And if there has been a theme of modern Wall Street,
it's that young men with PhDs who approach money
as science can cause more trouble than a hurricane.

Michael Lewis, 'In Nature's Casino'[1]

The best way to describe reinsurance is 'insurance for insurance companies' and as with insurance contracts a duty of utmost good faith applies to reinsurance agreements under the common law.

Reinsurance is the ideal mechanism for dissipating the potential losses of insurers and the EQC's Natural Disaster Fund, by extending them to broader market places. Reinsurance developed in response to events in 1842 in the city of Hamburg. Hamburg burned to the ground and bankrupted the entire German insurance industry. It is thought that the reinsurance industry as we know it today, grew from the ashes of Hamburg. Reinsurance was the entity that took on the risk that the insurance industry was unable to absorb through diversification. The established insurance companies continued to sell policies to Hamburg citizens but the insurers passed on some of the premium they collected to Cologne Reinsurance (Re) in exchange for taking on claims losses exceeding a particular amount. Cologne Re protected itself by diversifying at a higher level via retrocessional reinsurance (i.e. the practice of reinsurers themselves purchasing insurance). As time has gone on, the big catastrophe risks of the twenty-first century are less easily diversified 'away', as personal wealth has become concentrated in coastal areas and densely populated cities and the number of severe weather events have increased. Michael Lewis in 'In Nature's Casino' writes that the only way to deal with risk is to spread it widely. This results in removal of the risk from the insurance industry and places it in the capital markets. *"If you could take a magnitude 8 earthquake and distribute its shock across the planet, no one would feel it,"*[2] and so it is with the financial impact of an earthquake. If the risk is diversified sufficiently far and wide, the financial impact is felt only minimally... or so the theory goes.

Currently in New Zealand, high levels of reinsurance are carried. This means that the majority of privately insured losses are borne by global reinsurance companies rather than domestic insurance firms.[3] Aon Benfield[4] (a division of Aon Corporation) calculates that reinsurers by 2012 had already carried two-thirds of the losses from disasters in New Zealand since 2010.

For many years, few people outside the insurance industry were aware of the existence of the mechanism of reinsurance. In the USA the public was first introduced to reinsurance in the mid-1980s, during 'the liability crisis' (late 1984 – early 1986). At this time reports began to accumulate of remarkable developments in the world of business insurance. Some insurance customers suffered extraordinary increases in the price of liability coverage, of 60, 100 and even 1,500 percent. Other customers could not obtain any coverage, or where coverage was available, the scope of protection was often vastly reduced. A shortage of reinsurance was widely reported to be one of the factors contributing to the availability problems and high price of various kinds of liability insurance. Many anxious policyholders went on to form policy-owned insurance companies (mutual societies) with the help of brokers, relying less on traditional insurance companies and concentrating on their own underwriting practices.

Reinsurance has become a complex global business that is constantly evolving. Traditionally, and still most commonly, reinsurance transactions take place between two insurance entities: the primary insurer who sells the original insurance policy to the policyholder and the reinsurer. Primary insurers and reinsurers can choose to share both the premiums and losses, or reinsurers may decide to only assume the primary insurer's losses above a certain dollar limit. This is done in return for a fee. As the market has become more complex, other financial instruments have also been developed to diversify certain risks, particularly of natural disasters. The resulting mitigation products are being sold by insurers and reinsurers to institutional investors in the form of catastrophe bonds (CAT bonds, see Chapter 8) as well as other risk-spreading mechanisms. Increasingly we see these new products reflecting a gradual blending of reinsurance with investment banking. This is contributing significantly to the increasing complexity within the reinsurance and insurance marketplace. Arguably, it is also contributing to the uncertainty of the re/insurance 'safety net' in an ever increasingly uncertain global financial market.

Most reinsurance placements are shared between a number of reinsurers. For example, a NZD1.5 million reinsurance (due after the insurer excess of NZD 500,000) means that the reinsurer(s) assumes the risk between the NZD 500,000 and NZD 2 million. This NZD 2 million layer may well be shared by 30 or more reinsurers. The lead reinsurer sets the premium and contract conditions for the reinsurance contract. Other companies subscribing to the contract are known as 'following reinsurers'. Much of reinsurance is handled by reinsurance brokers who then place business with reinsurance companies. The other option is 'direct writing' reinsurers, who have their own staff and reinsure insurance companies directly. It is said that the choice of reinsurer is made with extreme care, as the primary insurers are essentially exchanging insurance risk for credit risk. *If the financial markets were to collapse it is highly likely that the reinsurance and primary insurance markets would also collapse.* Some of the reinsurers involved in Christchurch's financing include Munich Re of Germany, Swiss Re of Switzerland, Hannover Re of Germany, SCOR of France, Flagstone Re and Lloyd's of London in the United Kingdom. Hardy, Chaucer, Amlin, Novae, Partner Re, and Platinum are others.

In the relationship between the reinsurer and insurer there may be a contract which contains a clause obliging the reinsurer to follow the primary insurer's settlement decisions. The effect of these clauses depends on interpretation of the clause. Under a 'follow the fortunes' clause, a reinsurer is bound by the insurer's settlement where the claim falls within the reinsured risk and where the insurer has acted honestly and in a proper and business-like manner in effecting settlement.

The reinsurance contract will govern what information the primary insurer is required to give to the reinsurer with respect to claims. In order to avoid liability, the onus is on the reinsurer to prove bad faith or unprofessional behaviour in effecting settlement. Throughout the early months post-earthquakes in Canterbury there were firms employed specifically by the reinsurers to assess and audit insurers' decisions regarding quantum of damages in order to ensure that damage assessments are being carried out accurately and judiciously. In spite of this, very little was actually paid out by the insurers at that stage.

Reinsurance can be divided into two basic categories: *treaty* (the reinsurance company agrees to automatically reinsure a portion of the primary insurer's book of business); and *facultative* (where the primary insurer chooses individual risks). Both treaty and facultative reinsurance agreements can be structured on either a *proportional basis* (pro-rates all premiums, losses and expenses between the insurer and the reinsurer on a pre-arranged basis) or excess-of-loss basis. *Excess-of-loss* contracts require the primary insurer to keep all losses up to a predetermined level of retention, and the reinsurer to reimburse the company for any losses above that level up to the limits of the reinsurance contract. Excess-of-loss reinsurance has a greater orientation toward catastrophe.

In property coverage, a proportional agreement is most often applied. In this case the reinsurer and the primary insurer share both the premium from the policyholder and the potential losses. In an excess-of-loss agreement, the primary company retains a proportion of liability for losses (known as the ceding company's retention) and pays a fee to the reinsurer for coverage above that amount, normally subject to a fixed upper limit. Excess-of-loss agreements can apply to individual policies, to a stipulated event such as an earthquake, which affects many policyholders or to the primary insurer's aggregate losses above a certain amount per policy or per year.

There is also a third category of reinsurance known as *catastrophe reinsurance*. Reinsurance in this situation protects against catastrophic financial loss resulting from a single event, such as the total fire loss of a large manufacturing plant. Reinsurance in this case also protects against the aggregation of many smaller claims resulting from a single event, such as the recent Canterbury earthquakes or a major hurricane, which affects many policyholders, simultaneously. While the insurer is able to cover losses individually, the aggregate may be more than the insurer wishes to retain In the form of capital. This method enables the primary insurers to stay in business through large fluctuations in loss experience.

A primary insurer's reinsurance programme can be very complex. Robert Woodthorpe Browne[5] diagrammatically described the structure as a pyramid with increasing dollar levels of coverage for increasingly remote events which are then split among a group of reinsurance companies. Each of these companies assumes a portion of the risk. The programme would include layers of proportional and excess-of-loss treaties as well as perhaps a facultative excess-of-loss layer at the top. On Level I are the primary insurers who sell the homeowner their insurance. On Level II are the large professional reinsurers, e.g. many syndicates at Lloyd's as well as large and small broker market reinsurers worldwide. These are the 'leads' who quote the terms on contracts which other companies then 'follow'. On Level III are the companies who reinsure the primary reinsurers under retrocessional contracts. Level III companies also buy secondary retrocessional catastrophe covers which are known as London Market Excess (LMX). There is no distinct group of companies which write these but they are instead written as a subset of Level III companies themselves. This complex web of relationships and interrelationships explains in part why it is so difficult to trace how each of the New Zealand insurers spreads their risk; they are not particularly willing to share this information.

All of which leads us to an important point. The strength of your insurer to cover a risk is dependent upon the strength of its reinsurers, which leads to the question, 'How likely is systemic risk within the reinsurance market in this current global economic climate' (i.e. the collapse of an entire financial system)?

If the primary insurance sector in New Zealand is minimally regulated, as it is, the reinsurance industry is even less regulated.[6] The reasoning behind this, we are told, is that the primary insurers, as consumers of reinsurance, are considered to be 'sophisticated buyers' and therefore unlikely to invest in 'questionable' reinsurers. However, history shows this to be something of a fiction. In the early 1980s in the United States, state insurance officials became increasingly concerned about the reliability of reinsurance contracts, that is, the ability of the reinsurer to meet its contractual obligations when required and a primary company's (i.e. an insurer) use of them. Then again, in 2008, a large insurer, American Insurance Group (AIG), failed in the USA. Martin F. Grace of Networks Financial Institute, in a policy brief (April 2010), described AIG as having held a vast asset portfolio and also engaging in securities lending of the assets backing its insurance. This allowed AIG to lend its assets to others for cash collateral which AIG would then invest. A securities lender could invest in safe assets such as government securities or, for a higher return, a company such as AIG could invest the collateral in mortgage-backed securities. If the mortgage-backed securities lost value, (as they did in 2007/8) then AIG would have to meet the difference with its own money. This created a further liquidity problem for AIG. In addition these assets which were lent, were from AIG's subsidiaries, which, when allocated back to the subsidiaries exposed the insurers to increased solvency risk. State regulators were unaware of the significant size of the lending operation due to the 'off balance sheet' nature of the transactions.

So what is the probability that the failure of a re/insurance company can also take down a significant set of companies or influence the solvency prospects in other markets. It happened to AIG, so are there others? Or, more to the point, are there others operating in the New Zealand market?

The process of 'retrocession' (where a reinsurer insures with yet another reinsurer) can sometimes continue until the original reinsurance company unknowingly gets some of its own business (and therefore its own liabilities) back. This is called a 'spiral' and is not uncommon in some speciality lines of business such as the marine and aviation industries. For example, in the 1980s the London market created the 'London market spiral' (LMX) as a result of Hurricane Alicia in 1983, which essentially consisted of the same loss going round and round the market, thereby artificially inflating the market loss figures of big claims. The gross reinsured amount of loss grew year by year. This was ultimately due to the fact that market participants continued to receive additional claims and went on to submit additional claims to their own catastrophe covers, which in turn generated more reinsurance claims. Another example of this phenomena was the Piper Alpha oil rig scenario. Typically, these spirals develop when a company on a particular level reinsures another on the same level or higher levels and then feeds the exposure from those contracts back into their own retrocessional protections. In a catastrophe situation, the pyramidal hierarchy can form a pyramid where there is far more surplus available on Level I and not much on Level III. Yet, when the major catastrophe occurs, it is Level III (the reinsurance companies at the top of the pyramid) that are likely to receive the disproportionately large share of that loss.[7] It is said that sophisticated reinsurance companies are aware of this danger and through careful underwriting attempt to avoid it, but the reality is that the risk of major earthquake or other natural disaster is spread throughout the world by the property catastrophe reinsurance market. Inevitably this forms an extremely complicated web of contracts with many reinsurers reinsuring little pieces of each other's catastrophe covers. One could imagine that the likelihood of a spiral developing is considerable and further complicated by, for instance, a series of earthquakes such as Canterbury has recently experienced, which follow each other in quick succession and which are deemed to be separate claims events.[8] There is a blurring between damage caused by earthquake one and earthquake two or three and their resulting aftershocks, each claim representing yet another re/insurance event.

Risk/loss modelling

For the reinsurance industry, earthquake loss estimation is crucial not only to adequately price its product, but also to manage the accumulation risk in the face of the ever-increasing exposure in highly seismic regions. Changes in the built environment and a continuously evolving earthquake science make it a necessity for the industry to constantly refine earthquake loss estimation models. Current methods tend either to rely on the limited historical damage and loss data or on the numerical simulation of the response of individual buildings to the ground shaking produced by earthquakes.

As insurers and reinsurers become more sophisticated in their use of models, there will be continued pressure on the developers of models to provide more complete solutions that calculate all possible direct and indirect losses from a disaster, for example in the case of earthquakes: liquefaction, tsunamis and business interruption. Certainly the need for more sophisticated models was revealed by the Canterbury earthquakes, where the global models failed to correctly model liquefaction or business interruption. Some critics, such as Philip Geheb from the Washington University School of Law, state that catastrophe models are *"deterministic, based on uncertain science, and providing cover for insurance companies to raise premium rates to unjustifiably high levels"*.[9]

There is a legitimate concern that an 'unaccounted-for event', such as liquefaction, will cause the reinsurance industry to overreact, and make new assumptions about the rest of the country, leading to potentially higher premiums throughout the country. Along with liquefaction are the likelihood of slope failure, areas of potential subsidence, and the presence of other geological weaknesses. We do know that there are other parts of New Zealand particularly susceptible to some of these risks. The town of Lyttelton has highlighted the uniqueness of each event versus the events modelled. Numerous compounding anomalies have highlighted the fact that no tool has the ability to match the actual experience.

The current earthquake risk models include fire as a loss driver; tsunami is only included in a few models, and the increased seismicity after a large event is not included at all. Liquefaction is factored into some models but often very underestimated; business interruption is included in most models but the impact for business interruption-sensitive industries tends to be underestimated; contingent business interruption is often not modelled as exposure to it is not fully understood.[10] It is hardly a perfect science! The Christchurch events have highlighted the need to fully understand the aspects of loss not captured during modelling. While some consideration was given to potential ground damage this was greatly underestimated.

RiskScape is a multi-hazard risk/loss modelling system for use within New Zealand. It is a joint venture between the Institute of Geological and

Nuclear Sciences and the National Institute of Water and Atmospheric Research. RiskScape contains detailed data for a number of places in New Zealand, including Christchurch. Scientists have compiled data on the number, age and type of buildings, their size and condition, materials used in their construction, value of contents, and more. They have also gathered data on what the buildings are used for – homes, offices, schools, shops, factories and so on, and the number of people likely to be in them on any particular day and time. When the details of a real or projected hazard are combined with building, infrastructure and social information, RiskScape simulates the impact of the disaster on the buildings, and predicts the consequences in both human and economic terms.[11]

The EQC uses the modelling system Minerva which contains a full probabilistic Geographic Information System-based earthquake model. This model simulates earthquake losses up to 10 years into the future and two alternative 'Economic Scenario Generators' for modelling the risk faced by the Natural Disaster Fund. The earthquake model is designed to be used for scenario analysis of specified earthquakes, including past historical events, actual events and hypothetical events. The model has the ability to compare reinsurance prices with estimated prices based on the derived loss risk information and pricing theory. The system produces tables of balance sheet parameters at yearly intervals in statistical form as well as predicting the likelihood that certain parameters will be exceeded, for example the need to call on the Crown Guarantee.[12]

With each natural disaster, lessons are learned and observations are made that allow modellers to advance to the next generation in catastrophe modelling. There is also an accompanying growing appreciation of the limitations of models. The science and impact of natural hazards can never be completely understood and models are an approximation of a very complex suite of physical phenomena in an ever-changing global climatic landscape. Nothing has become clearer than the need for high quality data and the ability for rapid reporting. The lesson learned in Christchurch and environs must undoubtedly impact systems considerations and underwriting standards going forward.

Catastrophe (CAT) bonds

As the markets and the reinsurance industry become more sophisticated, alternative financial risk-spreading mechanisms are created. These include hedge funds, catastrophe-oriented funds and asset-management techniques. They are often structured as floating rate bonds.[13] One such mechanism is the Catastrophe (CAT) bond, which has attracted much interest in recent time. CAT bonds are risk-linked securities that transfer a specified set of risks from a sponsor to investors. They are a hedging instrument that offers multi-year protection without the credit risk present in reinsurance, by providing full collateral for the risk limits offered through the transaction. For investors, CAT bonds are said to offer attractive returns and reduction of portfolio risk, since CAT bond defaults are uncorrelated with the default of other securities. They do, however, present their own risks, as evidenced during the recent earthquakes in Japan where a lack of clarity over trigger points for existing catastrophe bonds led to broader questions over the ability of investors to accurately determine potential losses.[14]

CAT bonds initially had fairly simplistic and transparent structures, but as reinsurers have become active investors (as well as sponsors) in the products, deals have become increasingly complex. There are those who say that a better understanding by investors of the underlying portfolios is critical, as well as grasping the fundamental risk, now that the CAT bonds have become so sophisticated.

CAT bonds emerged from a need of insurance companies to alleviate some of the risk they would carry in the event of a major catastrophe which they would not be able to cover by premiums and/or returns from investments using those premiums received from policyholders. They were first used in the mid-1990s in the aftermath of Hurricane Andrew and the Northridge earthquake in the USA and have taken some time to become established.

The transaction begins with the formation of a single-purpose reinsurer. For example, if an insurer has built up a portfolio of risks by insuring properties in Christchurch, then it might wish to pass some of this risk on so that it can remain solvent after a large natural disaster. It could simply purchase traditional catastrophe reinsurance, which would pass the risk on to reinsurers, or it could sponsor a CAT bond, which would pass the risk on to investors. In consultation with an investment bank, it would create a special-purpose entity that would issue the CAT bond. Investors would buy the bond, which might pay them a coupon of the London Interbank Offered Rate (LIBOR) plus a spread, generally between 3 and 20 percent. If no natural disaster occurred, the investors would make a healthy return on their investment. But if a natural disaster were to occur and trigger the CAT bond, then the principal initially paid by the investors would be forfeit, and instead used by the sponsor to pay its claims to policyholders. Investors who object to CAT-bond investing usually say that it is merely another form of gambling. One investor phrased it this way: "my *boss won't let me buy bonds that I have to watch the Weather Channel to follow.*" Others claim it is gambling, but with the odds in your favour. However, with the ever-increasing incidence of natural disasters around the globe, the sagacity to rely on CAT bonds diminishes as the associated risk becomes ever more certain.[15]

Forcing primary insurers to capitalise, that is, maintain enough 'ready funds' for a one-off disaster, is currently unpopular with the insurance industry. It is likely to also have the consequence of raising premiums for the consumer, making insurance potentially unaffordable for many. This has happened in the USA in areas where hurricanes are prevalent. For this reason, issuance of CAT bonds or securities linked to specific potential catastrophes is considered to be a possible alternative and has been picking up traction around the globe. However, their use continues to be debated. In addition, consequent upon the European Union Solvency II requirements, which are intended to force European re/insurers to bolster and prove their capital adequacy for claims, these issues are likely to receive increasing scrutiny and attention[16] – and rightly so.

The Asia-Pacific region only accounts for around a quarter of the excess-of-loss catastrophe limit purchased in the world and this share of global catastrophe excess-of-loss premiums is just under 15 percent.

The share of premiums has doubled since 2007, demonstrating the Asia Pacific region's rapid growth. As reinsurance take-up increases, particularly in China, India and Southeast Asia, Asia is likely to contribute to a much higher proportion of global premiums. This will encourage, wisely or otherwise, the use of risk-transfer tools such as CAT bonds to hedge insurers' and reinsurers' risks in the region.[17]

CAT bonds 'financialise' natural disasters. Once there is a market for CAT bonds, there is money to be made, even as a storm strikes or an earthquake occurs, by those who over-rely on weathermen who are considered marginally better able to predict likely extreme weather events than their peers. As an example of this, prior to the 2005 hurricane season, a Bermuda CAT bond hedge fund, Nephila, found a team of oceanographers in Rhode Island (Accurate Environmental Forecasting) whose forecasts of the previous hurricane seasons had been surprisingly good. Nephila employed the company's services and traded bonds on the basis of the reports it was producing. Arguably the entire catastrophe risk-taking industry exists at the mercy of such modellers. The scientists were, in effect, the new odds-makers.[18] Rating agencies such as Standard and Poor's and Moody's also began to rely on the scientists to evaluate their exposure. When they predicted increased likelihood of catastrophic storms or other natural events, Standard and Poor's and Moody's demanded that the insurance companies raise more capital to cover their suddenly more probable losses. So in addition to the USD 40 billion-plus that the insurance industry had lost in Hurricane Katrina, the insurance companies, by edict of the ratings agencies, had to raise USD 82 billion from their shareholders just to keep their investment grade rating. Suddenly the primary insurance industry was not so eager to expose itself to losses from hurricanes.

This example also poses interesting questions around the links between government, research agencies and the re/insurance industry. How carefully is this research information guarded, how is it disseminated and who from the government 'oversees' what is released? Clearly the financial implications for what and how such information is released, are huge.

Systemic risk

Reinsurance companies are essential to the global private insurance industry and, to a large extent, have functioned relatively smoothly thus far. However, some concerns in relation to the possibility of systemic risk posed by reinsurance companies have been recently raised. Systemic risk has been defined by Kaufman as *"the breakdown in an entire system, evidenced by a high correlation and clustering of failures."*[19] Another definition involves the concept of 'contagion'; that is, one failure by an institution leading to failure in another/others. It is because of the links between and among firms, markets or sectors that this chain reaction evolves – not unlike the contagion we have seen take place within the banking sector. According to *Time* magazine, 92 US banks failed in 2011, 157 were wiped out in 2010 and 140 went bankrupt in 2009. A third definition of systemic risk focuses on a shock affecting one firm which creates uncertainty in the market about the value of other firms. The interrelationships between these firms leads to the core of the problem of systemic risk. One recent study shows that in the USA the top five reinsurance groups provided approximately 60 percent of the reinsurance worldwide in 2009. The USA Property/Casualty insurance market also depends heavily on the top reinsurance groups. Those top five reinsurance groups provide approximately 30 percent of unaffiliated reinsurance to USA Property/Casualty insurers. That equates to 1,315 companies of a total 2,492 Property/Casualty insurers in USA who had unaffiliated reinsurance with Swiss Re, Munich Re, and Berkshire in 2009. This fact places this group of reinsurers at the apex of the insurance sector's interconnectedness. Consequently reinsurance company failure would have a significant impact on primary insurers as those reinsurers potentially would be unable to pay the primary insurers' losses. The consequences for homeowners would be catastrophic. Another cause for concern is the finding that some companies are packaging together catastrophe risks in a similar way to the carving up of subprime mortgages by big banks occurred before the financial crisis of 2008. Many are increasingly turning to pension funds and other capital market investors. To date, little is known about the pattern and degree of damage likely to be caused by reinsurer failure on primary insurers and hence the systemic risk to the real economy. In addition it is difficult to isolate the impact of major reinsurer failure from the primary insurance industry and the economy, due in large part to the 'complexity and opacity' of reinsurance. There is a serious lack of transparency associated with the risk of reinsurance transactions. This is in part due to the international nature of reinsurance companies and lack of standardised prudential supervision. Are these the sort of risks New Zealand policyholders want to bear?

To some extent, rating agencies may help reduce some information asymmetry and perhaps also serve as the 'de facto' regulator in insurance. In light of recent global events, one has to wonder if they too are not exempt from political interference. There are those who suggest that the ratings agencies were a prime enabler of the credit crisis of 2007/8 and that they constitute some of the most corrupt institutions in the financial world and in particular in the USA, having sold their ratings to the highest bidder while the rating agencies themselves have been unable or unwilling to solve the lack of transparency and supervision issues. In addition, there are risks of retrocession spirals or reinsurance spirals of the kind previously mentioned (1988–92 in the London Market Excess). Such retrocession spirals could trigger failures of multiple reinsurers all at once through the retrocession channel, and this shock might cause a ripple-on effect among the primary insurers.

There have been several studies examining the systemic risk posed by the reinsurance industry; however, some were carried out by research institutions that were also sponsored by insurance companies. The reality is that history has shown there is no such thing as 'too big to fail' in the financial world (e.g. the 2007–08 financial crisis). Now again, during 2010 and 2011 with the crisis in Greece, many financial institutions have significantly depreciated their portfolio of Greek property. The Franco-Belgian Dexia suffered a record loss of EURO 11.6 billion, partly due to the bank loss of EUR 3.4 billion in Greece. In more recent times, a possible Greek exit from the eurozone could imply 'knock-on' effects which could be underestimated in the financial market place today. Credit Agricole, another large French bank, suffered a quarterly loss of over USD 3 billion, partly because it took an additional provision of EUR 220 million due to the expected loss on Greek debt. The German insurer Allianz saw its annual profit halved by natural disasters, but also because of depreciation of assets in the Greek quarter.[20] Also, the recent global interest-rate (LIBOR) rigging scandal involving Barclays is playing out; the depth of the fraud and final consequences for the bank are not yet known. Losses will no doubt continue to rise in the months ahead, reminding us of the fickle nature of the financial marketplace.

In addition, a decline in investment income in the 2000s and the 2008 financial crisis has caused a deterioration of the asset quality of reinsurers.[21] Contributing to this is the impact of 'global terrorism' and intensified natural disasters (hurricanes, floods and earthquakes). These have exposed reinsurers to greater liability risks, while simultaneously, the global reinsurance industry has never been more concentrated. This increased concentration, combined with a seeming deteriorating quality of reinsurers leading to a possibility of failure of the major reinsurance companies, magnifies concerns over potential reinsurer failure and the possible spill-over effect into the whole insurance industry and beyond. In the wake of the collapse of insurance giant AIG and other globally huge financial institutions, it is imperative that an improved understanding of the dynamics and risk of large reinsurer insolvency in the future is gained, with the intention of prior anticipation of such possibilities. Today, only a few top global insurers dominate reinsurance supplies. Failure of any one of these reinsurance giants would be likely to pose serious systemic risks. This would likely mean the end of the insurance market as we know it and reliance on government to 'bail out' its citizens in the event of a major disaster. Small sovereign states such as New Zealand, should take note.

Should any large financial institution in financial difficulty expect to be bailed out by public authorities on the grounds that it is 'too big to fail' or 'too interconnected to fail', or because it is a large and complex banking organisation with far-reaching consequences, or because it is 'a systemically important financial institution'? Certainly the turmoil that surrounded the failure of Lehman Brothers in September 2008 did lead politicians to believe they had to commit to unconditional support of any troubled financial institution whose failure might create major disruptions. We await the outcome of the next round of likely failures. In addition, the US Government gave AIG a USD 85 billion emergency loan, followed by another loan of USD 37.8 billion less than a month later, and another of USD 40 billion the month after that. Many have questioned how much in total has been doled out, how much has been paid back and who were the real beneficiaries? In 2008 the ordinary American was looking at a tab of around USD 800 billion. This kind of commitment is a highly contentious one in terms of moral hazard and market discipline, particularly in a nation which claims to be so 'market orientated'.

In New Zealand we have seen this again, with the recent AMI failure leading to a potential exposure of taxpayers to a NZD 1 billion bill. The New Zealand Government took the decision to bail out this failing insurer which had neglected to secure sufficient reinsurance cover to back-up the volume of claims it received as a result of the Canterbury earthquakes. There was now talk of the Government having to bail out the insurer to enable it to uphold its claims payments in relation to the earthquakes. Our government set aside NZD 500 million in funds as a reserve for AMI in the event the company should require it. AMI had NZD 600 million in reinsurance and NZD 350 million in cash, which it said would not be sufficient to pay claims. As it transpired, AMI was later bought by another large Australian corporate insurer, IAG, on the condition that the Government would pay for any existing liabilities resulting from the 2010–12 Canterbury earthquakes. What a sweet deal that was, and what food for thought for conspiracy theorists!

In addition Gary Dransfield, the chief executive officer of Vero Insurance, has called for the Earthquake Commission to be involved in providing insurance support for commercial properties, as it has in the past, and the suggestion that the EQC could also act as an aggregated buyer of reinsurance for local underwriters. With the private insurance industry constantly relying on government intervention, what is its true value in times of catastrophe to the citizens of New Zealand?

The lack or insufficiency of reinsurance cover is apparently not untypical of insurers and academic research suggests that many would not in fact have the requisite capital and reinsurance to meet the claims associated with a large catastrophic event. Usually a company will have enough reinsurance and capital to meet the demands of a one in 'X' years disaster based upon the risk modelling they have employed. In New Zealand, the industry-recognised 'benchmark' event for the calculation of earthquake liabilities is a major earthquake affecting Wellington, which is typically calibrated in a range between one in 600 – one in 800 years. The recent Christchurch earthquakes have been assessed at significantly more than a one in 1,000-year event, but it is unlikely these timeframes can ever be calculated accurately. There is no provision for direct risk relationship between the loss return period and the Richter scale magnitude or any other measure of physical severity of an earthquake.[22] The Reserve Bank has set the reinsurance levels after the Canterbury earthquakes accordingly in the 'Reserve Bank of New Zealand Bulletin':

> In respect of earthquake, the standard is calibrated to a 1 in 1,000 years requirement. This will be phased in over time, with a limitation of 1 in 500 years until September 2015 and then moved upwards to 1 in 1,000 years during 2016.[23]

So in light of the potential for catastrophe risk and the increasing natural disasters around the world, the capital markets have been proposed – no doubt by those who have more to gain from those same markets – as a method by which the insurance industry could secure additional cover. As mentioned, the industry increasingly believes it can achieve this through CAT bonds as part of a proactive risk management and reinsurance strategy, though the yields on cat bonds do drop and were at their lowest in 2012. According to Lane Financial LLC, an insurance consulting firm, natural disasters have saddled cat bonds with US682 million in losses since 1996, or 1.3 percent of the US51 billion issued.

The threats that seem the most unlikely are the ones the industry knows least about. Catastrophe risk is fundamentally different from normal risk. It deals with (what used to be) the most rare of events. Consequently, experience does not help to predict catastrophes because there is little prior experience. The less probable the event, clearly the greater the uncertainty. The greater the uncertainty, the more an investor should be paid to cope with it, or so the argument goes. The catastrophic risk-taker (investor) has been described by Michael Lewis as something akin to a card counter at the blackjack table, allowed to play only a few hands. The odds are in his favour, but the player does not always get to play long enough for the odds to determine the outcome.[24] While losses are said to be rare they can also be significant. Buyers of one bond that provided for claims tied to the Japanese earthquake on 2011 lost all their money. Fitch Ratings continues to view the reinsurance sector as ripe for consolidation, seeing this as producing a modest credit positive. In addition, there would be a reduction in the number of reinsurers and associated underwriting capacity, which would be likely to ease competitive forces and help precipitate a hardening of premium rates. These developments, in my view, would only go toward further increasing integration and systemic risk.

After Hurricane Katrina in the USA, Louisiana was unable to generate and preserve wealth without insurance. It could not obtain insurance except at the market price, but that price remained a mystery. Billions of dollars in insurance settlements were received by local businesses and homeowners as pay-outs on their pre-Katrina policies. These pay-outs now bloated the New Orleans banks and brokerage houses but the money was not moving because many people were financially paralysed. Businesses have subsequently found it harder than ever to buy insurance, and many homeowners received letters from their insurers telling them that their long relationship had now come to an end. It has been described as an entire city being reshaped by an 'invisible force' – the price of catastrophic risk. But there are also those who believe that the price is 'wrong' – that it is simply too high. As a result, the rebuild of New Orleans has been slow. John Seo, Co-founder and Managing Principal at Fermat Capital Management, states that, "*The insurance companies are basically running away from society.*"[25]

However, for the people on Wall Street, Hurricane Katrina is now the single most important event, as overnight it turned the CAT-bond business from a tiny backwater option into a multi-billion dollar market. Nevertheless, this market is still only a drop in the ocean when you consider that the USA insurance industry stands to lose not only trillions of dollars from claims associated with mega catastrophes such as Katrina – and most recently Hurricane Sandy – but also the additional trillions of dollars-worth of uninsured property premiums in the USA, which tend to be centred on precisely those places most likely to be destroyed by nature, for example in California. The reason they are not insured is because insurance has become too expensive.

Reinsurers provide financial facility to primary insurers, which in turn also means that reinsurers have the power and ability to place considerable pressure on primary insurers and affect their ability to make insurance available at affordable prices. Reinsurance prices clearly reflect the actual historical losses and the potential losses in a geographic area, which in turn results in higher prices in those same areas. The availability of specific coverage lines or of reinsurance can dramatically increase or decrease availability of some primary insurance coverage. If reinsurance is not available or only available at very high prices, the primary insurer may not obtain client premium increases that will sufficiently cover the increased cost of the reinsurance premium. Reinsurers may also ask primary insurers to cease writing certain classes of business that have generated excessive losses. Such pressure can reduce the availability of insurance for those classes of business. The reinsurance market is a very influential force in the primary insurance market. There are now numerous examples of its leverage around the world. For example in Florida, USA after the 2004 and 2005 damaging storms, reinsurers simply pulled out of the market, leaving homeowners without insurance. Florida must now rely on smaller, leveraged carriers that purchase hurricane protection from the largely offshore reinsurance industry, whose rates are unregulated and notoriously volatile.

The increasing frequency of natural disasters around the world is likely to push up prices for reinsurance globally. In Canterbury, the effects of the reinsurance industry on our local insurance market have begun to be seen, premiums rising and some homeowners also unable to secure any insurance for their new properties. As well, many insurers are changing the terms of their policies upon renewal. For example, changes to Vero's home insurance policy came into effect on November 1, 2011 and now include a standard limit of NZD 2,000 (including GST) per square metre for rebuilds and an excess of NZD 10,000 for swimming and spa pools, drains and pipes, garden walls, paths, driveways, retaining walls and tennis courts. Most companies have introduced 'sum insured' contracts in an attempt to better define and limit their liability. It is still too early to see what the ultimate effect on local property values from such changes will be, but the prediction is that they will rise substantially. Certainly the property market slowed initially and it was not hard to predict that in light of the ongoing earthquakes in 2016, Christchurch will continue to be seen as a financial risk, which will be reflected not only in premium pricing and the availability of coverage, but ultimately will affect the growth and prosperity of the city.

Insurance rates have already increased as much as three times due to the large number of claims and the perceived increase in catastrophe risk in the region. There are reports of some commercial business owners having to pay as much as 10 percent of the value of their properties for their renewed insurance.

The insurers have reportedly been able to renew and in some cases extend their reinsurance cover. After a year long 'mediation', the Christchurch City Council finally settled with its insurers and reinsurers (AIG, Axis and R+V) for NZD 635 million. The Council had lodged claims worth NZD 920 million for its above ground assets.[26] Their insurer, Civic Assurance, failed to renew its own reinsurance cover (though continues to operate with a provisional insurance licence) and will be unable to apply for a full insurance licence until it settles its Canterbury earthquake claims. It is likely to take several years for Civic Assurance to rebuild its insurance portfolio.[27] As a result the rates for Christchurch residents are likely to rise by more than 33 percent over the next four years.[28] In addition, the council intends to increase asset sales from NZD 550 million to NZD 750 million. It has been suggested that CAT bonds may be a more viable option for New Zealand's primary insurers, that in this way they will be able to secure their top layers of reinsurance cover at a fixed multi-year cost.

A lack of reliable reinsurance available from reputable reinsurers could cause a failure in the primary insurance market. Consumers take out insurance policies and assume that the primary insurer is able to cover a loss should it arise, without seeking to know all the detail of the insurer's reinsurance programme. However, that primary insurer's financial stability is only as good as the reinsurers who stand behind it. This is particularly true in the current environment, when so much reliance is placed on capital markets and so much is unknown about the strength and resilience of that market in the current delicate global economic framework.

The re/insurance market should be more transparent for consumers. Those corporates are at the top of the insurance sector network, and their failure may create financial instability within the broader insurance sector. This in turn could cause a spill-over effect into the whole economy. This risk could also be aggravated if the increased default risk of primary insurers (due to the failure of reinsurers) cannot be conceived transparently in the market. This is exactly what occurred relative to the banking industry during the recent financial crisis. Consumers should understand the reason for the complex interrelationships between primary insurers and reinsurers and the complexity of the contract terms and the number of parties involved in the cession and retrocession arrangements. This is also one of the arguments for moving away from the reinsurance market place to a 'home grown' solution for catastrophe risk that is more appropriate for a sovereign nation.

After the September 2010 earthquake, the New Zealand current-account deficit as a share of the economy was reduced to a value near the smallest in a decade as local insurance companies received reinsurance payments from overseas. The shortfall was 2.3 percent of gross domestic product in the year ended December 31, 2011, according to Statistics New Zealand. The gap in the year through September was revised to 2.2 percent from a previously reported 3.1 percent. There was a NZD 3.52 billion deficit in the fourth quarter. At this point in time it was clear that the reinsurers would fund a good portion of the damage arising from the September 4 earthquake. However, information on reinsurance payments for the later Canterbury earthquakes is far more elusive, leading to questions about increased government and insurance company liabilities. It has been stated that the domestic insurers would now foot 80 percent of the rebuild costs. Establishing the facts remains difficult and more transparency here is necessary. Whether the insurers will pay out all they were given is not easy to determine, though doubtful. The latest trend by IAG and other insurers forcing claimants to accept cash settlements rather than go through the repair/rebuild programmes would suggest that all is not rosy with the Industry. In 2015, IAG declared that it exceeded a NZD 4 billion insurance limit on the February 22, 2011 earthquake, meaning that it will have to dip into its own capital reserves for any outstanding claims relating to that earthquake.[29]

The recent catastrophes in Japan, New Zealand and Australia are expected to be 'earnings events', not 'capital events', for the reinsurance market. So the reinsurance industry is likely to see losses in earnings for several quarters, but these losses are not thought to be large enough to create a serious global balance-sheet impact, nor a reason to raise additional capital. This is said to be due to the fact that there have only been a few 'major' catastrophes in the past five years, and reinsurers had built up an excess of capital prior to the events in Japan. Losses from the disasters in Japan, New Zealand and Australia in 2010 and 2011 are estimated at USD 50 billion plus, with 35 to 50 percent of this figure expected to ultimately be provided by the reinsurance market. By contrast, the global reinsurance industry total capital was USD 470 billion at December 31, 2010. It has been suggested that the likely effects on the reinsurance market and pricing are that catastrophe reinsurance pricing for the Japanese earthquake and New Zealand and Australian exposures is likely to rise significantly, possibly by up to 50 percent. It is expected that the market will 'harden' as companies raise their prices for these specific types of reinsurance. This ensures that reinsurers will be able to charge higher prices than previously. Accordingly, the industry global contracts are unlikely to see catastrophe-reinsurance pricing experience much impact, rising only slightly. It has been stated that reinsurers in the USA and Europe are unlikely to change their risk perceptions for catastrophe risk except for Japan, New Zealand and Australia. However, recent massive premium increases in Florida would indicate that this may not be the case. No doubt Hurricane Sandy will have impacted outlooks in the USA.

For the New Zealand reinsurance sector, 2011 was a challenging year. The sector was in a period of heightened market uncertainty as it began to focus on the January 1, 2012 renewals. Much has gone on behind closed doors and there have no doubt been challenges.

Despite a series of devastating events in New Zealand, Japan, the USA and Australia which have resulted in insured losses of around USD 70 billion (five times higher than the first half average for the past ten years), the first half of 2011 was the most costly first half on record in natural disaster-year terms. The losses sustained in this six-month period have already surpassed those recorded in 2009 and 2010 combined. However, the reinsurance sector has asserted that it remains adequately capitalised, with a significant excess capital position. It is said that the quality and liquidity of overall dedicated reinsurance capital remains strong. Nevertheless, the macroeconomic environment remains challenging, as subdued economic growth and low interest rates continue to depress investment returns. In addition, there is growing concern over the sovereign debt crisis in Europe and the economic consequences following the downgrade of the USA's credit rating. Adding pressure to the reinsurance industry is the impact of major catastrophe model releases, particularly for earthquake and wind risks, which have caused disruption in the industry and significantly altered risk perceptions and unexpectedly changed calculated loss amounts. Re/insurers had to work hard leading up to the January 1, 2012 renewals in order to gain a better understanding of how the revisions would affect their business. The final insured loss figure for both the Tohoku (Japan) and Christchurch earthquakes has not yet been calculated, but current reports suggest that the events are the first and third most costly earthquakes on record, respectively. There remains considerable uncertainty over what the ultimate cost to the (re) insurance market will be, as earthquake losses historically take longer to accumulate than other natural disaster losses such as hurricanes.

In New Zealand, catastrophe programme rates are said to have increased from between 20 percent to more than 100 percent. It is expected that working through the current situation in Canterbury will ultimately produce an improvement in the current state of knowledge about New Zealand's natural hazards, e.g. liquefaction risks, which will also have the effect of helping inform the pricing of the New Zealand risk by international reinsurance companies. Following the events in Canterbury, one would expect to hear a number of insurance companies announcing capital-raising activities. Once these immediate issues are settled, one could expect to see the rating agencies begin to exert pressure on companies writing catastrophe-exposed business to further improve their catastrophe risk-management systems and controls, and provide stronger capitalisation to support the risks inherent in this type of business.

To what extent is the present government being directed by foreign reinsurers in their attempts to minimise their exposure to the contractual insurance rights of New Zealand homeowners? The insurers were initially happy to insure houses for full replacement so that their associates, the banks, could offer 95 percent mortgages. Now, after the earthquakes, the insurers are less willing to honour these policies. In fact it could be argued that the Government has been coerced into undermining the insurance policies of those people living in the red zone (see Chapter 2, The Politics). This was evidenced by the loss of their insurance entitlements and property titles in exchange for a Registered Valuation set at 2007 values. Only a government has the capacity to strip property titles in this way. Neither the EQC nor insurers normally 'take' insured property; the usual practice is to pay for reinstatement.

There are a number of difficulties in estimating the final liability for the Canterbury events, that is, in the summing up of estimates from individual insurers and reinsurers. For instance, not all insurers have released estimates, so those estimates which have been given, have to be 'grossed up' to adjust for missing company figures. Estimates of aggregate natural catastrophe losses have a tendency to develop upwards over time. The estimates are often stated on an inconsistent basis, for example, some are 'after-tax', while others are 'before-tax'. Some are in dollars, while others are a percentage of the ultimate total industry loss. Most are net of reinsurance, but a few are gross of recoveries. Where estimated losses are stated net of reinsurance, some companies may have included the cost of reinstatement premiums for their reinsurance, but some may not. Reinsurers typically include reinstatement premiums as an offset to their reported losses. Overall, one might expect that the property risk and property catastrophe reinsurance market will harden, and capacity may be reduced somewhat. To the extent that reinsurers rely on retrocessional protection, they will experience higher prices and less capacity to support them.

As an aside, it is probably not widely known that the New Zealand Superannuation Fund, a fund for the state-run retirement benefit (pension) available to all working New Zealanders, made an investment in insurance-linked securities, including CAT bonds, last year. They were the first investor in CAT bonds to make a statement regarding their potential exposure through their investment portfolio to the Japan earthquake and tsunami disaster. They claim that they do not expect to see any loss to their investments. However, the possibility of loss 'so close to home' serves to highlight the risks involved in the use of capital market instruments to bolster the reinsurance fund of a sovereign state. The New Zealand Superannuation Fund posted a loss of NZD 1.67 billion in July and August 2011, citing a tough two months on world share markets. It was not publicly noted that the Fund does invest in CAT bonds.[30] The rationale for doing so was stated that the Fund considers *"catastrophe bonds as [they are] a strong diversification play and offer attractive risk-adjusted returns".*[31] There is surely a more effective alternative than a sovereign government gambling on probabilities via catastrophe bonds? See Chapter 7.

Recent events in both Australia and New Zealand are likely to make government entities more open to risk-transfer instruments such as CAT bonds, using catastrophe bonds to transfer the peak risks to the capital markets. However, as discussed, CAT bonds, too, have their limitations. As yet the traditional re/insurance market is still considered the preferable option to alternative risk-transfer techniques. It has been stated that it is probably inevitable that some New Zealand earthquake risk, ends up being issued in CAT bonds in the future, given the likely extremely high costs of reinsurance. Other alternative risk-transfer techniques such as the use of 'captives' are also an option. A captive is established with the specific objective of financing risks emanating from an insurer's parent group or groups, but they sometimes also insure risks of the group's customers as well. They have the advantage of being only answerable to the parent and can provide insurance cover that is not available in the commercial market or not available at a realistic premium. As the captive matures, it is capable of retaining a greater proportion of its parent's risks which in turn diminishes the parent's dependence on commercial insurance. It also improves the parents company's negotiating position with insurance and reinsurance markets as the captive's ability to absorb risk grows.[32] Some of the larger insurance brokers are currently carrying out feasibility studies into the use of captives with Singapore a suggested domicile, according to a report by the ratings and analysis company A.M. Best.

Conclusion

As previously noted, there is growing evidence, according to the World Bank, that the losses associated with frequency and severity of natural disasters is increasing.[33] This is due to several factors, including the growing concentration of populations and assets in risky areas, together with increases in climate variability. As a consequence, the fiscal and economic exposure of countries is becoming larger with every passing year. There is a growing body of literature analysing government capacity to react in the aftermath of a major disaster and in particular, government capacity to finance relief and reconstruction needs and subsequently to ensure fair insurance premiums and economies of scale. What is required is a compulsory extension of coverage to include a bundle of natural disaster hazards. This would equate to a stop-loss reinsurance offered by a compensation fund and would establish the government as reinsurer of last resort. In this way risks become bearable and insurable and diversified effectively over time. An unusually severe catastrophe has the ability to make even a well-capitalised and profitable insurer insolvent. Reinsurers have similar problems to those of the insurers and will increasingly limit their exposure in catastrophe-prone areas. Investors in CAT bonds will want to obtain good returns on their investment in the form of higher than normal interest rates when no disaster occurs in order to justify the risk of losing principal and/or receiving a lower interest rate after a disaster. As the incidence of natural disasters increases around the world, high returns diminish and CAT bonds become less attractive.

The Asia Pacific re/insurance market accounted for two-thirds of the world's insured catastrophe losses during the first three-quarters of 2011 according to a report from Guy Carpenter (www.guycarp.com), a leading global reinsurance intermediary. This represents a record share of the world's insured losses, amounting to more than NZD 50 billion up to the 30 September 2011. This demonstrates both the exposure to catastrophe events in Asia Pacific and the growing value at risk in the region as insurance and reinsurance penetration grow. In light of the recent severe flooding in Thailand and neighbouring countries, there was continued catastrophe reinsurance demand in this area in 2012. The demand for catastrophe reinsurance in the region has expanded rapidly and is expected to grow even further. Underlying macro-economic factors also exist, such as the rapid economic growth and increases in both populations and wealth in, for example, China and India, together with the increasing sophistication of insurance organisations in the region, which in turn are helping to drive the growth. This means that there are significantly less funds to go round as the number of potential claimants' increases with the apparent ever-increasing natural disasters around the globe. It has been shown time and time again that re/insurers are quick to leave the market or penalise the market as soon as they are called in to 'fund' the very risks they have taken on. For instance, very few policyholders in Canterbury are yet able to reap the benefits of their primary insurer's reinsurance programmes. More than five years since the original event, many are still waiting for evidence of private insurance assistance. To add to this, the press in both Australia and New Zealand continue to report problems with acquiring re/insurance coverage for some government departments and assets, the most recent being Queensland's roads, which are largely uninsured and now leaving the taxpayer liable. Queensland Premier Anna Bligh stated that a worldwide search had failed to find any re/insurance company prepared to cover the state's 170,000 kilometres of roads *"because it's an enormous network that, as we've just seen, can suffer an enormous amount of damage and it's really hard to predict that damage."*[34]

So it would seem that where damage risk is unpredictable or a near certainty, reinsurers are unwilling to enter the market place. If the odds are too great, the industry shies away from coverage. So in light of these facts, where does that leave New Zealand, a country on the 'Pacific Ring of Fire' where the chances of a major catastrophic earthquake are reasonably high, where flooding is becoming more commonplace and sea level rises have begun? With systemic risk a reality in our modern economic climate, do New Zealanders want to continue to place their nation and the economic future of its citizens in such an uncertain environment?

By far the best reinsurance option for catastrophic risk mitigation is a sovereign government. It has a deep credit capacity, with the ability to borrow by issuing debt far more readily than can private insurers or reinsurers. It can also raise resources rapidly through its ability to tax and provide mechanisms for risk mitigation. The ability to borrow, tax or mitigate to meet cataclysmic obligations depends on political capacity and willingness. This places governments in a natural position to play the role of reinsurer. Such a system would displace private capital deployed in insurance and reinsurance companies and is one of the traditional rationales for mandatory participation in social security and other public insurance programmes. The New Zealand Government is already the natural reinsurer as it has been called in to cover catastrophe losses after they have occurred, whether it has contracted for them or not (as in the case of AMI). The private re/insurance industry has high insurance density in New Zealand (i.e. the total premium income per person in a country's population). If these premiums were transferred to government and removed from the private-sector insurers, the government would be well able to sustain major catastrophe re/insurance for an affected population, and be able to do so in a transparent manner.

CHAPTER 9

IMPLICATIONS FOR RECOVERY

...our communities also need to be inspired and we need to believe that life is going to get better. We need milestones that enable us to celebrate along the way because it is going to be a long, slow, arduous journey – and we know there will be setbacks along the way. And we also need to know that our 'new kind of normal' is going to be better than getting back to normal would ever be – because that is now lost to us forever. And most importantly we need to know that we can each contribute something of value and that we will be heard so that we can truly own our own recovery and own our own future.

Hon. Lianne Dalziel, Labour Member of Parliament[1]

As many continue to wait for their insurers to resolve their property claims after five long years, I wonder when and if life in Christchurch is going to return to its former state of 'normality'. Having witnessed the course of events in Canterbury, I find myself unable to hold out much hope for a successful recovery or rebuild, particularly of the residential areas. Peter Townsend of the Canterbury Employers' Chamber of Commerce is suggesting that we are only now at the midway point. That 2016 sees the 'job' only 45 percent complete.[2] There is little sense of the urgency that one might expect within the entities which are controlling the process. It is clear that the insurance industry is in no particular hurry; though there is clear evidence of a move away from the repair/rebuild programmes to cash settlements. This approach indicates that the industry is under some pressure to reach its self-imposed targets of having all claims settled. However, we are still a long way off. This is corroborated by recent reports in the media alluding to timeframes of four to eight years before many damaged residential homes will receive attention. With shoddy repairs now also on the horizon, these timeframes are likely to balloon even further into the future.

Natural disasters are extremely complex events and they can magnify pre-disaster social trends, particularly those relating to the levels of inequality in the society. Christchurch is experiencing this disparity. Many of the most vulnerable in our society are facing enormous hardship without assistance. Experience around the globe suggests that the most socio-economically vulnerable populations are generally more likely to bear the burden of a natural disaster – are more likely to be displaced, and for longer (clearly reflected in the experiences of the Haiti earthquake and the USA hurricanes Andrew, Katrina and Sandy and no doubt throughout countless other regions and events across the globe).

People need to have the ability to plan, prepare and implement adaptive options. Being able to do these things also assists in minimising community vulnerability and creating resilience. Factors that contribute to social vulnerability include a lack of access to resources, limited access to political power and representation and social capital in the form of social networks and connections. Without these in place, people feel powerless, with little control over their lives. These factors are very much weakened or missing for large numbers in Christchurch in these days.

While some segments of the Canterbury region have been minimally affected, other communities are simply still not able to begin the process of recovery as they continue to await decisions about flooding, the long term viability of their land, insurance pay-outs and grants. The frustration felt by affected Cantabrians is palpable. Many see Christchurch as a city divided into those who are able to live in their homes, some with only a little cosmetic damage, who want the rest of the world to think everything is 'fine' here and that the rebuild is under way, while the other half are either waiting for land reports, land decisions, remediation plans or the release of foundation codes so that land can be assessed as being uneconomical to repair or economical (a major issue for many). Many are living away from their homes, still paying mortgages, partial rates and storage of effects.

Declaring a disaster a 'national emergency' has profound political implications. The politicisation of the event only increases as the affected community moves from emergency response through to the recovery and the reconstruction phases. The immediate emergency response by any government is fairly predictable, as it should be, but the aftermath is completely uncharted political territory, highly susceptible to the circumstances and the political values of the day.

Disasters produce considerable media interest, which also leads to heightened political arousal. Events are monitored and reported (often selectively) to the wider population through 'politically tinted glasses'. Information about the true state of affairs becomes difficult to obtain, i.e. information on the number of people that have actually left the region, the numbers of jobs lost, the numbers of insurance claims settled – that is, honest answers to difficult, but quantifiable questions. The media should play a vital role in ensuring that these questions receive honest answers and that those answers are shared throughout the land. There has been a noticeable absence of nationwide reporting.

What has become clear from Canterbury's natural disaster is that even experienced, media-savy and proactive local leaders have little ability to influence change in process, law, regulation or policy. This highlights some serious questions about the democratic process in New Zealand. What are the hidden agendas currently being played out in respect to Christchurch? There were originally concerns about the likely compulsory acquisition of land within the central business district for four new anchor projects. These were launched. One of those projects is the new convention centre requiring the compulsory acquisition of 20,000 square metres of land within the central business district. The old conference centre was a mere 7,000 square metres. It is a fair question to ask why does Christchurch now need a conference facility almost three times larger when its population is not dramatically increasing? The Christchurch City Council does not own a parcel of land that size in the favoured location. "There's an opportunity to get it right and build a vibrant, exciting environment," according to Hamish Doig, Managing Director of property company Colliers, a Christchurch brokerage firm. "A lot of small titles are an obstacle."[3] Do the owners of those lots agree with him? He went on to say that CERA has the power to acquire property and land and if a landowner is an 'obstacle' to redevelopment, that power will come to the fore. This is just what has happened: coercion not cooperation.

Why are changes not being made as a response to the problems and complaints expressed by affected residents in relation to ineffective CERA/Government programmes and processes? And though efforts of the shadow government have been only dimly visible throughout the recovery phase, they have failed to call the Government to account and act as a voice for the constituent populations. It was unfortunate that people such as the former Labour Member of Parliament Lianne Dalziel was *"banned from dealing with anyone at CERA apart from one liaison person."*[4] Action and attitudes such as this seemed extraordinary when there was so much stress to be alleviated and are a fair barometer to measure the mindset of the Government of the day.

For many citizens, there is a sense that no one is being held to account and that, in the main, the national media have resisted or in some way been compliant in this outcome. There is a strong feeling that CERA and the Minister of Earthquake Recovery's views, possibly derived directly from policy, are accepted at face value, with no analysis or redress. Needless to say the Minister's popularity has slowly declined throughout the recovery.[5] It is currently at an all-time low.

Since critical services were re-established in the city, the focus has been the restoration of infrastructure services and there are now post-earthquake reconstruction works happening in the Avonside, Dallington and Burwood areas of Christchurch. Key urban services are being re-established, but many people are still displaced and debris is still being cleared. Throughout the city liquefaction damage and subsequent flooding caused by land subsidence has caused ongoing setbacks and many roads are still in a third-world condition.

Long term recovery tasks will require the cooperation of public and private agencies. First and foremost a viable plan for the city and environs is necessary; a battle ensues over who and how it will be developed. The list of needs is long, including: rebuilding, the restoration of transportation systems, hazard mitigation, reconstruction of permanent housing, reconstruction of commercial facilities, development and implementations of long term economic recovery, targeting impacted and critical industries. For businesses this will involve repair or reconstruction of economically viable commercial, industrial and retail establishments. Further down the track, recovery of retail sales as well as restoration of employment levels to pre-disaster levels are still necessary. This is also true in terms of broader infrastructure and the reinstatement of public transportation, parks and recreation. The repair and reconstruction of hospitals, schools, libraries, police stations and other important social service amenities will also be required as well as re-engagement with community projects which were underway before the earthquakes. Slowly, we have begun to see the building replacement and reconstruction phase begin, this should bring with it a return to economic and social activity.

Whilst commercial interests are undoubtedly vital to an economic recovery, I believe that the critical component is actually the settlement of insurance claims for personal property damage to ensure a return to pre-earthquake residential normality. It is this that will ensure the life of the central business district. A central business district with business only, without permanent residents added to the mix, will remain lifeless.

The recovery of the Canterbury region is perhaps the biggest challenge facing New Zealand in living memory. Times have of course changed since the 1931 Napier quake and, arguably, the task at hand now is a much more complex one. Today there is more legislation to regulate development and 'protect' the environment. District and regional plans, along with the Resource Management Act, and the building codes (which seem to be changing on a monthly basis) must be adhered to. The current legislation was not developed or designed to operate in times of natural disaster and there are few transparent provisions to short-cut lengthy processes in order to speed up recovery. CERA of course has 'extraordinary' powers in this respect and has the mandate to shorten many processes if it so chooses.

When is a recovery 'successful'?

Recovery from a disaster is a long and ongoing process and defining what constitutes a 'successful recovery' is problematic, with many elements defying measurement. However, the speed of repair or reconstruction of buildings and structures can be measured, as can the speed of evaluation and adjustment of existing building codes and land-use regulations to meet new requirements. Also quantifiable and measurable are the planning and administrative activities required for the identification and securing of resources necessary to accomplish the recovery. So where is Canterbury in the recovery process in 2016?

Confidence and certainty about the future among the citizens of a damaged community is vital in the recovery. The continued delays in insurance settlements have led to widespread uncertainty, which will ultimately have an enormous impact on how people feel about the recovery. The public perception of the presence of clear and authoritative leadership, whether in planning or in housing assistance is important as well. Also in this confidence equation is the availability and affordability of insurance, which remains a critical issue. A further element for judgement is whether development appears to be planned or is taking place haphazardly and whether the available money for development is being put to use or is simply sitting on the side-lines. The public will of course, come to some common understanding on these matters and, if not before, their opinion will be reflected in whether they stay to commit to Christchurch. Their choice in the next general election will also be an indicator of how they feel about recovery. There still remains a mismatch between residents' expectations and the decisions that are made by CERA and the Christchurch City Council without their input.

The delayed settling of claims leads to a community losing cohesion. Certainly people will leave a region in the early phases after natural disaster, but those who remain must be assisted and enabled to restore life to the previous 'state of normality' as quickly as possible in order that their surrounding environment is once again considered desirable. Psychologically speaking, people require a home base6 where they can express themselves, otherwise they begin to ask 'what am I doing here'? and they may decide to move on.

When people perceive that their present environment no longer works for them but against them, they may prepare to leave as soon as their insurance claims are settled. They feel manipulated and imprisoned by denial of access to information and by a decision making process in which they are allowed no part. They feel cheated by pay-outs which are often insufficient to properly repair or rebuild their homes. The City quickly becomes a place with little to offer those people unable to resolve their personal difficulties, the larger ones typically being damaged homes and businesses.

Capital is the key to either accelerating or decelerating a recovery process. The Government has set aside a limited budget for the recovery, meaning that there are multiple needs to be met from a fixed number of dollars. In 2013 a further NZD 2.1 billion in funding was added with a total cost of the recovery increasing to an estimated NZD 40 billion. The Government's contribution will increase from around NZD 13 billion to around NZD 15 billion. In 2015 the Government once again boosted funding for Christchurch's post-quake recovery by another NZD 27 million, taking the Government's contribution to the rebuild of the city to NZD 16.5 billion since 2010.[7] These needs include repairs to infrastructure, repairs to state-owned assets such as highways, schools and hospitals and welfare support through job-loss cover and wage subsidies. Decisions as to how those funds are to be allocated and over what period of time, will have a tremendous impact on the recovery. NZD 900 million has been set aside in new capital funding from the Future Investment Fund and an additional NZD 303 million has been earmarked for the Christchurch Central Recovery Plan, *"enabling Christchurch to rebuild and redevelop into a world class city."*[8] An immediate tension arises between the community's agenda and the Government's agenda. For instance, many people are frustrated by the energy they see being expended into rebuilding infrastructure which is not vital to everyday life, e.g. sports stadiums, 'cardboard' Cathedrals etc., while their own personal living circumstances are far from resolved. The situation worsens when authorities appear not to be communicating plans and ideas about the future of their city, but simply using the situation to further their 'pet' agendas e.g. the Government's insistence upon charter schools and the closure or the merger of others.

Disasters create a series of new problems for a community and, unsurprisingly, leadership is vital. In Christchurch, local officials quickly found themselves in a complex web of intergovernmental relationships while attempting to make locally appropriate policy, the success or failure of which would profoundly affect the citizens of the city and region, and its recovery. Certain leadership qualities facilitate recovery more effectively than others. These include flexibility and a creative problem-solving attitude, a strong vision of what the community might become, as well as being able to attract and motivate competent assistants.

Early on, Canterbury was judged by government to be unable to manage its disaster. This was the reason that officials suggested that catastrophic disasters need a strong command and control system (which came to Christchurch in the form of CERA) and that these circumstances might be best handled in a military, authoritarian fashion. However, CERA has become increasingly unpopular; it has demonstrated little understanding of community development, little empathy or comprehension of what is needed to rebuild resilience and social capital.[9]

In the community there is a sense that recovery planning should be devolved down to the affected communities so that the wealth of local knowledge can be tapped into, to ensure that everything 'is on the table', including all the potential opportunities that emerge from a disaster of this magnitude.[10] Many feel that the process must be truly apolitical – using Members of Parliament, councillors, community board members and leaders from community groups, residents associations, churches, sports clubs, and businesses as partners in the recovery, instead of perceiving them as 'political risks to be managed'.

Labour and resources are also critical to successful recovery. The current inability to source resources and labour, such as tradespeople, to build the approximately 75,000 new homes needed, will undoubtedly slow down recovery.[11] The city experienced material shortages, costly imports and opportunistic price increases, which ultimately affect the final rebuild price and speed of recovery. Builders inform that the costs of building have soared by approximately 25 percent already in the Canterbury area.[12] Throughout the last five years, the population has heard that the building boom will begin 'soon' and that Christchurch could expect to see a strong acceleration in the numbers of people moving into the region. Yet there has been an unacceptable loss of tradespersons from the area at what should have been a time of maximum need. As a result of insurance pay-out delays, many of the contractors and builders who came to Christchurch after the earthquakes have given up waiting for the rebuild to commence and in frustration and often financial hardship, have again left the city to secure work elsewhere. To an affected Canterbury resident this is totally inexplicable and represents a major failure of policy and process.

The principal economist from the New Zealand Institute of Economic Research, Mr Eaqub, has said that,

> Christchurch's economic recovery will be stunted if the earthquake rebuild does not get underway soon, and there is a chance the reconstruction will not be as big as some hope. It is up to leaders like the Canterbury Earthquake Recovery Authority and the Government to push ahead more strongly, otherwise the drain of people from the region could lead to significant shrinkage.[13]

Throughout the city, empty lots where once houses stood, are visible everywhere. The feeling is that many building owners in the central business district became disillusioned with being kept out of the area for almost three years because of what might be described as an overly conservative Civil Defence and CERA policy. In addition to this was CERA's desire to merge titles of land, insisting that landlords club together or sell their land to each other in order to meet 'whole-block size criteria'. This in turn was responsible for neatly locking out the small-parcel landowners, guaranteeing big money, big business with deep pockets and good credit. CERA wanted to see large scale block developments. Property owners experienced a large loss of rights during the government appropriations of land, so in response they instead took their insurance pay-outs and moved out of the central business district to other locations in surrounding suburbs. These companies and staff have now become accustomed to the lower rents, less traffic congestion and more accessible parking. They are unlikely to return to the central business district. Perhaps had Sir Bob Jones' suggestions back in 2011 been heeded, the City would look considerably different today. He proposed small, low level, low rise, low cost, modest, mixed retail and commercial development, surrounded by open natural parkland areas of wetland. He advocated abandoning thoughts of a central business district. Driving around the central business district today one is left with the impression that in large part the central business district has been abandoned. Instead, much of the early residents have moved West and South of the City to Addington, Middleton, Riccarton, Victoria Street, the Airport and Rolleston, where private enterprise is thriving.

There are still many unknowns and difficulties yet to be resolved to do with land and accommodation needs of the displaced population. Early estimates from the Canterbury Employment and Skills Board suggest that the earthquake rebuild would require 24,000 carpenters, painters, labourers, concrete layers and other tradespeople, plus a further 12,000 managers, accountants, engineers, shop staff and hospitality workers, to support them, though these estimates have recently dropped as many folk have taken some sort of insurance pay-out and moved out and on. Nevertheless, Christchurch is going to see massive issues relating to the supply and demand of Canterbury housing and rental stock. No visible plans have emerged for the establishment of quick housing solutions for temporary accommodation for incoming contractors.[14] The Earthquake Recovery Minister's response to the dilemma was, "Some of the contractors should be looking at ways to house their workers, who will be making them a lot of money".[15] The solution once again, clearly seen to be best left to the market and reflected in terms of 'private companies making money'.

Although 1,200–1,500 homes are scheduled to be under repair each month, there has been little official move or concerns expressed around the shortage of private rental accommodation left remaining in

Christchurch to cater for those unable to live in their properties while repair work is carried out.

There are of course those in the city who are cashing in on the shortage. One property management company is offering a NZD 95,000 caravan for rent to residents looking for a 'stop-gap' while their homes are repaired and is asking NZD 700 a week or NZD 120 a night if rented for less than a month. In addition, the number of hotel rooms in Christchurch was shrinking further as hotels that survived the earthquakes close for strengthening and repairs. Christchurch's hotel room inventory was said to have dropped to 853 rooms after the February 22, 2011 earthquake, from 3,717 before the quake. In 2014 it grew by 700 new rooms.[16] Many residents are said to be sleeping in cars, leading one Member of Parliament to state that Christchurch will turn into a *"third world this winter"*.[17] Christchurch International Airport reported that hundreds of people were sleeping in its terminal every night because there was nowhere for them to stay in the City.[18] The City is said to have lost up to 70 percent of its budget accommodation providers since the devastating earthquakes. Property managers say the accommodation shortage is still affecting all levels of the market, while social agencies believe that the situation has reached crisis point.[19] There is huge pressure on rental accommodation from people who have been forced out of the red zone, compounded by the large short-term work force assisting with the recovery and the normal rental demand from tertiary students. Landlords are said to be renting unfit, often damaged and unhealthy homes, for top dollars. Displaced residents can apply for funds from the Canterbury Earthquake Temporary Accommodation Service, but the subsidy is not sufficient to meet the actual costs. Desperate tenants are offering more than advertised to secure accommodation. It's not hard to see why many have left or are wanting to leave. The Government appears to have ruled out further intervention in Christchurch's worsening rental housing crisis – again the solution "best left to the market".[20] It was not until the middle of 2015 that the Christchurch rental market turned in favour of tenants and the rental fees began to slide and Landlords began to struggle to find tenants for their homes. The city's average weekly residential rent is now NZD 403 a week.[21]

The Canterbury Earthquake Recovery Authority stated that 26,000 sections should be coming to market for development in the devastated city in 2013, three years after the first earthquake. And while there are now plenty of sections available it is also unlikely that developers have any intention of placing that number of sections on the market simultaneously. Nor is it likely that the new sections would be affordable for most red zoned residents. In addition, there are serious problems with a lack of 'matching' of similar-sized sections for displaced residents with red zoned sections. The city is apparently to have up to 3,173 additional sections available in 2013, the majority being located in the south-west and Belfast areas, the two areas identified as best able to accommodate future urban growth and development. Some 35,000 new houses are required in Christchurch, so another 12,000 sections are expected to be made available over the next 12 years. The Land Use Recovery Plan (Lurp) indicates that by 2028, 42,606 greenfield sections could be available, with about 30,000 of those ready by 2016.[22]

Christchurch City Council's website states, *"Indications from developers are that there will be up to 6,600 greenfield sections released on the market during the next two years, about 3,170 of which will be in Christchurch City"*.[23] This numerical confusion does not instil great confidence in a community desperate to return to some semblance of normality. There appears to be no realistic or transparent plan to resolve this issue. At the same time, developments that were already in existence are being re-categorized; for example there are now questions over the new development of Pegasus Town after the partial completion of a NZD 500,000 geotechnical study. So while sections become available, other previously available sections have been withdrawn or their conditions for use modified.

Added to the land availability issue, is the concern of increases in property values and the current rapid speed of the sale of available sections. By the time people have settled with private insurers or the Government, it is likely that section prices will already be out of the financial reach of many. Despite this, the Government has once again made the decision to leave pricing 'to the marketplace'.

There has been widespread confusion about how to apply rates to the City. Central Government also needs to consider this issue. The law does not allow for changes to rates which are being paid during the currency of a financial year. So if a building is to be demolished, it would be revalued differently but the original rates would nevertheless continue to be required until the end of that financial year. For this reason, the Christchurch revaluation deadline was extended by a year. Christchurch's more affluent homes are now paying almost double the rates of their Auckland counterparts. This gap decreases as property values decrease.

The earthquake has contributed to considerable boosts to property values in undamaged parts of Christchurch. In the township of Lincoln, an ordinary four-bedroom home recently sold for NZD 200,000 more than its valuation. There is now a trend toward increased demand in less damaged suburbs such as Rolleston in the Selwyn District, which in turn has led to property price increases in those areas and the highest price inflation in the country.[24] These areas are green zone and have been cleared as safe, where houses can easily be repaired or rebuilt. Solid ground has become solid gold.

In September 2010, the median price fell from NZD 377,000 to NZD 316,500 in the suburbs of Avondale and Burnside. In Kaiapoi the median price fell from NZD 368,500 to NZD 262,500 in the same period. The November 2011 median price for Christchurch was NZD 325,000, down from NZD 338,000 in the previous two months, while the wider Canterbury prices fell from NZD 315,000 to NZD 307,000 in October 2010.[25] According to current QV values, the average sale price in Christchurch in 2012 was NZD 387,955, representing a considerable increase in two years. Yet in 2011 the housing market was said to face uncertainty because many residents were leaving the city. The large insurers had begun to stop accepting new house insurance business by then, which again slowed property sales. For example, AMI was not insuring any properties that were not currently insured with AMI. IAG followed suit, stating that 'this was standard company policy' following a major disaster. However, the housing market saw a 1.2 percent increase in values between 2014 and 2015. In early 2016 the average value sits at NZD 482,043.[26]

Local councils such as Waimakariri District Council, stated that they were attempting to provide a range of sections to suit all price ranges. The feeling at a 'Residential red zone workshop' held in Kaiapoi on January 7, 2012, was that the Government had a moral responsibility to help its citizens. How could people be expected to make up the shortfall in an inflationary situation? Placing thousands of people into the real estate market simultaneously has a clear effect on land and house prices, as well as on rental costs.

There has been considerable interest expressed by property owners of undamaged homes on affected land to be able to move their properties to new sections, which should be a cost-effective option for them. However, they are discovering that most property developers will not change the restrictive covenants in new residential subdivisions to allow for this, thereby severely limiting redevelopment options for owners who are then forced by the terms of the covenants to build more costly and larger homes than they necessarily require.[27] Creative solutions are desperately needed but few are being put forward. Is reform necessary?

Another challenge concerns land which has been severely affected by liquefaction. In some areas the liquefaction has caused upper surfaces of land to shift laterally by up to four metres, meaning that property boundaries are now unclear and resurveying and resolving such issues may take years.[28] Land in the green-blue zones has been stigmatised and panicked owners have been reported to be selling properties too cheaply, in some cases NZD 150,000 less than they might have been expected to fetch.[29]

Timeframes for making sections available have become a critical issue for many residents. In Kaiapoi, for instance, the physical task of bringing in fill and consolidating land to the point of sale was projected to take another two years. This means people in one of the red zones who settled claims in 2012 with their insurers or the Government, were faced with the unenviable task of buying property in an upward-trending market. Meanwhile, other people are defaulting on their rates payments as they are still having to pay 60 percent of their rates charges on uninhabitable homes, many of which are also still under mortgage.

Under the Building Act 2004, older buildings are required to be strengthened to 33 percent of the current building code, but when questioned as to what that means practically, the answers have been varied and unsatisfactory in their lack of clarity and consistency. In relation to the Central City Business District it is said that there are many unknowns for property developers (e.g. foundation designs) in the new city plan. It may be difficult for them to continue to wait or commit to Christchurch with the uncertainty of securing tenants, although there is evidence of some businesses re-establishing themselves via the Re:Start project (a container precinct in the City centre). Re:Start was to close in 2013, it is now 2016 and Re:Start is still open, filling in for the noticeable retail gap in the central city.[30]

Questions also arise around how land can be guaranteed in the future. Currently the technical categories allocated to land such as 'blue/grey' and 'yellow' determine the level of investigation required prior to construction commencing. Buying a section in a subdivision in the future will entitle the new owner to a geotechnical report from the vendor, which is a positive measure – when the reports are available....

The present inaccessibility to damaged areas will add significantly to construction delays. In addition, the restriction of land supply at the fringes of the city is likely to drive the costs of serviced residential sections up by approximately NZD 30,000 to NZD 60,000, resulting in section prices of around NZD 200,000 to NZD 320,000 and higher, well beyond affordability for many. This will have an effect on land values throughout the rest of the urban area.

Another issue is the inappropriateness of financing of the infrastructure required for new developments by loading the capital costs (with subdivision and builders' margins) onto the property purchaser, then requiring purchasers to 'gift' this infrastructure to the utility providers, typically a local council. This means that the developer's pricing structure compels the house buyer to pay 'their share' for the cost of roads, sewers, lighting, and water mains etc. in the price of the section/house, but then this infrastructure is 'given' to the local Council. So in essence the buyer is paying twice for services – once to the developer and again in rates to the local authority.[31]

There are also concerns that due to the rapid demand for sections, poor planning may result which will damage the residential construction sector.[32] Construction costs on a per-metre basis have risen significantly. There are, however, plans to try to provide affordable sections, such as the initiative by the Canterbury Co-operative Land Trust[33] - although in March 2012 the Trust failed to secure enough interest to buy a half-completed 14-section subdivision in Linwood. Looking at the land situation retrospectively, some believe that council planning and the Greater Christchurch Urban Development Strategy had effectively 'banned' the provision of affordable land on the good ground at the southern, western and northern fringes of Christchurch, severely inflating the price of fringe lots and forcing development to the poorer quality, swampy ground on the less-favoured east side of the city. Sound geotechnical and engineering advice was persistently ignored by local politicians and urban planners. Others are of the opinion that urban planning and the regional Greater Christchurch Urban Development Strategy, through the mechanism of land price inflation, artificially makes housing considerably more expensive, forcing greater intensification and Central Business District living.

Natural hazards risk management was seemingly not considered or was ignored. Earthquake, liquefaction and flooding risks were well understood within the development and engineering communities in particular. There is also a body of opinion that believes that the Christchurch City Council had a long history of discouraging the demolition of old commercial stock considered to be 'historic'. The 'over-listing' of historic buildings resulted in insufficient resources being available for necessary and adequate seismic upgrades of "truly historic" buildings, such as Christchurch Cathedral, the Catholic Cathedral of the Blessed Sacrament and the Arts Centre.

Another land issue which has sparked considerable debate relates to the costs of repair and strengthening of historic buildings in the city. A University of Canterbury architectural historian has said that if building owners who were keen to retain their buildings had been allowed to do so then there would have been much more happening in the city than is currently the case.[34] The New Zealand Historic Places Trust, local governments and the Ministry of Culture and Heritage collaborated to establish the Canterbury Heritage Buildings Earthquake Fund[35] to raise money to assist funding the repairs of heritage buildings. Funding will be targeted at the gap between insurance cover, and the actual cost of repairs and associated works, including conservation works, structural upgrading and Building Code compliance works.

Recovery is hampered by a diverse variety of insurance arrangements due in large part to inadequate insurance. This leads to a gap between what insurance or the property owners can pay and the cost of the repair and strengthening work required to achieve the public goals of safety, recovery and heritage.

Concerns are also raised about movement out of the Central Business District. For example, Inland Revenue and the Social Development Ministry have signed nine-year leases at the Airport Business Park, despite the draft central-city plan putting government departments to the fore in the return to the central city. Immigration New Zealand, which previously had staff in the central city, now has offices in the same Addington building as the Accident Compensation Corporation. Similarly, the Ministry of Health has left the central city area.

Industrial vacancy has also fallen considerably. A Colliers International Research report states that industrial vacancy had fallen by half in the main industrial precincts in Christchurch, from 8.9 percent vacancy over a year ago to 4.6 percent.[36] Latest reports indicate there is a continued vacancy increase of around 3 percent. Certainly, the Trademe property website in January 2016 would indicate that vacancies are numerous. Christchurch industrial rents have jumped and property values continue to rise. The largest demand is from those manufacturers who require sites of over 300 square metres. In 2003 the Canterbury region accounted for 12 percent of GDP, according to Statistics New Zealand.[37] According to the latest forecasts from Infometrics, GDP in Christchurch City increased by just 6 percent in the year ending March 2014. The construction sector is the biggest beneficiary with growth of more than 15 percent.

The Christchurch earthquake has taken a reasonably vibrant real estate market and made it 'better', while speculators try to buy properties on the cheap, hoping that the redevelopment of Christchurch will start a boom. This land/property rush has long term implications in a city where many of the poorest residents were red zoned and bought out. It raises serious questions as to the kind of housing – if any – that will be available to those without deep pockets. If Christchurch is to be a high-priced enclave, without a socio-economic mix, something vital will be lost. For now, though, it's a seller's market for habitable homes. Private insurance costs will continue to rise.

On top of these issues are the inherent, and blatant, self-serving activities of big business, as in the case of an engineer involved in awarding the multimillion-dollar Hotel Grand Chancellor demolition contract, who was also named as a consultant working for the winning bidder.[38] As a member of the panel, he was likely to have been privy to information on the competing tenders to demolish the hotel and involved in the final recommendation to award Fletcher the NZD 12.3 million contract. CERA denied any conflict of interest.

Immediately after the February earthquake, Air New Zealand provided reduced (NZD 50) domestic airfares in and out of Christchurch. People vacated the area in droves, to Auckland, Wellington and Otago, in the week immediately after the February 22, 2011 earthquake. Apparently, using cell-phone data, it was established that five weeks later most people had returned to the city. Preliminary observations of the impact of the February 22 earthquake showed that an estimated 65,000 people, or approximately 17 percent of Christchurch's population, left the city following the February earthquake. The loss of an estimated 16,600 people through net migration from Christchurch City in 2011 and 2012 which is said to have since reversed, with estimated population gains of over 5,000 people in Christchurch in each of the last two years.[39] Before the earthquakes of 2010–2012, Christchurch's population was growing and had been predicted by Statistics New Zealand to increase until 2031. The rate of increase has now been downgraded. In 2013 the population of Canterbury was 539,436. Net migration to Christchurch City has been high in recent years. In 2013 Christchurch was welcoming 22 migrants a day delivering a net gain of International migrants over the 1996 to 2014 period. This follows a similar national pattern.[40]

It is reported that the failure to get business back up and running since the earthquakes has caused the Christchurch population to shrink by at least 13,500, with about 26,800 job losses in the year to September 2011, and a further 18,000 jobs lost in the year to June 2012. Every week brings news of more job losses. Sanford saw 232 job losses; Tasman Insulation (Fletcher Building) 29 jobs; Christchurch Yarns, 85 jobs; JK Kids, 70 jobs; Independent Fisheries, 200 jobs; Delta Utility Services 40 jobs; Solid Energy, 105 jobs; Tait Communications, 74 jobs and an undisclosed number of teachers from Christchurch schools.[41] Lincoln University and CBRE (commercial real estate service provider) surveyed businesses in Christchurch in August 2011 and again early in 2012 as part of a project aimed at assessing the impact of the quakes on businesses and their plans. The initial survey showed 44 percent of businesses wanted to return to the Central Business District, but that figure fell to 32 percent in the second survey. In addition, Christchurch's tertiary sector is said to have experienced a 37 percent drop in international-student numbers.[42]

The National Bank index of regional activity estimates that in Canterbury in the year to September 2011, activity shrank 0.8 percent compared with the year to September 2010. A UBS senior economist along with many other Cantabrians, expressed concern as to the accuracy of the data, finding *"[it is] difficult that the official data shows so little impact but that's the data"*.[43] Certainly the local feeling is that these figures also underplay the real departure figures. Prime Minister John Key states:

You can't just pretend that Christchurch [the earthquake events] isn't there, it has a big impact and some people have said 'Well look, my home's in disarray, my job might be a little more uncertain,' and they've picked themselves up from Christchurch and gone.[44]

In January 2012 there is evidence of this, with the number of New Zealanders moving to Australia having hit a new high, with nearly 52,000 people taking a one-way trip on a permanent or long term basis.[45] By 2015 the figures had reversed and there are now more people moving from Australia to New Zealand, for the first time In 24 years.[46]

Conclusion

It is clear that a better understanding of the recovery process would assist national and local officials in managing the recovery more efficiently. The effectiveness of government efforts is vital in the healthy re-establishment of the community. Confused, slow-to-act or agenda-driven authorities, as demonstrated, can considerably exacerbate the problems. The literature on community recovery suggests that the manner in which bureaucratic activities match the public's needs and expectations, is vital. Saundra K. Schneider shows that the success or failure of an emergency response and recovery will ultimately "depend on the size of the inevitable gap between the collective behaviour of disaster victims and the bureaucratic procedures of public officials".[47]

This gap remains wide in Canterbury. Yet it is not too late for the stakeholders and the community together to create a better working relationship and a shared vision around how to proceed, thereby diminishing the present differences. The recovery period offers an opportunity to strengthen local organisational capacity to facilitate economic, social and physical development, as well as an opportunity to alter physical development patterns which have the ability to reduce future vulnerability. As well, longstanding community issues can finally be resolved, e.g. poor roading layout, provision of affordable housing stock, and expansion of parks and recreation areas, as well as modernisation of public facilities. In addition, adequate communications systems in the city will ensure that information flows freely between experts, policymakers and citizens. Local knowledge and development priorities must be identified and the geophysical risks must be communicated. Local participation in decision making through formal but truly democratic structures is also achievable by community involvement in local development projects.[48]

People's perceptions of the broader economic climate and progress in the area of disaster have a profound influence on whether people decide to stay or go. When these components are seriously out of balance for an individual or family, and where they have the financial means, people will tend to make the choice to leave the City for a new beginning elsewhere. Communities must be able to initiate collective action in order to ensure the timely and equitable distribution of resources, including those from insurers, and prevent the loss of significant opportunity.

Effective local public administration is vital and should be scrutinised and held to account at every turn. Equally vital is the uncensored reporting by the media of the facts concerning public opinion and objection to governmental and other corporate actions. Technical expertise, in the form of decisions regarding controls of land use and urban development plans, is essential. The use of tangible resources such as financial, personnel and grant monies, including the revenue from local taxes, needs to be publicly and regularly reviewed in terms of the priorities of their use. It is a judicious combination of these factors that will enable the recovery work in Christchurch to be accomplished.

The challenge for all stakeholders in the present Christchurch environment is to narrow the bureaucratic response–public perception gap, and if the citizens are to be served in a just and equitable manner, it is essential that the following changes soon be effected:

Maintenance of public confidence amongst the decision making bodies
Ongoing political turf wars, overlapping efforts and other impediments need to be addressed and resolved. This is as important as the actual physical rebuild as it will ultimately determine the kind of city that is rebuilt. Over the last five years the tensions between the Christchurch City Council and the Government related to the earthquake recovery, have heightened, with the Christchurch City Council still unsure of the level of state intervention that will occur in the form of CERA, the Christchurch Central Development Unit, the Minister and more recently the Regenerate Christchurch Agency (to replace CERA in April 2016).[49] It will be important that the Christchurch community is left with the feeling that they are in control of the future of the city. Many Cantabrians have expressed the need for the Council to push back against the influence of CERA and the current Government and take a greater role in Christchurch decision making. CERA and the City Council must re-establish the lines of engagement in a way that all parties are satisfied. Without this, the recovery is likely to be constantly hindered. There remain concerns about the loss of control over asset sales and the failure to take into account

community goals and the public good. There is also strong sentiment in the city around the need to repair basic infrastructure and community facilities and that these must take priority over the proposed Anchor Projects. For many, the proposed new convention centre and sports stadium are viewed as unnecessary ventures.

Sound prudential management of private insurers
Despite the Government's 'leave it to the market' attitude, it does have a responsibility to intervene in the private insurance sphere and assert its role as protector of the citizens of this nation, more particularly in the case where legal redress is not available by the public for a variety of reasons. There should immediately be put in place a mechanism by which policyholders can easily and effectively resolve their outstanding insurance claims in a timely and equitable manner, such as an independent mediation process described in Chapter 6, Policyholder Protection. This could be achieved along similar lines to regulations already implemented in other countries around the world. Implementing such a process will also do away with the need for specialist claims management services from companies such as the public adjusters currently in Christchurch, whilst they are often achieving results, are currently making considerable profits at the expense of people seriously affected by the earthquakes.

The balance between the need to restore economic activity and the need of citizens to return to homes
Many feel that there is an over-emphasis on rebuilding the city centre to pre-earthquake levels at the expense of interest in progress in rebuilding citizens' homes and consequently their well-being. If people are not comfortable in their homes and surroundings they will eventually move on. Accessible and affordable local community facilities remain a high priority for many, particularly in the area of New Brighton. There has been strong opposition to the closing of Rawhiti Golf Course and the South Brighton Camping Ground. There is also a sense that there is a lack of parity in that some suburbs receive more funding in comparison with others leading to the perception of political financial imperative driving and over-riding community wellbeing.

Availability of land
The ongoing availability of land and sections on which to rebuild is critical to the re-establishment of the community. What is required is the reigning-in of property developers and a well-thought-out centralised plan, to ensure that enough affordable sections will be provided. Policy regarding relocatable housing should be put in place and areas created for this purpose, possibly in the form of a heritage park.

Supply of affordable and social housing
The availability of affordable and social housing remains very high on the list of issues requiring priority. There is a need to increase the supply of both.

Heritage Buildings
Many of Christchurch's heritage buildings have been lost. The Civic Trust has identified 40 'must save' listed buildings which it thought would maintain the heritage integrity of the city. Of those only 15 remain today, and of these their fate is as yet unknown. There is a sense that there has been an inappropriate use of the CERA Act which has led to attempts to speed up the land swap processes leading to encroachment. The heritage debate will rage on for many years to come, I suspect.[50]

Accommodation for incoming labour force
Temporary accommodation has been significantly reduced, driving up rental costs and causing major population relocations. Stable surrounding communities have been required to take in considerable numbers, taxing their transportation arteries, schools and entire infrastructures. Large temporary housing sites are required to house thousands of incoming tradespeople. Worker accommodation needs cannot simply be left to the market, the market is currently already swamped and financially distorted.

Transport concerns
There is concern about the state of the city roads and the length of time it is taking to effect repairs, leading to heavy flows of 'diverted' traffic in some areas within the city.

Fairer distribution of work to local contractors
Local contractors are suffering as a consequence of a lack of work with most of the large contracts going to firms who are, arguably, well-connected with the Government. There should be a preferred-partner approach which favours local contractors who also have to live with their reputations through the quality of their work. What is currently occurring is that the large building giants are being awarded large contracts as the Government's preferred partners, leaving the smaller operators out of the future equation for the city. Fletcher Residential was recently awarded an NZD 800 million housing project to the dismay of other local contractors.[51] The Fletcher name has been remarkably prominent throughout the rebuild and notably, was the government's chosen partner for the EQC. There is probably some interesting research to be done on this topic.

Restoration of water networks
The recent flooding post-earthquakes has drawn the population's attention to the need for the prevention of flooding and sewage overflow concerns. Further funding is required for the repair and renewal of water, wastewater and storm water networks.

The consent process
The Christchurch experience indicates that substantial changes should be made to ensure the risks of natural hazards are fully considered in planning decisions across New Zealand. This may involve the creation of a standardised database on soil and sediment characteristics, e.g. mandatory borehole logs and soil test results sent to a central repository. Such information databases would prove useful not only for earthquake studies but also for soil erosion, building foundations, shrink-swell phenomena and Quaternary geology and geomorphology. Recent experience has shown that resource consents issued under the Resource Management Act for the development of land in some areas of Canterbury did not take into account identified liquefaction and flooding risks. Even post 2004, consents were being granted without any regard for this significant and, by then, well-documented risk. Not only was the information regarding identified risks not introduced into the zoning

and consent decision making about the development of these areas, but the risk of liquefaction was not clearly identified on Land Information Memorandum Reports for affected properties, despite awareness of this risk. The problems in Christchurch have identified a shortcoming in the current consents process, nationwide.

Without the implementation of these recovery elements the long term future of Christchurch will be uncertain. Christchurch is unlikely to recover until its people have recovered!

The Provision of Mental Health Services

It is critical for a community in recovery that there is enough health service funding to assist the population through the recovery phase. Sue Bagshaw's, director of the 298 Youth Centre statement suggesting that the next generation of Cantabrians will be *"costlier to New Zealand than any amount currently being spent on the rebuild"*, is not an understatement.[52] As an affected population we are experiencing higher incidents of stress, anxiety, cardiovascular issues, depression and post-traumatic stress disorder in both adults and children. New Zealand is a signatory to the International Covenant on Economic, Social and Cultural Rights which includes the right to the highest attainable physical and mental health, as well as adequate housing. The State is to extend special protective measures to vulnerable groups within society to ensure a degree of priority consideration. Cutting mental health funding to NZD 210 per head while the national average increases to more than NZD 250 requires address.

Citizens speak

Earthquake Outcasts: The story of Quake Outcasts is one of David vs Goliath, the victimised few who rose up and defended themselves against all odds. Why were a bunch of homeowners, land owners, and commercial building owners under the gun of the authority? What do they have to do with the overall recovery plan? And what do they all have in common?

To answer these questions, one has to understand that the creation of the 'Residential Red Zone' and buy-out scheme are intricately linked to insurance. Not just government rhetoric about insurance, but also the oddly complex relationships among the EQC, retail insurers, and their reinsurers. These are complex and convoluted relationships. The Quake Outcasts were mere collateral damage and had no relationship with the EQC whatsoever.

The government linked its buy-out offer to the status of insurance, or more precisely, status of the EQC cover. It could justify this by arguing that if no private house insurance was bought then there would be no EQC cover. So it became clear that the 'residential red zone' buy-out was targeted at reducing the EQC claims. This is the only way to explain why property owners were required to surrender their EQC land claims[53] under the buy-out options.

So imagine the horror government ministers felt when the Supreme Court ruled that the 'residential red zone' was unlawfully created.[54] Every policy, every order, every decree that came out of or was based on the 'colour zoning scheme' now sits on shaky legal ground. Even after the Supreme Court had ruled that insurance status should not be used as a factor in determining the buy-out, the Minister still used charged language in his media release in April 2015, announcing a public consultation process to discuss the issue of Quake Outcasts.[55] Many participants of Quake Outcasts share Labour's view that this is another attempt at side-slipping the Court judgement by subjecting the issue to a process which is no doubt heavily rigged in the Government's favour.[56]

By Ernst Tsao.[57]

~~~

Little did we realise, this was the beginning of a series of events which, 52 months later, (5 harsh winters duration) have only intensified for thousands of Canterbury families, elderly and vulnerable victims of a natural disaster... A story which has never ended.

I trained in Interior Architecture and have 24 years' experience in construction. I have also owned my own concrete manufacturing company. I offered my services to help in the assessment of structural damage to homes, and applied for multiple jobs. When inquiring why I was relentlessly unsuccessful, I was told 'you are far too over qualified, and EQC have chosen to employ people without construction experience, and train them themselves'. I was not alone – there were experienced architects, builders, roofers and tradespersons who were also now out of work, and their services deemed worthless, apparently 'a conflict of interest to employ local Canterbury people'. Meanwhile colleagues from Australia informed me of advertisements in local papers requesting 'persons with no construction experience required', to apply for jobs as earthquake damage assessors, all expenses paid, and a free trip home every 10 days for a week, paying AD 100.00 an hour.

Five months passed before we were scheduled for our first damage assessment - January 28, 2011. On the allotted day we were met in the driveway by a chap from Nelson and an experienced 'Contracts Manager'. This man was abusive, rude, and arrogant. It was quite obvious that he knew nothing about building structures, and it was also obvious by his comments that he had been instructed to minimise recognition of damage in his efforts to 'save money for EQC'. He muttered 'Historical damage and lack of maintenance' several times, stating that 'the house was built with a lean' and that 'I should have kept my sewer damaged carpet if it was to be included in my contents damage claim'.

I remember thinking *"if they are treating me like this, then how in God's name are they treating people without construction knowledge"*. I decided at that moment to become actively involved.

The assessed damage was deemed to be between NZD 10,000 and NZD 30,000, to fix a house I knew was not fixable. Now, four and a half years of stress, hardship and impeding ill health later, the property is deemed to be a NZD 850,000.00 plus rebuild!

Throughout the process I have been subjected to multiple assessments, from multiple teams of bullies, many of whom have known nothing about construction. Many of these teams consisted of retired policemen and police investigators, all too keen to tell of their past experiences within the force once they realised we too had been in the armed forces. Each assessment minimized more damage to my property.

I witnessed faulty assessment practices, where 1 metre spirit levels were used to measure wall verticality and floor levels and inappropriate use of laser levels and gas level equipment. I heard suggestions of repair which were impossible to achieve without the implosion of the roof structures occurring. I was subject to their blindly ignoring of obvious damage e.g. the separation of internal wall joins, and the separation of the concrete slab to the concrete ring beams, resulting in the concrete slab sinking, leaving a gap in excess of 30mm between the slab and skirting boards. I heard that phrase 'historical damage' again and again. So I wrote multiple complaints to the EQC head office and started cc'ing everything to the insurance ombudsman. I also got involved in Facebook earthquake victims fora, and advised everybody to send in Official Information Act requests for their earthquake damage assessments, and to write to the ombudsman. It *has* been a mitigated fiasco.

By Sarah O'Brien[58]

CHAPTER 10:

RECOVERY IN 2015?

"Two steps forward, one step back".

Prime Minister of New Zealand, John Key[1]

The recovery is considered to be perhaps the most challenging phase of the disaster cycle. This is in-part due to the need for clear allocation of responsibilities and the development of regulatory frameworks calling for close collaboration between professionals, agencies and interest groups from a diverse range of disciplines and perspectives. Without smooth collaboration, recovery is likely to be slow and painful. The financial and monetary underpinning of the recovery also play a major role in the recovery phase as well - as in any integrated long term action. Christchurch City Council finance spokesperson Raf Manji states that 2015 is the year of transition toward longer term planning. Canterbury is still only 25 percent of the way to recovery, according to the chief executive of the Canterbury Employers Chamber of Commerce, Peter Townsend. Mr Townsend envisioned that 2026 will mark the end of the reconstruction phase.[2]

2015 was marked by the earthquake emergency-phase being declared nearing its end and the Prime Minister's, acknowledgement of the frustrations of Cantabrians with the slow progress toward recovery. Handing the recovery reigns fully back to the local authorities still proves to be a step too far for the National Government, while their initially much-vaunted major building projects, such as the convention centre and sports stadium are still to be progressed, apparently with large Governmental financial stakes in these projects.

By March 2015 there are still 25,000 unsettled claims on properties with EQC land claims, 10,000 unsettled properties with EQC dwelling claims and 10,000 unsettled properties with private insurer dwelling claims. 46 per cent of the private insurer settlements have been cash settled, despite the fact that many policies were repair or rebuild policies.[3] 2016 marks the fifth year for many still living in severely damaged homes, with limited heating, and no repair strategies in sight. Progress in the city and in the settlement of residential claims is desperately slow. The roads in many areas, notably the East of the city, are still shambolic. Despite this, private insurers and the EQC declare significant progress on repairs and rebuilds while providing excuses for delays which the industry claims are caused by issues 'outside their control', including liability associated with replacing homes in flood risk areas and ongoing reports into land stability.[4] The New Zealand Insurance Council states that *"the majority of the insurer-managed rebuild programme would be complete by 2016"*. (By February 2016 there are still 4624 unresolved claims, of which 448 of those will probably go 'overcap', 442 claims where as yet the insurer has still not made an offer. These figures do not include the claims still sitting with the EQC, or the claims where a settlement has been reached but the repair or rebuild is yet to take place. Nor do these figures include the many thousands of faulty or dodgy repairs which will require revisiting).[5]

Then, there is another big blow to earthquake affected Cantabrians with the removal of popular journalist and reporter, John Campbell, from national television screens.[6] His departure see hashtags such as #Savejohn and #letCampbellLive and proves to be the most talked about subject in the country on Twitter.[7] He was one of the few reporters willing to explore the underlying questionable motives and drivers that required (and still require) exploration and exposure. Campbell Live was the only television programme that consistently brought the plight of the Canterbury people to the attention of the rest of the nation. He travelled down to Christchurch on several occasions and filmed live, often drawing large live audiences in venues such as the temporary 'cardboard cathedral'. Cantabrians and the rest of New Zealand saw him for the last time on their screens in May 2015. His questionable demise is another smack in the face for democracy in this country. His removal was widely seen as politically engineered. For the people of Canterbury he was the last hope of their voices being heard across the nation, which is almost certainly what the government wished to avoid. The demise of the 'Campbell Live' programme was unfortunate as those issues deserving ongoing public debate consist of the lessons to be learned. Until, and while we as a Nation remain unable to travel the road of self-reflection, nothing will change for the better. One has to ask - why the agenda? Is the Nation going to allow CERA and its swollen communications department to be the sole arbiters and editors of the tale of the Canterbury Earthquakes? Andrew Geddis, Otago University Law Professor hit it neatly on the head when he said "*Yes we do tend to be a bunch of lightweights... New Zealand is an outlier in allowing so much executive power to be focused in the hands of central government. We have no written constitution, no upper house, no federal division of power. The judiciary is restricted to ruling on technicalities. Even local government has no statutory standing on its own. A government can rewrite the rules at any time...*".[8] It is clear for all to see that there are few if any formal checks and balances on political power and behaviour in the City.

Christchurch's construction costs remain the highest in the country in 2015 due to rising labour costs and increasing subcontractor and supplier margins. These are expected to climb another 6 percent by the year's end.[9] This year (2015) it is said that the rebuild is at its peak. More than NZD100 million is now spent in Christchurch each week.[10] There are 31,000 workers in the construction sector. An additional 5000 construction workers are said to be required 'through to the crest of the rebuild in December 2016' but changes are required to immigration policy as migrant workers and human rights activists have spoken up against the tough conditions afforded migrants.[11] The building boom also brings with it an increase in financial crime.[12] The Inland Revenue Department begins to get tough with dodgy rebuild businesses.[13] Despite this, firms in the City continue to go bankrupt affecting migrant workers.[14] Almost 100 contracting companies have gone into receivership since the rebuild hit its stride. The rebuild boom has not materialized in the way the industry had expected, according to the Canterbury Master Builders president, Alistair Miles.[15] Another property developer attacks the council for its sluggish and 'extremely disappointing' 'can't do' attitude.[16] In an attempt to protect consumers, the Government introduces mandatory written contracts and builder requirements for residential work exceeding NZD 30,000.

House building too, continues to reduce pace and the number of new home approvals is down 30 percent from the previous year (Statistics New Zealand).[17] A survey conducted by the Canterbury Employers' Chamber of Commerce finds that businesses are taking a different tack to operations. Companies start looking and planning ahead for two or three years, rather than simply concentrating on just one. This is seen to be a result of having to function in a high growth and volatile environment. The survey reinforces the frustration felt over the pace of the rebuild. Christchurch developers claim that 'ludicrous' rules are delaying the city's rebuild - particularly in relation to the consenting process.[18] This is followed by an unanimous decision on the part of the city council to set up a one stop shop for investor and property developers – 'Development Christchurch'. Fletcher Building (again) manages to grab the lion's share of government–led residential developments in Christchurch City. This does not come as a surprise as once again, that building company is heralded as the Government's preferred partner… The NZD 800 million project is granted to Fletcher Building together with the sale of 7 hectares of inner city land. In true to form style, the Earthquake Recovery Minister fails to provide any of the financial details.[19] Leaving the three other contenders to miss out.[20] Many people question the propriety of this transaction and ask 'who benefitted'?

Meanwhile, in the east of the city, business leaders criticise local and central governments for neglecting the Eastern suburb of New Brighton.[21] The Mayor makes a tearful apology to those living in the East who feel that she has let them down, stating that more money should go to implementing the masterplan to regenerate the New Brighton area.[22] The anchor projects too, continue to cause consternation. One Canadian expert states that it is a mistake putting the Convention Centre in the middle of the Central City. There are further delays for the other anchor projects. The build of the metro sports facility is to be delayed until 2020 and the build of the convention centre will commence no sooner than late 2018. The Mayor calls for the Prime Minister to step in to address the embarrassing delays in the midst of a new low in Council-Government relations.[23] Talks for the need of a downsizing of the central city begin. There are also concerns around the renovation of Cathedral Square with ASB Bank pulling out of plans for a new regional office there, though they are expected to reopen elsewhere in the Central Business District in 2016.[24]

The council is again warned about the lack of social housing[25] and squatters begin to call empty quake damaged buildings their home. This produces predictable undesirable traits and an increase in criminality and other negative effects. Due to the unavailability of low-cost rental properties, many youth are living on the streets.[26] The earthquake settlements mean that there will be inadequate funding to return the city housing portfolio to pre-earthquake levels. An arson attack on the Barrington Park Playground also highlights the fragility of the City Council's insurance position. The Council does not have insurance cover on its public playgrounds which means that it will generally fall to the council to buy replacement equipment.

The City Council continues to express its disappointment and places pressure on the Government to tighten rules forcing building owners to strengthen the most dangerous sections first, as the Building (Earthquake-Prone Buildings) Amendment Bill does not require reinforced masonry, including facades, parapets, gables and chimneys, to be strengthened any sooner than the rest of quake-prone buildings. In August there is another round of public submissions on the Building (Earthquake-Prone Buildings) Amendment Act.[27] New Zealand has an estimated 15,000 to 25,000 earthquake prone buildings, the call goes out to strengthen these. Nevertheless experts in the field suggest that *"raising the earthquake prone threshold from 33 percent to 67 percent of the New Building Standard would be of questionable benefit"*.[28] Those involved in accidents and injuries relating to the earthquakes carry other views.[29] Anne Brower an earthquake victim herself states, *"We have to accept those who we trusted to keep our streets safe, failed"*. Surely, we must learn from the mistakes. However, despite the population's concern, the Ministry proposes a timeframe of 15 years to fix parapets and facades. The Bill does not prioritise the strengthening of unreinforced masonry buildings with hazardous features such as verandas and parapets despite their known dangers. During the earthquakes, forty people died as a result of failure of unreinforced masonry buildings. The Bill also ignores the recommendation from the local authorities for strengthening to be done faster and to a higher level than set by central government.[30] The Government is gambling with the lives of its citizens as mediocrity and bureaucracy prevail.

The issue of increased flood risk raises its head again and a decision is again delayed another four months. The council has requested CERA-agreement for having access to red zoned land so it can build and operate a storm water bypass channel or pipe.[31] The decisions for this proposal are continually pushed forward leaving people in the affected areas to deal with continual flooding.

The City Council heads to mediation with its insurer Civic Assurance. The initial estimate was that the Council would receive in excess of NZD 900 million but the losses 'calculated' are significantly below that figure and the Council ultimately receives NZD 635 million.[32] There are also internal issues with the Christchurch City Council itself. 10 days out from a release of the budget, six councillors release an alternate budget to the consternation of the Mayor.[33] Approval is expected of a phased release of NZD 750 million in capital from the sale of the Council's commercial assets over the following three years and a rate rise by about 27 percent over the next four years.[34] There is a last-ditch attempt to stop the sale of City Care, Red Bus, Enable, Lancaster Park, Horncastle Arena and Council-owned off-street parking buildings. The Council is said to be going to release up to NZD 200 million in capital over the next 12 months from the commercial assets it owns through Christchurch City Holdings, a further NZD 200 million in 2017 and up to NZD 350 million in 2018.[35]

The National Government of John Key and the insurance industry sold us promises of total replacement, quick fixes, transparency and honesty. It is clear early on in 2015 that insurers will not meet their promises, nor their self-imposed deadlines. The Insurance Council chief executive Tim Grafton states that the end of 2016 remains the target for the 'vast majority of residential claims completion'.[36] The Prime Minister states in a speech to the Middle East, during a visit there, that *"we are a country that stands for human rights"*. Five years on and Cantabrians are yet to see him stand up for the human rights of his own countrymen. Many citizens are now long past the conclusion that both the Government and the insurance industry are playing a game of cost minimization in every way possible.

Though the insurance 'wait for resolution' is over for some, it continues to plague many others. The evidence of this is visible everywhere in the city and thousands of residential claims are still to be settled. Many premises such as the Hotel All Seasons in Papanui are abandoned, while its owners wait for an insurance settlement.[37] IAG, now New Zealand's largest insurer, had committed to settling all claims by June 2016. IAG announces that it no longer wants to repair or rebuild properties but will instead make cash settlements for its outstanding claims. It is aware that it will no longer meet that deadline unless it cash settles. This produces concern amidst those still to settle, as they do not want to deal with the rebuild process nor do they want the additional expense of seeking expert opinion and the additional costs that that entails. Anecdotal studies carried out in the City show that cash settlement offers are inevitably 50 percent or more, short of the actual required sum and at least one legal group-action is based on this discovery. The unforeseen construction costs and the costs associated with managing a project efficiently are justified concerns. One couple manage to successfully oppose their insurer-imposed cash settlement.[38]

By August 2015, IAG makes a public statement that it has exceeded its NZD 4 billion reinsurance limit claiming that it is now dipping into its capital reserves to pay for the February 2011 earthquake and bringing the IAG group as a whole - on risk. Questions are raised by Christchurch accountant Cam Preston around the voracity in IAG's claims, suggesting that IAG Aus Group financial statements reveal that most of the retained profits and equity In their Singapore Captive (IAG Re Signapore Pte Ltd) are attributable to Its New Zealand operations.[39] IAG plans the assimilation of the AMI and Lumley brands, bringing both companies into the insurer's fold and placing IAG's monopoly status further in question. The Commerce Commission announced its decision that it has set no conditions on IAG, saying it's satisfied the acquisition *"will not have, or would not be likely to have, the effect of substantially lessening competition, for personal and commercial insurance products"*.[40] Many Cantabrians are sceptical. Tower Insurance increases its rebuild cover by an additional NZD 50 million. Tower also cash settles claims after reaching *"full capacity".* Cash settlement, they declare, will be the only option for Tower in situations where homes had previous existing conditions, such as weather tightness issues.[41] These solutions in many cases fall outside the wording of agreed insurance policies. Tower also requests a trading halt in its shares. Policyholders with Tower begin to ask some serious questions about the company's financial stability. The Tower chief executive declined to give details of the numbers of significant repairs it had completed, claiming to have settled 93 percent, by volume, of all claims related to the earthquakes. Speculation around Tower's position remains.[42] A fortnight later the company declares that there is likely to be a half year loss but that its general underlying profit, excluding the impact of the earthquakes, had grown strongly. Tower later reports a loss of NZD 4.9 million in the six months to March 31, though stating that they were well capitalized.[43] New Zealand's second largest insurer, Vero begins to call for a permanent national disaster reconstruction body to manage the rebuilding of communities declaring that the expertise garnered this far should not be lost once CERA winds down its role in 2016. Queensland in Australia had created a similar entity after the floods of 2010/2011. Its role covered historical and continuing disasters in the State as well as co-ordinating the Government's programme of infrastructure reconstruction. The New Zealand Government's rather short-sighted view was to retort that this would not constitute reasonable expenditure.[44]

The Government promises to back all Southern Response claims, even in the event it requires in excess of NZD 1 billion of Government support.[45] Southern Response keeps some cost information hidden from earthquake claimants to avoid 'confusion' over the amounts of their insurance settlements. Leaving out details of costs relating to contingency fees, professional fees, demolition and the "Grand Total House"- a sum which can be tens of thousands of dollars greater than the one they show the claimant. Claimants are of course entitled to know the true cost of reinstatement from the damage to their property. The Court of Appeal ruled in 2014 that Southern Response must pay the 'out of scope' costs to a customer as well. This will no doubt cost insurers millions of dollars in additional monies. Southern Response, a government funded/operated entity contested the case in the Supreme Court but the Supreme Court upheld the ruling.[46] This year also sees policyholder Cam Preston, (an accountant and vocal campaigner on insurance related matters), receive a visit from the local police in response to a series of letters he sent to Southern Response over the course of his claim. Southern Response declared that they were being threatened by Mr Preston. Most of the public, felt otherwise. This incident marks a new low in claimant relations.[47] Cam Preston is later to become the class representative for a group legal action against Southern Response. Southern Response takes aim at the class action law suit saying that customers who signed up are likely to have their claim pay-outs delayed and could end up worse off.[48] In a survey of its policyholders carried out by Southern Response, more than half said that life was a 'struggle' and that they felt 'bleak' about the future. Amongst that group, were those with as-yet unassessed claims or those who were yet to receive written communication from the insurer.[49] This is five years after the event and a government entity!

In a strange twist of fate, the private insurers declare that they have lost confidence in the EQC data and predictions.[50] The finger pointing begins in earnest. The insurers propose changes to the EQC Act. Changes include insurers managing the EQC claims. The EQC cover for future events is to increase from NZD 100,000 to NZD 200,000. Contents insurance to be the sole domain of the private insurance industry. The EQC is to no longer provide land cover for land damage that has not actually caused damage to the house and homeowners would no longer need to lodge their claim with the EQC but go directly to their private insurance company.[51] Do these changes go far enough?

A trite article appears in the *Christchurch Press* in which insurers state that they are worried about what their customers think of them. Price Waterhouse Cooper releases the results of a survey asking insurers to identify their top ten risks. Reputational risk comes in at number five. In 2013 reputational risk had ranked third. After repeated complaints from the public, discussion takes place about the revision to the Fair Insurance Code with minor amendments made, including potential industry fines of NZD 100,000. But in order to achieve this, a series of other steps must be taken by the policyholder first. These include negotiating one's way through a disputes resolution scheme, such as the Insurance Savings Ombudsman or Financial Services Complaints authority. Karen Stevens, the Insurance and Savings Ombudsman, along with many Cantabrians agree that the industry's self-regulation is not enough. If self-regulation is to exist effectively, it requires strenuous and active accountability mechanisms. Changing the words of the Fair Insurance Code and 'setting and forgetting' is not a viable answer to the problems Canterbury has experienced. If there is no accountability in place – and it would seem that there is not, then self-regulation is totally ineffective. Community cynicism regarding both the government and the inability of the insurance industry in the regulation of itself will undoubtedly have led to a general distrust of self-regulatory schemes unless it can be shown to operate effectively, transparently and produce confidence amongst consumers. Self-government of a profession or commercial entity is a franchise granted to the entity by Government. A Government regulator is therefore required to provide timely intervention where self-regulation is not working. This certainly has not happened in Christchurch. There has to date been no word from either the Commerce Commission or the Financial Markets Authority. Meanwhile, the Christchurch City Council agrees to put more monies into the Residential Advisory Service (RAS) to help those locked in insurance disputes. Local lawyers begin to urge disgruntled insurance policyholders to join 'no win, no fee' class action lawsuits, actions backed by third party Litigation Lending Services.[52] Group action litigation has a long history of changing the way businesses do business and of protecting the rights of a country's citizens. There are clear benefits to the disgruntled policyholder in becoming actively involved in class or group actions.

The EQC has set a deadline to close the Canterbury Home Repair Programme to all new customers and repairs from Monday, 1 June 2015, to ensure it has the right amount of resources necessary to complete the programme. Consequently the EQC repair deadlines also loom and homeowners have only a few months to be part of the Earthquake Commission's home-repair programme. This deadline causes stress for some, many of whom had been trying to organise repairs with the EQC for years. For others there is still disagreement about the nature of the repairs required, leaving them in severe limbo.[53] In 2014 the private insurers received 1963 over-cap claims from the EQC.[54] Five years on and there is still a steady dribble of over-cap (above NZD100,000 worth of damage) claims. Meanwhile Fletcher begins downsizing its earthquake repair programme, cutting its building contractors from 450 to 100, yet work is touted as continuing well into 2016.[55]

2015 sees many more Cantabrians complaining about the quality of repairs already completed to their earthquake damaged properties. Stories of 'notch-up' pile bearers and floor boards being replaced with melamine and chipboard abound.[56] There is a strong whiff of another big disaster on the horizon. The foundation 'repairs' are of particular concern.[57] Only one percent of the 66,769 earthquake repairs carried out in Christchurch were completed under a building consent or considered exempt from a consent. Considering that there was so much structural damage in the city this figure is very concerning and provides enough evidence of the need for an inquiry. There are serious implications for property owners whose repairs have been carried out without local authority consents. The EQC's figures show that there were approximately 6000 unconsented structural repairs and about 60,000 purely 'cosmetic' repairs.[58] In August, the findings of a repair survey are released which looked at a limited number of only 90 structural repairs, managed mostly by the EQC. Of these 90 repairs, 32 repairs are found to be non-complaint with a further 23 sporting minor defects. Extrapolating this citywide, it is not hard to understand the massive ramifications that lie ahead. In reality the true extent of the problem is unknown, though it is reasonable to assume that the numbers are very high. Most homes were assessed using the MBIE Guidelines and exempted from consenting requirements and will no doubt be subject to later disputes. The search for someone to blame has already begun and contractor 'exit plans' are no doubt already being planned. Despite this, no one is held accountable. Instead, in the *Christchurch Press*, a large full page EQC 'update' is published declaring that the EQC will put right non-compliant repairs followed by a few paragraphs under the heading *"Need support?"*[59] The EQC is to repair the repairs of 5500 homes and about 2300 underfloor repairs to re-inspect and potentially fix.[60] Meanwhile the EQC attempts to shut down the adverse findings about its top engineer, one Graeme Robinson, so as to avoid opening the cases of 2500 properties he is responsible for assessing. This would have wide implications for both the EQC, private insurers and the engineering profession.[61] Cantabrians clamour for an independent judicial inquiry or a royal commission with wide ranging terms of reference covering all aspects of the EQC and Fletchers' involvement in handling of earthquake damage and substandard repairs. In response, the earthquake Minister Gerry Brownlee pledges that all underfloor faulty repairs are to be properly fixed.[62] Without a doubt, the repair disaster is a direct result of a series of government bungles in the past starting with the introduction of the MBIE Guidelines in an attempt to reduce the cash strapped EQC's liability. The Government must take accountability for its causative role in what may easily develop into the next big disaster in Canterbury. The depressing reality of this situation is that government increased costs come at the expense of taxpayers. Taxpayers will ultimately end up paying for government negligence. The faulty building methodologies, faulty regulations, faulty building science, faulty local government practices are here for all to see. It is not that the government was not made aware of this. Over the course of the last four years there have been numerous professionals who have put New Zealand's building authorities on notice of the problems and issues arising, requesting that the authorities address these problems before a disaster does ensue – but both the Government and CERA have been content to ignore these early warning signals so long as immediate costs are contained. The cost to the country of the much discussed 'leaky home debacle' is estimated at NZD 11.5 billion. The cost of shoddy repairs in Canterbury will make this figure look insignificant in the years to come. Ironically the repair scandal in Canterbury will enrich the Government by billions of dollars, as the Government will reap at least 25c for every New Zealand dollar spent on fixing these shoddy repairs from the goods and services tax and company tax paid on materials, workmanship and experts' fees. (This too, happened during the leaky home crisis). This National Government will have to accept its liability for the deregulation experiment inflicted on the building industry and local government. It will also need to take full responsibility for the liability accumulated by the private sector builders, designers, architects and certifiers.

Unsurprisingly, it comes to light that the project manager for the EQC, Fletcher Construction Ltd, cannot be held responsible for the design of any works, the construction of any works or the work of any contractor or consultant. As one local lawyer put it, it seemed 'extraordinary' that the EQC agreed to such a clause.[63] The EQC gears up for litigation by hiring engineers to help with court cases involving quake repairs. A group of more than 100 homeowners will take the EQC to court over the standard of repairs.[64] A petition by homeowners is launched by lawyer Duncan Webb asking Parliament for a Royal Commission of Enquiry into the shoddy repairs, with a focus on the EQC, private insurers and the Christchurch City Council consenting processes.[65] The Earthquake Minister, not surprisingly, dismisses the need for a Royal Commission describing it as *"completely unnecessary"* claiming that regular customer audits carried out by the EQC and other insurers show generally high levels of satisfaction.[66] Once again the issue of accountability is side-stepped. Megan Woods, Labour's acting earthquake spokesperson and a Christchurch MP commented *"He [Brownlee] needs to realise we need some serious questions answered here"*.

The private insurers also play a major role in the shoddy repair saga. IAG repairs are also found to be deficient according to a Government investigation.[67] Six out of seven quake repairs were found to be deficient particularly in relation to unconsented foundation repairs. Questions begin to be asked about insurers taking advantage of the MBIE Guidelines in order to turn a blind eye to foundation damage.[68] IAG too, is accused of bullying its customers and a local lawyer states that this insurer *"threatens"* to cash settle its customers *"whenever there is a disagreement on the repair or rebuild strategy"*.[69]

There are further claims of nepotism within the EQC organisation as the highly remunerated daughter of one of the EQC's top bosses was removed from a case after complaints about her conduct.[70] The failures within the EQC are many and appear to flow from cultural and institutional flaws that have flourished largely unabated and without effective (or any) oversight by Government.

The restoration of historic buildings continues to produce high emotions amongst the Christchurch population. Jamie Gough, a City Councillor, declares that the Christchurch City Cathedral has become a symbol of 'negativity' looming over the city like a bad omen.[71] A decision on the Anglican Cathedral is still to be made. The Catholic Basilica decision has already been taken and the building will be partially retained.[72] Work on the restoration of the Town Hall began this year at an estimated cost of NZD 127.5 million.

The Government declares that it will consult the public on possible revised compensation for the red zone. Many red zoners feel that this is simply another delay tactic. The general sentiment is that the Government has shown no consideration whatsoever for people's real circumstances. CERA releases a revised proposal for the owners of vacant, uninsured and commercial property in the residential red zone, in which it is proposed that they will receive only 80 percent of the Rateable Value. The distinction made between the insured and uninsured is controversial particularly in light of the Supreme Court's ruling that the insurance status should not be 'determinative' in calculating compensation for red zoners.[73] The Christchurch City Council lashes out at the Government for its treatment of uninsured land owners declaring that the same offer should be made to everyone in the residential red zone regardless of their insurance status.[74] The red zone was due to be cleared last year. Again the Government misses its deadline. There is 'an intention' to consult the public on the future use of the land.[75]

Serious discussion takes place about the potential closure of yet another school, this time Redcliffs School. The general sentiment among the locals is that the school needs to remain open and is still viable.[76] The community is given until May 01 to respond to the news of closure.[77] Thousands of Cantabrians show their support for the local school staying open. The school vows to fight against its closure.[78] Nevertheless Education Minister, Hekia Parata, announces an interim decision to close Redcliffs at the end of the 2016 academic year.[79] Meanwhile Ms Parata unveils plans for six new 'charter' schools under public-private partnerships. Many Cantabrians find it hard not to view this as a small group of people in government, trying to control a national agenda, define issues in their own narrow right-wing terms and obfuscate their vested interests and motives. The point is made that the government had no mandate to do this. The charter/partnership issue is a case in point. It would seem that this small group of Ministers demand that they alone will determine the nation's future and are dismissive of anyone who would have the temerity to raise his or her voice or suggest that a democratic process should be followed. If New Zealanders' wishes are not acknowledged in this process - which was initiated without any mandate from the people - then one can safely say that as a population we have lost our hold of not only education but more fundamentally, of our democratic process.

The end of 2015 is marked by a rush on the Christchurch City Mission. The Mission usually hands out 20 to 25 parcels a day. This year that figure ballooned to between 90 and 100 food parcels. A study is released by Victoria University professor Ilan Noy detailing that on average every person in Canterbury has lost 150 days of *"healthy life"* since the February 2011 earthquakes.[80] He warns of the problems associated with long term survival. In mental health terms, Christchurch remains in the thick of it. Caroline Bell, psychiatrist, says that the *"damage is not acute, but it is chronic and cumulative"* and an expert on the Australia bushfire disasters says that much of the city may only be at the half way point.[81] Since the earthquakes, there has been a massive increase in the numbers of people requiring assistance in the form of mental health services and a 69 percent increase in the numbers of children and young people needing assistance. These figures do not account for the many others managing to get by with the services of their local GPs or other primary providers. In May 2015, the Government withholds funding from a counselling service: Relationships Aotearoa loses 15 staff members and further cuts are announced. Relationships Aotearoa alone, had seen 30,000 Cantabrians over the preceding four years. In addition, both local and central Government continue to neglect the housing needs of the region's most disadvantaged, creating a vicious cycle of mental health issues and dependence. For people struggling to afford rental housing or those who do not meet the criteria for social housing, options are very limited and certainly detrimental to their health.[82] The Ministry of Building, Innovation and Employment (MBIE) estimates that the population is facing severe housing deprivation which has likely increased by between 68 and 113 percent since the earthquakes. Average rents increased by 36 percent from December 2010 to April 2015, with the mean rental now sitting at NZD 408 per week, according to rental bond data.[83]

2016 is heralded in by desperate policyholders with unresolved claims. One Cantabrian, Philippa Corry, addresses the nation in a YouTube clip for all the world to see, in a 25 minute summary of events and the issues faced by Cantabrians.[84] As one *Christchurch Press* reporter aptly writes "*Middle class people complain, agitate, organise, petition, fight and go to court. They stick around to wait for answers. They have staying power. They use the media. Middle-class people push for things*".[85] I predict that in 2016 we will see the big 'push'.

Citizens Speak

It is February 2016. To reflect the current situation I am writing down a few words that reflect the total uncertainties many people in Christchurch are still living with, particularly those who still have unsolved land claims. The district plan is currently under review. 18,000 properties have been issued with hazard notices on their Land Information Memoranda. In a bizarre and manipulative process, homeowners' democratic rights to object to these hazard notices were negotiated away from those affected. All the new hazard notices take legal effect immediately; this releases both local and territorial authorities, as well as insurance companies from liability. Community consultation on the hazards has been 'parked' for a 'later date'. As it currently stands, insurance claims are being settled before the land damage and earthquake-introduced hazards have been adequately addressed. There is no protection for ratepayers against these unsustainable practices. In essence, this has the potential to lower the amount of many claim settlements and transfer much of the risk and liability to the unwary homeowner.

Standards remain outdated. The AS/NZS 1170.5 Earthquake Action Standard has still not been updated. If this standard is to be believed - seismic risk has not changed in Canterbury!

There is complete uncertainty about the city boundaries and individual properties as a result of lateral spread, some boundaries have moved between 1 and 2 metres. Legislation has now been proposed ruling that the legal boundaries have moved with the land. This lack of certainty assists no one. With respect to the boundary of Christchurch City - they are said to move with the rising sea levels, according to the Coastal Marine Act 2011. While it is reasonable to expect that Council does not have the responsibility of maintaining assets under sea level, we experienced an earthquake event after this law was enacted In April 2011. Consequently a large number of properties sank below the line of Mean High Water Springs, which is supposed to define the boundary of the city. Despite strenuous efforts to discuss the issues with the authorities, there has been a steadfast refusal to address the matter. We have raised this issue with the Hearings Panel on the District Plan, but whether anything comes from this remains to be seen. Neither the Crown nor the Christchurch City Council has been able to clarify where the boundaries lie.

CERA has declined to meet with residents' associations, community groups and experts on this and other issues. Meetings have been held with Insurance Council New Zealand, the EQC and the Council. When we raise the critical issues of boundaries and the lack of durability of the land, meetings have ground to a halt.

Erosion has been identified as land damage following the earthquakes. Thousands of trees had to be felled due to loss of ground bearing and salt water intrusion following the earthquakes. The properties around those areas have been identified as erosion-prone. Since erosion is an uninsurable risk, we have asked the EQC how they intend to address this particular form of land damage. Up until now, no answers have been forthcoming. The EQC has pointed the finger at the Council on the question of erosion, but has been unwilling to meet together with the communities and the Council to help clarify the situation.

Essentially, this stops all progress in its tracks. We urgently need these questions to be answered; we need a commitment to accountability and a commitment to sustainability. We need a Council and city planners that place the safety of residents and sustainability above potential savings on buildings and repairs on unsustainable and dangerous land.

If no changes are made, what I see happening is that tax and ratepayers who were sold some of the most extensive insurance covers available in the world will be left sitting in the water (literally), with hazard notices on their uninsurable properties, facing substantial risk of imminent loss following any natural disaster in the foreseeable future. We are already seeing examples of this on the banks of the Avon River, where properties are being exempted from regulations and being rebuilt up to 1.3 metres below that which would normally be required for a new building. The fact that only temporary emergency stop banks are being erected along the Avon also does not assist matters. Neither the houses nor the stop banks have sustainable standards of durability.

Such policies cannot be described as designated as either resilient, sustainable or classed as 'recovery'. Instead of the recommended approach of following a natural catastrophe, namely to 'build back better', what we are witnessing in Christchurch is the exact opposite. This will merely postpone the next disaster, which will no doubt leave the most vulnerable of homeowners sustaining imminent loss.

Is this a fair and equitable way to settle claims? What moral and social justification can there be for treating people in this way?

By Hugo Kristinsson[86]

CONCLUSION

- -

*Resilience is about the capacity to plan and prepare
for adversity, the ability to absorb the impact and
recover quickly, but more importantly it's about
the ability to adapt to a new environment or even
co-create a new kind of normal.*

Lianne Dalziel, Mayor of Christchurch[1]

'Christchurch' has become an ongoing saga about an unprecedented catastrophe, with a population largely left to wallow in its own misery. After some years of researching this sorry state of affairs, a story emerges of incompetence, dishonesty, professional vested interests, cynical corporate greed and government agendas, complicity and self-service. Should we not be afraid of power without impunity? It is clear that the manipulation of a community trickles down from the top of the ladder to the bottom; the power of the few is being exerted over the many. Time is now right for fundamental change to the system. Einstein once said that the definition of insanity was to do the same thing over and over again hoping for a different outcome. The outcome of another catastrophe somewhere else in the country will be no different unless fundamental change follows the Christchurch experience.

The insurance industry is in dire need of reform. For too many insurance companies, profit-making has replaced fair dealing with policyholders. The industry has done and continues to do all it can to maximise its profits by delaying settlement of claims and other sharp, dishonest practices. Private insurance companies are for-profit corporations and their goal is to increase profits. This tends to result in the implementation of business practices that hurt the insured, particularly when a private insurer is faced with a major catastrophe which is likely to impact heavily on its 'bottom line'. While insurance companies are in the business of making money, they cannot be considered 'just normal businesses'. They have special fiduciary duties requiring them to protect their customers both in statute and case law. Paramount amongst those duties are the duties to act fairly and in good faith. With this in mind, they should not be at liberty to act in the same manner as normal businesses. Yet despite this, following Hurricane Katrina in the USA the lawsuits against insurers numbered in their thousands. Litigation included: class actions on behalf of tens of thousands of policyholders; an antitrust action by the Mississippi Attorney General; and another class action by the Mississippi Attorney General, to name but a few. Hurricane Katrina exposed absolute failure of the insurance system from the viewpoint of the policyholders. The evidence is overwhelmingly clear that Canterbury too has suffered a similar fate. But the Government has not seen fit to put in place mechanisms to protect against corporate abuse. The Government standoff suggests vested interest by individuals, or policy that supports corporate interests above all else. Recent events concerning the TPPA trade agreement would tend to reinforce the latter. Regardless of which, it has done little to aid legal access to affected citizens or the possibility of class action.

Disaster mitigation, preparedness, response, rebuild and recovery are the end products of complex political and administrative interactions, the results of which cannot be guaranteed or easily controlled or anticipated. But there do have to be alternative solutions and those solutions should be presented by the 'other' political voices as distinct from a single governing entity. Though natural disasters themselves are not driven by politics as such, they are not immune from politics and the actions taken by human actors. Both, undoubtedly affect the prevention, mitigation, and effects of natural disasters and their aftermaths. The initial 'shock' is the natural act itself - the sequence of events post Christchurch earthquakes are recorded in this book and form the 'aftershock' which follows in the wake of the physical disaster. The aftershock I write about in this book, is actually man-made, as it reflects the way the EQC, the insurance industry and those professionals associated with it, together with CERA, the Christchurch City Council and the National Government of the day, equate to the generators of the net impact of the 'aftershock' on the population. The physical 'disaster' is far from the whole event. It is also made up of those shocking post-disaster events, such as delayed insurance pay-outs, top-down authoritarian decisions, ineptitude of government departments, corruption in the guise of free enterprise, corrupt professional bodies – and the list goes on. This conglomerate is responsible for an aftershock of a different kind which over these 5 years has seriously affected the recovery of the residents of the city of Christchurch, its economy and its surrounds.

There are those who would have us believe that political collaboration is a necessary foundation for dealing with a natural disaster, but the experience over the last five years has shown that a 'bipartisan' approach does not work. It was the former opposition Labour Leader, David Shearer who said *"I do believe we need to look at a way we can have a bipartisan approach on this. We do need a government/opposition united approach"* [and] *"as a result of that, I think we do need to be sitting down with the Government and looking at a bipartisan approach to the rebuild in Christchurch and its recovery."*[2] On the face of it, it is not hard to understand the appeal of bipartisanship. It sounds very mature and enlightened with a suggestion of the joint, harmonious pursuit of quick and beneficial solutions to a set of difficult circumstances. It seems an obvious choice in the case of *external* threat, such as war, yet there is little evidence that solutions to big *internal* problems are to be found through bipartisanship and there are plenty of examples throughout history that would suggest that they are not. When it comes to 'crisis' events, this is particularly the case. Democracy actually depends on the opposite - partisanship - in the form of strong, critical advocacy that opens public debate - forcing the parties to explain their ideas, which in turn clarifies choices for voters. Partisan-causes are often bold ideas and though these ideas can be divisive, they can offer citizens a genuinely new path forward, if the mechanism to take these views into account exists outside of a general election situation. It not only creates a system of checks and balances in the political arena but it also forces parties to take criticism and suggested alternatives politically seriously. That was clearly not the case, or even on the cards for the citizens of Christchurch and the political opposition was rarely seen or heard. By contrast, bipartisanship has the potential and the ability to 'cloak' corruption, obscure chasms between politicians and the people they serve, and agree to invest single individuals with absurd, almost dictatorial powers, or simply indicate that the leadership and direction of both parties has become a closed club, (often with an agenda). In principle and in practice, a serious partisan political structure is fundamental to a healthy democracy and partisan ideas are crucial for liberty. Bipartisanship, by contrast, has enabled some of the most shameful episodes in history, such as American slavery, the Iraq war, and others. In this respect the Labour opposition party, or any of the opposition political parties for that matter, have missed a huge opportunity in Christchurch and they have failed and continue to fail to protect the interests of the population in so doing. But it is not yet too late. The insurance aftershock and Christchurch fiasco is still an unfolding drama and far from over. There is a gaping great hole waiting for one or more of the opposition parties to step in. A deliberately established (by the media? Government?) invisibility of the true Christchurch situation in the rest of the country makes it difficult to enlist popular support for any other political party to exploit. If the rest of New Zealand really was aware of what has taken place in the second largest city, things might be different. It has become so abundantly clear that many of the introduced political and civil processes were not and are not functioning in a democratic way. Local and national authorities in our society fell short of protecting the interests of the people by whom they were elected into office. On the 'up-side' however it has awoken in some of us a renewed sense of citizenship. A better understanding of the fact that society functions at its best when we all participate and take responsibility for those things that require action. This can only happen when we all bring our energy and judgement to bear on a situation. It is the only way we have the potential to create a more honest, fairer and inclusive society. It helps to support a democracy in which people are willing to participate and feel that they belong. Through our media, I am often confronted with situations that remind me that many of the institutions that give structure to our society simultaneously betray our trust with the slow introduction of changes which seem to ignore the desires of the majority and thus simply impose that which those in 'power' happen to think is good for the majority or their political agenda. This often happens without any notice.

Confidence in a country's disaster-preparedness depends on confidence in the ability and willingness of its government to mandate and oversee levels of decency and fairness and how those matters are dealt with. In our modern society the power of 'the market' is enormous (and here I refer specifically to the private insurance industry). However, the market is driven by financial and economic incentives and has no inherent moral character, nor do the people who operate it and it is therefore arguable that it lies within the responsibility of the government to decide how to manage it. In times of crisis, the market must be tamed and tempered to ensure that it is first and foremost working for the benefit of its citizens. In this respect, the current New Zealand political system, post-earthquakes, failed to do so. It failed to check the growing inequalities and protect its earthquake victims from corporate abuse. In fact, the reverse is true, politics and economics coalesced. The government failed to use its available means, such as the Commerce Commission and other regulatory organs and turned a blind eye to the vagaries and distortions of so-called 'self-governing' professions. This failure in both politics and economics can be seen to be related and the evidence is that they reinforce each other. A political system that amplifies the voice of wealthy corporates fails to protect the ordinary citizen against corporate abuse at the overall expense of the society. Money speaks in politics as it does in the market place. Politics in New Zealand have shaped the market place in ways that advantage the corporates at the expense of the rest of the population. It could be argued that this reaches its zenith with the signing of the TPPA trade agreement, the content of which was not fully disclosed to the population prior to its signing but which has subsequently proved to be an act which surrenders the sovereignty of the nation to International corporatism.

Any system of disaster recovery must have and obey rules and regulations and operate within a legal framework. The seriousness of the circumstances in Christchurch post-earthquakes deserved and required a better balance between the marketplace and the government, based on the premise that the State has the best interests of the people as its mandate. In a neo-capitalist society and modern economy, the government still sets and enforces the rules of the game. In the absence of government support, the extent to which a population can recover post-disaster is severely challenged. In that respect 'Christchurch' was and *is* severely challenged! Private insurance will not be the risk management tool it claims to be when the proverbial 'poo hits the fan'. Let us also not forget the potential effects of a global financial crisis coupled with a global environmental crisis. Can you imagine…. So who will be paying for the fall out of climate change? National resilience to global risks needs to be a priority so that critical systems continue to function despite a major disturbance and this means being financially prepared to pick up the pieces. We do not want a repeat of the Christchurch insurance aftershock.

This book does not have the abolition of insurance as its motive, even though, ultimately that may be the best course, nor does it wish to tarnish all insurers with the same brush, some companies appear to have performed better, they tend to be mutual insurers and are in a minority. Generally speaking, insurers and their staff have tended to deal with their clients from the position of power, and many people have been unable to make inroads with legitimate claims. Insurance should be an essential protector of the 'middle class'. However, one sees little evidence among the major insurers in Canterbury of prompt and fair claims handling. Insurance does not work when insurers fail to honour their commitment to policyholders, exploiting the great asymmetry of corporate power and individuals and the high cost of justice. If insurance is to work and if insurance companies want to avoid costly litigation, class actions, demonstrations and the like, then the industry should adhere to the good-faith model that their marketing proclaims. If they show they are not doing this, guidelines or regulations designed to build honest business practices would eliminate the uncertainty of claims handling and protect the policyholders' as well as insurer reputations. The current profit-driven model demonstrates not only a breach of the fiduciary duty of good faith to the insured but also a breach of the company's duty to act in the best (long term) interests of its shareholders.

It is time for political and corporate accountability. The failure of good-faith action has provided a wake-up call to some of the realities of corporate culture and to New Zealand's current political landscape. Christchurch must remain an economically viable city with growth and investment opportunities. The only way this can be achieved, is with Local and Central Government intent and the insurance industry honouring its contracts in a timely manner. If that commitment is not forthcoming the future of the city will remain uncertain.

A diminishing trust in authorities tasked with insurance matters i.e. the EQC, Southern Response, Government Ministers and the private insurers, informs us that the present configuration is still the biggest barrier to residential recovery. The distrust slows down the negotiation process with all parties involved. I find myself continually amazed by the insurance industries' apparent complete control over that process. The insurance industry criticised a Labour Party proposal for an independent insurance commissioner to oversee the industry, stating that it did not see the value of an independent commissioner – of course, you would expect it to say that! What could be more repugnant than having an 'outsider' overseeing your activities when currently you have a seemingly free field? I would also argue that the self-imposed 'self-regulation' of the insurance industry is farcical and has failed utterly. If self-regulation is to exist effectively, it requires strenuous and active accountability mechanisms, plus regular government oversight. Changing a few words of the Fair Insurance Code and 'setting and forgetting' is not a viable answer to the problems policyholders have experienced. If there is no accountability in place – and it seems there is not in Christchurch, then self-regulation is totally ineffective. If the regulator then fails to lay down the law, then the fundamental purpose to be served by self-regulation is defeated and consumer welfare is compromised to the benefit of the corporate. This is exactly what has taken place in Christchurch. For self-regulation to be effective, the New Zealand Insurance Council must have the will to be able to harness the common interest and enlist the support and input of other stakeholders such as relevant government agencies and consumer organisations, and manage the self-regulatory scheme transparently. There should be regular and independent review for efficiency and effectiveness. This has not happened. Community cynicism regarding both the government and the inability of the insurance industry regulating itself will undoubtedly have led to a distrust of self-regulatory schemes generally. The regulator is required to provide timely intervention where self-regulation is not working. This certainly has not taken place in Christchurch and we are still waiting for this to happen.

Despite the fact that governments are primarily elected to care about the social welfare of their citizens, they also have an undeniable interest in maximizing government income. Though governments do spend on both preventative and palliative measures to lessen the impact of a potential natural shock, they also use a natural disaster to redistribute power through political effect by favouring disaster spending in some regions and on some projects that are politically aligned to the party in power. These dire circumstances provide opportunities for rapacious governments, and disaster can be used as a blunt policy instrument to target or reward populations and to enrich a government and the 'corporate classes'. It is well to remember that the Christchurch earthquakes sit within the nation's historical context as well. Prior to the 2010 September earthquake, the government bailed out South Canterbury Finance investors to the tune of NZD 1.7 billion.[3] This left the government decidedly short of ready cash. The Government was very cognisant of their funding short fall and knew that the Christchurch City Council was going to have to start finding funds from ratepayers or from debt and/or selling assets. So on the one hand, while the Government has pledged open handed support to Christchurch, we are also witnessing a slowing down/delay of anchor projects, silence over the fate of the red zone areas and a city left with a very expensive legacy of half mended roads and drainage problems.[4] Yet as time passes, we also witness enormous resource being pumped into the city in various directions within the central city recovery via private insurance, CERA and cost sharing arrangements with the Christchurch City Council, the work of SCIRT (Stronger Christchurch Infrastructure Rebuild Team) in the area of horizontal infrastructure (roads, underground pipes and bridges) and also the EQC in the repair and rebuild of homes. But let us not forget that a city and a community is foremost about the people, their health and their wellbeing. Here lies the priority: equal weight and resource should have been given to their recovery. It has been a substantial trauma that they have had to endure.

So after almost five years of 'organised' chaos, in a city which I have at times come to loathe and with levels of dishonesty that make my blood boil, I am left asking one question - Why has nothing changed? Five years have passed, no legislation has been implemented, no regulation endorsed, no accountability taken place. Yes, there have been several proposed changes to the Earthquake Commission Act, a cursory and ineffective rewording of the Fair Insurance Code, minimal changes to the Building Code, some discussion on the Building (Earthquake-prone Buildings) Amendment Bill and a few other minor revisions. I find myself thinking, we had better pray that we do not have another event any time soon because clearly the nation is still not ready for the next adverse event. The earthquakes and their aftermath have highlighted the need for forward thinking legislation particularly in light of predicted climatic changes. 6000 properties in Christchurch and Banks Peninsula will potentially be under threat of coastal erosion over the next century. A report written by engineering consultants, Tonkin and Taylor suggest that there will be a rise of 40 centimetres over the next 50 years and one meter over the next 100 years. Some 5971 properties fall in the coastal erosion zone and 17,819 lie within the coastal inundation zone.[5] Now is the time to mitigate. There is already discussion of Council discouraging new subdivisions and new building in high risk areas - but more than discouragement is required if the conscienceless 'developers' are to be controlled. Clear guidelines and regulations need to be put in place now while the disasters of the future can still be mitigated and managed.

Profound change is necessary, both for Christchurch now and for the country. New Zealand needs to develop an alternative system to cover the issue of the insurance of both commercial and private property. The experiences and reports of other disaster-affected communities around the world, where insurers are increasing their premiums and taking advantage of the fact that populations know little about the insurance industry, support this conclusion.

For those of us who have been party to this experience, it is more than likely to have a profound impact on the kind of property choices we make in the future: decisions about where to live, what kind of building to live in, and how much money to invest in our homes and businesses. In light of these events, it is also likely that locations which are now perceived as being higher earthquake risk or more liquefaction prone will become less desirable, suffer lower land prices or lower rents. It is also likely that for larger sites and any new developments, any insurer and lender will require more specific information, such as structural engineering and ground-condition reports. Because of the Canterbury events and New Zealand's known earthquake vulnerability, insurers and lenders will take a more critical view of 'construction type' in relation to buildings, with particular emphasis on unreinforced masonry buildings (pre-1975). This attention to detail is required. For too long assessment of risk has been a rather arbitrary science.

Present-day liberalised markets suit the needs of globally organised, corporate capitalism. Should we allow its agenda to define the lives of the citizens of New Zealand? Today, large corporations dominate consumerism. With the faceless services the big corporates provide, our lives may seem to run, on the surface at least, rather un-problematically. It is only when insurance companies' services are actually called upon that the consumer has the ability to assess the quality of their purchase. The opportunistic behaviour of the insurance companies, together with the lack of transparency within these corporations, is compounded by the failure of corporate watch-dogs such as government, the legal system and regulators to protect the public interest. In the background, behind closed doors, are the strategic alliances and the networked relationships between government, corporates, professionals and other major stakeholders.

In Christchurch we are now experiencing what has been labelled the 'new normal', i.e. civil chaos, dishonesty, self-service and flagrant profiteering. Dealing with insurers or other industry 'professionals' related to the settlement of my own residential property claim, I was daily reminded of the 'new normal' – my outlook on life has changed vastly in the past five years. I have found the whole experience sobering, disheartening and profoundly enlightening. I no longer live in the naive world of imagining that a government's function is to protect the populace or that corporates are essentially benign institutions. I have stepped away from this experience with a better understanding of what is wrong with this whole situation and, indeed, our society. I now have a more profound understanding of the Occupy Wall Street Movement – what it stands for and the goals it tries to achieve. Government has carved up our resources, given them to corporates who have in turn sold them back to us, demonstrating that they are quite prepared to engage in outright theft. As Christchurch moves into the phase of reconstructing its future, it has become overwhelmingly clear that this process only *"cuts deeper the ruts and grooves of social oppression and exploitation"*.[6] As each of the stakeholders vies for profit, power and control, as each weighs up the situation against their own economic or political interests, the politics of emergency management have become intense.

Many of the citizens of Canterbury feel themselves the victims of these 'stakeholder' struggles, unable to take action themselves, paralysed by the very institutions that were allegedly set up to protect them. We find ourselves the victims of political strife and the refusal of the insurance industry to front up. There is a deepening conflict over ends and means. It is clear that the central objective of capitalism is undermining our humanity and ordinary decency. While the Earthquake Recovery Minister, Hon. Gerry Brownlee suggests that we 'leave it to market forces', others, such as Christchurch Issues Earthquake Spokesman Denis O'Rourke, rightly interpret this as *"leave it to the wolves, the profiteers, and the law of the jungle"*.[7] Today we are surrounded by salivating corporations and authorities. How do we cope? And what is our response to be? This book proposes a solution, but it is one that will require our society to stand up and be counted, and require political courage and determination from a government willing to change.

Emergency management on a large scale is a government role and an overarching goal in the management of earthquake risk preparation. Recovery should be to ensure the sustainability and prosperity of New Zealand communities. Incredibly, despite the fact that the Christchurch earthquake is one of the most expensive insured natural catastrophes in history, triggering economic losses of in excess of USD 40 billion, the sales of insurance policies around the country have increased. This is a global phenomenon and it usually happens post-disaster. House insurance premiums for some homeowners have risen by 30 percent, while business premiums have more than doubled in some cases. Meanwhile, insurance industry sources state that as many insurance brokers and banks are paid commissions calculated as a percentage of premiums paid, they are enjoying substantial windfalls. The banks, which generally resell the house insurance policies of the large private insurers have been enjoying a similar windfall.

In light of the Insurance Council chief executive's comments in relation to the future of cover in New Zealand, the need for major change to our current system is clear. While 100 percent earthquake cover may remain in the market in the short term, there is no doubt that it will be the big issue for the next decade at least. For many, insurance is likely to become an unaffordable commodity, which could prove to be a social catastrophe.

In the push to maximise shareholder value, insurers' critical relationships with customers and the community have been sacrificed. This stance must not remain unchallenged, even if only from the perspective that long term shareholder value will be undermined. Corporate insurance giants are under the mistaken belief that their business practices are sustainable, but sustainability is built on the trust established with all stakeholders through past proper behaviour. The evidence suggests that repeated misconduct will ultimately lead to their downfall. The California Supreme Court in one of America's landmark insurance cases stated that the insurer's obligations are rooted in *"their status as purveyors of a vital service labelled 'quasi public in nature'"*. The suppliers of services affected with a public interest must take the public's interest seriously, where necessary placing it before their interest in maximising gains and limiting disbursements. Consequently as a supplier of a public service rather than a manufactured product, the obligations of insurers go beyond meeting reasonable expectations of coverage.

> ... The obligations of good faith and fair dealing encompass qualities of decency and humanity inherent in the responsibilities of a fiduciary, insurers hold themselves out as fiduciaries, and with the public's trust must go private responsibility consonant with that trust.[8]

The catastrophe that the Canterbury community has experienced will no doubt lead it to critique the response to these events for many more years to come. Many and diverse suggestions will be made; an article entitled 'lessons learned' will surely be written with the intention of others benefiting from the experience. However, history shows us that the same patterns and mistakes are repeated. The changes needed for New Zealand are of great urgency. If they are postponed or worse not made at all, we must expect a repeat of the fiasco that has taken place in Christchurch. Looking further ahead, aside from the immediate changes that need actioning, New Zealand has some important decisions to make with regard to the protection of the nation's social and economic well-being. These include a review of the current provisions and the implementation of strategies which address the following:

The development of an alternative catastrophe insurance structure and the expansion of the role and function of the EQC.

The insurance industry and its repeated poor performance in times of disaster has proven a global problem to be avoided. New Zealanders live in a country well known for its seismic risk. We need to prepare ourselves for future events of a similar nature and turn the Christchurch fiasco into an opportunity to find a more solid solution which will serve the interests of the citizens of New Zealand and better protect our economic and social interests. This must entail the elimination of private insurance for all property, to be replaced with an expanded EQC function to cover all property risk, including catastrophe.

The EQC has been vital to the whole of the government response to the Canterbury earthquakes and, although it has performed extremely poorly under the circumstances, it has had the lion's share of responsibility for claims. The Earthquake Commission has worked closely with CERA so that areas of mutual interest such as planning, mitigation and recovery can be addressed jointly. It is for this reason that the EQC should be the preferred residential property insurer during normal times and those of catastrophe. Catastrophe should be once again insured by the state. In order for the EQC to achieve its goal, a levy would be pegged to property values via the local authority rates system and linked to a sliding scale for building-code compliance, with an incentive attached to those properties that totally comply.

Many would argue that the EQC is not 'up to the job'. Based on the quality of their recent performance, that is a reasonable conclusion. However, with some major restructuring and inspired leadership this could be rectified. Given that the EQC's structure is already in place, extending this to a more comprehensive and formalised catastrophe scheme would not require too much more funding or implementation. In fact the 'bones' of a more comprehensive scheme are already in place; all that is required is some fleshing out. I also propose the EQC be structured as a Crown Entity and function as a corporation reporting to a Minister, with guidelines set or agreed by Parliament. This entity should be above political tinkering so that no matter the party in 'power', the EQC's mandate would be clear. In addition the corporation should function as a mutual, with the beneficiaries being New Zealand residential property owners.

In light of the EQC's recent performance there will need to be a major restructuring and overhaul of the EQC's internal framework, including a bolstering of trained staff nationwide. The proposition will also involve consideration of the Government's appetite for risk, i.e. the financial management of all risk, including catastrophe risk, which will require integration with economic, social and regulatory policies. The investment environment will have to be considered in terms of how the Natural Disaster Fund is to be managed. In addition, there is a necessity to create a balance between capital and the reinsurance needs of the Natural Disaster Fund in order to adequately provide for the population of New Zealand during times of catastrophe, i.e. the point at which the cost of capital and the cost of reinsurance provides a net benefit (see Chapter 4, the EQC and Earthquake Insurance). In my opinion, an unwilling and poorly delivering primary insurance market together with a nervous and 'frowning' reinsurance market indicates that the time is right for major reform of New Zealand's property insurance provisions (see Chapter 8, The Reinsurance Industry).

Regulatory change
The economic downturn around the world as a result of the 2008 financial crisis has increased the likelihood of greater attention and passage of

legislation geared toward an increase in oversight and transparency within the insurance industry in the form of legislation, such as the European Union Solvency II provisions – New Zealand should be no different. In the case where an EQC proposal such as the one outlined here is not acceptable, then some redesign of the regulation of the insurance industry is required in any case in order to prevent future 'bad faith dealings' and to restore policyholder confidence to the industry. This can be achieved by creating a truly independent consumer insurance oversight board, with substantial powers.

Safe-guarding the EQC Natural Disaster Fund
The time has now arrived to put pressure on our Government to ensure that the EQC Natural Disaster Fund is never again pillaged by present and forthcoming Governments for various reasons other than those that they were meant to serve. Now is the time to be saying to the Government – it is now time to do something serious about creating and growing very large EQC reserves. It is also the time to no longer be assuming private insurance will protect us. We now know the industry is 'not up to it'. Insurance works best for high-frequency, low-severity events, which are statistically independent and have probability distributions that are reasonably stationary over time. Catastrophic events, particularly mega-catastrophes such as Katrina, Northridge, Christchurch and Haiti, actually violate nearly all of the standard conditions for insurability. Together with the ever increasing threat of climatic change and the chance of increasingly violent weather events, there is even more urgency and reason to implement a national insurance scheme which enables New Zealand to be relatively self-reliant without the concern of reinsurers or insurers exiting the market place. As a nation we need to seriously revisit the potential for a better, replacement public insurance system. The benefits are beyond question.

Legislative change
Urgent legislative change is required in order to ensure that policyholders have a forum in which their insurance complaints can be truly independently heard in a timely and cost-effective manner and where insurers are held

accountable. Research during the course of this book shows clearly that access to 'justice' is out of the reach of the ordinary citizen. Currently there is no cost-effective method of holding private insurers to account. The insurance industry is only too aware of this, which is why Christchurch homeowners find themselves treated with disregard and blatant dishonesty. The courts are not seen as a risk as most claimants could not meet the cost. Where 'utmost good faith' cannot be enforced, there must be an option available for homeowners to defend themselves and protect their interests. Policyholder redress is required in both good and bad times.

In times of catastrophe, a comprehensive mediation structure should also be in place which can assist in the fast-tracking of mass claims settlement to ensure that people's lives are not disrupted for years while insurance claims are disputed and/or settled via the courts. This would represent an adequate recourse for unsatisfied policyholders (see Chapter 6, Policyholder Protection).

It is also clear that the Class Action Bill 2009 should be revitalized and a healthy class action regime developed. This is an important development for individuals' access to justice and their ability to effect social change in the realms of insurance. Law firms and litigation funders bringing class actions will continue to expand, the legislation should keep abreast of this development. We might ponder why the Bill has languished since 2009.

Cursory changes to the Fair Insurance Code and 'setting and forgetting' will not solve the problems faced by policyholders. Self-regulation of the insurance industry has clearly been an avid failure. The regulatory scheme has shown itself to be inconsistent with the underlying principles of the overall regulatory framework, or does not operate within the parameters of the framework. The regulators of the insurance industry have been strangely silent over the past five years. If the regulator fails to lay down the law then the fundamental purpose to be served by self-regulation is defeated and consumer welfare compromised. More must be done to protect policyholders.

Building codes
There is clear evidence that building codes need to be assessed and overhauled throughout the country. Earthquake engineering is a

major tool in mitigation of earthquake losses. It would seem that the interdependence between earthquake engineering and insurance is not always appreciated. The balance between the desire to retain heritage buildings and the need to protect these buildings from earthquake damage also needs to be clearly explored and addressed. Issues relating to earthquake risk include how to most effectively mitigate the effects of ground shaking on buildings and structures and whether areas particularly susceptible to liquefaction can be controlled more rigorously than areas of little or no risk. In other parts of the world, for example in Japan, there is an increasing integration of earthquake engineering and insurance activities. This interaction has the potential to significantly increase the effectiveness of both aspects in respect of the management of major disasters.

Already the insurers in New Zealand are working with the Government looking at the changes to earthquake regulations for commercial buildings and what the insurers would like to see in those buildings. The Insurance Council has said that from the Council's perspective they want to see more effort being directed into much better built buildings and more scrutiny of poor or under-strength buildings. It is also likely that commercial building cover might be more site-specific in the future. Engineers too have begun to call for the law to be changed so that authorities have the power to shut down buildings considered unsafe or not up to code.[9] Voluntary 'shut-down' is not enough. There is also the view that total quake safety is not viable and that the costs prevent any return on investment.[10] But safety is a return, preventing casualties and loss of life is a return. It's not about buildings but about the people who use them. In addition, the convenient altering of building codes post-event (e.g. the size of foundation cracks allowable and the tilt level of foundations), in order to minimise the sums of money payable to policyholders must stop.

In addition there is a need to rein in developers, to prevent them from making changes to subdivisions without informing residents and commencing development prior to consents having been issued. This practice makes a nonsense of the consent process.[11] In order to plan for a better future for New Zealand, developers should be more integrated with council city planning and development, with a shared responsibility to ensure that the needs, circumstances and interests of the local population are at the forefront of planning and decision making.

Public access to geotechnical information

It is now clear that the information about the risk of liquefaction and rockfall in the Port Hills etc. was already available prior to the Canterbury earthquakes. Reports had been written about the potential for damage and the expected extent of damage in various areas throughout the city. But such reports as these are apparently buried in local council office files, rarely seeing the light of day until a catastrophe occurs. A national database is required so that this information can be accessed, allowing people to make an informed decision about where to buy and where to build. This information availability will ultimately enable city councils, developers and individual citizens to mitigate risks for themselves. Yes, in the short term it may change the demographics of some areas, but this is a preferable organic process which will work towards minimising property loss in the long run. There are other cities in New Zealand which are highly prone to flooding and liquefaction; one wonders how many of the citizens, for example in Tauranga, parts of Wellington and Wanganui, are aware of the risks?

Consideration of climate change

Serious consideration needs to be given to the effects of climate change in light of the fact that natural disasters are causing re/insurance companies to evaluate their risk policies around the globe. A 2008 study conducted by Ernst and Young examined the top ten strategic business risks facing the insurance industry and found that climate change is the biggest threat to the industry.[12] Currently insurers are concerned about the level of uncertainty regarding the ability to accurately predict future risk resulting from climate change, the effect of disclosure on premiums, and the potential for increased litigation following disclosure.[13] We need to be increasingly wary of the impact of climate change on the re/insurance industry, in terms of solvency of operations and viability. As a nation we need to plan more for the future and find solutions to these ever-growing problems and the changes and potentialities need to be factored into the way the country structures its EQC Natural Disaster

Fund. Reliance on external insurers for protection is a false economy as weather events increase, private premiums increase or re/insurers simply extricate themselves from the market place, as they have done in parts of the USA and Australia. Prior planning is essential. Consequently there is also a need for good science to help reduce the uncertainty premium in any government model. In this way, catastrophe modelling should lead to price and cover improvements. It is necessary that the disaster policies and goals have provisions made on the basis of which government and the insurance industry communicate more effectively, align their policies and implement strategies together. Issues which are associated with climate change and which are now on the horizon make this an urgent requirement. There is a critical role for any government in adaptation to climate change. And what is so vitally clear is that the private insurance model simply will not work in a world with ever increasing natural disasters occurring.

Redefining the role and function of the EQC
Obviously homeowners need more information and guidance on the most effective measures they can take to prevent damage from natural disasters occurring. They also need to know what to expect from the EQC if these events occur. And while the EQC does have school education programmes in place and community information available through websites, long term sponsorships with the national museum Te Papa and the Auckland War Memorial Museum, advertising campaigns and published resources,[14] the general population is not very aware of the role, the function and the procedures of the EQC. What is required is public awareness in a personal sense – 'Christchurch yesterday, me tomorrow'.

Disaster Mitigation has to involve all stakeholders
Disaster mitigation cannot be a one sided discussion. It must involve government, (national and local), Civil Defence, the insurance industry and policyholders. Without a comprehensive alignment in policy and the allocation of responsibilities plus the development of a regulatory framework, the victims of any future disaster will continue to be victimized long after the event itself. Had this preparatory work taken place, or been

established in policy and understood by the parties, the time frames for residents, businesses and the City recovery would have been shortened, particularly in relation to insurance claim resolution.

Unless the people of Christchurch have the sense to combine their efforts to confront a lack of Government accountability and corporate greed, the EQC and the insurers will pick-off the 'little people' one by one, using pseudo-legal claptrap and misrepresentation. Now that these huge shortcomings have come to light, it remains to be seen whether or not the National Government will accept responsibility and try to equitably sort out the growing mess. Even more interesting will be whether or not those on the Labour, Greens and NZ First parliamentary benches will enforce an equitable remedy for the many defrauded homeowners. *That a Government agency could have visited this disaster on the nation's second largest city, is beyond comprehension.* We need accountability and we need remedy and we need them NOW.

In step with the increasing number of serious weather events, we are seeing an ever-increasing rise in property insurance rates for areas with catastrophe-exposed risks i.e. consumers have to pay more for their cover. Homeowners in the USA for instance, living in wind exposed areas, such as coastal regions or the Mid-West are seeing significant rate increases, while many insurers are restricting capacity, decreasing deductibles and requiring expensive wind mitigation construction. Insurers have to foot the costs of rising pay-outs while at the same time they are confronted with historically low investment returns and a dubious global economy. The insurance industry's overall financial performance according to Ceres (as measured by average return-on-equity), lags behind other industries.

The threat of rising catastrophic losses triggered by increasing concentrations of insured assets subject to natural disaster do present very real and significant challenges to the sector's financial future. Insurance sector losses and poor financial results have the potential to undermine the industry's financial ability to weather the storms. Another big risk for the insurance industry lies in that industry's interconnectedness and interdependency with the banking industry and the global marketplace. As we know, insurance has become so intrinsically woven into the very fabric of our society and in the event that its availability is lost or its stability undermined, then the outcomes look very gloomy for both consumers and governments. So the need to pre-empt the likely arrival of climate effects becomes critical for all parties. It is clear that if the effects of climate change were to become severe enough to impact the investment environment, which in turn drives insurers' investment yields, this circumstance would further compound the operating risk for the industry. Is this a risk that can be feasibly managed? For a certain period of time perhaps – but for how long – that is the trillion dollar question!

I remember post-quake Christchurch well. I remember that once the initial shock had worn off there was a palpable air of optimism in the City. It was so visible in the 'Share an Idea Wall' scattered with innovative and creative wishes of a people willing to do what was needed to rebuild. It was a city willing to rise to the challenge. Now in the sixth year post-earthquakes it is a city showing the signs of slow recovery, a city of tired, disillusioned citizens, worn down by the ongoing battles with insurance companies and the EQC – the two entities they thought were there to protect them in their time of most need. Many feel paralysed and cut off from the process of recovery by the heavy, ulterior and stubborn hand of bureaucracy in the form of CERA and the Earthquake Recovery Minister. In the background operates a new Council under the direction of Lianne Dalziel, urging people to get involved, to take responsibility for the things they want to take responsibility for. Once again there is an invitation to provide a vision for a succinct, sustainable, smart, healthy and resilient city. Mayor Dalziel's call to action, call to participation, is a genuine one I believe.[15]

When and how shall we respond to this open invitation to action?!

As I travel through the city I am regularly met with tails of heartache. People who have chosen to take out additional mortgages to complete the repairs on their homes. They simply could not 'fight the fight' with their insurer any longer. Middle class couples who, prior to the earthquakes lived in the centre of the city, had comfortable standards of living and were happy with their lives, now living in Kaiapoi, isolated from the community they once worked for, no income and desperate. These stories abound. Yes there are 'winners' and 'losers' in this saga - the winners are the happy few.

This experience and these times are crucial and critical to our futures, we are a people called to do great things - to rebuild a City, to improve income disparity, to constitute a self-aware middle class, to provide educational opportunities, and to reverse the rise of inequality. It is my hope that we all can all rise to that challenge.

My wish for the future of Canterbury and the future of New Zealand is that as a nation we challenge the injustices that many have experienced throughout this process, both as a result of sheer bureaucratic ineptitude and also dishonest vested interest, to ensure that this will never happen again. My wish is that as a nation we do not wait until another disaster takes place before starting to make the changes in the way we look at our cities and our ecosystem and their governance. My wish is that the country learns from the Canterbury experience and prepares itself better for the next one. If we do not take heed now, when the next disaster does take place then we will see a repeat of the insurance aftershock and the Christchurch fiasco. This challenge will require each of us to be more courageous – to insist on the respect for basic human dignity. To remember that it is the character and quality of our society and how we treat those in need that is all-important. All of our survival is tied to the survival of each one of us.

As I was completing the final touches to this book in February 2016, Christchurch experienced a magnitude 5.7 earthquake 15 km East of Christchurch. On February 22 the fifth year memorial service for the 185 people who had died as a result of the earthquakes took place. This solemn occasion was marked by the dowsing of the Hon. Gerry Brownlee, Minister of Earthquake Recovery, in a 'brown lumpy substance'..... It is fair to say that Cantabrians have had enough.[16]

~~~

I believe in the enormous power of the human spirit and the power within each of us to effect major change. Edmund Burke (1729–97), put it well:

The only thing necessary for the triumph of evil is for good men [and women] to do nothing.

NOTES

Introduction

1. www.searchquotes.com/quotes/author/Peter_Coyote/
2. Retirement savings go beyond the family home, Eloise Gibson, Christchurch Press, Feb 15, 2012.
3. www.icnz.org.nz/regulation/legislation7.php
4. earthquake.usgs.gov/learn/faq/?categoryID=11&faqID=95
5. earthquake-report.com/2012/02/21/christchurch-1-year-after-the-devastating-quake/
6. Rebuilding life tough for quake-paralyzed mums, Michelle Cooke, Christchurch Press, Jan 4, 2012.
7. Soil Risk may be Highest, Pail Gorman, Christchurch Press, Nov 2, 2011.
8. Warren Buffett, CEO of Berkshire Hathaway Inc., wrote in his annual letter to shareholders, www.bloomberg.com/news/2012-01-05/reinsurance-pricing-subdued-even-after-2011-s-disaster-record.html
9. Carolyn Bandel and Kevin Crowley, Reinsurance Pricing Subdued Even After 2011's Disaster Record, January 05, 2012: retrieved from http://mobile.bloomberg.com/news/2012-01-05/reinsurance-pricing-subdued-even-after-2011-s-disaster-record?BB_NAVI_DISABLE=PULSE
10. World Economic Forum, Global Risks 2007, at 4 (2007), available at www.weforum.org/pdf/CSI/Global_Risks_2007.pdf.
11. www.stuff.co.nz/business/industries/5989463/Vero-boss-calls-for-greater-EQC-role

Chapter 1: Sequence of Events

12. Farewell 2011, you won't be missed, Neil Irwin, Christchurch Press, Jan 7, 2012.
13. John Holiday, University of Canterbury doctoral student, All aftershocks still dwarfed by initial quake, 25 Sept, 2010.
14. www.chcheqjournal.com/2011/keythousands-homes-go/
15. www.stuff.co.nz/the-press/news/christchurch-earthquake-2011/canterbury-earthquake-2010/4472639/Call-for-ombudsman-to-oversee-insurance-claims
16. Call for ombudsman to oversee insurance claims, Ben Heather, Christchurch Press, 18 Dec 2010.
17. Little help available for struggling city firms, Ben Heather, Christchurch Press, Feb 7, 2011.
18. Huge jobs spinoff from quake, Ben Heather, Christchurch Press, Feb 8, 2011.
19. www.stuff.co.nz/the-press/news/4628028/Carter-push-for-quake-committee
20. www.stuff.co.nz/national/4643661/Quake-claims-by-uninsured-declined
21. www.stuff.co.nz/the-press/opinion/perspective/4673292/Ideas-for-an-ideal-quake-summit-result
22. 755 central buildings face demolition, New Zealand Herald, 28 February 2011.
23. Pay subsidy aids 62,000, Ben Heather, Christchurch Press March 23, 2011.
24. Brian Fallow, "Quake Money Reduces Deficit, 24 March, 2011: retrieved from www.nzherald.co.nz/business/news/article.cfm?c_id=3&objectid=10714558
25. www.thepledge.co.nz and www.stuff.co.nz/the-press/news/christchurch-earthquake-2011/4798166/I-love-the-place
26. www.stuff.co.nz/the-press/news/5275489/Insurance-freeze-crippling-Christchurchs-recovery
27. EQC levy to treble from February, Christchurch Press, John Hartevelt, 12 Oct, 2011.

28. Huge jump in home insurance cost likely: expert warns of San Francisco-type high excess policies, Kurt Bayer, The Star, Oct 9, 2011.
29. Insurance companies come round as residents speak to The Press, Martin van Beynen, Oct 1, 2011.
30. Determining your place in the claims queue, Christchurch Press, Marta Steeman, Oct 8, 2011.
31. City house values rise, but insurance issues delay sales, Christchurch Press, Tamlyn Stewart, 13 Oct 2011.
32. Daryl Hewitt, Letter to the Editor, *Christchurch Press,* Oct 12, 2011.
33. Carter Calls for Insurance Inquiry, Paul Gorman, 8 Nov 2011: retrieved from www.stuff.co.nz/the-press/news/christchurch-earthquake-2011/5923559/Carter-calls-for-insurance-inquiry
34. Protest Over Quake Recovery, Liz McDonald, 30 Aug 2012: retrieved from www.stuff.co.nz/the-press/news/7575569/Protest-over-quake-recovery
35. Give it to us, warts and all, Christchurch Press, Marc Greenhill, Oct 17, 2011.
36. www.rothbury.co.nz/News/The_Press_article.pdf
37. www.stuff.co.nz/the-press/news/christchurch-earthquake-2011/5989684/EQC-reports-7-1b-shortfall
38. EQC reports $7.1b shortfall as reinsurance costs continue to climb, Ben Heather, Christchurch Press, Nov 18, 2011.
39. www.stuff.co.nz/the-press/news/christchurch-earthquake-2011/6079569/Aussies-cash-in-on-EQC-contract
40. Aussies cash in on EQC contract, Martin van Beynen, Christchurch Press, Dec 3-4, 2011.
41. EQC accused of 'jobs for boys, girls', Martin van Beynen, Christchurch Press, Dec 7, 2011.
42. EQC reviews recruitment process, Martin van Beynen, Christchurch Press, Dec 8, 2011.
43. EQC criticism fuelled by 'gossip', Martin van Beynen, Christchurch Press, Dec 10, 2011.

44. EQC claims management criticised, Ben Heather, Christchurch Press, Jan 2, 2012.
45. Residents upset at red zone decision, Marc Greenhill, Christchurch Press, Nov 18, 2011.
46. Port Hills residents facing eviction, Christchurch Press, Nov 19, 2011.
47. Residents fear CERA special powers, Marc Greenhill, Christchurch Press, Dec 10, 2011.
48. Residents consider rates boycott, Marc Greenhill, Nov 26, 2011.
49. 6000 homes to be bowled, Ben Heather, Christchurch Press, Nov 26-27 , 2011.
50. www.stuff.co.nz/the-press/opinion/blogs/where-theres-a-will/5647890/Should-we-prosecute-quake-scientists.
51. Engineers insist they did their job, Ben Heather, Christchurch Press, Dec 01, 2011.
52. Expert voices insurance worries, Michael Wright, Christchurch Press, Dec 5, 2011.
53. www.rebuildchristchurch.co.nz/blog/2011/12/eqc-eqc-and-fletcher-eqr-announce-repair-timeframes
54. www.stuff.co.nz/business/rebuilding-christchurch/6176251/Extra-36-000-staff-needed-for-rebuild
55. Business split over return to Christchurch CBD, Tamlyn Stewart, Christchurch Press, Dec 12, 2011.
56. No quick fix for redevelopment of CBD, Mayor Bob Parker, Christchurch Press, Dec 12, 2011.
57. Offshore faults to blame for latest shakes, Paul Gorman, Christchurch Press, Dec 24, 2011.
58. Power cuts to 26,000, but city's infrastructure holds up, Charley Mann, Christchurch Press, Dec 24, 2011.
59. Residents in east lose faith in zoning: 'Green' land unfit for houses-owners, Ben Heather, Christchurch Press, Dec 28, 2011.
60. www.stuff.co.nz/national/christchurch-earthquake/6193749/Latest-Christchurch-earthquakes-costly
61. Rebuild top of priority list for PM, Fairfax New Zealand, Christchurch Press, January 27, 2012.

62. Now, Talk of Rates Revolt: Call to fire CEO, hold elections, Sam Sachdeva, Christchurch Press, Feb 2, 2012.
63. EQC, insurers to join forces on assessments, Michael Wright, Christchurch Press, Feb 1, 2012.
64. Brownlee warns about 'damage on damage', Michael Wright, Weekend Press, 4-5 Feb, 2012.
65. Quake toll lifted to 184, Keith Lynch, Nicole Mathewson and David Williams, Weekend Press, Feb 4-5, 2012.
66. Govt, Council debate NZD 100 m quake repair bills, Sam Sachdeva and John Hartvelt, Christchurch Press, Feb 7, 2012.
67. City loses property owners' money, Liz McDonald, Weekend Press, Feb 18-19, 2012.
68. Rebuild delayed by six months, Marta Steeman, Christchurch Press, Feb 6, 2012.
69. EQC keen to ease pain, Vernon Small, Weekend Press, Feb 11-12, 2012.
70. Delays with insurance frustrate port company, Alan Wood, Christchurch Press, Feb 14, 2012.
71. http://www.stuff.co.nz/business/money/6412014/Delays-with-insurance-frustrate-port-company
72. www.stuff.co.nz/the-press/news/christchurch-earthquake-2011/6643649/Govt-must-fix-insurance-limbo-group?comment_msg=posted#post_comment
73. Brownlee overruled green-zone go-ahead, Bean Heather, Christchurch Press, March 2, 2012.
74. Belfast's $600m village approved, Liz McDonald, Christchurch Press, March 15, 2012.
75. 'Wake up to the dangers of fracking', Vicki Anderson, Christchurch Press, March 17, 2012.
76. Fighting to make your claim, Tony Brazier, Christchurch Press, March 14, 2012.
77. CERA boss urges patience, Nicole Mathewson, Christchurch Press, March 23, 2012.
78. Request for faster rates relief, Sam Sachdeva, Christchurch Press, March 24, 2012.

79. www.stuff.co.nz/the-press/news/
    christchurch-earthquake-2011/6696504/
    Rates-hike-means-new-facilities-world-class
80. www.stuff.co.nz/the-press/news/
    christchurch-earthquake-2011/6711357/
    Meeting-on-insurance-shortfall
81. www.stuff.co.nz/national/christchurch-earthquake/6727253/
    Rates-rise-legacy-of-insurance-shortfall
82. www.radionz.co.nz/news/canterbury-earthquake/102357/
    quake-fund-overwhelmed,-applications-suspended
83. money.msn.co.nz/businessnews/national/8448004/
    iag-wants-nz-policyholders-to-share-risk
84. Government offers to red zone homeowners expire
    soon http://www.nzherald.co.nz/nz/news/article.
    cfm?c_id=1&objectid=10796675
85. www.stuff.co.nz/national/christchurch-earthquake/6730816/
    Mag-4-6-tremor-shakes-Christchurch
86. www.stuff.co.nz/world/asia/6727041/
    Huge-quakes-off-Indonesia-spark-panic
87. www.radionz.co.nz/news/world/103181/earthquake-in-mexico
88. www.stuff.co.nz/national/christchurch-earthquake/6734596/
    Fictional-repairs-cut-insurance-payout
89. www.legislation.govt.nz/regulation/public/2012/0063/latest/
    DLM4365601.html
90. www.stuff.co.nz/national/christchurch-earthquake/6741805/
    Pontius-Brownlee-sees-no-rental-housing-crisis
91. www.stuff.co.nz/national/christchurch-earthquake/6734583/
    Rental-shortage-State-must-step-in
92. www.radionz.co.nz/news/canterbury-earthquake/103722/
    govt's-quake-rebuild-unit-called-anti-democratic
93. www.stuff.co.nz/national/politics/6762210/
    Christchurch-CBD-rebuild-stripped-from-council-report
94. www.stuff.co.nz/business/rebuilding-christchurch/6821161/
    EQC-guarantee-to-cost-billions

95. www.nzherald.co.nz/christchurch-earthquake/news/article.
cfm?c_id=1502981&objectid=10807991

96. www.stuff.co.nz/the-press/news/christchurch-
earthquake-2011/city-blueprint/7380207/
Investment-unit-to-attract-private-sector-into-rebuild

97. www.stuff.co.nz/business/rebuilding-christchurch/6831407/
Compulsory-acquisition-could-reconfigure-Christchurch-CBD

98. www.stuff.co.nz/the-press/news/christchurch-earthquake-2011/
city-blueprint/7486704/Blueprint-land-grab-under-fire

99. www.stuff.co.nz/the-press/news/
christchurch-earthquake-2011/6849524/Housing-reports-blacked-out

100. www.radionz.co.nz/news/canterbury-earthquake/104871/
call-for-more-temporary-housing-in-christchurch

101. www.voxy.co.nz/national/
law-change-needed-kick-start-christchurch-rebuild/5/122642

102. tvnz.co.nz/national-news/
frustrated-christchurch-residents-stage-protest-4896847

103. www.voxy.co.nz/politics/
housing-activists-protest-outside-brownlees-office/5/124004

104. www.odt.co.nz/news/dunedin/207916/
quake-sees-church-premiums-rise

105. www.stuff.co.nz/business/money/7466764/
Tale-of-two-rental-markets

106. www.stuff.co.nz/manawatu-standard/news/7503953/
Councils-looking-to-go-it-alone

107. www.stuff.co.nz/the-press/news/6868165/
Fresh-calls-for-Garden-City-vote

108. www.radionz.co.nz/news/canterbury-earthquake/105215/
all-options- 'must-be-considered'-to-fund-rebuild

109. www.3news.co.nz/Christchurch-council-assets-in-dispute/
tabid/1607/articleID/253184/Default.aspx#ixzz26y1eyMWD

110. www.odt.co.nz/news/politics/210045/
govt-backs-council-asset-sales-christchurch-rebuild

111. www.stuff.co.nz/national/christchurch-earthquake/7704735/
Insurers-EQC-urged-to-settle-drilling-impasse

112. www.radionz.co.nz/news/canterbury-earthquake/106184/minister-urges-insurers-to-speed-up-quake-payouts
113. www.stuff.co.nz/the-press/news/christchurch-earthquake-2011/7370963/Poor-report-prompts-IAG
114. www.stuff.co.nz/the-press/news/christchurch-earthquake-2011/6968286/Disgruntled-residents-employ-lawyers-over-delays
115. www.stuff.co.nz/the-press/news/christchurch-earthquake-2011/7370954/Residents-to-protest-delays
116. www.stuff.co.nz/national/christchurch-earthquake/7440922/Christchurch-residents-protest-against-EQC-IAG
117. www.stuff.co.nz/business/rebuilding-christchurch/7405005/Anger-as-commercial-settlements-faster
118. www.voxy.co.nz/politics/jessica-mutch-interviews-gerry-brownlee/5/130280
119. www.3news.co.nz/Insurers-deny-dragging-feet-in-Canterbury/tabid/423/articleID/262797/Default.aspx#ixzz26yPhrT83
120. www.stuff.co.nz/the-press/news/christchurch-earthquake-2011/7267022/Council-asks-for-urgent-insurance-help
121. www.stuff.co.nz/the-press/news/christchurch-earthquake-2011/7248798/Call-for-council-backing-on-quake-insurance-tribunal
122. https://www.tower.co.nz/about-us/news/2011/tower-profit-pleasing-despite-earthquakes
123. www.nzherald.co.nz/business/news/article.cfm?c_id=3&objectid=10831720
124. www.nbr.co.nz/article/insurance-australia-group-reports-jump-nz-profit-has-optimistic-outlook-bd-126514
125. www.stuff.co.nz/marlborough-express/news/national-news/6943519/Negativity-on-quake-response-grows
126. www.stuff.co.nz/the-press/news/christchurch-earthquake-2011/7074536/Red zone-residents-threaten-UN-action
127. www.stuff.co.nz/business/rebuilding-christchurch/7683139/Laywers-called-in-over-red zone-offers

128. www.stuff.co.nz/the-press/news/
christchurch-earthquake-2011/7412765/Zone-revaluations-deplorable

129. www.voxy.co.nz/business/aon-cements-itself-christchurch/5/131648

130. www.stuff.co.nz/the-press/news/
christchurch-earthquake-2011/7601801/
Lumley-boosts-Christchurch-team

131. www.stuff.co.nz/the-press/business/7646803/
Policies-aim-to-break-Chch-insurance-deadlock

132. www.stuff.co.nz/the-press/news/
christchurch-earthquake-2011/7712787/
BNZ-offers-insurance-to-home-buyers

133. www.stuff.co.nz/the-press/news/7464949/
Homeowners-to-get-help-with-claims

134. www.stuff.co.nz/the-press/news/
christchurch-earthquake-2011/7490964/
Quake-claims-need-to-be-prioritised-better-Sutton

135. www.voxy.co.nz/business/
reinsurance-vital-christchurch-and-nz-vero/5/131965

136. www.nbr.co.nz/article/
too-much-criticism-rebuild-says-vero-ch-126518

137. www.3news.co.nz/Government-reviewing-EQC/tabid/423/
articleID/269816/Default.aspx#ixzz273Vn9Tkb

138. www.radionz.co.nz/news/political/116087/
earthquake-commission-to-be-reviewed

139. www.stuff.co.nz/national/christchurch-earthquake/7704359/
Give-back-our-democracy-Cantabs-tell-Govt

140. Naomi Klein, "The Shock Doctrine: The Rise of Disaster Capitalism",
Picador New York, 2007.

141. www.stuff.co.nz/the-press/news/6821198/
Signs-of-rebuild-but-pace-is-slow

142. www.3news.co.nz/IAG-responds-to-Canterbury-criticism/tabid/817/
articleID/268152/Default.aspx

Chapter 2: The Christchurch Fiasco Builds Momentum 2013 & 2014

1. https://www.hrc.co.nz/your-rights/social-equality/our- work/canterbury-earthquake-recovery/
2. http://www.stuff.co.nz/the-press/opinion/8949364/Quake-repairs-EQR-totally-incompetent; Are assessors scratching the surface? John McCrone, *Christchurch Press*, April 19, 2014.
3. http://www.stuff.co.nz/life-style/home-property/63226607/shoddy-repairs-but-big-markups
4. Human rights route by quake victims, Rick Jordan, *Christchurch Press*, July 11, 2014.
5. The EQC's cash reserves run close to wind, Charles Anderson, *Christchurch Press*, Sept 05, 2014.
6. ECQ bill shocks house owners, Marta Steeman and Brittany Mann, *Christchurch Press*, Nov 04, 2014.
7. Authorities 'ignore' most Maori post-quake, Shelley Robinson, *Christchurch Press*, Sep 23, 2014.
8. Stressed Cantabs turn to violence, Joelle Dally, *Christchurch Press*, April 03, 2013.
9. http://www.stuff.co.nz/national/health/76060300/Attempted-suicides-highest-in-Canterbury-twice-as-much-as-Auckland
10. Hair loss linked to quakes, Joelle Dally, *Christchurch Press*, July 06, 2013.
11. Ill health linked to quake silt, dust, Fairfax Media, *Christchurch Press*, Aug 15, 2013.
12. Alcohol use 'masks' quake troubles, Ashleigh Stewart, *Christchurch Press*, Nov 25, 2013.
13. Children suffering from stress aftershock, John McCrone, *Christchurch Press*, Feb 01, 2014.
14. http://www.stuff.co.nz/the-press/news/christchurch-earthquake-2011/5496495/Health-impact-of-Chch-quakes-investigated
15. Stress taking its toll, Marc Greenhill, *Christchurch Press*, March 19, 2014.

16. http://www.stuff.co.nz/the-press/news/
    christchurch-earthquake-2011/9696083/Plan-to-relieve-quake-stress

17. Alf, 92, waiting on tardy insurer, Ashleigh Stewart, *Christchurch Press*, March 25, 2014.

18. The EQC bosses meet Brownlee over plight of elderly victims, Fairfax NZ, *Christchurch Press*, March 08, 2014.

19. The EQC 'waiting for us to die', Charles Anderson, *Christchurch Press*, March 15, 2014; Why is Alf still waiting, 92 year-old pensioner stuck in damaged home, Ashleigh Stewart, *Christchurch Press*, June 07, 2014.

20. Writing this hurts, The EQC, because you don't care, Letters to the Editor, Gavin Tucker, *Christchurch Press*, May 14, 2014.

21. Anxious, depressed and now angry, Olivia Carville, *Christchurch Press*, April 02, 2013.

22. Aftershock of depression, anger still felt, Olivia Carville, *Christchurch Press*, April 15, 2013.

23. Issues and inconsistencies in latest rating valuations, Dr Duncan Webb, *Christchurch Press*, May 06, 2014.

24. Rise of wealthy changes Canty, Charlie Gates, *Christchurch Press*, Aug 12, 2014.

25. https://thechristchurchfiasco.wordpress.com/2013/02/01/
    my-insurance-nightmare/

26. Labour bids for 'fed up' claimants, Jody O'Callaghan, *Christchurch Press*, March 03, 2014.

27. The EQCs court costs with Cantabs exceed 45m, Michael Wright, *Christchurch Press*, Dec 30, 2014.

28. Quake stresses lead to threats, Cecile Meier, *Christchurch Press*, Jan 10, 2015.

29. 88 house checks and still waiting, Rick Jordan, *Christchurch Press*, Aug 12, 2014.

30. Tangled cases hard to unpick, The Editor, *Christchurch Press*, June 11, 2014.

31. A City stalled, John McCrone, *Christchurch Press*, March 08, 2014.

32. Rebuild 'at a turning point', Georgina Stylianou, *Christchurch Press*, June 03, 2014.

33. http://www.stuff.co.nz/business/69046908/
    Christchurch-rebuild-slows-industry-confidence-dips

34. Political players warned by Mayor, Lois Cairns and Glenn Conway, *Christchurch Press*, Feb 04, 2014.

35. Minister berates council, Lois Cairns, *Christchurch Press*, Nov 22, 2013.

36. Council, Brownlee tensions fester, Charlie Gates, *Christchurch Press*, Aug 02, 2014; Precinct drama: the conflict, anger and fluffed lines, Charlie Gates, *Christchurch Press*, Aug 02, 2014.

37. Letters reveal rebuild tensions, Georgina Stylianou, *Christchurch Press*, Aug 18, 2014.

38. CITY takes shape: Goodbye RED zone, *Christchurch Press*, Nov 29, 2013.

39. Concerns raised on Cera's expertise, Glenn Conway, *Christchurch Press*, Feb 05, 2014.

40. Migrants Bring World to the Rebuild, *Christchurch Press*, Jan 04, 2013.

41. http://www.radionz.co.nz/news/national/259693/
    migrant-workers-'ripped-off'

42. Brownlee questions figures, Lois Cairns, *Christchurch Press*, May 08, 2014.

43. Insurance firms must stop messing with our lives, Ross Williamson, Rangiora, Letters to the Editor, The Press, Feb 02, 2013.

44. http://www.stuff.co.nz/the-press/business/9773385/
    IAG-boss-defends-profits

45. IAG on track to save $30m after buyout, Marta Steeman, *Christchurch Press*, March 01, 2014.

46. Reinsurance only part of IAG's premium increases, Rob Stock, *Christchurch Press*, Aug 24, 2013.

47. http://www.stuff.co.nz/business/money/10006156/
    IAGs-Singapore-Sling

48. http://www.wilsonharle.com/earthquake-insurance-problems-of-successive-events-and-allocation-of-loss/

49. Clients lose plot at years of delays: Insurance anger leads to threats, as people with unsettled claims reach their wits' end, Cecile Meier, *Christchurch Press*, Dec 24, 2014.

50. Children the first victims, Olivia Carville, *Christchurch Press*, Feb 16, 2013.

51. Quake-hit families still in squalor, Olivia Carville, *Christchurch Press*, Feb 29, 2013.

52. Post-quake moves hurting kids, Jody O'Callaghan, *Christchurch Press*, Feb 22, 2014.

53. Rates hit on top of quake damage, Lois Cairns, *Christchurch Press*, Jan 13, 2014.

54. Residents find new land values perplexing, Marc Greenhill, *Christchurch Press*, Jan 13, 2014.

55. Investors snatch up city's homes: Landlords gazumping hopeful home-owners, Liz McDonald, *Christchurch Press*, Oct 11, 2014.

56. Insurers back record of written off homes, Lois Cairns, *Christchurch Press*, Feb 02, 2013.

57. http://www.stuff.co.nz/the-press/business/the-rebuild/69329787/As-is-where-is-houses-are-Christchurchs-new-gold-mine

58. http://www.stuff.co.nz/the-press/opinion/69428119/Editorial-Rigorous-study-of-quake-repairs-needed

59. http://www.stuff.co.nz/business/rebuilding-christchurch/8141492/F-grade-unfair-insurers-council

60. Repugnant insurance companies earn our distrust, Tom O'Connor, Letter to the Editor, *Christchurch Press*, Jan 19, 2013.

61. Insurance firms must stop messing with our lives, Letter to the Editor, Ross Williamson, *Christchurch Press*, Feb 02, 2013.

62. We're on track, say insurers, Ashleigh Stewart, *Christchurch Press*, Nov 04, 2013.

63. Sutton: Pick up pace on claims, Martin van Beynen, *Christchurch Press*, Nov 14, 2013.

64. Protesters' frustration boils over, Marc Greenhill, *Christchurch Press*, Dec 17, 2013.

65. Quake advocate dismisses claims by insurance boss, Charles Anderson, *Christchurch Press*, Jan 23, 2014.

66. We've listened and now we are acting, Peter Rose, *Christchurch Press*, Jan 24, 2014.
67. Insurer stands by mediation, Marc Greenhill, *Christchurch Press*, Jan 30, 2014.
68. Quake cases may overload courts, Marc Greenhill and Nicole Mathewson, *Christchurch Press*, Jan 09, 2013.
69. Quake issues rewrite legal textbooks, Stephanie Grieve and Tristan Sage, *Christchurch Press*, April 05, 2013.
70. Insurance adjusters defend role, Alan Wood, *Christchurch Press*, March 05, 2013.
71. https://thechristchurchfiasco.wordpress.com/
72. http://avonsidechch.blogspot.co.nz/?wref=bif
73. https://rebuildingchristchurch.wordpress.com/
74. http://www.therealrecovery.org/trrdrupal/?wref=bif
75. http://empoweredchristchurch.co.nz/
76. http://www.stuff.co.nz/the-press/business/the-rebuild/75695724/social-media-helps-isolated-cantabs-deal-with-quake-recovery
77. IAG rep tossed off TC3 forum, *Christchurch Press*, May 07, 2013.
78. Parker keen to explain service to Brownlee, Georgina Stylianou, *Christchurch Press*, April 29, 2013.
79. Rivals oppose IAG bid for Lumley, Marta Steeman, *Christchurch Press*, March 13, 2014.
80. Fences, pools cop big excesses, Marta Steeman, *Christchurch Press*, April 08, 2013.
81. Dismay over delays in insurance advice, Lois Cairns, *Christchurch Press*, Feb 28, 2013.
82. Razor wire comes down from fortress-like EQR hub, Michael Wright, *Christchurch Press*, May 04, 2013.
83. The EQC workers bullied, Georgina Stylianou, *Christchurch Press*, March 01, 2013.
84. http://thechristchurchfiasco.wordpress.com/2013/03/03/christchurch-insurance-victim-goes-on-hunger-strike/
85. 'Shoot' remark spurs police action, Georgina Stylianou, *Christchurch Press*, March 05, 2013.

86. http://www.stuff.co.nz/the-press/business/the-rebuild/67527169/
almost-100-rebuildrelated-firms-have-gone-bust-since-feb-11-quake

87. http://www.stuff.co.nz/the-press/business/the-rebuild/67532555/
Canterbury-homeowners-lose-all-their-savings

88. http://www.stuff.co.nz/business/industries/8279105/
Construction-firm-hopes-to-buy-Mainzeal

89. http://www.stuff.co.nz/business/industries/68957290/
Jenny-Shipley-among-Mainzeal-directors-facing-legal-action

90. Peters questions Brownlee over alleged frauds, Hamish Rutherford and Press Reporters, *Christchurch Press*, March 20, 2013.

91. Convention centre project is pivotal, Tamlyn Stewart, *Christchurch Press*, Feb 08, 2013.

92. MP calls for convention centre facts, Glenn Conway, *Christchurch Press*, Feb 27, 2014.

93. Stadium deal critical - mayor, Lois Cairns, *Christchurch Press*, Feb 01, 2014.

94. $30m aquatic centre on hold, Lois Cairns, *Christchurch Press*, Feb 27, 2014.

95. Rates up nearly 7 per cent to help pay rebuild costs, Lois Cairns and Rachel Young, *Christchurch Press*, June 28, 2013.

96. http://thechristchurchfiasco.wordpress.com/2013/03/31/
land-grab-in-christchurch/

97. Blueprint options 'reviewed', Georgina Stylianou, *Christchurch Press*, April 22, 2014.

98. CERA 'using bully tactics' to get land, Martin van Beynen, *Christchurch Press*, Sept 07, 2014.

99. Projects could be scaled back -Key, Caroline King, *Christchurch Press*, May 23, 2013.

100. Rebuilding homeowners stretched by higher rates, Lois Cairns, *Christchurch Press*, May 02, 2013.

101. Delays make firms wary of centre, Liz McDonald, *Christchurch Press*, Jan 24, 2013.

102. Soaring house costs have many causes, Gideon Couper, *Christchurch Press*, Feb 08, 2013.

103. Council to bolster housing stock, Lois Cairns, *Christchurch Press*, Feb 16, 2013.
104. Brownlee slams council 'inaction' on housing, Lois Cairns, *Christchurch Press*, Feb 01, 2013.
105. Council ponders move into affordable housing market, Vicki Buck, *Christchurch Press*, Feb 11, 2014.
106. City's poor housing is human rights concern, Lois Cairns, *Christchurch Press*, Feb 13, 2014.
107. Council battles insurer to get replacement value, Lois Cairns, *Christchurch Press*, May 08, 2013.
108. http://www.stuff.co.nz/the-press/news/67483938/Council-warned-over-social-housing
109. Millions of insurance dollars in jeopardy, Martin van Beynen, *Christchurch Press*, June 15, 2013.
110. https://thechristchurchfiasco.wordpress.com/2014/03/10/summary-of-the-marsh-risk-management-research-report-comparing-claims-from-catastrophic-earthquakes-feb-2014/
111. Investor pulls out, Liz McDonald, *Christchurch Press*, April 01, 2013.
112. No tenants left for the CBD, Georgina Stylianou, *Christchurch Press*, Jan 30, 2014.
113. Brownlee calls time on deadlock, Beck Eleven, *Christchurch Press*, July 09, 2013.
114. Bitterness at CCDU valuations, Georgina Stylianou, *Christchurch Press*, July 13, 2013.
115. Site-by-site solutions for residential rebuild, Alan Wood, *Christchurch Press, May 13, 2013.*
116. Rumblings of Rebellion, John McCrone, *Christchurch Press, Mainlander*, Aug 10, 2013.
117. Readers see Brownlee as clear No 1, *Christchurch Press*, May 04, 2013.
118. John's key to the city, Ric Stevens, *Christchurch Press*, May 04, 2013.
119. Rebuild funding gap remains, Marc Greenhill, *Christchurch Press*, May 17, 2013.
120. Stubborn money man won't back down, Charles Anderson, *Christchurch Press*, May 03, 2014.

121. Claim disputes head to court, Alan Wood, *Christchurch Press*, June 27, 2013.
122. http://www.stuff.co.nz/the-press/opinion/perspective/10230912/A-dispatch-from-the-front-line
123. The EQC lays complaint against recipient, Martin van Beynen, *Christchurch Press*, March 28, 2013.
124. Please explain, couple tell The EQC, Martin van Beynen, *Christchurch Press*, April 06, 2013.
125. The EQC blunder deepens, Martin van Beynen and Fairfax, *Christchurch Press*, March 26, 2013.
126. The EQC to review confusing text, Lois Cairns, *Christchurch Press*, Mar 28, 2013.
127. Overpaid claims of $100m by the EQC revealed, Michael Wright and Martin van Beynen, *Christchurch Press*, April 20, 2013.
128. Law firm gauges interest in the EQC case, Nicole Mathewson, *Christchurch Press*, Nov 09, 2013.
129. http://www.radionz.co.nz/news/national/283706/homeowners-to-take-class-action-against-the-EQC
130. http://www.ombudsman.parliament.nz/ckeditor_assets/attachments/300/information_fault_lines_-_accessing_the EQC_information_in_canterbury.pdf
131. http://www.stuff.co.nz/dominion-post/news/politics/9534271/Ombudsman-report-on-EQC-out-today
132. The EQC puts off tricky land settlements, Michael Wright, *Christchurch Press*, May 11, 2013.
133. http://www.stuff.co.nz/the-press/news/christchurch-earthquake-2011/9054065/Surveyor-calls-for- EQC-audit
134. A third of owners query home repairs, *Christchurch Press*, Aug 23, 2013.
135. Brownlee demands EQC survey probe, Martin van Beynen and Hamish Rutherford, *Christchurch Press*, Nov 08, 2013.
136. Start on inquiry into EQC, Hamish Rutherford, *Christchurch Press*, Nov 09, 2013.
137. EQC cash falls short for frustrated owner, Charles Anderson, *Christchurch Press*, Dec 11, 2013.

138. Pay-outs may come up short, Marc Greenhill, *Christchurch Press*, Feb 15, 2014.

139. http://www.radionz.co.nz/news/regional/278050/the EQC-review-moots-insurance-changes

140. Worth saving or beyond repair? Charles Anderson and Anna Pearson, *Christchurch Press*, 22 Aug, 2014.

141. Professor warns of a 'shabby' future, *Christchurch Press*, July 12, 2014.

142. Harding Resigns before Hearing, Marc Greenhill, *Christchurch Press*, July 04, 2014.

143. Engineer for EQC to face hearing, Martin van Beynen, *Christchurch Press*, July 30, 2014.

144. http://www.stuff.co.nz/business/better-business/70606425/EQC-engineer-Graeme-Robinson-wins-appeal

145. https://thechristchurchfiasco.wordpress.com/2015/08/12/mbie-a-seismic-slight-of-hand-and-at-worst-fraud/

146. Rising flood risk in a sunken city, John McCrone, *Christchurch Press*, Nov 09, 2013.

147. http://www.geosociety.org/gsatoday/archive/25/3/article/i1052-5173-25-3-4.htm

148. Brownlee cautious on flood-risk link to quakes, Georgina Stylianou, *Christchurch Press*, March 03, 2014.

149. http://www.stuff.co.nz/the-press/news/9832174/Solving-the-citys-flood-problems

150. EQC 'covers flood damage', Lois Cairns, *Christchurch Press*, March 08, 2014.

151. City on flood alert, Nicole Mathewson, Sarah-Jan O'Connor and Olivia Carville, *Christchurch Press*, March 05, 2014.

152. Residents: Why are we still living like this? Blair Ensor and Georgina Stylianou, *Christchurch Press*, March 05, 2014.

153. Melanie Tobeck works in the area of change and communications management, facilitation, and business coaching. She set up the website Claimants4claimants to assist Canterbury homeowners

with unresolved insurance claims as well as organised a series of information evenings at the Transitional Cathedral.

Chapter 3: The Politics

1. Ratepayers lose power as city modernizes, John Cookson, Christchurch Press, Dec 5, 2011.
2. Martin Luther King in August 1966
3. Canterbury States of Emergency Lifted, Otago Daily Times (16 September 2010), www.odt.co.nz
4. www.stuff.co.nz/national/christchurch-earthquake/4693868/Key-announces-national-state-of-emergency
5. tvnz.co.nz/national-news/death-toll-75-national-emergency-declared-4038747
6. For additional reading see Jonathan Orpin, Constitutional Aftershocks, New Zealand Law Journal, November 2010, pp. 386-388 and Dean Knight, Canterbury Earthquake Response and Recovery Bill: Constitutional Outrageous, Fairness and Justice, Victoria University of Wellington, 14 September 2010.
7. www.legislation.govt.nz/bill/government/2011/0286/latest/whole.html
8. www.stuff.co.nz/national/christchurch-earthquake/4995119/Roger-Sutton-appointed-quake-recovery-czar
9. www.parliament.nz/en-NZ/PB/Legislation/Bills/BillsDigests/3/b/3/49PLLawBD18551-Canterbury-Earthquake-Recovery-Bill-2011-Bills-Digest.htm and www.russellmcveagh.com/_docs/WatchingBrief14Apr2011_385.html#NewBills
10. news.msn.co.nz/nationalnews/8440073/report-criticises-response-to-chch-quake
11. See p. 2 of www.eqc.govt.nz/downloads/pdfs/CRP-Review-Report-final-280509.pdf
12. A 20/20 vision for rebuild and recovery Lianne Dalziel, Tuesday, Oct 18, 2011.

13. www.stuff.co.nz/national/christchurch-earthquake/4919892/
Cera-labelled-militaristic
14. Liquefaction data ignored-report, Ben Heather, Christchurch Press, Dec 3, 2011
15. www.stuff.co.nz/the-press/news/6197060/
Rehiring-of-Marryatt-hits-raw-nerve
16. Council review 'no solution', Sam Sachdeva, Christchurch Press, Jan 21-22, 2012.
17. City Council crisis deepens, Sam Sachdeva, Christchurch press, Jan 24, 2012.
18. 'Rise Above Pettiness', Mayor Urges, Paul Gorman, Christchurch Press, Jan 24, 2012.
19. 'Leakers to blame' for city's woes, Paul Gorman, Christchurch Press, Jan 25, 2012.
20. Meeting with minister set for council 'on a precipice', Sam Sachdeva, Christchurch Press, Jan 25, 2012.
21. Marryatt may yet reconsider, Sam Sachdeva and Fairfax, Christchurch Press, Jan 26, 2012.
22. Marryatt gives back pay rise, Rachel Young, Weekend Press, Jan 28-29, 2012.
23. Cracks in City Confidence, David Killick, Christchurch Press, Jan 26, 2012.
24. www.stuff.co.nz/the-press/news/6299843/
Council-is-tearing-itself-apart-Sue-Wells
25. Government observer appointed to council, Sam Sachdeva, Weekend Press, Jan 28-29, 2012.
26. $1.5m payout for Marryatt possible- expert, Sam Sachdeva, Christchurch Press, Feb 6, 2012.
27. Minister against an early election, Cate Broughton, Christchurch Press, Feb 15, 2012.
28. Threat to quit scared Parker, John Hartevelt, Christchurch Press, March 15, 2012.
29. Three year plan, http://www.ccc.govt.nz/thecouncil/
policiesreportsstrategies/ltccp/index.aspx

30. Annual Plan, http://www.ccc.govt.nz/thecouncil/policiesreportsstrategies/annualplan/index.aspx

31. Area Plans,http://www.ccc.govt.nz/thecouncil/policiesreportsstrategies/districtplanning/districtplanreview/ourdistrictplanreview/whatshappeninginyourarea.aspx

32. Christchurch Transport Strategic Plan,http://www.ccc.govt.nz/thecouncil/policiesreportsstrategies/transportplan/index.aspx

33. District Plan,https://thechristchurchfiasco.wordpress.com/2013/02/01/my-insurance-nightmare/http://www.ccc.govt.nz/thecouncil/policiesreportsstrategies/districtplanning/districtplanreview/ourdistrictplanreview/aboutthedistrictplanreview.aspx

34. Land Use Recovery Plan, http://cera.govt.nz/recovery-strategy/built-environment/land-use-recovery-plan

35. Blue Print Plan, https://ccdu.govt.nz/the-plan

36. Greater Urban Development Strategy, http://www.greaterchristchurch.org.nz/

37. The Rebuild an outsider's view, Peter Robb, *The Christchurch Press*, April 07, 2014.

38. Marryatt regrets letter surprise, Lois Cairns and Rachel Young, *Christchurch Press*, June 15, 2013.

39. City Council's resource consents face scrutiny, Rachel Young, *Christchurch Press*, July 11, 2013.

40. New city boss fit and ready to go, John McCrone, *Christchurch Press*, May 31, 2014.

41. Marryatt takes an $800,000 final walk, *Christchurch Press*, Oct 24, 2014.

42. Players differ on CBD growth, Georgina Stylianou, *Christchurch Press*, Feb 08, 2014.

43. Recovery leaders miss forum on CERA's role, Georgina Stylianou, *Christchurch Press*, March 11, 2014.

44. Asset sales to fill 'black hole', *Christchurch Press*, Aug 02, 2014.

45. City asset sales back on the table, Lois Cairns, *Christchurch Press*, Jan 24, 2014.

46. Warning on cost of quake repairs, Lois Cairns and Glenn Conway, *Christchurch Press*, Feb 04, 2014.

47. Council fund plunges $175m, Lois Cairns, *Christchurch Press*, Jan 27, 2014.

48. Will council fall short on rebuild? Lois Cairns, *Christchurch Press*, Dec 04, 2013.

49. Dalziel speech raises hackles, Glenn Conway, *Christchurch Press*, Feb 15, 2014.

50. Parker criticises Dalziel over staff spending, Glenn Conway, *Christchurch Press*, Feb 20, 2014.

51. Cash runs short for repairs, Lois Cairns, *Christchurch Press*, May 08, 2014.

52. http://www.stuff.co.nz/the-press/business/the-rebuild/70819020/top-cop-dave-cliff-gets-canterbury-earthquake-recovery-authority-job

53. http://www.stuff.co.nz/the-press/business/the-rebuild/69943847/council-claws-back-rebuild-power

54. http://www.stuff.co.nz/business/industries/68152533/christchurch-city-council-to-set-up-rebuild-agency.html

55. http://www.stuff.co.nz/the-press/news/70503456/government-needs-to-step-back-says-christchurch-city-council

56. www.stuff.co.nz/business/rebuilding-christchurch/6170837/Earthquake-Minister-scolds-council

57. Govt poised to seize control, says Dalziel, Ben Heather, *Christchurch Press*, April 5, 2012.

58. www.stuff.co.nz/the-press/news/christchurch-earthquake-2011/6696503/Govt-poised-to-seize-control-says-Dalziel

59. www.3news.co.nz/Insurance-loophole-a-nightmare-for-ChCh-red zone/tabid/817/articleID/216665/Default.aspx

60. Red zoners 'bullied' in Govt buyout, Ben Heather, Christchurch Press, Jan 18, 2012.

61. Sep 24, 2011, 08:49:09, myquakereality.wordpress.com/2011/09/11/share-your-quake-reality-2/

62. www.stuff.co.nz/the-press/news/christchurch-earthquake-2011/5826012/Red zone-challenge-proposal-scrapped

63. Acceptance would be foolish-village owner, Francesca Lee, Christchurch Press, Feb 13, 2012.

64. www.stuff.co.nz/national/christchurch-earthquake/6641105/Dalziel-distressed-by-Brownlees-attack

65. www.stuff.co.nz/the-press/news/christchurch-earthquake-2011/7109380/Some-land-zoning-decisions-to-be-reviewed and The World Conference on Human Rights. 1993, Fact Sheet No.25, Forced Evictions and Human Rights

66. Catherine Ryan, Radio New Zealand interview with Renee Walker on 12, April, 2012 and www.stuff.co.nz/national/christchurch-earthquake/6727056/Homes-assessed-as-writeoffs-become-repairs

67. www.stuff.co.nz/national/christchurch-earthquake/6727056/Homes-assessed-as-writeoffs-become-repairs

68. Brownlee cut pay out for owners, Michael Wright, *Christchurch Press*, Jan 28, 2013.

69. Brownlee denies he ignored CERA advice, Marc Greenhill, *Christchurch Press*, Jan 29, 2013.

70. Valid questions on red zone values, Michael Wright, *Christchurch Press*, March 30, 2013.

71. Quake 'sorry' riles victims, Ashleigh Stewart, *Christchurch Press*, Aug 29, 2013.

72. Quake Outcasts file legal challenge, Michael Wright, *Christchurch Press*, May 02, 2013.

73. http://www.stuff.co.nz/national/8946555/Complex-red zoner-High-Court-case-opens

74. Unique risks in deals with Crown, Mai Chen and Nick Russell, *Christchurch Press*, Aug 30, 2013

75. http://www.nbr.co.nz/article/brownlee-appeal-outcasts-win-no-quick-fix-ch-144972

76. Brownlee takes swipe at Judge, *Christchurch Press*, Nov 18, 2013.

77. Welcome to the Pay 100 Website: The facts: retrieved from http://sbitnz-web.sharepoint.com/Pages/NewsLetters.aspx

78. http://www.stuff.co.nz/the-press/news/
    christchurch-earthquake-2011/67321207/
    Quake-Outcasts-win-in-Supreme-Court

79. http://www.stuff.co.nz/the-press/news/8711140/Red
    zone-reprieve-option-kept-quiet

80. Red flag 'unfair' in green zone, Hamish Rutherford, *Christchurch
    Press*, June 07, 2013.

81. Residents' rights 'breached', Emily Murphy, *Christchurch Press*, July
    16, 2013.

82. http://www.voxy.co.nz/politics/
    devaluations-new-nightmare-residents-nz-first/5/185047

83. Invercargill City Council v Hamlin 3 NZLR 513, New Zealand Court of
    Appeal.

84. www.buildingdisputestribunal.co.nz/site/buildingdisputes/files/
    Court%20Decisions/Invercargill%20City%20Council%20v%20Hamlin%20
    (1996)%201NZLR.PDF

85. www.stuff.co.nz/business/rebuilding-christchurch/6661138/
    Insurance-companies-fail-performance-survey

86. www.stuff.co.nz/the-press/opinion/perspective/5665147/
    Brownlee-gives-reinsurers-the-facts

87. www.stuff.co.nz/the-press/news/
    christchurch-earthquake-2011/6321356/
    Rebuild-top-of-priority-list-for-PM

88. www.stuff.co.nz/the-press/
    news/6158995/70-000-pay-boost-for-council-boss

89. Legal concept ensures that you do not suffer any unreasonable
    harm or loss.

90. Legal concept which suggests that persons who are so closely and
    directly affected by an act that the perpetrator ought reasonably to
    have those persons in contemplation.

91. National or Local Disaster? www.mkweb.co.uk/
    emergencyplanning/.../NationalOrLocalv1_1.pdf

92. Taxpayer-backed quake insurance on Govt list: retrieved from www.
    nzherald.co.nz/nz/news/article.cfm?c_id=1&objectid=10751886

93. www.nzherald.co.nz/nz/news/article.
cfm?c_id=1&objectid=10751886

94. Cameron Preston is a Christchurch accountant, representative for a class action against Southern Response and homeowner with a longstanding unresolved quake insurance claim.

Chapter 4: EQC and Earthquake Insurance

1. Bruce Emerson at www.eqc.govt.nz/news/assessment-phase-complete

2. http://www.eqc.govt.nz/canterbury-earthquakes/progress-updates/scorecard

3. The head office is now In the Majestic Centre in Willis Street in Wellington's Willis Street.

4. http://www.eqc.govt.nz/about-eqc/people/commissioners

5. http://www.eqc.govt.nz/what-we-do/eqc-insurance

6. www.scoop.co.nz/stories/BU1108/S01029/sp-keeps-eqcs-aaa-credit-rating-despite-blow-out.htm

7. www.eqc.govt.nz/what-we-do/eqc-insurance

8. www.stuff.co.nz/the-press/opinion/editorials/6553936/EQC-admits-some-of-its-errors-but-does-not-say-how-it-will-correct-them

9. www.parliament.nz/NR/rdonlyres/C39E56B4-0B5E-402C-BCC6-B753455815A8/181835/49SCCO_EVI_00DBSCH_FIN_10135_1_A158877_EarthquakeC.pdf

10. www.rebuildchristchurch.co.nz/blog/2011/12/stuff-co-nz-eqc-staff-selected-without-interviews

11. www.stuff.co.nz/the-press/news/christchurch-earthquake-2011/6176265/EQC-to-audit-work-of-staff-on-drug-charges

12. www.stuff.co.nz/business/rebuilding-christchurch/6096870/EQC-accused-of-jobs-for-boys-girls

13. www.stuff.co.nz/the-press/news/christchurch-earthquake-2011/6344433/EQC-insurers-to-join-forces-on-assessments

14. www.stuff.co.nz/the-press/news/
christchurch-earthquake-2011/6648753/Confusion-over-fixing-homes

15. www.stuff.co.nz/the-press/news/
christchurch-earthquake-2011/6321590/Ruling-a-year-in-the-making

16. http://www.stuff.co.nz/national/10470247/
EQC-complaint-numbers-a-disgrace-Cosgrove

17. www.stuff.co.nz/the-press/news/
christchurch-earthquake-2011/6205917/
EQC-cops-shoddy-jobs-complaints

18. Lisa, Jan 02 2012, www.stuff.co.nz/the-press/
news/christchurch-earthquake-2011/6205917/
EQC-cops-shoddy-jobs-complaints

19. www.dbh.govt.nz/UserFiles/File/Publications/Building/
Guidance-information/pdf/guide-canterbury-earthquake-revised.pdf

20. www.dbh.govt.nz/canterbury-earthquake-technical-guidance

21. Who can we trust, John McCrone, *Christchurch Press*, March 23,
2014.

22. Study backs homeowners on floor flaws, Marc Greenhill,
Christchurch Press, July 08, 2014.

23. Fears Homes Won't be Fixed, Ben Heather, Christchurch Press, Feb
20, 2012.

24. www.stuff.co.nz/national/christchurch-earthquake/6445349/
Fears-foundations-won-t-be-fixed

25. Brent Cairns in a letter to the editor of the Christchurch Press

26. www.stuff.co.nz/the-press/opinion/perspective/6465450/
If-in-doubt-get-a-second-opinion

27. http://www.stuff.co.nz/the-press/news/68135509/
eqc-fights-adverse-findings-against-its-top-engineer

28. http://www.stuff.co.nz/business/71021676/
eqc-foundation-repair-shortcomings-revealed

29. http://architecturenow.co.nz/articles/what-lies-beneath/

30. http://www.stuff.co.nz/national/christchurch-earthquake/8446726/
Health-timebomb-lurks-under-Chch-homes

31. http://thechristchurchfiasco.wordpress.com/2014/09/11/
mould-issues-this-is-a-must-see/

32. http://www.stuff.co.nz/the-press/business/the-rebuild/10724259/The-dangers-from-dust

33. Family live in fear of asbestos exposure, Cecile Meier, *Christchurch Press*, July 01, 2014.

34. Deadly Dump: Asbestos mountain fills Kate Valley, Rachel Young, *Christchurch Press*, Feb 01, 2014.

35. Asbestos in homes a 'health landmine', Charlie Gates, *Christchurch Press*, Jan 09, 2013.

36. http://www.stuff.co.nz/national/health/63956823/eqc-slated-after-asbestos-inquiry.html

37. http://www.stuff.co.nz/the-press/business/the-rebuild/69329787/As-is-where-is-houses-are-Christchurchs-new-gold-mine

38. Property- check, check, recheck, Ingrid Taylor, *Christchurch Press*, Nov 25, 2013.

39. http://thechristchurchfiasco.wordpress.com/2013/03/07/demand-surge-and-the-implications-for-policyholders/

40. http://www.stuff.co.nz/business/rebuilding-christchurch/7438808/Builders-wages-rise-faster-in-Canty and http://www.stuff.co.nz/the-press/news/8144749/Christchurch-wages-show-big-increase

41. http://www.stuff.co.nz/business/industries/4786567/Quake-exposes-skill-shortages

42. http://www.theinstitute.com.au/journals/Journal_FebMar_2008_34-40.pdf

43. 'As-is' sales go upmarket, Liz McDonald, *The Christchurch Press*, April 17, 2014; Luxury home snapped up, Liz McDonald, *Christchurch Press*, May 20, 2014.

44. Construction prices still rising, Alan Wood, *Christchurch Press*, April 24, 2014.

45. http://www.eqc.govt.nz/news/eqc-welcomes-declaratory-judgement-ruling

46. Flood modelling omitted in road repair, Marc Greenhill, *Christchurch Press*, March 13, 2014.

47. Flockton Basin red zone ruled out, Anna Pearson, *Christchurch Press*, March 19, 2014.

48. http://thechristchurchfiasco.wordpress.com/2014/12/10/the EQC-v-insurance-council-the-flockton-litigation-guest-post-by-lane-neave/
49. Floods push city rates up, Lois Cairns, *Christchurch Press*, June 21, 2104.
50. http://www.stuff.co.nz/the-press/news/69901937/6000-christchurch-properties-at-risk-from-coastal-erosion
51. Flood fear for city, Shirley Robinson, *The Star*, Jan 08, 2014.
52. City urged to take harder line, Georgina Stylianou, *Christchurch Press*, Feb 04, 2014.
53. Flood-hit families ineligible for claims, Georgina Stylianou, *Christchurch Press*, July 19, 2014.
54. http://www.stuff.co.nz/the-press/news/9995017/Flood-insurance-harder-to-get
55. Minor to moderate land damage from liquefaction is possible in future significant earthquakes. You can use standard timber piled foundations for houses with lightweight cladding and roofing and suspended timber floors or enhanced concrete foundations.
56. Moderate to significant land damage from liquefaction is possible in future large earthquakes. Site-specific geotechnical investigation and specific engineering foundation design is required.
57. http://thechristchurchfiasco.wordpress.com/2013/03/10/why-fixed-sum-insurance-is-not-the-answer-for-policyholders/
58. Hon. Gerry Brownlee in Biggest Challenge is quake-ravaged city, John Hartevelt, Christchurch Press, Nov 2, 2011.
59. http://www.stuff.co.nz/the-press/news/71970100/Royal-Commission-for-earthquake-repairs-unnecessary-Brownlee-says
60. http://www.stuff.co.nz/the-press/news/christchurch-earthquake-2011/69382563/canterbury-earthquake-repair-survey-a-whitewash.html
61. Jo **Byrne,** lives in **flood**-prone Flockton Basin and is a spokesperson for some **affected** residents. She is also a community board member for Shirley Papanui.

Chapter 5: 'Good Faith': The Insurance Industry and Catastrophe

1. The policyholder pays the premium now and the insurance company must later pay a claim. Insurers have certain time frames within which they must act after the policyholder has supplied the relevant information.

2. American Association for Justice, The Ten Worst Insurance Companies in America: How They Raise Premiums, Deny Claims, and Refuse Insurance to Those who Need it Most: retrieved from www.justice.org/docs/tenworstinsurancecompanies.pdf and American Association for Justice, Tricks of the Trade: How Insurance Companies Deny, Delay, Refuse and Confuse: retrieved from www.howardlawpc.com/files/11-_tricks_of_the_trade.pdf

3. www.bloomberg.com/apps/news?pid=nw&pname=mm_0907_story1.html

4. Crawford and Company: A large, claims and third-party administration solutions provider to insurance companies and self-insured entities.

5. Neil Campbell, Claims for Damages Against Insurers in New Zealand, University of Auckland (no date): retrieved from www.nzila.org/conferences/docs/christchurch/Neil%20Campbell%20-%20Damages%20Against%20Insurers.pdf

6. In Oakland Investments (Aust) Ltd v Certain Underwriters at Lloyds [2012] QSC 6 it was decided that if an insured is able to prove greater losses as a result of late payment, then insurers will be exposed to those losses. This case should serve as a warning to insurers to pay on time, or risk paying more. The court also ordered them to pay interest on those damages.

7. David Dietz and Darrell Preston, The Insurance Hoax, Bloomberg News San Francisco: retrieved from www.bloomberg.com/apps/news?pid=nw&pname=mm_0907_story1.html

8. J. M. Feinman, Delay, Deny, Defend: Why insurance companies don't pay claims and what you can do about it, Penguin Books, London, U.K., 2010.

9. Brenda Snook and Toni Hannah, New Beginnings Christchurch Central Business District: Evolution from an Earthquake, The Field Connection Ltd, 2011: retrieved from www.fieldconnection.co.nz/ New%20Beginnings%20-%20Christchurch%20CBD.pdf
10. http://www.interest.co.nz/insurance/74910/ general-insurance-industry-making-its-highest-profits-nearly-decade
11. Stimulated yet sobered by sheer size of disaster, Roeland van den Bergh, Christchurch Press, Jan 11, 2012.
12. Dean has worked in the insurance industry for the last 29 years, since 2010 Dean has helped over 1000 Cantabrians negotiate their claims with the insurance industry and was nominated KiwiBank New Zealander of the year for his work in relation to the earthquake claims in Canterbury.

Chapter 6: Policyholder Protection

1. http://www.theguardian.com/law/2015/nov/10/ human-rights-and-the-cost-of-justice
2. https://www.courtsofnz.govt.nz/business/high-court-lists/ earthquake-list-christchurch/150930EarthquakeLitigationListRepo rt.pdf
3. http://www.icnz.org.nz/issues-submissions/regulations/ registration-and-dispute-resolution-requirements/
4. https://thechristchurchfiasco.wordpress.com/2013/03/11/ possible-causes-of-action/
5. David Dietz and Darrell Preston, The Insurance Hoax, Bloomberg Markets, September 2007: retrieved from www.bloomberg.com/ apps/news?pid=nw&pname=mm_0907_story1.html
6. H. Macfarlane, Investor Losses: A Fruitful Ground for Class Actions?, Retrieved from www.heskethhenry.co.nz/news/archives/docs/ InvestorLossesFruitfulGroundForClassActions.pdf
7. Jamie Gray, Law Firm seeks funding for class action, Business, NZ Herald News, Jul 4, 2011: retrieved from www.nzherald.co.nz/ business/news/article.cfm?c_id=3&objectid=10736141

8. H. Macfarlane, Investor Losses: A Fruitful Ground for Class Actions?, Retrieved from www.heskethhenry.co.nz/news/archives/docs/ InvestorLossesFruitfulGroundForClassActions.pdf

9. http://www.aminz.org.nz/

10. https://advisory.org.nz/

11. http://www.cias.org.nz/

12. Queensland Floods Commission of Inquiry, see: www.floodcommission.qld.gov.au/announcements/ inquiries-into-flood-insurance

13. Collins Center Managed Mediation Program at www.collinscenter. org/mediation/

14. Mel Rubin, Disaster Mediation: Lessons in Conflict Coordination and Collaboration, Cardozo J. of Conflict Resolution, Vol. 9:351: retrieved from cardozojcr.com/issues/volume-9-2/

15. Notice of Rule Adoption-Final Rule, State of Mississippi Department of Insurance: retrieved from www.mid.state.ms.us/ regulations/20073reg.PDF

16. Louisiana Register Vol. 32, No. 01 January 20, 2006, Rule 23- Suspension of Right to Cancel or Non-renew Residential, Commercial Residential or Commercial Property Insurance Due to Hurricane Katrina or Hurricane Rita: retrieved from www.ldi. state.la.us/docs/CommissionersOffice/legal/rules/Rule23_arc_ SuspensionOfRightToC.pdf

17. Susan Zuckerman, Mediation Program Helps Miss. and La. Rebuild After Katrina and Rita, Dispute Resolution Journal, Vol. 61, no. 3 (August-October 2006), a publication of the American Arbitration Association, 1633 Broadway New York, NY 10019-6708, 212.716.5800, www.adr.org.

18. Elizabeth Baker Murrill, Mass Disaster Mediation: Innovative, ADR, or a Lion's Den? Pepperdine Dispute Resolution Law Journal Vol. 7:3, 2007: retrieved from www.adr.org/si.asp?id=4281

19. Mass Claims ADR Programs and Federal ADR Programs, The American Arbitration Association: Dispute Resolution Services Worldwide: retrieved from www.adr.org/aaa/ ShowPDF?doc=ADRSTG_004209

20. Susan Zuckerman, Mediation Program Helps Miss. and La. Rebuild After Katrina and Rita, Dispute Resolution Journal, Vol. 61, no. 3 (August-October 2006), a publication of the American Arbitration Association, 1633 Broadway New York, NY 10019-6708, 212.716.5800: retrieved from www.adr.org/aaa/ShowPDF?doc=ADRSTG_004328

21. http://www.eqc.govt.nz/about-eqc/make-complaint/mediation-service/guide-mediation-service

22. Class actions needed in New Zealand, says lawyer, March 18, 2013: retrieved from http://www.nzherald.co.nz/business/news/article.cfm?c_id=3&objectid=10871862

23. https://www.tvnz.co.nz/one-news/new-zealand/-quake-outcasts-win-court-battle-6254650

24. https://thechristchurchfiasco.wordpress.com/2015/11/16/eqc-action-group-to-file-proceedings/

25. http://www.stuff.co.nz/the-press/business/71470352/southern-response-class-action-launched.html

26. http://www.scoop.co.nz/stories/AK1505/S00016/new-backers-for-1-billion-southern-response-class-action.htm

27. Stephen Patterson B.Com, A.C.A (*former*), LL.M holds a masters in International Human Rights Law from the University of Essex.

Chapter 7: Catastrophe Insurance

1. Tim Woods from Collected Quotes on Politics: retrieved from politicalquotes.blogspot.co.nz/

2. Brenda Snook and Toni Hannah, New Beginnings Christchurch Central Business District: Evolution from an Earthquake, The Field Connection Ltd, 2011. Retrieved from www.fieldconnection.co.nz/New%20Beginnings%20-%20Christchurch%20CBD.pdf

3. Rawle O. King, Hurricane Katrina: Insurance Losses and National. Capacities for Financing Disaster Risk, Congressional Research Service Report for Congress, Sep 15, 2005.

4. Should the Government Provide Insurance for Catastrophes? J. David, Cummins, Federal Reserve Bank of St. Louis Review, July/August 2006, 88(4), p. 362

5. Howard Kunreuther, Catastrophe Insurance: Challenges for the U.S. and Asia, 1st International Conference on Asian Catastrophe Insurance Innovation and Management University, Kyoto University, Dec 3-4 2007.

6. J. David Cummins, Should the Government Provide Insurance for Catastrophes?, Federal Reserve Bank of St. Louis Review, July/August 2006, 88(4), p. 362.

7. J. David Cummins, Should the Government Provide Insurance for Catastrophes?, Federal Reserve Bank of St. Louis Review, July/August 2006, 88(4), p. 337-79.

8. See Centrelink Website: www.centrelink.gov.au/internet/internet.nsf/emergency/index.htm

9. The European Union introduced a single authorization system whereby an insurance undertaking whose head office is in one of the Member States of the Community may open branches and carry on business by way of the freedom to provide services under the supervision of the Member State in which its head office is based. The aim is to allow policy-holders to find the cover best suited to their needs.

10. George L. Priest, The Government, the Market and the Problem of Catastrophic Loss, Journal of Risk and Uncertainty, 12:219-237 (1996): retrieved from portal.uni-freiburg.de/empiwifo/lehre-teaching-1/summer-term-09/materials-seminar-in-risk-management/catloss_govern_priest.pdf

11. http://www.stuff.co.nz/the-press/business/the-rebuild/70000338/Major-changes-to-EQC-Act-proposed

12. Quotable Value produces rating valuations. These are compiled by statute, under the Rating Valuations Act 1998, mainly as a uniform basis for levying local authority and regional council rates. Rating valuations also serve as a useful guide for property owners and other interested parties, as they are impartial and independently assessed.

13. Full evidence text- New Zealand Parliament, Earthquake Commission: Briefing for the Minister in Charge of the Earthquake Commission (Summary): retrieved from www. parliament.nz/NR/rdonlyres/C39E56B4-0B5E-402C-BCC6-B753455815A8/181835/49SCCO_EVI_00DBSCH_FIN_10135_1_A158877_EarthquakeC.pdf

14. Recently, the Earthquake Commission has increased its reinsurance cover for the 2012–13 year at a cost of NZD 130 million to ensure cover of NZD 7 billion for a Wellington event. See www.stuff.co.nz/business/industries/7962539/eqc-reinsurance-cover-gets-a-boost

15. NZ's finance company bail-out fund to end, 20 Dec 2011: retrieved from business.scoop.co.nz/2011/12/20/nzs-finance-company-bail-out-fund-to-end/

16. New support for quake-hit firms, Lois Cairns, 27 March 2011: retrieved from www.stuff.co.nz/the-press/news/christchurch-earthquake-2011/4814597/New-support-for-quake-hit-firms

17. Mike Coleman is a School Counsellor, Anglican Priest and former teacher of Accounting and Economics. He became a Community Advocate and Media Spokesperson for the Wider Earthquake Communities Action Network (WeCan) which he Co-founded.

Chapter 8: Reinsurance Industry

1. Michael Lewis, 'In Nature's Casino', The New York Times, August 26, 2007: retrieved from www.nytimes.com/2007/08/26/magazine

2. Seo, Co-Founder and Managing Principal at Fermat Capital Management, LLC. Based in Westport, Connecticut, Fermat Capital manages over USD 2 billion in catastrophe bond investments, making it one of the leading catastrophe bond investors in the world.

3. Alan Bollard, Opinion piece: the implications of the Canterbury Earthquakes for the Reserve Bank, 13 May 2011:retrieved from www.rbnz.govt.nz/speeches/4398500.html

4. Aon Benfield, a division of Aon Corporation (NYSE: AON), is one of the large reinsurance intermediary and full-service capital advisors.

5. Robert Woodthorpe Browne, The London Insurance and Reinsurance Market, 3 Feb 2010: retrieved from www.gresham.ac.uk/lectures-and-events/ the-london-insurance-and-reinsurance-market

6. Gary St. Lawrence, AIG's CEO says 'Trust Us to Self Regulate', Third Party and Independents Archives, June 24, 2011: retrieved from www.watchblog.com/thirdparty/archives/007599.html

7. For a mathematical explanation of how this works see James N. Standard and Michael G. Wacek, The Spiral in the Catastrophe Retrocession Market: retrieved from www.casact.org/pubs/dpp/ dpp91/91dpp529.pdf

8. In the High Court of New Zealand Wellington Registry CIV-2011-485-1137 and CIV-2011-485-1116.

9. Phillip J.F. Geheb, A risky Proposition: Proposed Use of Catastrophic Modelling for the National Flood Insurance Program, August 2011: retrieved from www.realestatedevelopmentlawupdate. com/2011/08/02/a-risky-proposition-proposed-use-of-catastropohic-modelling-for-the-national-flood-insurance-program/

10. Lessons from Recent Major Earthquakes, Swiss Reinsurance Company Ltd, Economic Research and Consulting, Jan 2012: retrieved from media.swissre.com/documents/Exp_Pub_Lessons_ from_recent_major_earthquakes.pdf

11. S. Giovinazzi and A. King, Toward the Seismic Assessment of Lifelines within the Regional RiskScape Model in New Zealand, GNS Science. Retrieved from ir.canterbury.ac.nz/ bitstream/10092/3664/1/12623495_Giovinazzi%20%26%20King%20-%20 ANIDIS2009%20-%20MEMORIA.pdf

12. This would be required if the Natural Disaster Fund and reinsurance arrangements are exhausted following a major catastrophe.

13. en.wikipedia.org/wiki/Cat_bonds; a floating rate bond is a bond that has a variable coupon, equal to a money market reference rate, like Libor, plus a spread. The spread is a rate that remains constant.

14. Thomas Whittaker, Japan Earthquake Raises Cat Bond Uncertainty, April 2011: retrieved from www.risk.net/credit/news/2040264/japan-earthquake-raises-cat-bond-uncertainty
15. Ron Fraser, Why Have Natural Disasters Increased?, The Trumpet: retrieved from standeyo.com/NEWS/10_Earth_Changes/100305.nat.diz.increasing.warning.html
16. NZ Government to Bail out Insurer Without Enough Reinsurance, by Admin. on April 7, 2011: retrieved from www.artemis.bm/blog/2011/04/07/nz-government-to-bail-out-insurer-without-enough-reinsurance/
17. Asia Pacific Accounts for Two-thirds of Worlds Insured Catastrophe Losses, by Admin. on Nov 1, 2011: retrieved from www.artemis.bm/blog/2011/11/01/asia-pacific-accounts-for-two-thirds-of-worlds-insured-catastrophe-losses/
18. An odds-maker is a mathematical method for computing optimal strategies for a class of problems, in this case the likelihood of hurricanes in a particular region.
19. G.G. Kaufman and K. E. Scott, What Is Systemic Risk, and Do Bank Regulators Retard or Contribute to It?, Independent Review, v. VII, n. 3, Winter 2003.
20. nos.nl/artikel/344225-verlies-banken-door-griekenland.html (in Dutch)
21. http://www.aon.com/attachments/AON_Reinsurance_Market_Outlook_2009.pdf
22. www.radionz.co.nz/news/business/91291/vero-wants-working-party-on-quake-insurance
23. Insurer solvency standards – reducing risk in a risk business, Richard Dean, Reserve Bank of New Zealand: Bulletin, Vol. 74, No. 4, December 2011, p32: www.rbnz.govt.nz/research/bulletin/2007_2011/2011dec74__4dean.pdf
24. Michael Lewis, In Nature's Casino, New York Times, Aug 26, 2007: retrieved from www.nytimes.com/2007/08/26/magazine
25. Co-Founder and Managing Principal at Fermat Capital Management, LLC. Based in Westport, Connecticut, Fermat Capital manages over

$2 billion in catastrophe bond investments, making it one of the leading catastrophe bond investors in the world.

26. http://www.stuff.co.nz/the-press/news/75073343/record-635-million-insurance-payout-for-christchurch-city-council
27. http://www.civicassurance.co.nz/docs/civicAR/Civic_AR14_Web.pdf
28. http://www.stuff.co.nz/the-press/news/68630196/Rates-hike-will-drive-people-from-Christchurch
29. http://www.stuff.co.nz/business/71340053/IAG-hits-reinsurance-limit-on-Feb-22-2011-quake
30. https://www.nzsuperfund.co.nz/news-media/new-zealand-superannuation-fund-appoints-leadenhall-capital-partners-us275-million
31. Sarah Watson, Asia Catastrophe Prone, International Travel Insurance Journal, 12 Dec, 2012 retrieved from www.itij.co.uk/story103
32. http://www.nzcia.org.nz/captive-basics.htm
33. http://www.worldbank.org/en/news/feature/2013/06/24/climate-change-natural-disasters-stress-food-energy-production-south-asia
34. Francis Tapim, Melinda Howells and Chris O'Brien, Roads insurance Difficulties 'incredible', ABC News, 23 Sep 2011 retrieved from www.abc.net.au/news/2011-09-23/government-gives-up-too-soon-on-qld-insurance/2919906/?site=westqld

Chapter 9: Implications for Recovery

1. Lianne Dalziel, Turning Disaster into Opportunity, Keynote Address to Australian & NZ Institute of Insurance & Finance Conference, Sky City Convention Centre, Auckland, Nov 30, 2011: retrieved from https://www.labour.org.nz/node/4478
2. John McCrone, What's the word for 2016?: Another year in the Christchurch Recovery, Jan 16, 2016: retrieved from http://www.stuff.co.nz/the-press/news/75900337/whats-the-word-for-2016-another-year-in-the-christchurch-recovery

3. Rob O'Neil, Compulsory Acquisition Could Reconfigure Christchurch, 30 April 2012: retrieved from www.stuff.co.nz/business/rebuilding-christchurch/6831407/Compulsory-acquisition-could-reconfigure-Christchurch-CBD

4. Charlie Gates, Lianne Dalziel Claims CERA Ditched Her, 24 April 2012: retrieved from www.stuff.co.nz/the-press/news/christchurch-earthquake-2011/6795039/Dalziel-claims-Cera-ditched-her

5. Cecile Meier, OPINION: Gerry Brownlee menus a step too far, July 23, 2015: retrieved from http://www.stuff.co.nz/the-press/opinion/70474561/OPINION-Gerry-Brownlee-menus-a-step-too-far

6. Kia Kaha: a Personal Account of the New Zealand Earthquakes, Herman van der Kloot Meijburg, Bereavement Care, Vol. 30, Issue 3, 2011, p.8.

7. Budget 2015: $27m boost for Christchurch recovery, New Zealand Herald, May 21, 2015: retrieved from http://m.nzherald.co.nz/christchurch-earthquake/news/article.cfm?c_id=1502981&objectid=11452500

8. Gerry Brownlee, Additional $2.1b for Christchurch's recovery, May 16, 2013: retrieved from http://www.beehive.govt.nz/release/additional-21b-christchurch%E2%80%99s-recovery

9. TRP- Submissions 38-72, received 17-23 July 2015: retrieved from http://cera.govt.nz/sites/default/files/common/dtrp-submissions-38-72-received-17-23-july-2015.pdf

10. Hon Lianne Dalziel, Dalziel: Turning Disaster into Opportunity, Nov 30 2011: retrieved from http://www.scoop.co.nz/stories/PA1111/S00521/dalziel-turning-disaster-into-opportunity.htm

11. Resourcing of the Canterbury rebuild: Changes and emerging there, Alice Chang-Richards, Susanne Wilkinson and Erica Seville, June 2012: retrieved from http://www.resorgs.org.nz/images/stories/pdfs/report%20june%202012%20-%20resourcing%20the%20canterbury%20rebuild%20changes%20%20emerging%20themes.pdf

12. Red tape still boosting home build costs, Christchurch Press, May 11, 2015: retrieved from http://www.stuff.co.nz/business/industries/68360997/red-tape-still-boosting-home-build-costs.html

13. Christchurch-rebuild Must Speed Up-Economist, 2 Dec 2011: retrieved from www.stuff.co.nz/business/rebuilding-christchurch/6073005/Christchurch-rebuild Must Speed Up-Economist

14. Myths and Realities of Reconstruction Workers' Accommodation, February 2013, Alice Chang-Richards, Susanne Wilkinson, Erica Seville, and David Brunsdon: retrieved from http://www.resorgs.org.nz/images/stories/pdfs/Reconstructionfollowingdisaster/report%20on%20workers%20temporary%20accommodation.pdf; http://www.resorgs.org.nz/images/stories/pdfs/Reconstructionfollowingdisaster/case_study_report_resourcing.pdf

15. Rent crisis 'best left to market', Michael Berry, Christchurch Press, March 20, 2012.

16. Alan Wood, Christchurch hotel rooms on the rise, survey shows, Aug 6, 2015: retrieved from http://www.stuff.co.nz/business/70883978/Christchurch-hotel-rooms-on-the-rise-survey-shows

17. Housing dearth forces poor to sleep in cars, Fairfax Media, 29 March 2012: retrieved from tvnz.co.nz/national-news/housing-dearth-forces-poor-sleep-in-cars-4804904

18. Hundreds sleeping in Christchurch airport terminal, Radio New Zealand, March 27, 2012: retrieved from http://www.radionz.co.nz/news/national/101884/hundreds-sleeping-in-christchurch-airport-terminal

19. Olivia Carville, 11 into four bedrooms won't go – national, 31 March 2012: retrieved from www.stuff.co.nz/national/6670704/11-into-four-bedrooms-won-t-go and Christchurch renters under 'huge pressure'- Business News TVNZ, 11 April 2012: retrieved from tvnz.co.nz/business-news/christchurch-renters-under-huge-pressure-4826259

20. Christchurch rental crisis 'best left to market'-Govt-National News, 20 March 2012, Fairfax Media: retrieved from tvnz.co.nz/national-news/christchurch-rental-crisis-best-left-market-govt-4785067

21. Liz McDonald, Christchurch rents on downward slide, landlords finding it tougher, June 11 2015: retrieved from http://www.stuff.co.nz/the-press/news/69210910/christchurch-rents-on-downward-slide-landlords-finding-it-tougher

22. Rachel Young, Christchurch needs over 35,000 new houses, March 22, 2013: retrieved from http://www.stuff.co.nz/business/rebuilding-christchurch/8457986/Christchurch-needs-over-35-000-new-houses

23. Plenty of land for rebuild: retrieved from http://www.greaterchristchurch.org.nz/News/PDF/PlentyOfLandAvailableForRebuild.pdf

24. Lois Cairns, Selwyn district population booming, 03 Ag, 2013: retrieved from http://www.stuff.co.nz/the-press/news/canterbury/8997848/Selwyn-district-population-booming

25. House prices fall in areas of severe quake damage, Liz McDonald, Christchurch Press, 15 Dec, 2010.

26. QV property valuation: retrieved from https://www.qv.co.nz/, January 2016

27. Restrictive Covenants - Is there a case for public plans to control private planning instruments in new Zealand?, David Mead and Stuart Ryan: retrieved from http://www.hillyoungcooper.co.nz/assets/Uploads/Restrictive-Covenants-Mead-Ryan.pdf

28. Property boundaries for survey after quake, Ben Heather, Christchurch Press, 27 Nov, 2011. For further explanation see www.sssc2011.com/assets/Papers/Professional/SmithMarketal-Re-establishmentofCadastralBoundariesfollowingthe2010-2011Canterburyearthquakes.pdf

29. Panicked owners sell too cheaply, Liz McDonald, Weekend Press, Feb 25-26, 2012.

30. Cecile Meier, Re: Start pop-up mall no High St, 9 April, 2015: retrieved from http://www.stuff.co.nz/business/67650835/Re-Start-Pop-up-mall-no-High-St

31. Hugh Pavletich, Opinion: Hugh Pavletich accuses Christchurch City Council of blindness, blunders and chain dragging, 20 Jul 2011: retrieved from www.interest.co.nz/opinion/53947/

opinion-hugh-pavletich-accuses-christchurch-city-council-blindness-blunders-and-chain-

32. John McCrone, Will heads roll in Christchurch's beleaguered planning department?, June 6, 2015: retrieved from http://www.stuff.co.nz/the-press/business/the-rebuild/68972257/Will-heads-roll-in-Christchurchs-beleaguered-planning-department

33. Selling sections at a reasonable price, Glenn Livingstone, Christchurch Press, March 6, 2012 and Cheaper land for quake-hit buyers, Liz McDonald, Christchurch Press, March 9, 2012.

34. Feasible to repair and strengthen heritage buildings says UC architectural historian: retrieved from http://www.rebuildchristchurch.co.nz/blog/2014/2/feasible-to-repair-and-strengthen-heritage-buildings-says-uc-architectural-historian

35. Canterbury Earthquake Heritage Building Fund Operational Guidelines: retrieved from resources.ccc.govt.nz/files/CanterburyEarthquakeHeritageBuildingFundOperationalGuidelines.pdf Industrial vacancy at a low, Christchurch Press, Nov 9, 2011.

36. Shortage of Space pushes up rents for industry, Liz McDonald, Christchurch Press, Feb 13, 2012.

37. Statistics New Zealand, 2011.

38. Ben Heather, Panel member on HGC winning bidder's list, 11 April 2012: retrieved from www.stuff.co.nz/the-press/news/christchurch-earthquake-2011/6719877/Panel-member-on-HGC-winning-bidders-list?comment_msg=posted#post_comment

39. Population estimates, 25 Nov 2015: retrieved from http://ecan.govt.nz/about-us/population/how-many/Pages/estimates.aspx#growth

40. International migration to and from Canterbury region: 1996-2014: retrieved from http://www.stats.govt.nz/browse_for_stats/population/Migration/international-travel-and-migration-articles/international-migration-canterbury-1996-2014.aspx

41. Reported job losses 2013-2014: retrieved from http://www.interest.co.nz/news/job-losses-reported

42. Charley Mann, Foreign student revenue slumps in Canterbury, 29 March, 2012: retrieved from http://www.stuff.co.nz/national/education/6655750/Foreign-student-revenue-slumps-in-Canterbury

43. Christchurch quake caused more Kiwis to leave- Key, 3 News, 6 March 2012: retrieved from www.3news.co.nz/Christchurch-quake-caused-more-Kiwis-to-leave---Key/tabid/1607/articleID/245284/Default.aspx

44. Exodus to Australia hits record, Michael Berry and Sam Sachdeva, Christchurch Press, March 6, 2012.

45. Sandra K. Schneider, Flirting with Disaster: Public management in crisis situations, 1995, Armonk, New York.

46. Kathy Marks, More people moving from Australia to New Zealand than in the other direction for first time in 24 years, Independent, May 22,2015: retrieved from http://www.independent.co.uk/news/world/australasia/more-people-moving-from-australia-to-new-zealand-than-in-the-other-direction-for-first-time-in-24-10268060.html

47. Mark Pelling, The vulnerability of cities: natural disasters and social resilience, Earthscan Publications Ltd, London and Sterling, VA, 2003.

48. Philip R. Berke, Jack Kartez and Dennis Wenger, Recovery after Disaster: Achieving Sustainable Development, Mitigation and Equity, in Disasters Vol. 17, No. 2.

49. Regenerate Christchurch agency confirmed, 25 Sept, 2015: retrieved from http://cera.govt.nz/news/2015/regenerate-christchurch-agency-confirmed-25-september-2015

50. Christchurch Civic Trust, Newsletter March 2012: retrieved from http://www.christchurchcivictrust.org.nz/wp-content/uploads/news/March-2012-Newsletter.pdf

51. Marta Steeman and Alan Wood, Fletcher snares the big prize but local bidder not happy, 4 July, 2015: retrieved from http://www.stuff.co.nz/the-press/69949237/Fletcher-snares-the-big-prize-but-local-bidder-not-happy

52. Ashleigh Stewart, Health 'costlier than the rebuild' 19 Feb, 2016: retrieved from http://www.stuff.co.nz/national/health/77018384/

youth-expert-warns-next-generation-of-cantabrians-may-be-costlier-than-rebuild

53. Residential red zone offer package - sample letter (May 2012 version), Cera.

54. New Zealand Supreme Court judgement [2015] NZSC 27 *Quake Outcasts v The Minister for Canterbury Earthquake Recovery, The Chief Executive of the Canterbury Earthquake Recovery Authority.*

55. New process for red zone Crown offers, 21 April 2015: retrieved from http://www.scoop.co.nz/stories/PA1504/S00258/new-process-for-red zone-crown-offers.htm

56. More angst and anguish for red zone locals, 22 April, 2015: retrieved from http://www.scoop.co.nz/stories/PA1504/S00288/more-angst-and-anguish-for-red zone-locals.htm

57. Ernest Tsao has a Bachelor's degree in Mathematics and an MBA degree. He was a homeowner in Avondale, Christchurch. He was the formal representative of homeowners in the Quake-Outcasts group. He lodged a complaint with the Universal Postal Union. http://www.chchplan.ihp.govt.nz/wp-content/uploads/2015/08/3261-Tsao-Evidence-of-Ernest-Tsao-24-11-2015-redacted.pdf

58. Sarah O'Brien studied Interior Architecture at CIT Heretaunga, Wellington, training in seismic design and flood plain control elements. She has had 25 years construction experience. She has been the Owner/Director of a concrete manufacturing business in Nelson.

Chapter 10: Recovery In 2015?

1. http://www.stuff.co.nz/the-press/business/67805954/john-key-opens-new-tait-communications-building

2. http://www.stuff.co.nz/the-press/news/75900337/whats-the-word-for-2016-another-year-in-the-christchurch-recovery

3. Christchurch Four years on – Cam Preston – Insurance Update: retrieved from http://www.slideshare.net/Jotomero/christchurch-four-years-on-cam-preston-insurance-update

4. "Insurers slower to react' in New Zealand, *Christchurch Press*, Feb 21, 2014.

5. http://www.stuff.co.nz/business/76453260/4600-stuck-homeowners-need-more-help-settling-quake-claims-mayor-says

6. https://thechristchurchfiasco.wordpress.com/2015/04/10/bread-and-games-and-the-plight-of-campbell-live/

7. http://www.stuff.co.nz/entertainment/tv-radio/68022219/John-Campbell-greets-Save-Campbell-Live-marchers

8. Legal challenge expose hasty process, Andrew Geddis, *Christchurch Press*, Nov 02, 2013.

9. http://www.stuff.co.nz/the-press/business/the-rebuild/67429541/building-costs-expected-to-climb-further

10. http://www.stuff.co.nz/the-press/business/the-rebuild/70335758/experts-differ-on-whether-christchurch-rebuild-has-peaked.html

11. http://www.nzherald.co.nz/nz/news/article.cfm?c_id=1&objectid=11447976

12. http://www.stuff.co.nz/the-press/news/67556930/building-boom-brings-out-predators

13. http://www.stuff.co.nz/the-press/business/the-rebuild/67569705/ird-gets-tough-with-rebuild-businesses

14. http://www.stuff.co.nz/business/The-Rebuild-Black-Hole.html

15. http://www.stuff.co.nz/the-press/business/the-rebuild/67527169/almost-100-rebuildrelated-firms-have-gone-bust-since-feb-11-quake

16. Developer slams council for sluggish city rebuild, Liz McDonald, *Christchurch Press*, April 27, 2015

17. Canty home building continues to slow, Liz McDonald, *Christchurch Press*, July 01, 2015

18. http://www.stuff.co.nz/the-press/business/the-rebuild/67961922/Ludicrous-red-tape-delaying-Christchurch-rebuild

19. http://www.stuff.co.nz/business/industries/69904053/Fletcher-Residential-wins-800m-Christchurch-housing-project

20. http://www.stuff.co.nz/the-press/69949237/Fletcher-snares-the-big-prize-but-local-bidder-not-happy

21. http://www.stuff.co.nz/the-press/business/the-rebuild/67535901/New-Brighton-neglect-is-moral-injustice-Paul-Zaanen

22. http://www.stuff.co.nz/the-press/news/68804410/ mayor-to-east-i-am-really-sorry

23. Mayor calls for PM to stop delays to centre, Alan Wood and John McCrone, *Christchurch Press*, June 20, 2015

24. http://www.stuff.co.nz/the-press/business/the-rebuild/68407247/ Christchurch-anchor-projects-delays-causes-frustration

25. http://www.stuff.co.nz/the-press/news/67483938/ Council-warned-over-social-housing

26. Squatters call quake buildings home, Shelley Robinson, *Christchurch Press*, April 27, 2015.

27. http://www.nzherald.co.nz/opinion/news/article. cfm?c_id=466&objectid=11495333

28. Quake proofing: How far to take it, Tony Taig, *Christchurch Press* , Feb 04, 2013

29. Dr. Anne Brower at Seismics in the City, https://www.youtube.com/ watch?v=Hcc2fqEsoyA

30. Quake's lessons 'not in new law', Lois Cairns, *The Christchurch Press*, April 12, 2014.

31. http://www.stuff.co.nz/the-press/news/67483946/ Flood-plan-decision-delayed-yet-again

32. http://www.stuff.co.nz/the-press/opinion/67844274/city-council-and-insurer-headed-for-mediation; http://www.ccc.govt.nz/ the-council/news-releases/show/284

33. http://www.stuff.co.nz/the-press/news/67984099/ The-era-of-peace-and-love-is-over

34. http://www.stuff.co.nz/the-press/news/69582168/ live-stream-christchurch-city-council-long-term-plan-meeting

35. http://www.radionz.co.nz/news/regional/267010/ christchurch-faces-big-rates-rise

36. http://www.stuff.co.nz/business/industries/68545276/ Insurers-unlikely-to-meet-own-settlement-deadlines

37. http://www.stuff.co.nz/the-press/news/67449005/ from-all-seasons-to-hotel-cesspit

38. http://www.stuff.co.nz/the-press/news/
    christchurch-earthquake-2011/67639610/
    insurers-uturn-delights-quakehit-couple
39. http://www.stuff.co.nz/business/71340053/iag-hits-reinsurance-limit-
    on-feb-22-2011-quake; http://www.interest.co.nz/property/69847/
    cam-preston-Investigates-how-iag-uses-reinsurance-arrangements-
    its-nz-business-and
40. http://www.lifehealthinsurancenews.com.au/general-insurance/
    iag-gets-green-light-for-nz-monopoly
41. http://www.stuff.co.nz/the-press/business/the-rebuild/67961922/
    Ludicrous-red-tape-delaying-Christchurch-rebuild
42. http://m.nzherald.co.nz/christchurch-earthquake/news/article.
    cfm?c_id=1502981&objectid=11440393
43. http://www.stuff.co.nz/business/68189175/
    Higher-earthquake-costs-may-cause-half-year-loss
44. Vero: Cera skills needed, Marta Steeman, *Christchurch Press*, Aug 21,
    2015
45. http://www.stuff.co.nz/business/industries/68769247/
    Southern-Response-to-get-more-Government-money-if-needed
46. Insurance info held to avoid 'confusion', Michael Wright,
    Christchurch Press, May 28, 2015; http://www.stuff.co.nz/
    business/70445749/Supreme-Court-awards-extra-300k-insurance-
    for-quake-damaged-property
47. http://www.3news.co.nz/nznews/christchurch-insurance-critic-gets-
    police-visit-over-emails-2015081109#axzz3wspFz1Xj
48. http://www.stuff.co.nz/business/71811037/
    Southern-Response-hits-back-at-class-action
49. http://www.pressreader.com/new-zealand/
    the-press/20151130/281479275334184/TextView
50. http://www.stuff.co.nz/the-press/business/the-rebuild/68408780/
    Insurers-have-lost-confidence-in-poor-EQC-data
51. http://www.stuff.co.nz/the-press/business/the-rebuild/70000338/
    Major-changes-to-EQC-Act-proposed; http://www.stuff.co.nz/
    business/73907221/Insurers-want-EQC-Act-overhaul

52. http://www.stuff.co.nz/the-press/business/71470352/southern-response-class-action-launched.html

53. http://www.stuff.co.nz/the-press/business/the-rebuild/67734451/EQC-home-repair-deadline-causes-stress-and-confusion

54. http://www.stuff.co.nz/the-press/business/the-rebuild/68171009/Christchurch-residents-in-EQC-limbo

55. Fletcher cuts contractor roster, Michael Wright, *Christchurch Press*, April 04, 2015

56. http://www.stuff.co.nz/the-press/business/the-rebuild/67805459/Shoddy-EQC-repairs-leave-Christchurch-homeowner-with-wonky-floor

57. http://www.stuff.co.nz/business/71021676/EQC-foundation-repair-shortcomings-revealed

58. http://www.stuff.co.nz/business/72002002/Only-1-per-cent-of-EQC-repairs-done-with-building-consent; http://www.stuff.co.nz/the-press/business/the-rebuild/72283618/extent-of-shoddy-quake-repair-work-exposed-in-reports

59. EQC Update, Keeping You informed, Aug 22, 2015

60. http://www.stuff.co.nz/the-press/business/the-rebuild/75682640/eqc-has-about-5500-shoddily-repaired-homes-to-fix

61. EQC fears fallout from decision, Martin van Beynen, *Christchurch Press*, April 30, 2015.

62. Audit must ensure that earthquake repairs meet codes, *Christchurch Press*, Aug 15, 2015; http://www.stuff.co.nz/the-press/news/10441327/Cheap-fixes-devaluing-thousands-of-homes

63. Repairs deal 'extraordinary, Celcile Meier, *Christchurch Press*, Aug 15, 2015.

64. https://thechristchurchfiasco.wordpress.com/2015/11/16/eqc-action-group-to-file-proceedings/

65. http://www.stuff.co.nz/business/71938905/Petition-for-Royal-Commission-inquiry-into-shoddy-repairs-launched

66. http://www.stuff.co.nz/the-press/news/71970100/Royal-Commission-for-earthquake-repairs-unnecessary-Brownlee-says

67. http://www.stuff.co.nz/business/71419970/Six-out-of-seven-IAG-repairs-found-to-be-deficient-in-Govt-investigation

68. http://www.stuff.co.nz/the-press/business/the-rebuild/71493791/Christchurchs-rocky-foundations-and-cheap-fixes

69. http://www.stuff.co.nz/the-press/business/the-rebuild/71861334/IAG-accused-of-bullying-customers

70. http://www.stuff.co.nz/the-press/news/70407760/EQC-assessor-is-just-so-rude-and-treats-you-like-you-are-a-criminal

71. http://www.stuff.co.nz/the-press/news/69784941/christ-church-cathedral-a-symbol-of-negativity

72. http://www.3news.co.nz/nznews/new-plans-for-christchurch-catholic-cathedral-revealed-2015052812#axzz3wmUjiMeA

73. http://www.stuff.co.nz/the-press/69691497/red zoners-set-for-more-compo

74. http://www.stuff.co.nz/the-press/news/70087549/Red zone-discrimination-against-uninsured-says-city-council

75. Red zone date extended, Cecile Meier, *Christchurch Press*, July 01, 2015

76. Redcliffs School is safe, Mark Robberds, *The Christchurch Press*, Feb 04, 2015

77. http://www.stuff.co.nz/the-press/news/74401956/Redcliffs-School-to-fight-closure-decision

78. http://www.stuff.co.nz/national/education/74500409/Redcliffs-School-considering-court-action-to-stay-open

79. http://www.stuff.co.nz/the-press/news/74751713/Redcliffs-reflects-on-a-broken-promise; http://www.newstalkzb.co.nz/news/education/government-announces-six-new-public-private-schools/

80. http://www.radionz.co.nz/national/programmes/morningreport/audio/2562648/academic-is-concerned-chch-will-struggle-to-fully-recover

81. http://www.stuff.co.nz/the-press/news/christchurch-earthquake-2011/67919822/Christchurch-quake-survivors-and-the-long-road-to-mental-recovery

82. http://www.stuff.co.nz/the-press/news/christchurch-earthquake-2011/68063552/ive-had-enough--canterbury-caravan-mum; http://www.stuff.co.nz/the-press/news/christchurch-earthquake-2011/68295946/christchurch-quake-

mums-sleeping-in-chairs-dining-rooms; http://www.stuff.
co.nz/the-press/news/christchurch-earthquake-2011/69010881/
here-for-the-christchurch-rebuild-living-in-a-van

83. http://www.stuff.co.nz/the-press/news/69115205/
Christchurch-housing-recovery-too-little-too-late

84. https://www.youtube.com/watch?v=VemqVxmAFQQ; Homeowner
seeks class action, Cecile Meier, *Christchurch Press*, June 11, 2015

85. http://www.stuff.co.nz/the-press/opinion/72139804/
eqc-wasnt-equipped-to-deal-with-the-middle-classes

86. Hugo Kristinsson is an Icelandic computer consultant and
publisher who migrated to Christchurch with his wife (Emma)
twenty years ago. Their home in South New Brighton borders
the estuary. He has an unresolved claim with Southern
Response. He has been an active community advocate and
set up website Empowered Christchurch. http://www.stuff.
co.nz/the-press/news/christchurch-earthquake-2011/8744573/
Quake-hit-residents-now-face-flood-risk

Conclusion

1. Lianne Dalziel, It's time to re-engage and listen to the
people, Nov 25, 2015: retrieved from http://www.stuff.co.nz/
the-press/christchurch-life/a-great-place-to-be/74315953/
its-time-to-reengage-and-listen-to-the-people

2. Cullen Smith, Shearer wants bipartisan response to quakes,
The Star, Jan 17, 2012; https://thechristchurchfiasco.wordpress.
com/2013/03/25/why-a-bipartisan-approach-to-disaster-recovery-is-
not-working-for-christchurch/

3. http://www.stuff.co.nz/business/money/7066704/
SCF-bailout-means-lessons-not-learnt

4. http://www.stuff.co.nz/the-press/business/the-rebuild/70084887/
How-much-is-the-Government-really-spending-to-fix-Christchurch

5. http://www.stuff.co.nz/the-press/news/69901937/6000-
christchurch-properties-at-risk-from-coastal-erosion; Council

approves risk area restriction, Lois Cairns, *Christchurch Press*, July 04, 2015

6.   Neil Smith, There's no such thing as a natural disaster, in Understanding Katrina: Perspectives from the Social Sciences, 11 June 2006: retrieved from understandingkatrina.ssrc.org/Smith/

7.   Earthquake Recovery Grinds to a Halt, 28 March 2012: retrieved from business.scoop.co.nz/2012/03/28/earthquake-recovery-grinds-to-a-halt/

8.   D.J. Berardinelli, An insurer in the grip of greed, in Trial: The insurance industry exposed, July 2007, Vol. 43:7: retrieved from www.erisa-claims.com/library/Berardinelli%article.pdf

9.   'Fix or shut' buildings calls: Enforce standards, engineer urges, Ben Heather, *Christchurch Press*, March 1, 2012.

10.   Total quake safety not 'viable', Marc Greenhill, *Christchurch Press*, March 22, 2012.

11.   Surprise Subdivision changes rile residents, Sam Sachdeva, *Christchurch Press*, March 22, 2012.

12.   Ernst & Young (2008a). Strategic Business Risk: Insurance.

13.   Kevin W. Weigand, Climate Change Disclosure: Ensuring the Viability of the Insurance Industry While Protecting the Investor, College of William and Mary Environmental Law and Policy Review, Vol 34 Issue 1, Article 9.

14.   Annual Reports, ECQ Earthquake Commission: retrieved from www.eqc.govt.nz/downloads/eqc-annual-report-2010-11.pdf

15.   http://www.stuff.co.nz/the-press/christchurch-life/a-great-place-to-be/74315953/its-time-to-reengage-and-listen-to-the-people

16.   http://www.stuff.co.nz/national/77147819/arrest-after-brown-substance-poured-on-gerry-brownlee-at-service

GLOSSARY

AA Insurance	General purpose New Zealand insurer
AAJ	American Association of Justice
AIG	American insurer, sponsor of the All Blacks
Allstate	The second largest personal lines insurer in the United States
AMI	A subsidiary of IAG Insurance
CAT Bond	Catastrophe bond
CCDU	Christchurch Central Development Unit
CDEM	The Civil Defence Emergency Management Act
CERA	Central Earthquake Recovery Authority
CER Act	Canterbury Earthquake Recovery Act
CERC	Canterbury Earthquake Royal Commission
CERRA	Canterbury Earthquake Response and Recovery Act 2010
CBD	Central Business District
CHRP	Canterbury Home Repair Programme
CIAS	Canterbury Insurance Assistance Service
GST	Goods and Services tax.
IAG	Insurance Australia Group, New Zealand's largest insurer. IAG's subsidiaries include State, AMI, Lumley, NZI and holds 47 per cent of the general insurance market in New Zealand.
ISO	Insurance and Savings Ombudsman
KiwiBond	A New Zealand Government issued bond to assist fund the recovery in Christchurch
EQR	Fletcher Construction Business Unit
LIBOR	London Interbank Offered Rate

Lumley	Lumley General Insurance (NZ) Ltd, part of the Australian Wesfarmers Group
Lurp	Land Use Recovery Plan
MBIE	Ministry of Business, Innovation and Employment's
Ngai Tahu	New Zealand South Island Maori tribe
NDF	The New Zealand Earthquake Commission's Natural Disaster Fund
OECD	Organisation for Economic Co-Operation and Development
OIA	Official Information Request
PMA	Project Management Agreement
RAS	Residential Advisory Service
Red Zone	Areas in the flat land residential red zone have area-wide land and infrastructure damage, and an engineering solution to repair the land would be uncertain, costly, and is likely to be highly disruptive
SCIRT	Stronger Christchurch Infrastructure Rebuild Team
Selwyn District	Part of the wider Canterbury region, adjacent to Christchurch
Southern Response	A government-owned company responsible for settling claims by AMI policyholders for Canterbury earthquake damage which occurred before 5 April 2012
TC1	Technical Category 1 (grey) future land damage from liquefaction is unlikely
TC2	Technical Category 2 (yellow) minor to moderate land damage from liquefaction is possible In future significant earthquakes
TC3	Technical Category 3 (blue) moderate to significant land damage from liquefaction possible in future large earthquakes

Vero	Insurance company owned by the Australian Suncorp Group.
Waimakariri	A district forming part of the wider Canterbury region, adjacent to Christchurch
WeCan	Canterbury earthquake community action group

Song of Silence

Often we see evil triumph by walking
the way of pain to achieve its ends.
Yet, its victory is for today alone,
it has no place in tomorrow.
Only good intent is of the wider dream, of the source
that is everlasting.

Barry Brailsford, Insights: touching hope, knowing love, living magic, finding self, remembering spirit (Stoneprint Press Ltd, New Zealand, 2011)

www.ingramcontent.com/pod-product-compliance
Lightning Source LLC
Chambersburg PA
CBHW060959220326
41599CB00023B/3769